Consequences of Party Reform

CONSEQUENCES OF PARTY REFORM

NELSON W. POLSBY

OXFORD UNIVERSITY PRESS
Oxford   New York   Toronto   Melbourne
1983

Oxford University Press
Oxford London Glasgow
New York Toronto Melbourne Auckland
Delhi Bombay Calcutta Madras Karachi
Kuala Lumpur Singapore Hong Kong Tokyo
Nairobi Dar es Salaam Cape Town

and associate companies in
Beirut Berlin Ibadan Mexico City Nicosia

Library of Congress Cataloging in Publication Data
Polsby, Nelson W.
Consequences of party reform.
Includes index.
1. Presidents—United States—Nomination. I. Title.
JK521.P58 1983 324.5'0973 82-14509
ISBN 0-19-503234-9
ISBN 0-19-503315-9 (pbk.)

Printing (last digit): 9 8 7 6 5 4 3 2 1

Printed in the United States of America

The Democratic party of the nation ain't dead, though it's been givin' a lifelike imitation of a corpse for several years. . . . The trouble is that the party's been chasin' after theories and stayin' up nights readin' books instead of studyin' human nature and actin' accordin' . . . .

. . . Have you ever thought what would become of the country if the bosses were put out of business, and their places were taken by a lot of cart-tail orators and college graduates? It would mean chaos.

William L. Riordan, *Plunkitt of Tammany Hall* (1905) (New York: Dutton, 1963), pp. 88, 81.

It has become fashionable among a certain group of pundits and political scientists to blame the reforms undertaken by the Democratic Party after its 1968 convention for all manner of political ills—declining voter participation, the proliferation of single-issue groups, weak presidential leadership, poor congressional performance, and, above all, the decay of the political party. So great has been the hostility to these reforms, to the reformers who perpetrated them and to the proliferation of presidential nominating primaries that followed in their wake, that one expects any day now to see a book published that blames these reforms, not only for our political ills, but for cancer, heart disease, and falling arches.

Curtis Gans, "How the White House is Won," *Book World, Washington Post* (August 12, 1979), p.10.

The processes of government are essentially educational processes.

Felix Frankfurter, letter to Franklin D. Roosevelt, November 8, 1928. In Joseph P. Lash, *From the Diaries of Felix Frankfurter* (New York: Norton, 1979), p.40.

For
Allen I. Polsby
and
Daniel D. Polsby

Contents

Preface

This book comes to its readers through the courtesy of Watergate. For many Americans, Watergate was a profoundly unsettling business, including, as it did, the unprecedented resignation of a Vice President under a cloud of criminal charges, the near impeachment and resignation of a President, and numerous other misfortunes. Some of us who study American politics felt during those difficult times that it was a part of our professional obligation to stop whatever we were doing and pay attention to Watergate so that we could make an effort at interpreting for our fellow citizens—perhaps only slightly more confused than we were—what was going on in the light of our understanding of the ongoing patterns and requirements of the American constitutional order. For a few of us, the experiences of those years turned out to be more than a temporary detour; they more or less permanently changed our intellectual agendas. I count myself as one of those who as a result of the concerns of the Watergate era have undertaken to attend on a more or less regular basis to the state of the American political system as a whole. I thus have become interested in monitoring changes in the vital signs of the system, and—no matter how unreasonably ambitious the effort has seemed—in tracing out how changes in one part of the system affect changes in others.

As it happens, the last twenty years have been rich in these sorts of systemic changes,[1] and the purpose of this book will be to follow one set that has caused particular concern: the reform of the presidential nomination process. Because the consequences of reform in this sector have rippled out very widely into the political system, it would have been impossible to render a full account of my views within the pages of the text on presidential elections that Aaron Wildavsky and I have written together in happy intermittent collaboration since 1964.[2] It gives me great pleasure to acknowledge the constructive influence that my friend and colleague has had on this offshoot of our common enterprise.

I owe to a number of former students a debt of gratitude for the intellectual stimulation they have given me as I have wrestled with the issues of this book. Many of them are now well launched on promising careers of their own that have spread more widely the insights that once circulated around the seminar table in Berkeley. As will be readily apparent from the footnotes, I have frequently drawn from their published work, but in addition I wish to mention here James I. Lengle, Elaine Kamarck, Robert T. Nakamura, Bill Cavala, and the late Jeffrey Pressman. In a category all his own is Byron Shafer, whose prize-winning doctoral dissertation on the reforms of the Democratic party[3] provided many occasions of enlightenment, and whose energy, generosity, and high intellectual standards have contributed a great deal to these pages.

A year in England (in 1977–78) and a month in Australia and New Zealand (June 1980)—the former under John Simon Guggenheim Foundation and the latter under USICA auspices—convinced me that the proper workings of the American political system are not exclusively the concern of Americans. In the course of fifty or so talks to foreign audiences, and in response to their comments and queries, I shaped much of the argument of this book. Notable among those friends who have shared with me their valuable comparative outlooks on American politics are Leslie Stone of the BBC overseas service, Greg Armstrong at Melbourne, John Hart at Australian National University, Louis Heren, formerly of *The Times* of London, the late Robert McKenzie of the London School of Economics, Jim Sharpe and Philip Williams at Nuffield College, Oxford, Anthony King and Graham Wilson of Essex, Esmond Wright in London, Colin Seymour-Ure and Alec Barbrook at Kent, Malcolm Shaw of Exeter, Richard Hodder-Williams of Bristol, and those two pillars of American political studies in the United Kingdom, John Lees of Keele and David Morgan of Liverpool. Douglas Wilson and, especially, the incomparable Allan Croghan, sometime cultural affairs officers at the U.S. Embassy in London, were extraordinarily helpful in providing the introductions that mean so much in a society where one needs to be introduced. Geoffrey Smith of *The Times* of London has over the last few years been the foreign observer of American politics whose questions and observations have stimulated me most. Two great cosmopolitan spirits, Constance and William Drower, have also taught me much about America, in part from the fund of knowledge they accumulated in the decade Bill was the British embassy's brilliantly successful specialist on Capitol Hill in Washington.

Many of the ideas expressed in these pages have found preliminary expression in essays I have written on earlier occasions.[4] I doubt I should ever have pulled together the entire argument that was floating around in bits and pieces in my head if I had not been invited to try my hand first at one, then at another part of the overall problem. And so I am grateful to William Lee Miller, Robert Goldwin, Seymour Martin Lipset, James Sterling Young, and Walter Dean Burnham and Martha Wagner Weinberg for chances to do some thinking out loud.

I am also very grateful for three opportunities to meet with students of various aspects of reform of the presidential nomination process under the auspices of the American Bar Association: in Tiburon, California, in April 1975; in Washington

D.C., in February 1976; and at the Johnson Foundation's conference center, Wingspread, in July 1981. I likewise acknowledge the hospitality of the American Enterprise Institute and Kenyon College for inviting me to participate in a most illuminating conference at Kenyon in April 1979, and of James Sterling Young for his generous invitations to a series of Miller Center meetings on the presidency and the party system at the University of Virginia in 1979–80. Among my mentors on one or more of these occasions were Joel Fleishman, Herbert Alexander, George Agree, William Crotty, Roger Allan Moore, John Sears, William Brock, John Hoving, Stephen Gottlieb, Richard Scammon, Robert Horwitz, Tom Mann, James Ceaser, Michael Robinson, Richard Cheney, Wayne Grandquist, Norman Ornstein, David B. Truman, and Richard E. Neustadt. I emphasize that none of these distinguished people necessarily agrees with any part of my analysis, but that I found their comments thoughtful, stimulating, reassuring, informative, or all of the above. In some cases we spent hours together in informal dialogue, the infallible sign of a well-run conference.

Closer to home, I am pleased to acknowledge the intellectual influence of Allan P. Sindler, Austin Ranney, Raymond E. Wolfinger, John Zaller, Eric Davis, Herbert McClosky, Paul Sniderman, Richard Brody, and Charles O. Jones on my understanding of many of the problems discussed in this book.

The following friends and colleagues read a draft of this manuscript and offered comments, criticisms and numerous improvements: Aaron Wildavsky, Daniel D. Polsby, Larry Bartels, John Zaller, Leon Epstein, Herbert Alexander, Adam Clymer, Roger Allan Moore, John Bibby, James I. Lengle, David B. Truman, Eric L. Davis, Joel Fleishman, Douglas Bennet, James Ceaser, David Cohen, Richard Stearns, William J. Crotty, Charles O. Jones, Byron Shafer, Stephen Snyder, David Price, Patricia Brown, Morley Winograd, Donald Pfarrer, Christopher Arterton, and Everett Carll Ladd. In addition, Anne Wexler very kindly and promptly looked over a portion of the manuscript in which her name appears, and Edwin Epstein and

Pamela Goldschmidt helped dig up some hard to find data. As the length of this list should indicate, I have been the recipient of so much good advice and encouragement that it is without doubt my pig-headedness alone that accounts for the mistaken ideas in the pages that follow.

I have had the benefit of cheerful and highly competent research assistance in bringing this book to completion from Deborah Cichon and Lynne Gordon, and in addition collegial support and entrepreneurial energy of a special kind from Michael Goldstein and Peverill Squire. The Department of Political Science, the Committee on Research, the Survey Research Center, the Institute of Governmental Studies and its National Policy Studies Program, the Graduate Division and the Office of the Chancellor, all of the University of California, Berkeley, have in one way or another contributed to the ongoing enterprise that made this book possible. In this connection I would like to thank Sanford S. Elberg, William A. Shack, William K. Muir, Eugene C. Lee, and Percy Tannenbaum, each of whom gave at the office. In all these thank-yous, a reader will be unable to find an extraordinary extra-mural grant of funds. This book was produced without one, a tribute to the resourcefulness of the University of California at Berkeley, and to its commitment to routinely providing assistance, and the right sort of atmosphere, for scholarship.

The two learned attorneys to whom this book is dedicated have not only given me shelter, support, laughter, and good counsel for most of my life, but have done so in a spirit for which the term brotherhood is, as it happens, an excellent approximation.

Finally, I thank Daniel R. Polsby, Emily A. Polsby, and Lisa S. Polsby for being unusually bountiful with their affections and sparing with their disaffections all these years. My most skilled editor and closest friend Linda O. Polsby shares with me the responsibility for the three last named, but wishes to be excused along with everyone else from responsibility for the various mistakes and lapses in judgment that not even her unblinking eye, sharp pencil, and impeccable judgment could prevent in the pages that follow.

Like many others who are concerned with political parties, presidential selection, and reform, I am looking forward to reading the results of the many projects, study groups, and commissions that have lately been formed and funded to consider these and related matters. As an early offering in the field, this book can hope to do a little agenda-setting for those that follow, and contribute to ongoing discussion as much through the questions it has formulated but answered inadequately as through those it has settled. At least it would be nice to think so.

Berkeley, California   N. W. P.
March 15, 1982

Consequences of Party Reform

Introduction

It is not at all unusual for Americans to find fault with the alternatives available to them on any given election day. No presidential election within living memory has been totally devoid of dissatisfactions focused on the shortcomings, real or imagined, of the main candidates and of the processes that brought them forward.[1] Yet it may not be wholly an optical illusion stimulated by the proximity in time of the last few elections that suggests that the contemporary presidential selection process does pose serious problems for the American political system. Consider one straw in the wind: by the simple criterion of prior experience in national politics and government no newly elected President in the entire history of the republic was ever less well prepared to take office than Jimmy Carter, unless it was Ronald Reagan.[2] That our two most recent Presidents should be arguably the two most nationally inexperienced in American history cuts directly across the grain of common sense that tells us that the duties of the Presidency are not smaller today than when more seasoned candidates—whatever their other qualifications and limitations—were routinely the only ones considered suitable for the job.

A criterion such as prior experience is an elite, if not an elitist, gauge with which to measure a presidential candidate in that it is likely to be invoked primarily by those who are well enough informed about politics to have some notion of the on-the-job benefits that a fund of exact information may confer on a newly elected President. This may suggest the extent to which the American system of presidential selection has moved away from elite and toward mass criteria in providing means for assessing the qualifications of presidential candidates.[3] To observers accustomed to democratic political systems that routinely choose their heads of government only from a pool of those previously elected to the national parliament and then selected by colleagues to lead a parliamentary party, the inattention of the American presidential selection process to the issue of prior preparation seems unfamiliar, uncomfortable, and even dangerous.[4] Some of them are genuinely puzzled that the American political system has in recent years appeared to move, if in any direction, away from concern with the political education, the intellectual capital, of what many of them conceive to be the most important leader in the world.

Even more interesting is the possibility that such a trend might be accounted for in part by a series of explicit choices made by politicians. The purpose of this book is to explore this possibility. It seeks to establish a few connections between causes and effects in the loosely coupled, overdetermined, busy world of American politics, and attempts to trace through some of the effects of some political reforms, choosing from a wider menu of possibilities those recent reforms that seem to have had an impact on later events sufficiently important to warrant thoughtful reconsideration. It is not the argument of this book, however, that the explicit choices entailed in the political reforms presently to be considered are completely responsible for the consequences I may seem to be fastening on them. I wish rather to argue that they are partially responsible, and facilitative in character, that they were necessary but not sufficient pre-conditions of a particular set of institutional problems toward which the American political system evolved in the wake of the turmoil of the late 1960's. Although other forces of varying sorts were also at work—technological, demographic and institutional changes that were bound, for example, to increase the independent influence of the news media on American politics—it does not seem to me unreasonable to focus on the contribution to social change made by the explicit choices of political actors. To study political choices in light of their consequences is not to claim they are the only determinants of consequences but merely to acknowledge that they are a set of determinants through which people took a direct hand in managing their own affairs, and might have managed differently, and that studying how these choices are made, their factual premises, their results, and their theoretical justifications can hope to add to usable knowledge.

Given the rumbles of dissatisfaction in both major parties about the political arrangements resulting from the last wave of reform, the practical implications of a study of this sort seem clear enough. In addition, this study may also contribute in at least three ways to political science: as an opportunity explicitly to consider interrelations among institutions of the American political system normally studied in isolation from one another; as an exploration of the process of reform and of ways to manage it so as to minimize the burden of unexpected and unwanted consequences; and as an example of the sort of policy analysis that falls squarely within a subject matter area where political scientists carrying a brief primarily for the understanding of process might supplement and criticize recommendations of actors more concerned with the manipulation of outcomes for their own partisan or intramural advantage.

The argument to be made in this book may or may not prove to be appealing when its underlying assumptions about political life and human behavior are taken into account: that changing the rules of politics changes the incentives for political actors; that changing incentives leads to changes in political behavior; and that changing behavior changes political institutions and their significance in politics. Thus we shall be exploring the

educational impact of political reform, the capacity of rules of
conduct actually to guide and to influence the activities of a
varied cast of political actors: candidates for public office and
their managers, state and local party leaders, interest group
leaders, delegates to national party conventions, journalists and
television news producers, and ordinary voters.

The discussion begins with a short historical account of the
reasons for the adoption of the two main sets of party reforms
whose interaction together and with broader trends has produced significant consequences, namely, reforms of the delegate selection process and reforms of party finance.[5] The second chapter outlines major consequences of these reforms
within their intended sphere of influence, the political parties,
and shows how the system of party competition as well as the
individual party organizations have been affected by reform. Because parties and the party system have been changed, the chief
results of party activity at the national level—recruitment of
presidential candidates—have in turn had an impact upon the
conduct of the presidency. This, at any rate, is the argument
of Chapter Three. Chapter Four examines wider consequences
of reforms in the political system, for interest groups, for the
news media, and for processes of political intermediation more
generally, and for the political mobilization and participation
of ordinary citizens. The final chapter returns to the general
subject of reforms and, in the light of the consequences considered in previous chapters, reformulates the criteria by which
changes in the party system might be justified and evaluated.

It is to be expected that there might well be reasonable disagreement with many of the conclusions reached in the course
of this inquiry. Even if this proves to be the case, it is desirable
to narrow the ground upon which policy disagreement might
rest to differences of opinion rather than differences in empirical knowledge. Thus at every feasible juncture I have taken
pains to establish the factual premises of my argument with
such empirical information as I could gather, and to indicate
those instances where the empirical information I could bring

to bear on a given question seemed to me to fall short of being satisfactory. On the whole, I am content to say that the line of argument taken in this book does no great violence to the facts as best I presently can marshal them, but one must concede that in a world as tumultuous and diverse as the world of American politics, there are quite likely more than enough facts available to lend themselves to arrangement in still other patterns, some of which may flatly contradict some of the conclusions of this book. Indeed, one of the scientific purposes of a book of this sort is to so sharpen the perceptions of its readers as to make more visible the bases for rejecting, modifying, and reformulating, not merely for accepting its central propositions. This invitation to disagreement is, perhaps, the chief distinction which ordinarily separates a work of political science from a work of political persuasion, and should, unlike the case of a work of political persuasion, make it more persuasive.

I

The Party Reforms
and How They Grew

Handwritten annotation: to anyone who has the misfortune to study this to the end this is... "I totally agree — this has to be one of the most depressing pieces of work ever undertaken!"

1. Eyewash? Primaries Before Reform

Perhaps the most famous remark ever made about American presidential primary elections was Harry S Truman's declaration on January 31, 1952, that they were "eyewash." The circumstances under which he said it were suspect: Senator Estes Kefauver of Tennessee, whom he disliked, was running hard and essentially unopposed in the New Hampshire Democratic primary, then as now the first of the election season.[1] Moreover, recent memory suggested that primaries could not be quite so lightly dismissed. In 1944 Wendell Willkie's presidential candidacy had been done in by the Wisconsin primary just four years after he had won the Republican nomination on the eighth ballot at the National Convention of 1940.[2] In 1948 Harold Stassen had risked a radio debate with Thomas E. Dewey as a feature of his campaign in the Oregon primary. He lost the debate, the primary, and the nomination.[3]

Later on in 1952—on March 18—Dwight D. Eisenhower received 100,000 write-in votes in the Minnesota Republican primary. Though it was less than the vote accorded favorite son Harold Stassen, it overshadowed Eisenhower's New Hampshire

9

victory of the previous week and launched his successful campaign for the nomination of his party.[4]

On the Democratic side, however, primaries that year did
prove to be eyewash: Kefauver won most of them but lost the
nomination.[5] He entered the Democratic National Convention
with 257½ delegates pledged to his candidacy, many more than
the 161½ pledged to Senator Richard Russell of Georgia, the
112½ pledged to New York's Averell Harriman, the 45½ to
Senator Bob Kerr of Oklahoma, or the 41½ to Governor Adlai
Stevenson of Illinois. His total still fell far short of the 616
needed to win the nomination. As the convention opened, 611½
votes, nearly a majority, were spread among minor candidates,
were formally uncommitted, or were in dispute.[6] It was the last
major party convention in American history—there have been
fourteen conventions since—to have taken more than a single
ballot to nominate a presidential candidate.

On the first ballot Kefauver got 340 votes, more than any of
the other thirteen candidates for whom votes were recorded.
On the second ballot he peaked at 362½ votes, and on the third
he slipped back to 275½ votes, as Adlai Stevenson gathered in
just enough of the scattered votes to win with 617½.[7] There
was nothing unexpected about Stevenson's eventual win. He had
been the choice of the incumbent President of his own party,[8]
acceptable to labor, as another attractive centrist candidate, Vice
President Alben Barkley, was not,[9] moderate enough to be un-
threatening to the South—as his Illinois colleagues had under-
scored by voting earlier in the convention to seat challenged
delegates from Virginia[10]—and well connected with the Eastern establishment—as Averell Harriman's well-timed withdrawal in his favor attested.[11] Indeed, with so many of the forces
in the Democratic party moving in his direction, it was a wonder that his nomination took so long. The delay can be accounted for mainly by Stevenson's obdurate reluctance to seem
to be doing anything at all in his own behalf.[12] This momentarily stalled his bandwagon and exasperated many of his supporters, but in the end did not prevent the Democratic party
from making him the nominee.

Stevenson had entered no primaries, and initially won no delegates pledged by primary elections. He beat Kefauver, the winner of 174 delegates in this fashion, and the leader in number of committed delegates until the convention's third ballot. In 1952, though primaries counted for enough to damage a candidate's chances or dramatically boost them, winning even a large proportion of them was not a sufficient condition for winning the nomination. Indeed, from the time of their introduction into American politics around the turn of the twentieth century, until well into the 1960s, primary elections were never the sole determinant of party presidential nominations.[13]

The fact that Kefauver was a serious candidate at all was not merely a tribute to his indefatigable campaigning. He was the

Table 1.1   Winner of most primary elections: 1912–1980

Year	Republicans	Democrats
1912	Theodore Roosevelt	*Woodrow Wilson
1916	Albert Cummins	*Woodrow Wilson (incumbent)
1920	Hiram Johnson	William McAdoo
1924	*Calvin Coolidge	William McAdoo
1928	*Herbert Hoover	*Alfred E. Smith
1932	Joseph France	*Franklin D. Roosevelt
1936	William Borah	*Franklin D. Roosevelt (incumbent)
1940	Thomas Dewey	*Franklin D. Roosevelt (incumbent)
1944	*Thomas Dewey	*Franklin D. Roosevelt (incumbent)
1948	Harold Stassen	*Harry S Truman (incumbent)
1952	Robert Taft	Estes Kefauver
1956	*Dwight Eisenhower (incumbent)	Estes Kefauver
1960	*Richard Nixon	*John Kennedy
1964	*Barry Goldwater	*Lyndon Johnson (incumbent)
1968	*Richard Nixon	Eugene McCarthy
1972	*Richard Nixon (incumbent)	*George McGovern
1976	*Gerald Ford (incumbent)	*Jimmy Carter
1980	*Ronald Reagan	*Jimmy Carter (incumbent)

* Party nominee

Sources: Robert A. Diamond (ed.), *Guide to U.S. Elections* (Washington, D.C.: Congressional Quarterly Inc., 1955), pp. 58–95, 309–35; Diamond (ed.), *Presidential Elections Since 1789* (Washington, D.C.: Congressional Quarterly Inc., 1975), pp. 110–14, 119–55; Paul T. David, Ralph M. Goldman, and Richard C. Bain, *The Politics of National Party Conventions* (Washington, D.C.: Brookings Institution, 1960), pp. 213–44; *Congressional Quarterly Weekly Reports* (July 10, 1976), pp. 1794–99, (August 14, 1976), pp. 2188–96, (July 12, 1980), pp. 1928–37, (August 9, 1980), pp. 2268–76.

first national politician in American history to attain prominence by means of television. As chairman of a special Senate
committee investigating organized crime, he had earned the
enmity of "regular" Democratic politicians well beyond the states
of Illinois and Florida, where early committee hearings embarrassing to the party had been held. It was widely believed that
his committee's activities had damaged the re-election chances
in 1950 of the Senate Democratic leader, Scott Lucas of Illinois.[14] Something of a loner in the Senate, considered a rene-
gade by many of his less liberal southern colleagues, Kefauver
was not popular with Democratic officeholders—President
Truman, in particular.

But his popularity was high with television viewers after the
broadcast of the New York hearings of the Kefauver Committee, the week of March 12, 1951.[15] As Kefauver's biographer
said:

> Overnight, millions had become familiar with the tall, lanky forty-
> seven-year-old Tennessean, whose soft Southern accent exhibited
> just a trace of Appalachian influence and whose firm but fair di-
> rection of the hearings evoked almost universally favorable com-
> ment. The dignity and easily shocked innocence of Kefauver and
> the other committee members allowed millions of viewers to iden-
> tify with them . . . .[16]
>
> The New York investigation became the most discussed topic in
> the country, and to millions the crime committee members be-
> came overnight celebrities . . . .[17]
>
> The twelve months preceding the Kefauver Committee's hear-
> ing in New York City had seen the percentage of homes in the
> New York metropolitan area with TV sets rise sharply, from 29
> to 51 per cent. . . . In the morning hours, the hearings created
> seventeen times the normal viewing audience (26.2 per cent of
> homes vs. the normal 1.5 per cent); in the afternoon there was
> also a dramatic increase in viewing (from 11.6 per cent of homes
> to 31.5 per cent). It was estimated that an average of 86.2 per
> cent of those viewing television watched the hearings, and that an
> average of 69.7 per cent of the TV sets in the New York area
> were on during the hearings, twice as many as during a weekday
> World Series game in October 1950.[18]

[The hearings] were eventually carried by TV stations in twenty cities along the eastern seaboard and in the Midwest . . . .[19]

Life magazine commented:

The U.S. and the world had never experienced anything like it . . . All along the television cable . . . [people] had suddenly gone indoors—into living rooms, taverns and clubrooms, auditoriums and back offices. There, in eerie half-light, looking at millions of small frosty screens, people sat as if charmed. For days on end and into the nights they watched with complete absorption . . . the first big television broadcast of an affair of their government, the broadcast from which all future uses of television in public affairs must date . . . Never before had the attention of the nation been riveted so completely on a single matter. The Senate investigation into interstate crime was almost the sole subject of national conversation.[20]

Kefauver's biographer continues:

Newspapers were full of stories of neglected housework, and deserted movie theaters and department stores; in New York, Consolidated Edison had to add a generator to supply power for all the TV sets being used . . . .[21]

The televising of the New York hearings . . . transformed Kefauver into a genuine national hero and vastly heightened his availability for the Presidency.[22]

The year 1952 marks the beginning of the interaction between television popularity and success in the primaries. Because primary elections did not select most delegates to the Democratic National Convention in that year, criteria other than television popularity retained their importance and determined the outcome of the nomination process.

Even in 1952, however, primaries were not negligible. At a minimum they provided information to the political leaders in whose gift the presidential nomination still remained: information about the popularity of various candidates in assorted states of the Union and among admittedly restricted but indubitably mass electorates in trial-heat situations, and information also about candidates' abilities to conduct the sort of arduous

Primaries growing in importance

face-to-face campaigning that the primary contests traditionally
demand. Performance in primaries would communicate something about a candidate's stamina, perhaps about the strength
of his desire to capture the Presidency, his capacity to mobilize
resources in his own behalf, to meet the press early in the
morning and late at night without committing some fatal error,
to attract support from local party organizations, to find the
right grounds in differentiating himself from competitors, yet
at the same time appealing to voters. National party leaders
could draw contrary inferences from data of this sort if they
chose to do so. But often enough some measure of consensus
arose: that Willkie had alienated too many regular Republicans
by 1944, for example, that Stassen had blundered in his handling of the Oregon debate of 1948, that Eisenhower's popularity at the grass roots was overwhelming in 1952.[23] Moreover,
primary elections were not all beauty contests, separated from
delegate selection procedures. Some delegates were selected in
primaries which might, given a close convention, make a difference in the outcome. A resourceful candidate, faced with a
scattered field of competitors, with no incumbent President or
heir-apparent to block his way, could use primaries to pick up
some delegates and change a few minds.

But no candidate would risk embarrassment by a poor showing in the primaries if an easier pathway to the nomination was
open. The rule of thumb among party tacticians was that the
earlier a candidate put himself in the field, the weaker the candidacy.[24] As candidate Hubert Humphrey explained to Theodore White during the 1960 primary season, on his campaign
bus one bone-chilling Wisconsin winter night:

> You have to be crazy to go into a primary. A primary, now, is
> worse than the torture of the rack. It's all right to enter a primary
> by accident, or because you don't know any better, but by fore-
> thought . . . .[25]

In 1960 John F. Kennedy's candidacy was regarded as deeply
flawed by a number of Democratic party leaders owing to their

concerns that a Roman Catholic could not be elected President. Many of these leaders, themselves Roman Catholics, still remembered the doomed presidential candidacy of Alfred E. Smith thirty-two years earlier.[26] And so Kennedy had to take the risks of running in primary elections. As White describes his calculations:

> If he could carry the Tenth [congressional district] he would carry all of Wisconsin. If he swept the entire Wisconsin delegation, he couldn't see how "they" (the big Eastern bosses) could deny him the nomination . . . He mused on the effect a victory here would have on the thinking of Governor Lawrence, boss of vital Pennsylvania . . . .[27]

Of course it was a primary victory, in largely Protestant West Virginia, that more than any other event of 1960 overcame the doubts that party leaders had about the burden of Kennedy's religion.[28] As the results of the general election later demonstrated, they were far from foolish in their apprehensions.[29] But Kennedy's other assets, and the inability of the rest of his competitors to match them, made the risk worth taking.

Kennedy worked hard to reduce his dependency upon party leaders. On one occasion rivalry between leaders within a state party played into his hands. In Ohio, Governor Mike DiSalle wanted to head an uncommitted delegation. But Ray Miller and the Cuyahoga County faction, from Cleveland, threatened to run Kennedy against DiSalle in the primary. As Aaron Wildavsky describes it:

> The astute governor, when he saw how the land lay, entered the primary as a favorite son pledged to Kennedy so long as he had a chance to win the nomination.[30]

In this small event we can catch the beginnings of change: primary elections not merely as an appeal to party leaders but also, and for the time being only in special circumstances, as an appeal against them as well. Primaries had the potential of shifting the balance of initiatives from party leaders and their organizations to candidates and their organizations, if the grip of party leaders was infirm, or their organizations incapable of restricting, or controlling, or dominating a state-wide party electorate, or the candidate in question was especially glamorous, or popular, or a good campaigner, or had friends or allies within the state.

Otherwise, prospective candidates had to calculate carefully whether or not to enter primary elections at all. As V. O. Key described the situation in 1964, in the last edition of his magisterial text:

> An early victory in a pivotal state may win the delegation and impress the party in other states with the aspirant's vote-pulling power. On the other hand, a defeat may bring the boom to a premature end. Yet a refusal to enter the primary may be interpreted as a manifestation of lack of confidence. Since the primary choice may be governed by the wishes of the state organization, it would be rash to enter a primary unless the candidate has the support of the organization or of an important faction, or feels that he could defeat the state machine.[31]

Before 1968, in short, the pursuit of a presidential nomination principally by entering primaries constituted a high-risk strategy. The increasing presence of television, the decline in the influence of political parties on voters generally in many localities, the success of John Kennedy, and the remarkable showing of Estes Kefauver all suggested that it would prove to be more useful to prospective candidates in the years ahead. None of this, however, prefigured the earthquake that was to shake the political system in 1968.

2. The Transformation of 1968

The year 1968 spawned more violence than most years before or since. There were coups in Iraq, Mali, Peru, Sierra Leone, Panama, and Congo (Brazzaville). Congress was suspended in Brazil. There were general strikes in Italy and Pakistan. Severe, protracted riots took place in Poland, Northern Ireland, Mauritius, Mexico, the United Arab Republic, and West Germany. Riots were accompanied by general strikes and demonstrations and the fall of the government in France. Terrorists exploded a bomb in a Jerusalem market, killing eleven people. Czechoslovakia was invaded by the armies of its allies of the Warsaw Pact—notably the Soviet Union—and the Czech leadership that had sponsored a measure of liberalization was forcibly removed. Civil war continued in Nigeria, and there was widespread starvation in what was then known as the secessionist province of Biafra. Universities around the world were visited by demonstrations, disturbances, violence, and disorder and were closed by police or by armies in Mexico City, Paris, and Cairo. The French and the Chinese tested—that is, exploded—thermonuclear devices. The North Vietnamese army and/or the Vietcong launched a major offensive in South Vietnam during the Tet holiday. During the 25-day-long battle of Hue alone an estimated 11,000 people—soldiers and civilians—were killed.

Conditions were very little better for the United States. As a major participant in the war in Vietnam, the United States was greatly affected by the Tet offensive and by the prolongation of the war. During the first six months of 1968, some 9,557 Americans died due to military action, more than the 9,419 Americans who died in Vietnam in the entire year of 1967. By the end of the year, a grand total of more than 30,000 Americans had died since the war began.[32]

In Memphis, Tennessee, Martin Luther King was shot and killed. There followed several days of rioting in more than 120 American cities, with much looting and burning of property. More than forty people lost their lives. The U.S. Ambassador to Guatemala was gunned down, as was presidential candidate Robert F. Kennedy. North Korea seized the U.S. vessel *Pueblo*. Students at Columbia University ransacked and occupied the president of the university's office and closed the school for more than a week. In Miami, Florida, riots broke out during the Republican National Convention in nearby Miami Beach. Three people were killed.

So it went, all year. At least the disorders accompanying the Republican convention took place away from the coverage of television. The Democratic party was not so lucky with its August Chicago convention. There, in full view of television cameras, many ugly incidents of violence took place. These frequently were instigated by peace officers, guards, or the police. The U.S. government was moved to inaugurate a statistical series based on data collected in the Justice Department. Titled "Civil Disturbances and Related Deaths," it showed 1968 to be a peak year for "major" civil disturbances in the United States.[33] A "major" disturbance was defined as having all of the following characteristics: vandalism, arson, looting or gunfire, the presence of outside police forces or troops, more than 300 participants, excluding police, and a duration of 12 or more hours. Twenty-six such events were recorded in 1968, up from twelve the previous year. Between June of 1967 and June the next year, 148 persons were recorded as having died in civil disturbances. The body count receded to thirty in the following year, and thirty-two in 1969–1970, and then tapered off, as Table 1.2 shows.

Table 1.2   Civil disturbances and related deaths: 1967 to 1973

Period	Total	Disturbances Major¹	Other²	Related deaths	Period	Total	Disturbances Major¹	Other²	Related deaths
1967, June–Oct.	52	12	40	87	1970				
					July–Sept.	20	3	17	6
1968	80	26	54	83	Oct.–Dec.	6	–	6	6
Jan.–Mar.	6	2	4	9					
Apr.–June	46	19	27	52	1971	39	10	29	10
July–Sept.	25	5	20	21	Jan.–Mar.	12	4	8	6
Oct.–Dec.	3	–	3	1	Apr.–June	21	5	16	4
					July–Sept.	5	–	5	–
1969	57	8	49	19	Oct.–Dec.	1	1	–	–
Jan.–Mar.	5	–	5	–					
Apr.–June	27	5	22	8	1972	21	2	19	9
July–Sept.	19	3	16	9	Jan.–Mar.	3	–	3	5
Oct.–Dec.	6	–	6	2	Apr.–June	8	1	7	–
1970	76	18	58	33	July–Sept.	5	1	4	1
Jan.–Mar.	26	8	18	10	Oct.–Dec.	5	–	5	3
Apr.–June	24	7	17	11	1973, Jan.–Mar.	4	1	3	2

– Represents zero.   ¹Characterized by all of the following: (a) vandalism; (b) arson; (c) looting or gunfire; (d) outside police forces or troops used; (e) more than 300 persons involved, excluding police; (f) 12 hours or longer duration.   ²Characterized by: Any three elements (a)–(d) described in footnote 1; duration of at least three hours; and more than 50 persons involved, exclusive of police.

Source: U.S. Dept. of Justice, Internal Security Division, unpublished data. *Statistical Abstract of the U.S. 1973* (Washington, D.C.: Government Printing Office, 1973), p. 148.

Not all these events were equally important in supplying a context for the movement toward political reform that culminated in the transformations which provide the occasion of this book. It is important nevertheless to remind ourselves of the atmosphere in which the changes took place. More proximately, three 1968 events were especially significant in shaping the changes as they occurred. They were President Johnson's precipitate withdrawal from the nomination process, the assassination of Robert Kennedy, and the election of Richard Nixon.

3. The Hasty Departure of President Johnson

Preliminary plans for the Democratic National Convention were drawn mostly for the convenience of Lyndon Johnson. The convention was to be held in Chicago, Mayor Daley's city, and was timed a shade later than was customary so as to coincide with the President's August 27 birthday.[34] By early in 1968, however, it had become apparent that it would be no ordinary birthday party. A goodly portion of the political activists in the Democratic party were in revolt, open or tacit, against President Johnson's continued prosecution of the Vietnam war. Some were dismayed that it should have become an American war. Others, that there was a Democratic President in charge. Many were convinced of the immorality of the entire enterprise. Some felt they had been deceived at the time of the Tonkin Gulf resolution, which was widely interpreted in Washington as having granted President Johnson broad powers. There was distress at the President's concealment of the actual magnitude of the American commitment and his unwillingness to face the economic costs of the war.[35]

Sentiment out in the country was not much happier. Public opinion surveys told a story of escalating disapproval of the war and of President Johnson's conduct of the Presidency. In early February of 1968 the Gallup poll for the first time showed more respondents agreeing than disagreeing with the proposition that the U.S. had made a "mistake" in getting involved in Vietnam. By March the Gallup poll reported 69 percent in favor of phas-

ing out of Vietnam, with Democrats 70 percent to 18 percent
in favor and Republicans 68 percent to 25 percent in favor.
President Johnson's overall job rating sank from 48 percent approval and 39 percent disapproval in January 1968 to 41 percent approval and 47 percent disapproval in February.[36]

For some activists in the Democratic party—notably Allard K.
Lowenstein of New York—the coming 1968 election seemed an
appropriate vehicle for the expression of their deep disapproval of the war and of President Johnson's policy of heavy
and increasing American involvement.[37] For the purposes of
spreading that message, and of eliciting a response from the
electorate, the primary elections seemed ideal. The problem was
to find a candidate who would carry the dump-Johnson banner. After some false starts and disappointments,[38] the mantle
finally fell on the shoulders of Senator Eugene McCarthy of
Minnesota. McCarthy campaigned in New Hampshire, the location of the earliest primary, against the war, against Lyndon
Johnson, and against the Presidency itself, arguing that the office had become "personalized" and its powers subject to abuse.[39]

A Johnson write-in movement was hastily organized by regular Democratic politicians in New Hampshire, and it succeeded in beating McCarthy in the March 12 preference primary by 48.5 percent to 42 percent. Far more salient was the
virtually unanimous opinion in the news media that McCarthy
had pulled off the coup of the year by doing so well.[40]

McCarthy's moral victory emboldened many Democrats
around the country to support him and also brought Senator
Robert Kennedy of New York into the race. Kennedy in the
beginning had refused to oppose the President, and it was only
after he had earlier decided against contesting the New Hampshire primary and given his tacit blessing to the effort to find
someone else to do the job that McCarthy had agreed to campaign.[41]

The timing of Kennedy's entry into the contest, immediately
on the heels of McCarthy's New Hampshire success, did nothing to endear him to McCarthy or to McCarthy's strongest en-

thusiasts. As one of them, Mary McGrory of the Washington *Star,* wrote:

> Kennedy thinks that American youth belongs to him at the bequest of his brother. Seeing the romance flower between them and McCarthy, he moved with all the ruthlessness of a Victorian father whose daughter has fallen in love with a dustman.[42]

There was a further rationale to Kennedy's candidacy. He was, no doubt in part through the bequest of his brother, more broadly based and more widely acquainted within the Democratic party than McCarthy, notably among black and Hispanic leaders and urban politicians. He was also more widely but not necessarily more favorably known among labor leaders and southern Democratic politicians. There was in addition the sizable cadre of Kennedy loyalists throughout the country who had never been comfortable with Lyndon Johnson or his Presidency and who looked with favor on a restoration of a political status quo that had been interrupted by the assassination of John Kennedy five years before.

As a practical matter, Kennedy people maintained McCarthy could not actually win the nomination whereas Kennedy could. McCarthy was arguing for a drastically scaled-down Presidency, which meant that even if by the unlikeliest turn of events he was nominated and elected he could not or, perhaps worse, would not govern. Kennedy, on the other hand, understood and appreciated the uses of power and could succeed where McCarthy could only fail. Kennedy represented not an anti-establishment but an alternative establishment.[43]

On March 16, Kennedy threw his hat in the ring and entered the next major primary election open to him, the May 7 Indiana primary. Allard Lowenstein's aspiration to make of the primaries a parade of referendums on Lyndon Johnson and his conduct of the Vietnam war was about to be realized.

On March 31, Lyndon Johnson greatly confused the issue by withdrawing as a candidate.[44] This gave the sizable fraction of Democratic party activists that wanted to dump Johnson a stunning victory: Johnson had dumped himself. Still another sizable fraction of the Democratic party remained, however, consisting not only of Johnson loyalists but also of those Democrats who for one reason or another found themselves outside both the McCarthy and the Kennedy camps.

Although taken somewhat by surprise, and inconveniently in Mexico City when the President sprang his announcement, Vice President Hubert Humphrey moved promptly to spread the word of his impending candidacy and announced several weeks later, on April 27.[45] Humphrey's strategy did not include contesting the primary elections. His natural advantage lay in his long-time friendships with party leaders all over the country and especially with labor leaders active in Democratic politics. He wrote:

> Enjoying people as I do, I naturally seek new friends and keep old friendships going. As a matter of course, some of these friendships do have political value, and every politician is human enough to develop some friendships primarily for their potential political value. So I suppose it is honest to say that, within the limitations of my position and the strictures placed on me, I did instinctively try to develop a political base while I was Vice President, building primarily on the base I already had from my senatorial career—my long, happy relationships with the labor movement, the Jewish and black communities, liberal farm organizations. I had also been expanding my contacts in the business world.[46]

While Kennedy and McCarthy were busy campaigning hard against one another in the primary elections, Humphrey pursued a more traditional path:

> An enormous amount of work was done by the key staff people and our labor supporters, the kind of work that is crucial to a solid campaign and is not often seen, because it is not in the forefront: lining up delegates; working the states where delegates were selected in caucuses; getting commitments; putting together the coalition.[47]

This made sense if for no other reason than because so many delegates were not selected in primaries and because as a late entry Humphrey would have had difficulty in securing money and forming a campaign organization quickly. Primaries, moreover, were a risk. Humphrey as Vice President could be burdened with all the disadvantages of having to defend the most unpopular aspects of President Johnson's administration. But as Vice President he had no power to mobilize the Johnson administration or orchestrate events in his own behalf. Journals of opinion—not excluding those liberal organs which had commended him to President Johnson as his vice presidential candidate four years earlier—were already beginning to experiment with the theme that a vote against Humphrey would be a way of striking at the absent Johnson, and that a vote for either Kennedy or McCarthy in a primary election was a repudiation, therefore, of both the President and the Vice President.[48]

There was some evidence that public opinion did not see things quite that way. The Gallup poll of April 28 showed Humphrey, not Kennedy, as the second choice of McCarthy supporters (42% to 31%, with 27% undecided). Only 35 percent of Kennedy supporters, on the other hand, preferred Humphrey. McCarthy was the second choice of 50 percent with only 14 percent undecided.[49]

The climax of the primary season came in early June with what was then the winner-take-all contest for the giant California delegation and its 174 delegate votes. As of May 15, Democratic rank-and-file respondents around the country were split three ways: 40 percent favored Vice President Humphrey, 31 percent were for Senator Kennedy, and 19 percent for Senator McCarthy, with 10 percent undecided.[50] This constituted a nine-point gain for Humphrey over comparable April figures, and losses for Kennedy and McCarthy of four points each. As of the first of June, Democratic county chairmen were overwhelmingly for Humphrey—70 percent Humphrey to 16 percent for Kennedy and 6 percent for McCarthy.[51] Two days before the California primary *Newsweek* claimed 1,279 delegates out of the 1,312 needed to win were solid for or leaning to Humphrey, with 713½ for Kennedy, 280 for McCarthy, and

349 uncommitted.[52] *U.S. News* on the same date put out a much
more cautious estimate, with 998 delegates uncommitted or
pledged to favorite sons, and Humphrey leading Kennedy by
1,020 delegates to 357, with 247 for McCarthy.[53] Humphrey
had campaigned in no primaries and won none. Kennedy had
by then won three primaries, and McCarthy had won four.[54] It
could reasonably be said on the eve of the California primary
election that the Democratic party was split three ways, but with
Humphrey comfortably in the lead. His standing with party
leaders, with labor, with Johnson loyalists, and in the South,
where Kennedy and McCarthy were both notably weak, was
considerably greater than either of his main rivals. He was,
however, short of victory according to non-partisan calculations, and his rivals were able to make much of the fact that he
had not contested any of the primaries, where they had con-
centrated so much of their effort.

4. The Assassination of Robert Kennedy

What happened next, at approximately 12:20 a.m. on June 5,
1968, was one of the most extraordinary and consequential
events in modern American political history. On the night of
his victory in the California primary, Robert Kennedy was shot
and killed. It was widely and immediately assumed that Vice
President Humphrey was the obvious beneficiary of this dread-
ful act. Events were presently to reveal, however, that nothing
could have been farther from the truth.

As Kennedy's friend Dick Tuck disclosed more than a decade later, speaking of the six regional coordinators of the
Kennedy campaign who kept track of every delegate and every
potential delegate to the 1968 Democratic convention:

> Once their best-kept secret was that Bobby didn't have enough
> delegates to win the nomination.[55]

Of course it was no secret; most impartial sources put Humphrey far ahead of Kennedy at the time of the California primary.

There was, however, a Kennedy battle plan for the post-primary period: television broadcasts, a twenty-six-state tour, an overseas junket. Humphrey delegate counts were considered soft by Kennedy people, and they thought McCarthy's hold on young people would slip. Of these sorts of wistful thoughts a large and poignant literature has been made.[56] The plausibility of the claim that Kennedy would have been nominated is of less interest than the fact that wishes, made irretrievably contrary to fact by the assassination, for a time dominated the thoughts of those who had been most active in Kennedy's behalf.

As Jules Witcover said:

> For most of the old Robert Kennedy team . . . there was no stomach at this juncture for any more politics in 1968. The pro, Larry O'Brien, hopeful he could help stitch the splintered party together, went over to his friend Humphrey, and [speechwriter Richard] Goodwin returned to McCarthy. But the other key figures . . . sat out the preconvention doldrums . . .
>
> Part of letting go, among most of the Robert Kennedy followers, was the hope and the anticipation that they could ignore the approaching Democratic National Convention. It would be too painful for them, and it seemed almost irrelevant now . . .
>
> In all the pulling and hauling [of the convention] over the platform plank on Vietnam, the assassinated candidate's influence was ever-present; in the deep pessimism that infected the convention from the start and inevitably produced a yearning for a viable alternative to Humphrey and McCarthy, the prospect that he could have been nominated, had he lived, seemed infinitely more possible than it had appeared to be on that last night in California.[57]

Although more than a decade has elapsed since the spring of 1968, it is impossible to read the yellowed newspaper clippings, or the outpouring of memoirs from participants in the politics of that difficult time without sensing the intensity of feeling that overcame nearly everyone. Large numbers of Democrats, disgusted with the war and unable to abide the leadership of Lyndon Johnson, had turned to Eugene McCarthy. He in turn had been undercut, as many of his supporters thought, by Rob-

ert Kennedy's unwillingness to endorse their effort and by
Kennedy's belated decision to capture the nomination for himself. Many of Kennedy's people, who had been deeply devoted
to him, were ready enough to adopt a politics of pragmatism
and coalition-building while they were winning, but, overwhelmed by his assassination, afterward turned bitter and de-
spondent.

Humphrey was appalled and immobilized by the assassination of his chief rival:

> Bob Kennedy's death was a national tragedy . . . that shook our
> entire political world. Once more, the poison and hate demon-
> strated in the new act of assassination traumatized the survivors
> and permeated the nation.
>
> To campaign in such a situation was unthinkable, even if one were
> not affected by the act, as I deeply was. This was particularly so
> for a man connected, as I was, with Lyndon Johnson. So I im-
> mediately put a stop to our campaign efforts. We withdrew from
> the New York campaign entirely, even though we'd already spent
> considerably more than any sensible organization should have. We
> lost a month of campaign activity, since it wasn't until July that we
> really geared up once again. Momentum was lost, and now we
> reeled under the strain.[58]

By the end of the pre-convention period, an ugly mood had
settled on the Democratic party. Robert Kennedy's death had
left a gaping wound. Rather than acting as a force for reconcil-
iation Kennedy's partisans joined McCarthy supporters in the
belief that somehow Vice President Humphrey would win the
nomination illegitimately.[59]

The intellectual foundations of this position were set in place
by McCarthy supporters fairly early in the election year. Finding themselves prevented by state party rules from exploiting a
number of opportunities to convert their indignation about the
war into solid delegate votes, McCarthy strategists cried foul.
They put together a blue ribbon commission on the delegate
selection process under the chairmanship of Governor Harold
Hughes of Iowa which served as a clearing house for atrocity

stories about the management of the nomination process by party leaders in various states throughout the country,[60] even in the face of strong challenges by McCarthy and anti-war groups. Among the most telling stories were these:

(1) Unfair representation of McCarthy among the 65 of New York's 190 votes who were appointed by the Democratic State Committee. McCarthy won a slight majority of the 125 elected delegates but received only 15 of the 65 appointed delegates. New York State Chairman John Burns said: "If I ignored the people who have helped me with the organization work and appointed strangers just because they're for McCarthy, I'd have a revolution on my hands."

(2) Walk-outs by McCarthy delegates from state conventions in Connecticut and Kentucky when conventions, controlled by pro-Humphrey majorities, refused to give them what they regarded as adequate representation, in spite of the Humphrey national staff's expressed desire that proportional representation be permitted.

(3) Manipulation by party leaders of access to delegate nomination processes. "In at least two counties in Oklahoma and one congressional district in Missouri, conventions were held in secret. In three Indiana district conventions, McCarthy delegates tape recorded nominating sessions at which the chairman heard the nomination of the regular party slate, entertained a motion to close the nominations and declared an affirmative vote with McCarthy delegates shouting for recognition. One tape records a complete nominating session lasting twenty-two seconds."[61]

Stories of this kind were given wide circulation and fueled resentment of Humphrey and his candidacy by McCarthy supporters, and later by Kennedy supporters. Protests from the Humphrey camp that they had played by the rules were met by many McCarthy and Kennedy partisans with derision. The "old" rules were "old" politics. "New politics" demanded new and more democratic rules.

The Hughes Commission report, *The Democratic Choice*, released on the eve of the Democratic National Convention, concluded that "state systems for selecting delegates to the national convention and the procedures of the convention itself, display considerably less fidelity to basic democratic principles than a nation which claims to govern itself can safely tolerate," and it advocated that an official party commission be appointed to examine problems they had identified. McCarthy delegate Anne Wexler of Connecticut, through her position on the Rules Committee of the Democratic National Convention, was able to bring the commission report to the Committee, which accepted the idea of an ongoing rules commission, and referred Hughes Commission recommendations onward to it.

These complaints raised an issue with which the delegate selection machinery as it existed in 1968 could not cope: what to do about a relatively late-blooming but very strong wave of feeling among a large number of political activists when many delegate positions had already been filled at an earlier time, and when access to the rest of the delegate slots would be hard fought. Not all American political institutions are designed to respond to the sentiments of a given moment. The rationale for electing one-third of the Senate every two years, for example, is expressly to buffer the institution against the effects of a landslide in any one election. So it can hardly be argued as an abstract proposition that responsiveness to contemporary sentiment is an unfailing hallmark of American political institutions. Moreover, support for timely responsiveness to contemporary feelings is not necessarily either a "left-wing" or a "right-wing" policy position. Being for an "open" delegate selection process and favoring McCarthy meant backing timeliness of delegate selection against institutional continuity and was in the context of 1968 politics a more-or-less left-wing position. But to favor up-to-date sentiments a few years later meant supporting the right of state legislatures to overthrow an earlier endorsement of a constitutional amendment favoring the Equal Rights Amendment.

This suggests that a political analysis of real-world consequences underlying the "principles" of timeliness on one hand or of institutional protection from momentary swings of sentiment on the other is appropriate. Emphasis on timeliness in delegate selection gives advantages to candidate enthusiasts and argues for the use of primary elections to select delegates within the calendar year of the election; state party leaders, on the other hand, gain in influence when delegates are selected earlier than the election year and in less public circumstances. So there is a necessary trade-off between the satisfaction of urgent needs for the representation of current feelings and the maintenance of the stability of the party organization. In practice, in 1968, the particular solution to this problem that prevailed in the Democratic party proved unsatisfactory to many of those who sought a reflection of their views, especially about Vietnam, in the delegate selection process. Feelings of having been unjustly treated on the part of some of those who were thus rebuffed were directed against their party's eventual nominee.

Events of the convention week did little to soothe the sensibilities of those outside the Humphrey camp, and the fact that Humphrey was treated little better than they was lost on them. A strenuous effort to write a peace plank on Vietnam for the party platform foundered on the intransigence of the absent Lyndon Johnson. Convention planning was entirely in the hands of Johnson, who rejected Humphrey's plea to move the site from Chicago and refused to cooperate with Humphrey or his allies on technical arrangements of all kinds. Johnson's evident hostility to the McCarthy camp on similar issues—telephones, floor passes, gallery seats—merely convinced McCarthy supporters that the convention was being run, as they told Allen Otten of the *Wall Street Journal,* "as part of a Johnson-Humphrey plot."[62]

The convention itself was tightly managed by large numbers of functionaries in charge of "security" alleged to be taking orders variously from President Johnson, the Secret Service, or Mayor Daley. Numerous disgraceful incidents took place on the floor of the convention itself or nearby involving the manhandling or arrest of delegates.[63] One delegate was hand-cuffed and hauled off to jail because he had succeeded in activating a machine guarding an entrance to the convention hall by using an ordinary credit card instead of the plastic card issued him by the Democratic National Committee. Another delegate was ejected from the floor bodily, in the full view of the television cameras, because he was alleged to be wearing faulty identity cards. This occurred over the objection of his delegation chairman, who vouched personally for his identity. Security guards attacked CBS news reporter Dan Rather and knocked him down on the floor of the convention hall. The event was broadcast nationwide, and audiences could hear the most trusted nonpartisan voice in America, that of CBS anchorman Walter Cronkite, refer to the employees of the Democratic party who did it as "thugs."[64]

The convention hall was barricaded off from the crowds of protesters, demonstrators, ill-wishers, and hangers-on who had come to Chicago for the convention, but the streets and hotels where delegates stayed were filled with manifestations of their discontent. These grew greatly in pitch and volume as Mayor Daley's police herded delegates about and, seemingly at random, attacked people crossing the path of the police.

After it was all over, an official investigation of irregular conduct that took place in the surrounds of the convention yielded the following description of a part of what went on:

> During the week of the Democratic National Convention, the Chicago police were the targets of mounting provocation by both word and act. It took the form of obscene epithets, and of rocks, sticks, bathroom tiles and even human feces hurled at police by demonstrators . . . .

> The crowd included Yippies come to "do their thing," youngsters working for a political candidate, professional people with dissenting political views, anarchists and determined revolutionaries, motorcycle gangs, black activists, young thugs, police and secret service undercover agents. There were demonstrators waving the

Viet Cong flag and the red flag of revolution and there were the simply curious who came to watch and, in many cases, became willing or unwilling participants . . . .

[I]ncidents of intense and indiscriminate violence occurred in the streets . . .

Demonstrators attacked too. And they posed difficult problems for police as they persisted in marching through the streets, blocking traffic and intersections. But it was the police who forced them out of the park and into the neighborhood.

On the part of the police there was enough wild club swinging, enough cries of hatred, enough gratuitous beating to make the conclusion inescapable that individual policemen, and lots of them, committed violent acts far in excess of the requisite force for crowd dispersal or arrest. To read dispassionately the hundreds of statements describing at firsthand the events of Sunday and Monday nights is to become convinced of the presence of what can only be called a police riot.[65]

Needless to say, unofficial observers, drawn to Chicago to witness the Democratic convention, and some of them deeply engaged politically, were not always so restrained in their accounts. A particularly ripe specimen—not greatly atypical of much left-Democratic "coverage" of political events of 1968— appeared in the *New York Review of Books* in late September from the pen of the well-known novelist and Eugene McCarthy supporter, William Styron:

It was perhaps unfortunate that [Mayor Richard J.] Daley, the hoodlum suzerain of the city, became emblematic of all that the young people in their anguish cried out against, even though he plainly deserved it. No one should ever have been surprised that he set loose his battalions against the kids; it was the triumphant end-product of his style, and what else might one expect from this squalid person whose spirit suffused the great city as oppressively as that of some Central American field marshal. . . . It was too bad that Daley should have hogged a disproportionate share of the infamy which has fallen upon the Democratic party; for if it is getting him off the hook too easily to call him a scapegoat, nonetheless the execration he has received . . . may obscure the fact that Daley is only the nastiest symbol of stupidity and desuetude in a political party that may die, or perhaps is already dead, because it harbors too many of his breed and mentality. Humphrey, the departed John Bailey, John Connally, Richard Hughes, Muskie—all are merely eminent examples of a rigidity and blindness, a feebleness of thought, that have possessed the party at every level.

Recalling those young citizens for Humphrey who camped out downstairs in my hotel, that multitude of square, seersuckered fraternity boys and country club jocks with butch haircuts, from the suburbs of Columbus and Atlanta, who passed out Hubert buttons and Humphrey mints, recalling them and their elders, mothers and fathers, some of them delegates and not all of them creeps or fanatics by any means but an amalgam of everything— simply well-heeled, most of them, entrenched, party hacks tied to the mob or with a pipeline to some state boss, a substantial number hating the war but hating it not enough to risk dumping Hubert in favor of a vague professorial freak who couldn't feel concern over Prague and hung out with Robert Lowell—I think now that the petrification of a party which allowed such apathy and lack of adventurousness and moral inanition to set in had long ago shaped its frozen logic, determined its fatal choice months before McCarthy or, for that matter, Bobby Kennedy had come along to rock, ever so slightly, the colossal dreamboat. And this can only reinforce what appears to me utterly plausible: that whatever the vigor and force of the dissent, whatever one might say about the surprising strength of support that the minority report received on the floor, a bare but crucial majority of Americans still is unwilling to repudiate the filthy way. This is really the worst thought of all.[66]

A significant feature of many accounts of violence at the Democratic convention was the effort to pin the blame on the Democratic nominee, Hubert Humphrey. On the night of the nomination several of the worst incidents took place, and they were shown on national television, sometimes in embarrassing juxtaposition to coverage of Humphrey's nomination, as Theodore White graphically described:

[San Francisco Mayor Joseph] Alioto rose on screen to nominate him; back and forth the cameras swung from Alioto to pudgy, cigar-smoking politicians, to Daley, with his undershot, angry jaw, painting visually without words the nomination of the Warrior of Joy as a puppet of the old machines. Carl Stokes, the black mayor of Cleveland, was next—to second Humphrey's nomination—and then, at 9:55, NBC's film of the bloodshed had finally been edited, and Stokes was wiped from the nation's vision to show the violence in living color.

The Humphrey staff is furious—Stokes is their signature on the Humphrey civil-rights commitment; and Stokes' dark face is being wiped from the nation's view to show blood—Hubert Humphrey being nominated in a sea of blood.[67]

Amidst all the anger and turmoil of the convention week Humphrey made several efforts to build some bridges to disaffected delegates. In the main, he was ineffectual and, worse, was seen to be buffeted by events rather than in charge of the Democratic party. His efforts to be conciliatory on the Vietnam peace plank of the platform came to naught.[68]

But on one matter, largely unnoticed at the time, Humphrey was able to make a concession unimpeded by President Johnson. This was on the liberal minority report of the Committee on Rules and Order of Business, which used language similar to a resolution adopted with the report of the Credentials Committee and called for abolition of unit voting in state delegations at future national party conventions, and throughout the delegate selection process, and for efforts to assure that in the future "delegates are selected through party primary, convention or committee procedures open to public participation within the calendar year of the National Convention." This report was more or less the result of Hughes Commission recommendations, and unlike the Credentials Committee resolution, called for prompt implementation in the 1972 convention. The Credentials Committee resolution provided only that changes of this sort should be studied by a special commission and a report presented to the 1972 convention.[69] This rather muddled set of overlapping resolutions was the seed from which the most significant party reforms grew, providing the rationale for the formation after the election of a commission of the Democratic party on delegate selection, and for possible implementation of its report in the convention of 1972.

The Commission on Party Structure and Delegate Selection was the formal name given to the McGovern—later the McGovern-Fraser—Commission of the Democratic Party.[70] It was formed in February 1969,[71] and reported to the Democratic National Committee by April 1970. It pieced its own mandate together from the two convention resolutions, one of them calling for "full and timely," the other for "meaningful and timely," opportunities for Democrats to participate in the delegate selection process.[72] Its report, *Mandate for Reform*, contains several elements, notably, (1) endorsements of itself by various Democratic party leaders and strong claims about its legal authority to issue orders to state parties;[73] (2) a compendium of complaints reminiscent of the Hughes Commission about selection procedures for delegates in 1968; and (3) eighteen detailed "guidelines." The importance of these guidelines and their various requirements for subsequent events was very great.[74]

They were put forward, in the words of the report, as ". . . the minimum action state Parties must take to meet the requirements of the Call of the 1972 Convention."[75] Thus, formerly more or less independent state party organizations were put on notice that they would be expected to follow requirements of the national party as outlined by the McGovern Commission. Most of the guidelines dealt with the processes by which delegates were to be chosen. Two selection systems were banned entirely. Byron Shafer describes them as follows:

> *The Party Caucus.* In party caucus systems, the bottom level of party officers—usually precinct committeemen and committeewomen—meet to select delegates to some higher-level convention, which eventually chooses the national convention delegation. States using this system varied according to the level at which the process began and the number of levels which intervened between the bottom and the top. But in toto, the device was the oldest and most widely used delegate selection institution in American history.

campaigns. An overwhelming majority favors action to prevent recurrence of the scandalous features that infect the system by which money is raised and the uses to which it has been put.[82]

It is not obvious that Watergate was a scandal about political finance at all. If it was, it could be argued that Watergate was about the expenditure of campaign funds for purposes that were already thoroughly illegal, and conceivably also about raising money illegally as well. By this reasoning, no new laws with respect to the regulation of political finance were germane to righting the wrongs of Watergate.

New laws were nevertheless what ensued. It is a common experience for political innovations to be enacted in the wake of situations widely perceived as crises.[83] These innovations are not necessarily rigorously related to the causes of crises or to their amelioration, however. Thus, in the wake of the alarm in the United States about growing technological proficiency in the Soviet Union set off by the launching of Sputnik in October of 1957, the condition of American rural libraries was greatly improved. This was, among other things, an entrepreneurial achievement of a particularly shrewd legislative craftsman in the House of Representatives named Carl Elliott, who understood how an urgent need for Congress to be seen to be doing something could be dovetailed to the requirements of his longer-term political agenda.[84]

No doubt some similar process was at work in producing the 1974 amendments to the Federal Election Campaign Act, which introduced sweeping innovations having broad effects on presidential selection.[85] The new law set limits on the amount of money individuals, political committees, and political parties could contribute to a single election campaign for federal offices.[86] Limits were also set to the amount of money a candidate could spend to get elected. Candidates for a presidential nomination were prohibited from spending more than $10,000,000, and candidates running in the general election were limited to $20,000,000, all as conditions for receiving public finance in election campaigns. The 1974 amendments also developed the rules under which public financing of presidential campaigns, which had been created by the 1971 Act, could be implemented. National party conventions were to be subsidized by public funds. A six-member Federal Election Commission was created. Changes were also made to strengthen campaign finance disclosure laws, in large part by requiring candidates to establish a single central campaign committee, and to report contributions and expenditures in some detail.[87]

The law was challenged in the courts almost immediately after it took effect on January 1, 1975, by a group of political activists from varying parts of the political spectrum.[88] The Supreme Court found some elements of the new scheme unconstitutional: thus, limits on total expenditures by a candidate, limits on independent expenditures in behalf of a candidate, and limits on contributions by a candidate to his own campaign were invalidated.[89] So was the method by which Federal Election Commission members were to be appointed. The Court did, however, uphold limits on individual, political committee, and party contributions. Likewise, the spending limits imposed on recipients of public funds for presidential campaigns were allowed.

Since the Court decision, rendered in early 1976 at the start of a presidential campaign, in effect shut down the new Federal Election Commission, Congress was put in the position of having to rewrite the procedures for appointing commissioners speedily, before the 1976 campaign progressed much further. While they were at it they added a few new amendments to the law.[90] These changes limited individual contributions to political parties[91] and to political committees,[92] and allowed political committees to contribute no more than $15,000 to a political party in a given year.

In sum, the new arrangements provided for in the Federal Campaign Practices Act Amendments of 1974, as modified by the decision of the Supreme Court in *Buckley et al. v. Valeo,* and subsequent laws drastically changed the face of campaign finance. The innovations included (1) provision for federal subsidy of presidential elections, nominating conventions, and primary election campaigns under certain conditions; (2) strict requirements on the reporting by candidates of contributions to and expenditures of their campaigns; (3) limitations on the amounts of money candidates could spend in behalf of their candidacies as a condition of the receipt of federal financing both in presidential primary and general elections and; (4) finally, restrictions on the amounts of money individuals might give to or spend in coordination with (but not independently of) candidates of their choice. This entire panoply of new provisions and regulations was to be presided over by a newly created regulatory agency, the Federal Election Commission.[93] As we shall see, this sizable package of reforms in presidential campaign finance have interacted with reforms directly focused on the presidential selection process to produce wide-ranging consequences.

Appendix

THE OFFICIAL GUIDELINES OF THE COMMISSION ON
PARTY STRUCTURE AND DELEGATE SELECTION TO THE
DEMOCRATIC NATIONAL COMMITTEE

*On November 19 and 20, 1969, the Commission, meeting in open session in
Washington, D.C., adopted the following Guidelines for delegate selection.*

PART I—INTRODUCTION

The following Guidelines for delegate selection represent the Commission's interpretation of the "full, meaningful, and timely" language of its mandate. These Guidelines have been divided into three general categories.

A. Rules or practices which inhibit access to the delegate selection process—items which compromise full and meaningful participation by inhibiting or preventing a Democrat from exercising his influence in the delegate selection process.

B. Rules or practices which dilute the influence of a Democrat in the delegate selection process, after he has exercised all available resources to effect such influence.

C. Rules and practices which have some attributes of both A and B.

A. Rules or practices inhibiting access:

1. Discrimination on the basis of race, color, creed, or national origin.
2. Discrimination on the basis of age or sex.
3. Voter registration.
4. Costs and fees.
5. Existence of Party rules.

B. Rules or practices diluting influence:

1. Proxy voting.
2. Clarity of purpose.
3. Quorum provisions.
4. Selection of alternates; filling of delegate and alternate vacancies.
5. Unit rule.
6. Adequate representation of political minority views.
7. Apportionment.

C. Rules and practices combining attributes of A and B:

1. Adequate public notice.
2. Automatic (ex-officio) delegates.
3. Open and closed processes.
4. Premature delegate selection (timeliness).
5. Committee selection processes.
6. Slate-making.

PART II—THE GUIDELINES

A-1 Discrimination on the basis of race, color, creed, or national origin

The 1964 Democratic National Convention adopted a resolution which conditioned the seating of delegations at future conventions on the assurance that discrimination in any State Party affairs on the grounds of race, color, creed or national origin did not occur. The 1968 Convention adopted the 1964 Convention resolution for inclusion in the Call to the 1972 Convention. In 1966, the Special Equal Rights Committee, which had been created in 1964, adopted six anti-discrimination standards—designated as the "six basic elements"[1]—for the State

---

[1] *Six basic elements, adopted by the Democratic National Committee as official policy statement, January 1968:*

1. All public meetings at all levels of the Democratic Party in each State should be open to all members of the Democratic Party regardless of race, color, creed, or national origin.

2. No test for membership in, nor any oaths of loyalty to, the Democratic Party in any State should be required or used which has the effect of requiring prospective or current members of the Democratic Party to acquiesce in, condone or support discrimination on the grounds of race, color, creed, or national origin.

3. The time and place for all public meetings of the Democratic Party on all levels should be publicized fully and in such a manner as to assure timely notice to all interested persons. Such meetings must be held in places accessible to all Party members and large enough to accommodate all interested persons.

4. The Democratic Party, on all levels, should support the broadest possible registration without discrimination on grounds of race, color, creed or national origin.

5. The Democratic Party in each State should publicize fully and in such manner as to assure notice to all interested parties a full description of the legal and practical procedures for selection of Democratic Party Officers and rep-

Parties to meet. These standards were adopted by the Democratic National Committee in January 1968 as its official policy statement.

These actions demonstrate the intention of the Democratic Party to ensure a full opportunity for all minority group members to participate in the delegate selection process. To supplement the requirements of the 1964 and 1968 Conventions, the Commission requires that:

1. State Parties add the six basic elements of the Special Equal Rights Committee to their Party rules and take appropriate steps to secure their implementation;

2. State Parties overcome the effects of past discrimination by affirmative steps to encourage minority group participation, including representation of minority groups on the national convention delegation in reasonable relationship to the group's presence in the population of the State.[2]

A-2 Discrimination on the basis of age or sex

The Commission believes that discrimination on the grounds of age or sex is inconsistent with full and meaningful opportunity to participate in the delegate selection process. Therefore, the Commission requires State Parties to eliminate all vestiges of discrimination on these grounds. Furthermore, the Commission requires State Parties to overcome the effects of past discrimination by affirmative steps to encourage representation on the national convention delegation of young people—defined as people of not more than thirty nor less than eighteen years of age—and women in reasonable relationship to their presence in the population of the State.[2] Moreover, the Commission

resentatives on all levels. Publication of these procedures should be done in such fashion that all prospective and current members of each State Democratic Party will be fully and adequately informed of the pertinent procedures in time to participate in each selection procedure at all levels of the Democratic Party organization.

6. The Democratic Party in each State should publicize fully and in such manner as to assure notice to all interested parties a complete description of the legal and practical qualifications for all officers and representatives of the State Democratic Party. Such publication should be done in timely fashion so that all prospective candidates or applicants for any elected or appointed position within each State Democratic Party will have full and adequate opportunity to compete for office."

[2] It is the understanding of the Commission that this is not to be accomplished by the mandatory imposition of quotas.

requires State Parties to amend their Party rules to allow and encourage any Democrat of eighteen years or more to participate in all party affairs.

When State law controls, the Commission requires State Parties to make all feasible efforts to repeal, amend, or otherwise modify such laws to accomplish the stated purpose.

A-3 Voter registration

The purpose of registration is to add to the legitimacy of the electoral process, not to discourage participation. Democrats do not enjoy an opportunity to participate fully in the delegate selection process in States where restrictive voter registration laws and practices are in force, preventing their effective participation in primaries, caucuses, conventions and other Party affairs. These restrictive laws and practices include annual registration requirements, lengthy residence requirements, literacy tests, short and untimely registration periods, and infrequent enrollment sessions.

The Commission urges each State Party to assess the burdens imposed on a prospective participant in the Party's delegate selection processes by State registration laws, customs and practices, as outlined in the report of the Grass Roots Subcommittee of the Commission on Party Structure and Delegate Selection, and use its good offices to remove or alleviate such barriers to participation.

A-4 Costs and fees; petition requirements

The Commission believes that costs, fees, or assessments and excessive petition requirements made by State law and Party rule or resolutions impose a financial burden on (1) national convention delegates and alternates; (2) candidates for convention delegates and alternates; and (3) in some cases, participants. Such costs, fees, assessments or excessive petition requirements discouraged full and meaningful opportunity to participate in the delegate selection process.

The Commission urges the State Parties to remove all costs and fees involved in the delegate selection process. The Commission requires State Parties to remove all excessive costs and fees, and to waive all nominal costs and fees when they would impose a financial strain on any Democrat. A cost or fee of more than $10 for all stages of the delegate selection process is deemed excessive. The Commission requires State Parties to remove all mandatory assessments of delegates and alternates.

The Commission requires State Parties to remove excessive petition requirements for convention delegate candidates of presidential candidates. Any petition requirement, which calls for a number of signatures in excess of 1% of the standard used for measuring Democratic strength, whether such standard be based on the number of Democratic votes cast for a specific office in a previous election or Party enrollment figures, is deemed excessive.

When State law controls any of these matters, the Commission requires State Parties to make all feasible efforts to repeal, amend or otherwise modify such laws to accomplish the stated purpose.

This provision, however, does not change the burden of expenses borne by individuals who campaign for and/or serve as delegates and alternates. Therefore, the Commission urges State Parties to explore ways of easing the financial burden on delegates and alternates and candidates for delegate and alternate.

A-5   Existence of Party rules

In order for rank-and-file Democrats to have a full and meaningful opportunity to participate in the delegate selection process, they must have access to the substantive and procedural rules which govern the process. In some States the process is not regulated by law or rule, but by resolution of the State Committee and by tradition. In other States, the rules exist, but generally are inaccessible. In still others, rules and laws regulate only the formal aspects of the selection process (e.g., date and place of the State convention) and leave to Party resolution or tradition the more substantive matters (e.g., intrastate apportionment of votes; rotation of alternates; nomination of delegates).

The Commission believes that any of these arrangements is inconsistent with the spirit of the Call in that they permit excessive discretion on the part of Party officials, which may be used to deny or limit full and meaningful opportunity to participate. Therefore, the Commission requires State Parties to adopt and make available readily accessible statewide Party rules and statutes which prescribe the State's delegate selection process with sufficient details and clarity. When relevant to the State's delegate selection process, explicit written Party rules and procedural rules should include clear provisions for: (1) the apportionment of delegates and votes within the State; (2) the allocation of fractional votes, if any; (3) the selection and responsibilities of convention committees; (4) the nomination of delegates and alternates; (5) the succession of alternates to delegate status and the filling of vacancies; (6) credentials challenges; (7) minority reports.

Furthermore, the Commission requires State Parties to adopt rules which will facilitate maximum participation among interested Democrats in the processes by which National Convention delegates are selected. Among other things, these rules should provide for dates, times, and public places which would be most likely to encourage interested Democrats to attend all meetings involved in the delegate selection process.

The Commission requires State Parties to adopt explicit written Party rules which provide for uniform times and dates of all meetings involved in the delegate selection process. These meetings and events include caucuses, conventions, committee meetings, primaries, filing deadlines, and Party enrollment periods. Rules regarding time and date should be uniform in two senses. First, each stage of the delegate selection process should occur at a uniform time and date throughout the State. Second, the time and date should be uniform from year to year. The Commission recognizes that in many parts of rural America it may be an undue burden to maintain complete uniformity, and therefore exempts rural areas from this provision so long as the time and date are publicized in advance of the meeting and are uniform within the geographic area.

B-1 Proxy voting

When a Democrat cannot, or chooses not to, attend a meeting related to the delegate selection process, many States allow that person to authorize another to act in his name. This practice—called proxy voting—has been a significant source of real or felt abuse of fair procedure in the delegate selection process.

The Commission believes that any situation in which one person is given the authority to act in the name of the absent Democrat, on any issue before the meeting, gives such person an unjustified advantage in affecting the outcome of the meeting. Such a situation is inconsistent with the spirit of equal participation. Therefore, the Commission requires State Parties to add to their explicit written rules provisions which forbid the use of proxy voting in all procedures involved in the delegate selection process.

B-2 Clarity of purpose

An opportunity for full participation in the delegate selection process is not meaningful unless each Party member can clearly express his preference for candidates for delegates to the National Convention, or for those who will select such delegates. In many States, a Party member who wishes to affect the selection of the delegation must do so by voting for delegates or Party officials who will engage in many activities unrelated to the delegate selection process.

Whenever other Party business is mixed, without differentiation, with the delegate selection process, the Commission requires State Parties to make it clear to voters how they are participating in a process that will nominate their Party's candidate for President. Furthermore, in States which employ a convention or committee system, the Commission requires State Parties to clearly designate the delegate selection procedures as distinct from other Party business.

B-3 Quorum provisions

Most constituted bodies have rules or practices which set percentage or number minimums before they can commence their business. Similarly, Party committees which participate in the selection process may commence business only after it is determined that this quorum exists. In some States, however, the quorum requirement is satisfied when less than 40% of committee members are in attendance.

The Commission believes a full opportunity to participate is satisfied only when a rank-and-file Democrat's representative attends such committee meetings. Recognizing, however, that the setting of high quorum requirements may impede the selection process, the Commission requires State Parties to adopt rules setting quorums at not less than 40% for all party committees involved in the delegate selection process.

B-4 Selection of alternates; filling of delegate and alternate vacancies

The Call to the 1972 Convention requires that alternates be chosen by one of the three methods sanctioned for the selection of delegates— i.e., by primary, convention or committee. In some States, Party rules authorize the delegate himself or the State Chairman to choose his alternate. The Commission requires State Parties to prohibit these practices—and other practices not specifically authorized by the Call— for selecting alternates.

In the matter of vacancies, some States have Party rules which authorize State Chairmen to fill all delegate and alternate vacancies. This practice again involves the selection of delegates or alternates by a

process other than primary, convention or committee. The Commission requires State Parties to prohibit such practices and to fill all vacancies by (1) a timely and representative Party committee; or (2) a reconvening of the body which selected the delegate or alternate whose seat is vacant; or (3) the delegation itself, acting as a committee.

When State law controls, the Commission requires State Parties to make all feasible efforts to repeal, amend or otherwise modify such laws to accomplish the stated purposes.

B-5 Unit rule

In 1968, many States used the unit rule at various stages in the processes by which delegates were selected to the National Convention. The 1968 Convention defined unit rule,[3] did not enforce the unit rule on any delegate in 1968, and added language to the 1972 Call requiring that "the unit rule not be used in any stage of the delegate selection process." In light of the Convention action, the Commission requires State Parties to add to their explicit written rules provisions which forbid the use of the unit rule or the practice of instructing delegates to vote against their stated preferences at any stage of the delegate selection process."[4]

B-6 Adequate representation of minority views on presidential candidates at each stage in the delegate selection process

The Commission believes that a full and meaningful opportunity to participate in the delegate selection process is precluded unless the presidential preference of each Democrat is fairly represented at all levels of the process. Therefore, the Commission urges each State Party to adopt procedures which will provide fair representation of minority views on presidential candidates and recommends that the 1972 Con-

---

[3] UNIT RULE. "This Convention will not enforce upon any delegate with respect to voting on any question or issue before the Convention any duty or obligation which said delegate would consider to violate his individual conscience. As to any legal, moral or ethical obligation arising from a unit vote or rule imposed either by State law by a State convention or State committee or primary election of any nature, or by a vote of a State delegation, the Convention will look to each individual delegate to determine for himself the extent of such obligation if any."

[4] It is the understanding of the Commission that the prohibition on instructed delegates applies to favorite-son candidates as well.

vention adopt a rule requiring State Parties to provide for the representation of minority views to the highest level of the nominating process.

The Commission believes that there are at least two different methods by which a State Party can provide for such representation. First, in at-large elections it can divide delegate votes among presidential candidates in proportion to their demonstrated strength. Second, it can choose delegates from fairly apportioned districts no larger than congressional districts.

The Commission recognizes that there may be other methods to provide for fair representation of minority views. Therefore, the Commission will make every effort to stimulate public discussion of the issue of representation of minority views on presidential candidates between now and the 1972 Democratic National Convention.

B-7 Apportionment

The Commission believes that the manner in which votes and delegates are apportioned within each State has a direct bearing on the nature of participation. If the apportionment formula is not based on Democratic strength and/or population the opportunity for some voters to participate in the delegate selection process will not be equal to the opportunity of others. Such a situation is inconsistent with a full and meaningful opportunity to participate.

Therefore, the Commission requires State Parties which apportion their delegation to the National Convention to apportion on a basis of representation which fairly reflects the population and Democratic strength within the State. The apportionment is to be based on a formula giving equal weight to total population and to the Democratic vote in the previous presidential election.

The Commission requires State Parties with convention systems to select at least 75% of their delegations to the National Convention at congressional district or smaller unit levels.

In convention or committee systems, the Commission requires State Parties to adopt an apportionment formula for each body actually selecting delegates to State, district and county conventions which is based upon population and/or some measure of Democratic strength. Democratic strength may be measured by the Democratic vote in the preceding presidential, senatorial, congressional or gubernatorial election, and/or by party enrollment figures.

When State law controls, the Commission requires State Parties to make all feasible efforts to repeal, amend or otherwise modify such laws to accomplish the stated purpose.

C-1 Adequate public notice

The Call to the 1968 convention required State Parties to assure voters an opportunity to "participate fully" in party affairs. The Special Equal Rights Committee interpreted this opportunity to include adequate public notice. The Committee listed several elements—including publicizing of the time, places and rules for the conduct of all public meetings of the Democratic Party and holding such meetings in easily accessible places—which comprise adequate public notice. These elements were adopted by the Democratic National Committee in January 1968 as its official policy statement and are binding on the State Parties.

Furthermore, the Commission requires State Parties to circulate a concise and public statement in advance of the election itself of the relationship between the party business being voted upon and the delegate selection process.

In addition to supplying the information indicated above, the Commission believes that adequate public notice includes information on the ballot as to the presidential preference of (1) candidates or slates for delegate or (2) in the States which select or nominate a portion of the delegates by committees, candidates or slates for such committees.

Accordingly, the Commission requires State Parties to give every candidate for delegate (and candidate for committee, where appropriate) the opportunity to state his presidential preferences on the ballot at each stage of the delegate selection process. The Commission requires the State Parties to add the word "uncommitted" or like term on the ballot next to the name of every candidate for delegate who does not wish to express a presidential preference.

When State law controls, the Commission requires the State Parties to make all feasible efforts to repeal, amend or otherwise modify such laws to accomplish the stated purposes.

C-2 Automatic (ex-officio) delegates (see also C-4)

In some States, certain public or Party officeholders are delegates to county, State and National Conventions by virtue of their official position. The Commission believes that State laws, Party rules and Party resolutions which so provide are inconsistent with the Call to the 1972 Convention for three reasons:

1. The Call requires all delegates to be chosen by primary, convention or committee procedures. Achieving delegate status by virtue of public or Party office is not one of the methods sanctioned by the 1968 Convention.

2. The Call requires all delegates to be chosen by a process which begins within the calendar year of the Convention. Ex-officio delegates usually were elected (or appointed) to their positions before the calendar year of the Convention.

3. The Call requires all delegates to be chosen by a process in which all Democrats have a full and meaningful opportunity to participate. Delegate selection by a process in which certain places on the delegation are not open to competition among Democrats is inconsistent with a full and meaningful opportunity to participate.

Accordingly, the Commission requires State Parties to repeal Party rules or resolutions which provide for ex-officio delegates. When State law controls, the Commission requires State Parties to make all feasible efforts to repeal, amend or otherwise modify such laws to accomplish the stated purpose.

C-3   Open and closed processes

The Commission believes that Party membership, and hence opportunity to participate in the delegate selection process, must be open to all persons who wish to be Democrats and who are not already members of another political party; conversely, a full opportunity for all Democrats to participate is diluted if members of other political parties are allowed to participate in the selection of delegates to the Democratic National Convention.

The Commission urges State Parties to provide for party enrollment that (1) allows non-Democrats to become Party members, and (2) provides easy access and frequent opportunity for unaffiliated voters to become Democrats.

C-4   Premature delegate selection (timeliness)

The 1968 Convention adopted language adding to the Call to the 1972 Convention the requirement that the delegate selection process must

begin within the calendar year of the Convention. In many States, Governors, State Chairmen, State, district and county committees who are chosen before the calendar year of the Convention, select—or choose agents to select—the delegates. These practices are inconsistent with the Call.

The Commission believes that the 1968 Convention intended to prohibit any untimely procedures which have any direct bearing on the processes by which National Convention delegates are selected. The process by which delegates are nominated is such a procedure. Therefore, the Commission requires State Parties to prohibit any practices by which officials elected or appointed before the calendar year choose nominating committees or propose or endorse a slate of delegates— even when the possibility for a challenge to such slate or committee is provided.

When State law controls, the Commission requires State Parties to make all feasible efforts to repeal, amend, or modify such laws to accomplish the stated purposes.

C-5   Committee selection processes

The 1968 Convention indicated no preference between primary, convention, and committee systems for choosing delegates. The Commission believes, however, that committee systems by virtue of their indirect relationship to the delegate selection process, offer fewer guarantees for a full and meaningful opportunity to participate than other systems.

The Commission is aware that it has no authority to eliminate committee systems in their entirety. However, the Commission can and does require State Parties which elect delegates in this manner to make it clear to voters at the time the Party committee is elected or appointed that one of its functions will be the selection of National Convention delegates.

Believing, however, that such selection system is undesirable even when adequate public notice is given, the Commission requires State Parties to limit the National Convention delegation chosen by committee procedures to not more than 10 percent of the total number of delegates and alternates.

Since even this obligation will not ensure an opportunity for full and meaningful participation, the Commission recommends that State Parties repeal rules or resolutions which require or permit Party committees to select any part of the State's delegation to the National Convention. When State law controls, the Commission recommends that State Parties make all feasible efforts to repeal, amend, or otherwise modify such laws to accomplish the stated purpose.

C-6 Slate-making

In mandating a full and meaningful opportunity to participate in the delegate selection process, the 1968 Convention meant to prohibit any practice in the process of selection which made it difficult for Democrats to participate. Since the process by which individuals are nominated for delegate positions and slates of potential delegates are formed is an integral and crucial part of the process by which delegates are actually selected, the Commission requires State Parties to extend to the nominating process all guarantees of full and meaningful opportunity to participate in the delegate selection process. When State law controls, the Commission requires State Parties to make all feasible efforts to repeal, amend or otherwise modify such laws to accomplish the stated purpose.

Furthermore, whenever slates are presented to caucuses, meetings, conventions, committees, or to voters in a primary, the Commission requires State Parties to adopt procedures which assure that:

1. the bodies making up the slates have been elected, assembled, or appointed for the slate-making task with adequate public notice that they would perform such task;

2. those persons making up each slate have adopted procedures that will facilitate widespread participation in the slate-making process, with the proviso that any slate presented in the name of a presidential candidate in a primary State be assembled with due consultation with the presidential candidate or his representative;

3. adequate procedural safeguards are provided to assure that the right to challenge the presented slate is more than perfunctory and places no undue burden on the challengers.

When State law controls, the Commission requires State Parties to make all feasible efforts to repeal, amend or otherwise modify such laws to accomplish the stated purpose.

II

Consequences for Political Parties

1. Changing the Structure of Incentives

A large body of commentary now exists discussing the consequences for parties of party reform. Those critical of the reforms have argued the view that they brought significant unanticipated changes to American politics;[1] those more favorable have argued that they have had a far more limited impact, except as intended.[2] It may not be possible to find empirical grounds for settling all the disagreements about the effects of party reform in a definitive way, but it is, perhaps, possible to make headway in establishing the plausibility of at least some of the details on which the contrary positions rest.

In general the argument proceeds mostly through the discussion of what happened in the Democratic party. In many respects, the Republican party remains unreformed: its apportionment formula for delegates to national conventions is still weighted toward the electoral college; the 1976 recommendations of its Rule 29 Committee to provide for monitoring of state delegation selection processes were rejected by the Republican National Committee and the 1976 Convention; the Republicans have no enforceable demographic quotas or affirma-

tive action standards; convention committees reflect state
equality in apportionment of members; and the confederate legal structure of the party has been retained.[3] Yet important
consequences of the reforms of the Democratic party have been
visited upon the Republicans as well; the laws having to do with
campaign finance operate equally on both parties, and so do
the effects of the mass media. The impulse to reform the nomination process came out of the turmoil of the Democratic experience of 1968, but because the delegate selection procedures
disapproved of by the McGovern-Fraser guidelines in many
states were perfectly legal and established in state law, changes
in the election laws of the several states were necessary in order
for many Democratic state parties to come into compliance with
the demands of the emerging enforcement machinery of the
Democratic National Committee. Where state laws were
changed, willy-nilly, Republican practices had to be adjusted as
well, presumably because changes in the rules under which delegate selection was to take place changed the structure of opportunities for Republican as well as for Democratic politicians.

Thus the notion that party reforms have had a significant
impact upon the parties relies upon the argument that party
leaders in the various states responded to the imposition of
McGovern-Fraser guidelines and to other changes in the political climate by modifying their own behavior in accord with a
newly emerging set of incentives.

At least five such incentives can be identified, all working in
mutually reinforcing ways to transform the presidential nominating process. In brief, they are: (1) centralization of control
over the certification of delegates, arising from the uncertainties introduced by the McGovern Commission guidelines; (2)
federal subsidies for candidates to contest primaries, interact-
ing with the mass media and with the public commitment of
delegates to candidates so as to push critical decisions earlier
and earlier on the calendar; (3) restriction of sources of money
other than the subsidy; (4) changes in primary election rules
promoting ease of candidate entry; and (5) the separation of

state conventions from delegate selection procedures owing to the risks of contamination of state conventions by candidate enthusiasts. The first and last of these have affected the leaders of state parties, inducing them to establish primaries for candidates to contest, while the middle three chiefly affected presidential candidates, enticing them into entering primary elections.

(1) The promulgation by the McGovern Commission of its eighteen guidelines introduced a new order of complexity, of uncertainty, and of centralized control to the selection of state delegations to national party conventions. Complexity meant the possibility of widely differing interpretations of what constituted adequate compliance with guidelines, and the possibility of conflict over the issue of compliance within the state parties. Uncertainty meant that state party leaders could not be sure whether the full range of options theoretically open to them in designing a presidential selection process would in fact pass muster with the compliance machinery being evolved by the Democratic National Committee or with the credentials committee of the next national convention. Neither body could be presumed in advance by state party leaders to be purely ministerial in character, devoid of political coloration. Centralization meant that as far as state party leaders were concerned, the ultimate determination of the adequacy of their compliance would be out of their hands. The burden of proof concerning a state delegation's fitness to be seated at a national convention had been shifted onto the shoulders of state party leaders, and this left them vulnerable to possible challengers within the state to the delegation's credentials before the national convention credentials committee.[4]

As the 1972 delegate selection season approached, the uncertainties of party leaders were palpable. R. W. Apple of the *New York Times* wrote:

> The delegates will have been chosen in a bewildering variety of ways—but all or nearly all by methods sanctioned by the reform

commission headed during the months of its most active work by Senator George McGovern of South Dakota. . . .

In 22 states and the District of Columbia, the delegates will be selected in some form of primary election.

In 24 states, a convention system with procedures already set will be used. In four others, a convention system will also be used, in all probability, but the situation is too murky at the moment to say for sure.

Delaware is one of the places where confusion reigns (the others are Georgia, Louisiana and Michigan). Under the rules as they now stand, delegates to the state convention, which would pick the delegates to the national convention, would not even be chosen until July 8, two days before the national convention is scheduled to begin. . . .

In all, more than 60 per cent of the delegates will be elected in primaries. . . .

But the McGovern commission requirement that at least 75 per cent of a state's delegation be elected by Congressional district (to avoid submerging minorities) forces more complicated systems on most convention states. The only exceptions are the six states that have only one Congressional district. . . .

The minutiae of election law and party regulations are usually of interest only to political insiders. But they can influence major political decisions.

For example, one of Governor [John] Gilligan's main reasons for coming out for Senator Muskie, rather than simply throwing the state open to all comers, was the fact that the Ohio election law requires all candidates for delegate to state a preference. All Ohio delegates will be chosen in the primary. So if Mr. Gilligan did not want to run as a favorite son, he either had to state his choice or give up any plan to attend the convention.[5]

Selecting delegates by primary election offered a quick and simple solution to most of the problems state party leaders were experiencing since it was evidently widely presumed that a primary conducted in the usual way would almost certainly meet the requirements of the guidelines.[6]

It has been denied that the proliferation of primaries in the delegate selection process—from 17 Democratic and 16 Republican in 1968, before the guidelines were promulgated, to 23 Democratic and 22 Republican in 1972, the next presidential election year—was inspired by McGovern-Fraser Commission reforms. Two former staff members of the Commission—conceivably in a mood to defend their work from well-meant erosion or from political attack—have generated a short list of other possible motives for switching to primary elections.[7] These include a desire on the part of state party leaders to attract the coverage of the national television networks for the purposes of drawing attention to state or regional problems. In addition, there is the simple financial attraction of having a primary, since:

> The candidates, their campaigns, and the press who cover them are known to spend a great deal of money in "crucial" primary states.[8]

These authors also mention several states—Texas, North Carolina, Georgia—in which they believe that primary elections were instituted because such elections were going to be helpful in 1976 to the favorite son presidential candidacies of Lloyd Bentsen, Terry Sanford, and Jimmy Carter, respectively. This ignores the changes of the 1968–72 period, but raises the possibility that by the time the leaders of state parties began thinking about the 1976 elections a whole raft of reasons to switch to primary elections might have occurred to them. It is not entirely clear, however, why primary elections were necessarily superior to the methods of delegate selection they replaced, at least from the standpoint of favorite son candidates. In Georgia, for example, prior to the reforms "the entire national convention delegation was chosen by the state party chairman, in consultation with the Democratic governor."[9] Even though the Georgia state chairman in 1976 was no friend of Jimmy Carter's, it is easy to envisage such a system being even more advantageous than a primary to a favorite son. If being selected by delegates picked in a primary election rather than by other means could be regarded as particularly helpful to candidates

Table 2.1 Major changes in delegate selection procedures: 1968–72, 1972–76, 1976–80

State	1968	1972
Illinois	direct primary, caucus	clsd pref primary
Maryland	(d) committee, (r) caucus	clsd pref primary
Michigan	(d) caucus	(d) clsd pref primary
New Mexico	caucus	clsd pref primary
North Carolina	caucus	clsd pref primary
Pennsylvania	clsd pref primary, committee	clsd pref primary
Rhode Island	(d) committee, (r) caucus	clsd pref primary (+ *inds*)
Tennessee	caucus	open primary

State	1972	1976
Arkansas	caucus	open primary
Georgia	caucus	open primary
Idaho	caucus	open primary
Kentucky	caucus	clsd pref primary
Michigan	(r) caucus	(r) clsd pref primary
Montana	(d) caucus	(d) clsd pref primary
Nevada	caucus	clsd pref primary
New Mexico	clsd pref primary	caucus
Texas	caucus	open primary

State	1976	1980
Arkansas	(r) open primary	(r) caucus
Connecticut	caucus	clsd pref primary
Idaho	(d) open primary	(d) caucus
Kansas	caucus	clsd pref primary (+ *inds*)
Louisiana	caucus	clsd pref primary
Michigan	(d) open primary	(d) caucus
Mississippi	(r) caucus	(r) direct primary
New Mexico	caucus	clsd pref primary
New York	(d) direct primary, committee	(d) direct primary
South Carolina	(r) caucus	(r) open primary
Puerto Rico	caucus	open primary

(r) Republicans only; (d) Democrats only; (*inds*) open to Independents as well; *caucus*, Delegates chosen by state and local caucuses and conventions; *committee*, Delegates chosen by state party committee; *clsd pref primary*, Delegates chosen or bound by presidential preference primaries open only to voters preregistered as members of the particular party; *direct primary*, Delegates chosen directly by voters in primaries, without a presidential preference poll; *open primary*, Delegates chosen or bound by presidential preference primaries open to all registered voters without regard to party pre-registration.

Sources: Austin Ranney (ed.), *The American Elections of 1980* (Washington, D.C.: American Enterprise Institute, 1981), pp. 366–68, and *Congressional Quarterly Weekly Reports*.

because delegates picked in this fashion would be perceived to be more legitimate by press and public, or less vulnerable to credentials challenges, then of course one must ask why. The answer seems plain enough: because of the changes in party regulations inspired by the McGovern Commission.

The other reasons given make sense as possible excuses for switching to primary elections at any time; what they do not explain is why all these reasons so suddenly occurred to so many state party leaders, and only after the guidelines had come into being. Could the compulsion of newly instituted guidelines have coincidentally stimulated an interest in publicizing state problems, or in raising money for the tourist industry? Perhaps; but it is more likely that the Winograd Commission of the Democratic Party—a commission set up after the 1976 election to examine the effects of reform—was expressing the view of many state party leaders when it said that "many states . . . felt that a primary offered the most protection against a challenge at the next convention."[10] The primary election was in any event a solution that was adopted in most cases where states changed from one election to the next in the period after 1968.

(2) The creation, by the Federal Election Campaign Act Amendments of 1974, of a federal subsidy for candidates in primary elections encouraged candidates to enter primaries.[11] In order to qualify for the subsidy, candidates had to raise $5,000 or more in small amounts (the federal subsidy only matches each donor's first $250) in twenty different states, a requirement that has not turned out to be onerous.

This subsidy also creates an objective device through which journalists can sift the various candidates, declaring those that have qualified for the subsidy as "serious" contenders. Although the actual payments of the subsidy do not occur until the election year begins, slowness in acquiring what Terry Sanford referred to as this "license to practice" could restrict the amount of favorable news coverage a candidate might receive.[12]

Not only participation in primaries but in early primaries is thus encouraged. The media coverage attending announcements of participation in early primaries has provided a means for qualifying for the subsidy, since the publicity surrounding entry into the race can help to generate the name recognition necessary to inspire a sufficient number of recipients of mailed appeals for funds to contribute a small amount, thus activating the matching federal payment. A further incentive to early entry into primaries is created because early choices color the way later alternatives are perceived. R. W. Apple said in 1972:

> Because the process in Iowa and in most of the other convention states is so structured and so open to public view, it appears likely that, beginning at the lowest level, the preferences of delegates will be known. From step to step, it will be relatively easy to assess Mr. Muskie's strength, Mr. McGovern's and so on.
>
> Thus, it will be far harder than in the past to remain uncommitted. Some analysts believe that fewer than 15 per cent of the delegates at Miami Beach will actually be uncommitted.[13]

As this suggests, the news media have learned to give enormous coverage to, and tend to extract a coherent story from the results of, the earliest primaries and state conventions.[14] More delegates are bound to candidates by rules prohibiting delegate primaries, and "uncommitted" delegates selected by state conventions tend to be ignored in news stories, as happened most conspicuously in the coverage of Iowa in 1976. The strategic options for political leaders, candidates, and party influentials alike are increasingly foreclosed by the publicity blitz of the early primaries, and the competitive pressure among newspapers, magazines, and the networks for reaction stories. Thus early participation becomes a necessity for a serious candidate. As Michael Robinson says, "In proportionate terms, each Democratic vote [in 1976] in New Hampshire received 170 times as much network news time as each Democratic vote in New York. Media reality—television reality—implied that a victory in New Hampshire totally overwhelmed a victory in New York."[15]

Candidates must allocate as well as raise their money early because of the way early results influence later outcomes. As reports filed with the Federal Election Commission show, this leads to great disparities in the investments candidates make in the different state selection processes, depending on the timing of delegate selection.

Table 2.2 Amount of money candidates receiving public financing spent per vote in selected states

State (Delegates selected in)	1976	1980
Iowa (Jan.)	$9.46	$13.89
New Hampshire (Feb.)	7.22	8.90
Florida (March)	2.02	2.21
Wisconsin (April)	1.15	1.36
Nebraska (May)	1.30	.45
California (June)	.68	.23

Source: *Congressional Quarterly Weekly Report* (December 26, 1981), p. 2566. See also F. Christopher Arterton, "Dollars for Presidents: Spending Money under the FECA," in Campaign Finance Study Group, *Financing Presidential Campaigns* (Mimeo), (Institute of Politics, John F. Kennedy School of Government, Harvard University, January 1982), chap. 3, pp. 11–12.

(3) Candidates were also encouraged to enter primaries, seek early publicity and qualify for the federal subsidy because access to the principal alternative source of funds to run any sort of campaign at all—heavy financial backing by a small circle of friends—was after 1974 forbidden by law.[16] Thus the principal sources of funds outside the federal subsidy itself became small individual contributions: money raised by direct-mail advertising, through anonymous donations at large fund-raising events like rock concerts, at $250-a-plate dinners, and similar activities.[17]

(4) Candidates were even further encouraged to enter early primaries by the abolition of the unit rule at the 1968 Democratic convention and consequently of winner-take-all primary elections. This meant that several candidates in any given election might anticipate garnering at least some pledged delegates, that even a modest effort might produce a modest harvest, and that it would be less likely that candidates would be

shut out altogether from receiving representation on a state delegation. Whether in response to these incentives or for some other reason, as Table 2.4 indicates, the number of candidates contesting primary elections—especially in the party where no incumbent President was trying to succeed himself—grew sharply after the reforms of 1968–72.[18]

Table 2.4   Number of candidates running in presidential primaries in more than one state, 1952–80

	Republicans	Democrats
1952	4	3
1956	2*	3
1960	3	5
1964	4	2*
1968	3	3
1972	3*	13
1976	2*	13
1980	9	5*

Mean 1952–68 (pre-rules changes): Rep. 3.2, Dem. 3.2
Mean 1972–80 (post-rules changes): Rep. 4.7, Dem. 10.3

*Party of an incumbent President running for renomination

Sources: Robert A. Diamond (ed.), *Presidential Elections Since 1789* (Washington, D.C.: Congressional Quarterly, Inc., 1975); *Congressional Quarterly Weekly Report* 34, nos. 9–24 (1976); Jonathan Moore (ed.), *The Campaign for President* (Cambridge, Mass.: Ballinger Publishing, 1981), pp. 280–88.

(5) With candidate initiatives so thoroughly dominating the delegate selection process, an incentive was created for state parties to separate their internal affairs from the presidential nominating process, thus removing a further impediment to the use of primaries by state parties. A state convention could do all sorts of business. If such a convention were overrun with the zealous supporters of various presidential candidates, politicians with concerns lying closer to home might find themselves inconveniently outnumbered. This created organizational incentives for party regulars—not just party reformers—to switch to primary elections. As Mark Siegel observed preparations for 1972 in New York state:

. . . the state organization was subject to strong criticism [in 1968] for the manner in which . . . non-primary delegate slots were filled. It seemed that the majority of the "regulars" at the guideline adoption meeting, including the organization's leadership, wanted no part of a repetition of the 1968 experience. Indeed, one member of the committee said, "they want a primary, let them have a primary, everything by primary; we don't need more headaches." Thus the committee endorsed all the guidelines and opted for primary election of all delegates and alternates.[19]

Former McGovern-Fraser Commissioner Austin Ranney said, in summary:

Most of the fourteen states which adopted presidential primaries after 1968 did so as a direct response to the McGovern-Fraser rules. Some decided that primaries were the best way to provide genuine "full, meaningful and timely participation." Others decided that the best way to keep the new national delegate-selection rules from upsetting their accustomed and preferred ways of doing state and local party business would be to establish a presidential primary and thereby split off presidential nomination matters from all other party affairs. And still others calculated that the new rules made caucuses and conventions much more vulnerable than a primary to being captured by small but dedicated bands of ideologues.[20]

This bundle of new incentives produced a genuine transformation of the presidential nominating process.[21] From a system in which primaries played a supporting rather than a leading role the United States rapidly moved toward a nominating system in which primaries dominated the process. In 1968, 49 percent of the delegates to the Democratic and 45 percent of the delegates to the Republican National Convention were chosen in states with primary elections, and 36 percent of all the delegates to each convention were committed to candidates by primaries. By 1972 the figures were 66 percent selected and 58 percent committed for the Democrats, and 53 percent selected and 41 percent committed for the Republicans; as Table 2.5 shows, the numbers have increased since then.

We shall be exploring the strategic implications of this set of

Table 2.5   Proportion of delegates selected in primaries, 1952–1980

DEMOCRATS

Year	Number of primaries	Convention total	Delegates selected in primaries		Delegates committed to candidates by primaries	
			Number	Percent	Number	Percent
1952	17	1230	570	.46	224	.18
1956	21	1372	690	.50	523	.38
1960	17	1521	686	.45	311	.20
1964	18	2316	1177	.51	943	.41
1968	17	2623	1276	.49	936	.36
1972	23	3016	1977	.66	1737	.58
1976	29	3008	2264	.75	1982	.66
1980	31	3331	2378	.71	2366	.71

Mean 1952–1968: Selected 48.2%; Committed 30.6%
Mean 1972–1980: Selected 70.7%; Committed 65.0%

REPUBLICANS

Year	Number of primaries	Convention total	Delegates selected in primaries		Delegates committed to candidates by primaries	
			Number	Percent	Number	Percent
1952	15	1206	558	.46	290	.24
1956	18	1323	628	.47	572	.43
1960	15	1331	550	.41	468	.35
1964	17	1308	623	.48	462	.35
1968	16	1333	601	.45	480	.36
1972	22	1348	715	.53	555	.41
1976	28	2259	1501	.66	1219	.54
1980	33	1993	1502	.75	1374	.69

Mean 1952–1968: Selected 45.4%; Committed 34.6%
Mean 1972–1980: Selected 64.6%; Committed 54.7%

Source: Compiled from summaries in *Congressional Quarterly Weekly Reports.*

changes for the workings of the party system and major actors within that system for the rest of this chapter.

2. Factions and Coalitions: Changes in Candidate Strategies

As the Democrats learned in 1972, candidates must behave differently in a presidential nominating process dominated by primary elections than in one in which primaries play a smaller part. Rather than build coalitions, they must mobilize factions.

A political faction is easy enough to define: it is a group acting through a political party in pursuit of a common interest. Factions may give to political parties the loyalties of voters, which contributes to the party's mass base, ideological justifications for party programs, and organizational linkages between leaders and followers. When factions do not operate directly through political parties they are described as "interest groups" or "pressure groups."[22] Whether they are organized and act outside parties or within them, factions, by providing a political focus for the expression of the perceived needs of citizens are by virtue of that fact fundamental entities in any complex political system.

Coalitions are less fundamental structures than factions, in that they are alliances among groups organized for the purpose of achieving goals common to their constituent parts. They arise not out of the natural bedrock interests of people but rather out of their capacity to calculate their advantage over a protracted period, and their ability to see their best interests in light of the complexity of the political world in which they exist. Coalitions come into existence in political systems where two conditions are met: first, no faction is large enough to get its preferences directly enacted by the government without seeking help; second, the system operates by some sort of stable rules giving incentives for factions to undertake strategic behavior. One set of rules common in democratic regimes is majoritarian, in which the assent of majorities or their representatives is necessary for governmental policy to be made. Thus the type and character of coalitions, their durability and their strategies, are determined not only by the sorts of demands made on government, and by the size and strength of the factions that arise to make these demands, but also by the constitutional organization of the polity, with its prescriptions that provide incentives for factions to make alliances with one another.

James Madison claimed that the Constitution he and his colleagues had written was a means for abating the mischiefs of faction.[23] Of course he was right: that is what all constitutions do that provide for institutions meant to be responsive to majorities or their representatives. The means for accomplishing that end are the construction by constitutional provision of institutions that force factions to behave strategically, thus forming coalitions. In the American case there are a number of important coalition-forcing institutions: single-member congressional districts, for example, the bicameral Congress, the electoral college. It is a peculiar feature of a political system so constituted that the task of making and tending the coalitions which feed their preferences through these institutions is itself performed by an extra-constitutional entity, namely, the political party. American political parties organize Congress and almost all the state legislatures, bring voters to the polls, and make nominations for the Presidency. Where party organizations are strong, coalition-building flourishes; where they are weak, the politics of factional rivalry prevails.

This can be seen vividly at the state level. Primary elections have traditionally played the role in state politics of weakening the grasp of political parties. Where any faction can run its candidate for governor, and where many factions frequently do, the capture of state government is determined as if by lottery: as each new candidate enters the gubernatorial race, it reduces the number of votes it takes to vault into the run-off. Thus, the more candidates there are in any given race, the greater the incentive for the next entrant to enter. In states where gubernatorial elections are run in this fashion, factional warfare is frequently at fever pitch. When the incentives are weak for politicians of divergent views to work together, they rarely overcome their natural antipathies. Thus the poisonous political strife of such places as Texas.[24] Meanwhile, even in such an unlikely place as Connecticut—with its deep-seated ethnic rivalries—balanced tickets and mutual accommodations are the norm, owing to nomination processes that make heavy use of such consensus-forcing institutions as state party nominating conventions and the challenge primary.[25]

In the race for the Presidency, the same logic obtains. One of the hidden virtues of the electoral college system—with its aggregation of votes state by state, and the custom of casting all the electoral votes of a state for the winner within the state— is that coalition-building within each state, looking toward the assembly of a majority vote, is encouraged. Under a direct election system, incentives would run in the opposite direction. Instead of pressing politicians toward coalitions that would assemble a majority in each state, factionalism would be encouraged. Each new entrant into the presidential race, carrying with him an unknown potential for capturing the loosely attached votes of a front runner, would create an invitation for the next presidential hopeful and the next until, in a crowded electoral field, differentiation—however marginal—and not consensus-building would emerge as the best strategy for victory. This scenario is, of course, hypothetical for general elections so long as the electoral college persists in something like its present form. There is nothing hypothetical about the impact of its logic on the nomination process, however.

Why must a presidential candidate in the new circumstances created by the proliferation of primaries mobilize his faction rather than build coalitions? The task of a presidential hopeful, threading a path through the minefield of successive primary elections, is not to win a majority but rather to survive. Survival means gaining as high as possible a rank among the candidates running for election. Coming in first in early primaries means achieving the visibility that ensures that a candidate will be taken seriously by the news media. This makes it a little easier to raise money and therefore to contest the next primary. All this hangs on the candidate's being able to attract, let us say, 29 percent of the vote in an early state primary rather than 24 percent of the vote. In a state the size of New Hampshire, in a Democratic primary the difference in absolute numbers of voters between those two percentages may be fewer than 5,000 votes.[26] The candidate's best strategy is therefore to differentiate himself from the others in the race and persuade more of his supporters to come out and vote. A premium is placed on building a personal organization, state by state, and in hoping that the field becomes crowded with rivals who cluster at some other part of the ideological spectrum, or who for some other reason manage to divide up into too-small pieces the natural constituencies that exist in the primary electorate.[27]

It may not be entirely clear at first blush why a system dominated by primaries exhibits these characteristics more than one dominated by caucuses. Devoted observers of the contemporary nomination process note that the early Iowa caucus presents much the same survival problem to candidates as the early New Hampshire primary. It is reported every bit as thoroughly by the news media and it provides much the same sort of momentum to winners and handicap to losers. Indeed Senator McGovern in 1972 did unexpectedly well not just in primaries but also in caucus states, as Norman Miller described in the *Wall Street Journal:*

> The reforms created conditions made to order for the well-organized McGovern campaign with its legions of zealous volunteers. District-by-district elections of delegates gave the McGovern people an incentive to organize early and effectively, even in states that didn't look like good bets at first. When the Muskie campaign sank, the McGovern forces were already positioned in such states as Massachusetts, Pennsylvania and Ohio to exploit the opportunity.

> The McGovern organization's effective exploitation of the reform rules has been most striking in little-noticed contests in the 28 non-primary states. Time and again, bands of McGovern backers have "blitzed" precinct-level caucuses and seized power to name delegates from outnumbered regulars, who have either backed another candidate or wanted to remain uncommitted. The tactics have insured Sen. McGovern delegates from a number of unlikely states—Texas, Virginia and Oklahoma, to name a few—enough that it now seems likely he'll attain his goal of 300 delegates from the non-primary states.

> Not even organized labor has been able to deliver reliably under the new rules. In many places, observes one political operative close to the unions, labor has "let a bunch of long hairs and college kids beat them." He adds glumly, "The new rules ruined the unions—absolutely ruined them."

While this is obviously an overstatement, it is clear that the traditional convention power brokers—labor leaders, governors and other political figures—will have their power diminished this year. For the reform commission also took action to reduce the number of delegates who can be relied on to take orders from bosses.[28]

The reforms not only facilitated the conversion of the nomination process into a system dominated by primaries. They also vastly increased the role of the news media in the overall process by requiring that delegate selection be done under conditions of great public visibility and in the year of the election. Thus the early Iowa caucus became a significant early media event, as Senator Howard Baker described it in 1980, "the functional equivalent of a primary."[29] Morris Udall discovered the same thing in 1976, and at the last minute changed his plans to stay out of Iowa. It was not because the number of delegates being selected in Iowa were irresistible. Rather, as F. Christopher Arterton reports:

> Their discovery that the media planned to cover the Iowa caucuses as extensively as they would the early primaries led Udall's advisors to conclude that they could not let the other candidates . . . get the jump on them.[30]

Earliness is not the only attribute of a delegate selection process that attracts media coverage. At least three criteria readily come to mind that might predispose a news organization to give coverage to a series of delegate-selecting events: the number of delegates at stake, the competitiveness of the race, and uncertainty about the outcome. Certainly the latter two characteristics are present to a far greater degree early than late in the election year, and while the careful systematic study of 1980 campaign news coverage by Michael Robinson and Margaret Sheehan shows some media attention to large states, it is clear that early states whether large or small, and pre-eminently Iowa and New Hampshire, dominated news coverage.[31]

As in baseball, to understand the strategic implications of the selection process, and changes therein, it is important to focus not only on individual games but on the entire season. What

Table 2.6 News coverage of selection processes, 1980

Date of delegate selection process	State	Number of delegates selected (Dem. and Rep.)	Percentage of total news coverage given over to state primaries and caucuses, 1980	
			CBS	UPI
Jan. 21	Iowa	87	14%	13%
Feb. 10	Maine	43	4	3
16	Arkansas	52	0[a]	0
17	Puerto Rico	55	1	2
26	New Hampshire	41	14	15
	Minnesota	109	1	0
March 4	Massachusetts	153	7	3
	Vermont	31	1	1
11	Florida	151	3	2
	Alabama	72	1	0
	Alaska	30	0	0
	Georgia	99	0	–[b]
12	Delaware	26	–	0
18	Illinois	271	10	7
25	New York	405	7	6
	Connecticut	89	2	2
April 1	Wisconsin	109	6	5
	Kansas	69	0	1
5	Louisiana	82	0	0
12	South Carolina	62	2	3
	Arizona	57	–	1
17	North Dakota	31	0	0
19	Mississippi	54	0	–
22	Pennsylvania	268	9	7
May 3	Texas	232	2	2
6	D.C.	33	1	2
	Indiana	134	1	1
	North Carolina	109	–	1
	Tennessee	87	–	0
13	Nebraska	49	0	1
	Maryland	89	0	2
17	Dems. Abroad	4	–	0
	Virginia	115	–	0
20	Michigan	223	1	7
	Oregon	78	1	1

raising, mostly by mail solicitation. Anonymous givers by mail are far more likely to send money to candidates of whom they have heard.

(3) Money helps candidates contest primary elections, which are very expensive because of the need to use the mass media. Newspaper and television advertising and television production and all the other modern devices for reaching mass electorates demand far more money than whatever it used to take to reach state party leaders and prospective delegates.

Developments like these have given rise to the displacement of state party leaders and leaders of interest groups associated with them in the presidential nomination process—the demise, so to speak, of presidential nominations as repertory theater. It does not mean that candidates shun all party leaders or factional leaders within the states, but rather that selected state leaders may be invited to participate in a candidate's campaign rather than the candidate being a recruit and representative of the state party or faction. The balance of initiatives, and of responsibilities for the overall organization of the effort, has definitively shifted. It has also meant that a new group of political decision-makers has gained significant authority. These are the fund-raisers by mail and by rock concert, media buyers, advertising experts, public relations specialists, poll analysts, television spot producers, accountants and lawyers who contract themselves out to become temporary—or in the case of a successful candidate, perhaps longer than temporary—members of the entourages of presidential aspirants. They work not for the party but directly for candidates.

The growth of campaign management as a profession demanding the mastery of increasingly arcane and complex bodies of knowledge was noted early and has been carefully monitored by students of presidential nominating politics.[33] In two respects political reform has accelerated this process of professionalization.

First and most important, technocrats in the candidates' entourages have enjoyed enormous increases in their influence because of the decline in the power of party politicians. Second, the techniques that technocrats master have become more complicated and more demanding. The Federal Election Commission, created by the 1974 reforms of campaign finance, now issues streams of memoranda regulating the receipt, reporting, and expenditure of campaign funds.[34] Knowing what needs to be complied with is itself a sizable challenge, not to be undertaken without the assistance of a lawyer and an accountant.[35] Candidates used to find out all they thought they needed to know about public opinion by talking to other politicians, or by reading the newspaper, or by taking the temperature of the crowds to which they spoke.[36] Nowadays, professionally drawn and certified public opinion surveys have largely supplanted seat-of-the-pants methods.

Owing to the stern prohibitions of the federal law, financial angels now fear to tread in the precincts of the candidate. Rushing in to take their place are the professionals who run mail solicitation operations, impresarios who can put together and deliver authentic media stars to fund-raising events, and increasingly, the access-maximizing professional agents of Political Action Committees, who invest in candidates in behalf of groups of contributors. Only the last of these are employed independently of the candidate's entourage.[37]

Commercial messages broadcast on radio or television touting the merits of candidates have never been in the hands of amateurs. The sophistication of the professionals who now do this sort of work is nevertheless easily visible to those who remember the election night broadcasts of 1952 and 1956 and can compare them with the sort of thing broadcast today, just as today's network evening news program bears only a faint resemblance to the old Camel News Caravan.

The great issue of democratic theory that arises in connection with the decline of one set of political elites and the rise of another is of course the issue of accountability, as we will see later in tracing through the implications of party change for interest groups. For now it is enough to ask: what values animate and constrain the behavior of these new political elites? How do these compare with whatever the values were that animated and constrained the old?

In some cases the answer is professional values. Lawyers, accountants, and even managers of public opinion polls have standard ways of doing business that as a matter of professional ethics they require their colleagues to observe. A polltaker who knowingly divulges to his client the name of a respondent who has been offered anonymity, or an accountant who claims to have audited an account when he has not done so, risks severe professional sanctions.

There is also the sanction of the law: accepting or spending more money than the law will allow is not a professional error in accountancy—it is a crime. The existence of far more regulations in the political environment, the violation of which lead to criminal charges is, however, less a constraint upon new political elites than an opportunity for them, since this creates a situation in which candidates feel—and may indeed be—unsafe without professional help.

Whatever the professional constraints on the behavior of technicians of political campaigns, however, it cannot be said that they represent anyone. The access they gain to candidates serves no legitimate interest beyond that of their own careers, and presumably the careers of the candidates whom they serve. The peopling of a campaign organization with specialists thus makes no coalitions, cements no alliances, seals no deals in the world of grass roots electoral politics. In this sense the professionalization of campaigns has served to isolate candidates even though, in another sense, they may be better informed than ever before.

4. National Party Conventions

It follows that the institution of the national party convention, as everyone has noticed, has been transformed. Instead of a body of delegates from the state parties meeting to ratify the results of a complex series of negotiations conducted by party leaders at the convention, the convention is now a body dominated by candidate enthusiasts and interest group delegates who meet to ratify a choice made prior to the convention mostly through primary elections. A major part of the responsibility for this change can be assigned to the effects of television, which has the power to start bandwagons very early in the delegate selection process. Reforms have not been intended to increase the influence of television: abolition of the unit rule, for example, was in part a device to spread the rewards for candidate effort and to prevent the premature consolidation of delegates by an early winner. On the whole, however, the enhancement of incentives for candidate initiative has had as its dominant consequence the weakening of state party leaders, and this has in turn given to primary voters and contributors to mail financial solicitations—both populations overwhelmingly dependent for their information about politics on television and other forms of mass publicity—the major role in the pre-convention nomination process. Thus the publicity effects of television have overridden the efforts of party leaders to tinker with party rules to contain their influence.[38]

So bandwagons have not merely survived the changes in the presidential selection process; they have flourished. They operate earlier and earlier in the process. Indeed, everything consequential occurs earlier than ever before. Candidate initiatives must begin earlier as well, indeed so much earlier that it is now accounted an advantage for a serious presidential candidate to be unemployed or at least without major distracting responsibilities for a full year or more preceding the nomination.[39]

Delegates are for the most part pledged to a candidate before setting foot in the convention hall.[40] Much ink has been spilled worrying over the legal enforceability of such a pledge, made in one state according to state primary law but to be redeemed in another state, the locus of the national convention, in a body controlled by its own rules and backed by federal law.

The 1980 Democratic convention was briefly amused by a pre-liminary skirmish—predominantly a thinly disguised attempt to prevent the nomination of Jimmy Carter—over a proposed procedural rule making the honoring of a delegate's pledge en-forceable by the convention itself and by the candidates.[41] Without such a rule, it was argued, delegates could exercise their obligation freely to deliberate on the business of the con-vention. As a practical matter, delegates pledged to candidates in each state are cleared if not actually named by the candidates and their agents. Such delegates represent nobody but the can-didate to whom they are pledged. It is difficult to see in whose behalf they might presume to deliberate in the unlikely event they were to decide to do so. Delegates pledged to a candidate and elected on a candidate's slate in a primary have no stand-ing to deliberate except as that candidate's representative even if called upon to make the attempt.

Since the transformation of 1968–72, of course, no delibera-tion over the nomination has taken place at conventions. Dark horses—candidates who arrive at the conventions with fewer delegates than the front runner and who hope to pick up del-egates as a plausible second choice when more favored candi-dates cancel one another out—have become an endangered species. Indeed all strategies based on second choice strength have disappeared. Such strategies entail coalition-building, not factional mobilization.

So today national conventions survive primarily as specta-cle—an ingathering of the multitudes who by their good behav-ior can reward their foreordained nominee with favorable pub-licity, or by their bad behavior can cripple the party's ensuing presidential campaign. More and more conventions are de-signed as entertainment, although interstitially they may still conduct business of great importance to the future of the party, as, for example, when they pass resolutions governing the fu-ture conduct of party affairs, such as the Democratic resolution in 1980 forbidding national committee funds to be used in sup-port of party candidates not in favor of the Equal Rights

Amendment[42] or the Democratic resolutions in 1968 establishing a commission on delegate selection.

5. *Central Control vs. Voluntarism*

Centralization within each national party has resulted as a consequence of new rules. Each national convention under the law has firm control of its own membership, and can set criteria which state parties must meet in order to be seated at conventions. Broad party principles require means of enforcement and particular application, which emanate from the national committees. Well in advance of national conventions compliance review must take place, so that state party adherence to criteria laid down by the previous national convention or by other nationally sanctioned instrumentalities can be assured. Immediately prior to national conventions this review can be undertaken by credentials committees run by delegates themselves.

Before the convention is constituted, however (bearing in mind that delegates may not be selected too far ahead of time without violating rules requiring timely delegate selection),[43] consultation, persuasion, and informal adjudication on state party delegate selection procedures and activities are necessary. The differential between the major parties on this matter has been sharp, with the Republicans having few centrally mandated criteria to enforce, and little appetite for centralized enforcement activity. Among the Democrats, the exercise of rule-application functions has to all intents and purposes become a prerogative of national committee employees. Not all these employees have in the past been perceived by state party leaders as embodying the soul of tact; in some cases senior, or at least duly elected leaders of state parties have taken unkindly to jawboning from zealous young agents of a formerly moribund and—despite the best literary efforts of the Supreme Court[44]— still only questionably legitimate central party bureaucracy.

The sense of loss of autonomy among state party leaders in national affairs has conceivably turned their concerns inward toward state level concerns and reduced their incentives to contest with various interest groups and candidate enthusiasts for influence over the presidential nomination process. Thus centralization of power through the compliance review process in the hands of national party functionaries can lead to a weakening of party organization at the intermediate level of the state parties. Whether this in turn permits the grass roots to flourish is a matter for consideration in a later chapter.

A further consequence of the new atmosphere of regulation, professionalization, legal responsibility, and legal sanctions is the centralization of political activity within each candidate's campaign, a logical concomitant of the centralization of political authority and of criminal liability. Richard Cheney, who ran Gerald Ford's campaign in 1976, testifies eloquently on this point:

> One of the major results of the spending limitations has been to encourage the development of highly centralized campaign organizations with elaborate controls over spending. Unless a campaign develops such an organization, there is virtually no possibility that it can account for all of the funds expended or adequately comply with federal regulations. While this makes for a more efficient campaign operation, it has had the effect of choking off the kind of grass-roots activity that historically has been a part of American presidential campaigns.

> The experience of the Ford campaign in 1976 showed conclusively that it was easier to discourage grass-roots activity than to try to control and report it. In previous campaigns, it was possible to tell a local campaign or party official to go ahead with a project as long as he could raise the money to finance it. Now, federal law places a premium on actively discouraging such activity because of the danger that it could well lead to a violation of contribution or spending limits in the primary. Furthermore, in the general election, because no contributions are permitted once federal funds become available, it is even more important to discourage such activity.

> Such considerations lead to shifts in spending priorities and, therefore, campaign strategies. State-by-state primary spending limitations, the overall limitation on prenomination spending, and the requirement that none of the money raised before the con-

vention be used to promote the general election effort (which has
to be totally financed with federal funds), all serve to discourage
organizational activities. We found it much easier during the 1976
Ford campaign, for example, to spend money on identifiable goods
and services, such as electronic media and production costs, in the
general election campaign than to spend it intelligently on local
and state organizational efforts. This was especially true because
we had discouraged organizational activity that was not directly
under our control during the primaries. The case of the Florida
primary, held in March 1976, is illustrative of the difficulties posed
by the new law. The Ford campaign poured significant resources
into the Florida effort and won our second major victory over
Governor Reagan. Within days of the election, the entire Florida
operation had to be totally shut down because of the various limitations we faced. As a result, there were no resources available to
keep even a symbolic operation going through the summer in
preparation for the fall campaign—no headquarters facility, no
phones, no paper clips, and no staff.

The same thing happened in virtually every state where we contested a primary in 1976. It was hardly surprising, then, that with
only a little more than two months for the general election campaign, we found it difficult to spend money on organizational efforts at the state and local level when we had dismantled the nucleus of our organization at the end of each primary campaign. It
made a lot more sense to spend it on media.

I firmly believe that the effect of the campaign finance laws in this
area has been to discourage grass-roots political activity, to discourage participation, and to place a premium on strategies that
rely on activities that are easily controlled and reported. Given a
choice between local spontaneity and enthusiastic participation, on
one hand, and control over spending, on the other, the cautious
campaign manager has little choice but to opt for activities that
are "controllable."[45]

The net effect on state and local party organizations of this
discouragement of grass roots political activity during a presidential election year is hard to assess. At a minimum, it tends
to diminish the value of state and local party leaders in their
dealings with candidates, thus reinforcing trends that already
have ample momentum. Further, on the assumption that presidential campaigns are a good way to build party solidarity at

the constitutional forms of American politics: single-member districts and plurality elections, sometimes with run-off provisions, create their well-known premium on coming in first. The electoral college, likewise, operates at the presidential level to encourage the building of a winning coalition broadly based among the states, and by depriving those who lose narrowly in a state from sharing any of that state's electoral votes it discourages weak candidates and penalizes third parties.[51]

Finally, there are many and varied discouragements to third parties written into election laws and regulations having the force of law. Ironically, many of these disabilities are the consequence of an intention to foster party competition. In most cases if they encourage competition at all, it is distinctly two-party competition. These problems are not new, for, as an example, some state statutes have long constituted election boards only from members of the two major parties.

Recent reform activity has nevertheless increased the burdens upon third parties and independent candidates. A massive example is provided by the Federal Election Campaign Act Amendments of 1974 and later years, which provide public financing for the campaigns of the two major political parties but delay payment to new parties until it is determined—after the election—that they got enough votes to qualify as nonfrivolous and may exclude independent candidates altogether, while subjecting them all to the same limitations in their receipt of funding from private sources.[52] Major parties are allocated public funds for holding their nominating conventions; minor parties are not.[53]

Congress has likewise frequently suspended equal time and fairness doctrine requirements on F.C.C. broadcast licenses so as to make debates between major candidates possible—and to make possible the exclusion of minor party candidates and independents.[54] Minor parties are also disproportionately burdened by the strict disclosure requirements of the new federal election law with respect to financial contributions, since they have reason to believe that prospective contributors may be shy of being publicly identified with political candidates who are out of the mainstream and who may, indeed, be widely considered to be odd. This is sometimes known as a "chilling effect."[55]

There is a practical way out of a dilemma which confronts the presumed chilling effect on third party contributors who might fear social stigmatization or worse with the presumed civic advantages that follow from public disclosure—and prior knowledge that public disclosure will take place—of contributors to and financial backers of the candidates who will almost certainly win the election. And that is to offer small deviant parties exemptions from reporting requirements, as courts have been asked to do in the case of the Communist and Socialist Worker parties of New York and Pennsylvania, respectively, and that of a self-identified homosexual candidate running for county commissioner in Ohio. There may, however, be no other practical way to hold a televised debate between the two candidates who monopolize the real chance of being the next President than arbitrarily excluding the rest. The reinforcement effect is important, however. When television networks exclude candidates from a debate or a joint appearance with the front runners they are denying them visibility, publicity and, most of all, a social definition as being worthy of serious consideration. An attempt to find a formula based on the standing of a candidate in public opinion surveys, as was tried in 1980 with John Anderson, suffers from a possible confusion between cause and effect: the easiest way to ensure that Anderson met the threshold number would have been to put him on television, visibly equal to the major party candidates. His exclusion, conversely, was the best guarantee that he would diminish in public esteem.[56]

Much the same problem arises when we consider public finance. Some rational basis for the expenditure of public funds has to be established if candidates are to be publicly funded. Otherwise, incentives are created for frivolous candidacies. Limitations on subsidy, however, are unavoidably limitations upon political expression and have the effect of entrenching the two major political parties.

7. *Competition Between the Major Parties*

Perhaps the most startling effect of political reform has been its influence on the competitive balance between the two major parties. The smaller, more ideologically cohesive of the two, the Republican, has reaped enormous benefit from changes weakening the internal organizational integrity of both parties.[57] Where ideology must substitute for institutional rules in maintaining organizational cohesion, a party with a strong ideological core and not much periphery may be better off at least over the short run than a party like the Democratic that attempts to embrace a wider range of ideological perspectives.

It may not be immediately apparent why political reforms established across the board might affect the two major parties somewhat differently. In some respects, to be sure, they do not. Although most of the dramatic examples of changed circumstances come from the Democratic side, Ronald Reagan's almost-successful challenge to President Ford in 1976 would have been far less likely under a system with fewer primary elections. Nevertheless, the two major parties are somewhat different in their organizational, coalitional, and ideological makeup, and the impact of the reforms has differed accordingly.

The key difference is ideological. Factionalism in the Democratic party, a failure to build a broad coalition, exposes Democratic candidates in the general election to the full force of the wide variation that Democrats of different stripes maintain in their policy concerns and commitments. Failure to embrace a coalition-building strategy risks defection in such circumstances far more surely than in the Republican case, where the party maintains a high rather than a broad church of co-believers and where, consequently, serious contestants for the Republican nomination are much more likely to think more or less alike about public policy. The classic Republican problem in presidential elections has not been the shaky loyalty of Republican voters but rather the party's too narrow base in the general electorate. Thus, Republicans internally have less to fear from a nomination process that encourages factionalism and discourages coalition building since Republicans are already more nearly factionally cohesive and like-minded on political issues.

Centralization has also posed less of a problem for the organizational side of the Republican party, because central management of an organization with a narrow ideological dispersion means that party managers will be making fewer choices fraught with political implications as far as party members are concerned, and a broader range of functions will be considered to be purely ministerial in character. Moreover, Republicans have a lot more money to devote to party management. The central offices of the Republican National Committee have in general been better staffed and its business more stably and professionally conducted than has been true of the Democrats.[58] Under the innovative management of William Brock, professional services were expanded for identifying, recruiting, training, and supporting Republican candidates for elective office at state and local levels.[59] But party rules have forbidden meddling: in 1980 the Convention adopted a rule requiring state party consent before the Republican National Committee could contribute from its bulging war chest to candidates within a state.

A stunning consequence of the differential impact of reform on the two major parties is that in two out of the last three presidential elections the minority party has won and the majority party has lost.[60] Thus, it is at least arguable that party reforms have worked disproportionately to the disadvantage of the majority party, the Democrats, by leading to the nominations of candidates unable to command widespread support within the party. The reforms in effect have institutionalized the disequilibrium suffered by the party in 1968 and facilitated Republican victories in 1972 and 1980. In 1968, as we have seen, the majority party tore itself to tatters. Even so, it took an

assassination to destroy their otherwise reasonable chance for
victory.[61] The Democratic rules changes of 1968–72 weakened
the state parties and so strengthened candidates in the nomination process that in 1972 a candidate widely perceived as an
extremist, and certainly supported by extremists,[62] could win
the nomination and singlehandedly in the general election ward
off a Democratic landslide. While the Democrats won the 1976
election, I shall presently argue that who their candidate was
and what he felt able to do in office were importantly shaped
by the constraints, or lack thereof, of the nomination process.
And of course the majority party candidate in 1980—and the
loser of that election—was an incumbent President; hence responsibility for his nomination in that year rests primarily with
the workings of the process in 1976. If majorities are supposed
to win in a democracy, then the American presidential election
process has not lately been mobilizing them.

Some of the underpinnings of this argument can be readily
noted. We can certainly begin with the fact, already established,
that the Democratic party is without question the larger of the
two major parties in terms of long-term self-identified adher-

Table 2.14 Defection levels from party in presidential voting,
1952–80

| Year | Democrats | | | By comparison, Republicans (to anybody) |
	To Rep. candidate	To 3d party (if signif.)	Total	
1952	23%		23%	8%
1956	15		15	4
1960	16		16	5
1964	13		13	20
1968	12	14%	26	14
1972	33		33	5
1976	18		18	9
1980	26	4	30	13

1952–1968 mean defection: 18.6% Democratic; 10% Republican
Post 1968 mean defection: 27% Democratic; 9% Republican

Source: The Gallup Opinion Index Report No. 183, December 1980, pp. 6–7.

ents.[63] Republican Presidents have repeatedly been elected by the votes of Democratic defectors, who give as their major reasons for voting Republican their dissatisfactions with the Democratic alternative.[64]

Claims that Republican Presidents are elected not by Democrats but by formerly inactive or disaffected or latent Republicans founder on all sorts of difficulties: the fact that at or around the time of the elections in question heavy majorities rejected Republican positions on many controversial political issues,[65] that Democrats retain the nominal loyalties of more voters than Republicans,[66] that Democratic votes have consistently outnumbered Republican for all other offices.[67]

We can establish as well that the reforms put in place organizational features of party structure that made it difficult for anyone to do anything effective about forestalling the nomination of candidates who may have been extremely unpopular with large numbers of party members. This is a clear cost of the automated, nondeliberative national nominating convention in which state party leaders and officeholders play increasingly passive roles, and where proceedings are dominated by candidates who have previously secured a majority of pledged delegates by accumulating sufficient first-place wins in state primaries and conventions to stampede the uncommitted remainder onto their bandwagon.[68]

All this adds up to a plausible, perhaps even compelling case for the proposition that various reforms of the presidential selection process have had a sizable impact on American political parties and the party system. To be sure they were intended to affect the parties, though perhaps not to the extent, or in each and every way, that they have done. But because the parties are the principal agency in our political system through which future Presidents are recruited, it might have been foreseen that the effects of presidential selection reform would not stop with the parties, or even the party system, but would also influence the conduct of the Presidency as well.

III

Consequences for Governing:
The Conduct of the Presidency

Since the election of 1968, the Democratic majority has been able to pull itself together sufficiently to elect a President only once. This adds up to twelve years of Republican rather than Democratic control of the federal government in the sixteen years between 1968 and 1984, a rather sizable effect to be attributed in more than trivial ways to party reform. I believe it can reasonably be maintained, in addition, that party reform also had an impact on the four intervening Democratic years. For the Democratic incumbent, Jimmy Carter, was a President whose conduct in office to a remarkable extent faithfully reflected the learning experiences available along the pathway he followed in order to achieve the Presidency. The argument in brief is that President Carter conducted himself in office in ways that were fully consonant with his personal predilections and his views of public administration but which would have been harder for him to pursue if he had been educated in the course of the nomination process to the need to build a governing coalition. What it takes to achieve the nomination differs nowadays so sharply from what it takes to govern effectively as to pose a problem that has some generality. This problem can conveniently be illustrated by a closer look at the Carter Presidency and its difficulties in the context of recent Presidents.

1. The Cabinet: Recent Historical Experience [1]

There was, to begin with, the early evidence of the composition of President Carter's cabinet. In general, the pattern of cabinet appointments a President makes can be informative about what sort of Presidency he means to have. Like the campaign rhetoric that precedes the election, a newly appointed cabinet can be read in a variety of ways. And it affords less than comprehensive evidence about how the president plans to run the government. But fragmentary though it is, this sort of information is hard to ignore, for unlike the rhetoric of campaign promises, cabinet members do not disappear into thin air.[2] Rather, they assume office and to a greater or lesser extent actually administer the affairs of the nation. President Eisenhower's appointment of "nine millionaires and a plumber" gave a good forecast of the sort of status-quo-defending Presidency he wanted. It could not have come as much of a surprise when the plumber, Secretary of Labor Martin Durkin, was the first to leave the cabinet. When John F. Kennedy became President he struck a dominant theme of self-consciously moving beyond his own range of personal acquaintance to form a governing coalition. As Douglass Cater said:

> While consulting a senior statesman about the selection of a Secretary of State . . . Kennedy remarked that he had suddenly discovered he didn't know "the right people." During his campaigning he had, of course, met practically every politician in the country. But as far as picking a cabinet was concerned, his large circle of acquaintances seemed inadequate. The truth of these remarks . . . was subsequently borne out when Mr. Kennedy appointed men not previously known to him to several key posts in his administration.[4]

In one conspicuous case, of course, Kennedy was well acquainted with a cabinet appointee: His appointment of his brother as Attorney General telegraphed—among other things— his strong desire to keep close control of the civil rights issue.[5]

It is possible to see in Richard Nixon's cabinet appointments a mirror of his emerging view of the role of the President vis-à-vis the rest of the government. After beginning with a group of cabinet appointees that was both politically diverse and reasonably visible, Mr. Nixon increasingly appointed people with no independent public standing and no constituencies of their own.[6] In this shift we can read a distinctive change in the fundamental political goals and strategies of the Nixon administration from early concerns with constituency building to a later preoccupation, once Mr. Nixon's reelection was assured, with centralizing power in the White House.

Table 3.1 Decline in prior experience of Nixon cabinet

	President Nixon's First Cabinet, 1969	*President Nixon's Last Cabinet, 1974*
Prior political experience extensive (includes office-holding)	William Rogers, State Melvin Laird, Defense Walter Hickel, Interior Maurice Stans, Commerce Robert Finch, HEW George Romney, HUD John Volpe, DOT	Rogers C. B. Morton, Interior Earl Butz, Agriculture
Prior political experience moderate (active in state party, etc.)	Winton Blount, Post Office	Frederick Dent, Commerce Peter Brennan, Labor Caspar Weinberger, HEW
Prior political experience slight	David Kennedy, Treasury John Mitchell, Attorney General Clifford Hardin, Agriculture George Shultz, Labor	Henry Kissinger, State William Simon, Treasury James Schlesinger, Defense Robert Bork, Acting Attorney General James Lynn, HUD Claude Brinegar, DOT

From Nelson W. Polsby, *Congress and the Presidency*, 3rd edition, (Englewood Cliffs, N.J.: Prentice-Hall, 1976), p. 53.

Nixon's first Secretary of Labor, George Shultz, though unknown to begin with, became an early star of the cabinet owing
to his intelligence and quick grasp of problems. The first major
reorganization of the Nixon Presidency shuffled Mr. Shultz into
the White House.[7] He was replaced by an efficient but unpre-
possessing figure (James Hodgson), who in turn gave way to a
maverick union official (Peter Brennan), who was not even on
speaking terms with the head of the AFL/CIO.[8] This was not
the only example of a movement away from clientele concerns
in cabinet building and toward the accretion of managerial capacity within the White House. Seemingly by design the access
of large and significant interest groups to the President was
greatly hampered. Labor, education, the scientific community,
conservationists and others felt not merely that Richard Nixon
was a President whose goals differed from their own but that
their voices were being choked off, that they were shut out from
the White House and that their cases were being rejected before they were heard.[9]

If Mr. Nixon's administrative appointments were designed to
be increasingly weak in their capacity to carry messages from
interest groups to policymakers, they were far stronger in executing orders, in providing a conduit from the various arms of
the White House executive apparatus—the Domestic Council,
the Office of Management and Budget, the National Security
Council—to the levels of policy execution.

Centralization of policy making was only half of the latter
day Nixon administrative program. The other half consisted in
systematic attempts to place functionaries who can best be described as political agents in the bureaus and departments, ad-
ministrators whose job it was to report to the White House on
the political fidelity of the executive branch.[10]

✻ Presidents and their political appointees have frequently
puzzled over the problem of making the enormous apparatus
of the executive branch responsive to their wills.✻ The legitimacy
of this claim is based upon the results of the last election; presumably a President is elected and makes appointments at least

in part to carry out his promises with respect to the future conduct of public policy.[11] The necessary instruments of that conduct reside in the unelected agencies of the executive branch.

Executive agencies, however, are seldom merely passive receptacles, awaiting the expression of the President's preferences. Rather they embody a number of persistent characteristics that from time to time may serve as bases for conflict with presidential directives. Expertise, for example, a body of doctrine about the right way to do things, may well thwart responsiveness to presidential demands. So may alliances between agency executives and the Congressional committees that have program and budgetary oversight over them. So may strong ties between agencies and the client groups they serve.

The case of a conservative President facing an executive agency doing what he believes is liberal work is especially poignant. The very existence of a bureaucratic apparatus attests to the mobilization at some time in the past of a majority of sufficient strength to pass a law and put an agency to work. So long as the law is on the books and Congress appropriates funds, the agency presumably has some sort of legitimate standing. Yet it was precisely the existence of all too many of these federal activities, all staffed with people devoted to the execution of their programs, that Mr. Nixon wished to challenge. In one famous instance, the case of the Office of Economic Opportunity, President Nixon attempted prematurely to put an agency out of business altogether.[12]

In each of Mr. Nixon's attempts to organize and reorganize the executive branch, an observer can note efforts to cope with what was evidently being defined as a hostile administrative environment. Revenue sharing, of course, had the intended effect of removing responsibilities altogether from federal agencies.[13] Mr. Nixon vastly strengthened the White House National Security Office and invented a domestic counterpart in the Domestic Council, politicized and reincarnated the Bureau of the Budget as the Office of Management and Budget, attempted on a sizable scale to impound and redirect funds appropriated according to law, and drastically increased the number of employees in the Executive Office of the President.[14] Just as the storm of Watergate was breaking over his head, he proposed a reorganization plan that would have officially denied cabinet officers direct access to the President by shifting supervisory power to four super-cabinet officers who were supposed to act as special presidential assistants.[15]

These devices for limiting the power of government departments, agencies, and bureaus were in general not illicit. They reflect a distinctive view of executive branch legitimacy and its monopoly in the presidential office. Mr. Nixon's view, it became clear, was that his reelection in 1972 by a landslide not only provided him with a special entitlement to pursue his vision of public policy, but it had in addition delegitimized all other major actors in the system.[16]

The last pre-Watergate months of the Nixon Presidency saw neither the first nor necessarily the last official manifestation of the view that the President is the source of all the legitimacy on which the entire government runs. Indeed even today the theory is widely held that, because the President is the only elected official in the executive branch, political choice by the executive branch is legitimized only insofar as it can be plausibly seen to have radiated down from a presidential choice or order or preference.

Sustenance for this view comes from a conception of the American political system in which legitimacy arises chiefly, if not exclusively, from the electoral process. If the direct results of elections are the only source of political legitimacy, then it follows that the legitimacy of the entire executive branch flows as though down the sides of a gigantic pyramid from the source: the quadrennial election of the single member of that branch who is elected—the President. Given this view of the situation, there can be no grounds upon which hierarchical subordinates of the President might legitimately act to thwart, undermine, delay, modify, or attenuate the will of the President in public policy once it is expressed.

This is not, however, the only possible view of political legitimacy in the executive branch. Another view is that even though the electoral process does provide a significant measure of legitimacy for the acts of government, this process by itself is neither adequate to the task of providing accountability, nor is it the only process actually provided for in the constitutional design and in the pattern of American politics that has since evolved in harmony with the spirit of the Constitution. In contrast with this hierarchical or pyramidal or plebiscitary view of legitimacy, there is the check and balance or multiprocess view favored, for example, by the authors of the *Federalist* in which the rightful power to govern is spread about in the government and even, in a more modern version, extended to interest groups and other mobilizers and organizers of popular desires, needs and sentiments.[17]

It is interesting to contemplate the extent to which the Presidency-centered view of the proper relations between the Presidency and bureaucracy survived intact through Watergate and indeed through the fashionable disparagement of the imperial Presidency.[18] This was reflected in President Carter's initial address to the problem of cabinet building and what appeared consequently to be his first perspective on the permanent government of the United States.

2. *Five Strategies of Cabinet Building*

There are at least five different ways to build a cabinet. The first option takes account of the fact that each of the great departments of government serves clientele in the population at large. Each has custody over a range of policies that tend to affect some Americans more directly than others. Thus one strategy for building a cabinet is to enter into a coalition with the client groups of the departments by finding appointees who already have extensive relationships or political alliances or management experience with relevant client groups. A cabinet

in which this alternative is dominant is frequently one heavy
with former political officeholders.

Characteristic costs of this mode of cabinet building include
those associated with complaints from interest groups whose
competitors have succeeded where they have not. So, for example, conservationist groups may feel exceedingly well served
by the appointment of one sort of Secretary of Interior. Gra-
zers, miners and loggers may feel quite differently about the
matter. The impossibility of accommodating all the groups into
which Americans may legally divide themselves for the purpose
of pursuing a common interest is no doubt one of the facts of
life that give vitality at the presidential level to a competitive
two-party system. The fact that ungratified client groups can
form alliances with the out party helps to legitimize the inevitable choices that Presidents must make among contending interests. This is one mechanism for expressing dissent from governmental policy which, if it becomes loud enough or effective
enough, can limit the extent to which any incumbent may persist in a line of policy without risking electoral defeat.

An advantage of this strategy is that by drawing from a pool
of politicians associated with clientele of the agencies, presidents may cement electoral alliances with interest groups and
draw them into collaboration with his administration, forming
a governing coalition that resonates throughout the population
at large.

A second option is available to a President who may, if he
chooses, select a cabinet of substantive specialists. Specialists
possess technical mastery, knowledge of programmatic alternatives and understanding of particular governmental agencies
and their impact on the world. Whereas the client-oriented cabinet member seeks to do his job to the satisfaction of the customers, the specialist cabinet member's internal definition of
success depends on satisfying the norms of performance that
the agency itself and its associated professions generate.

Since most federal bureaucratic agencies have histories, they
also have built up over the years a population of leaders and

former leaders, for example former assistant secretaries grown older, from which a president may draw members of his cabinet. A characteristic cost of this sort of leadership is a tendency for experts to know where too many of the agency's bodies are buried. Their knowledge gives them the means to use the agency's basic political capital if they succumb to the temptation to sacrifice the long-term interests of the agency in behalf of short-run goals or alliances that will make their incumbency of office look good. An advantage of a strategy of appointing specialists is that specialists are frequently highly competent managers, know the strengths and weaknesses of the organization intimately, and can draw the best work out of their former colleagues of the permanent government.

 A third possibility is to call upon the Washington careerist. There is a very large group of possible cabinet officials who always live in Washington, whether or not they hold public office, and whose main expertise is general knowledge about how the federal government works within the Washington community. When these people are not serving in government, they may frequently be found in Washington law firms, public relations organizations, journalistic enterprises, or think-tanks. It is common for Washington careerists to associate themselves predominantly with the fortunes of one political party or another, but they only rarely have grass roots political knowledge or experience. Rather, these are typically bright graduates of the best universities who wash into government at an early age on the tide of some fresh incoming administration, and then stay around Washington once their tour of duty is ended, giving general advice—some of it very expensive—about how to work the American political system.

Frequently senior people in this group are considered eligible for a wide range of cabinet positions when a new cabinet is being formed, and in this sense they are interchangeable. They may have only tenuous ties to the electoral base of their political party and may or may not maintain special expertise with respect to the operations of one or another of the great bureaucracies. What they do offer is access to and knowledge about the byways of the Washington community and the modes in which it functions. Such officials offer general managerial skills, quite frequently of a high order, and the capacity to do policy analysis.

The great cost to a President who chooses a cabinet member from this population is the difficulty he may encounter in interpreting such a cabinet official's resistance—when it occurs— on substantive policy. When a client-oriented cabinet member disagrees with the White House, he can be presumed to be sending a message from a meaningful slice of the population at large, and it is a foolish President who ignores such a signal. Regardless of whether the President yields or persists in his line of policy, the signal means something to him, informs him about real political risks and costs. The specialist or expert is especially capable of vibrating to the pitch of his agency, and signs of disagreement from such a source may be the best early warning available to a President that a proposed plan of action will not work in a technical sense. A Washington careerist, however, may be vibrating only to the siren song of his own career. A Washington careerist's career may well entail longer time horizons than can be useful to the incumbent President, who must mobilize his influence and that of his administration so that it can be applied—spent, invested, even dissipated—before his term runs its course. Or the Washington careerist may simply be substituting the conclusions of his own policy analysis for an analysis in favor at the White House—or farther down in the bureaucracy.

On occasion, a Washington careerist can perform a significant service for a President by presenting to him the massed opinion of one or another policy Sanhedrin of resident senior Washingtonians that a contemplated plan of administration action will have highly damaging consequences for the professional reputation of a President, or for the welfare of the party or nation, or all of the above. This, evidently, was the great contribution of Washington careerist Clark Clifford, newly appointed Secretary of Defense, toward the termination of the Vietnam war. Clifford, with his delicate sense of touch in these matters, orchestrated a highly explicit show-and-tell session to persuade Lyndon Johnson that further prosecution of the war was futile.[19] The fact that this was needed for Johnson, a man himself so thoroughly embedded in the Washington milieu, is a very strong indication that resistance from a Washington careerist to a President's plans is normally inscrutable to the President.

 A fourth option available to a cabinet-building President is to choose presidential ambassadors. These are officials who arrive in office principally because they are pre-presidential friends and allies of the President. Such officials frequently hail from the President's home state and—although there are exceptions—typically return there after their service with their particular President concludes.[20] These officials may be counted upon to respond with special alertness to presidential priorities, plans, and orders and to carry the President's message both to the agency and to its client groups. The rationale for a cabinet dominated by executives of this stripe is already familiar. Such executives are strongest in defending the presumption that the President, being the most recently elected chief executive, is entitled by his electoral mandate to command the resources of the executive branch and to shape its program according to his desires. The careers of presidential ambassadors are tied not to interest groups or to agencies or to the Washington community, but to the President personally.

Until the beginning of President Nixon's second term, commentators were not terribly alert to the possibility of pathology, cost, or difficulty in the pursuit of this alternative. Yet Presidents, it now appears, can ask members of the executive branch to do illegal or at least questionable acts, acts not contemplated and in some cases prohibited by the charters of the agencies involved. A President or his agent can seek to close down activities provided for by law or can repudiate political alliances with devastating future effects for himself, his party, and/or his successors. Those executives who are without expertise or independent standing with interest groups, the bureaucracies, or the Washington community are presumably least well situated to resist these tendencies when they appear.

To some observers it may seem odd and inappropriate that resistance to a President's expressed desires might occur as an administrative issue at all. This view, for example, seems to infuse the incredulity with which President Nixon's former speechwriter William Safire treats the difficulties Mr. Nixon had in getting World War I "temporary" government buildings cleared off the downtown Washington ceremonial parkland known as the Mall.[21] As Mr. Safire describes it, Mr. Nixon made an essentially aesthetic judgment. Flying overhead in his helicopter, it offended Mr. Nixon's sensibilities that the Mall had never been restored to its pristine state after the incursions of hasty wartime construction half a century before. So he ordered the buildings demolished forthwith. In fact, it took several years, a matter of great consternation to Mr. Nixon, and also, it appears, to Mr. Safire, who uses this as an example of the mindless bureaucratic inertia with which all Presidents must cope. Yet an off-with-their-heads proclamation is all very well when there is nothing more complicated involved than seeing that a glass of Fresca appears at the touch of a button on the President's desk.[22] A blazing fire can always be lit in the presidential fireplace if the President insists—as Nixon did—regardless of the temperature of the real world, since the presidential air conditioning can see to the overall comfort of the incumbent.[23] But Mr. Nixon made no constructive suggestion about what to do with the government employees who worked in the buildings he wanted obliterated, their files, equipment, office furniture, or functions. As luck would have it, given the vagaries of the Washington market in commercial real estate, it took time and not a little inconvenience and effort on the part of others, who also presumably had their ordinary jobs to do, to cleanse Mr. Nixon's vista.

It is, in short, one thing for a President to sit atop the administrative machinery of the government, blending and harmonizing the various contending interests that clamor for attention. The outcome is always bound to entail some administrative friction, some dissatisfaction, some reluctance, foot dragging, disagreement, and so on. In such circumstances there is no doubt that a President's political judgments ought to prevail. And sometimes, given the expenditure of sufficient resources, it does.[24] But when a President is merely taking his prerogatives, real or imagined, out for a morning stroll, it should come as no surprise when he has difficulty getting his way. Presidential ambassadors are likely to be the least well equipped of all his aides to see the distinction.

 Finally, a President may choose his cabinet from representatives of symbolic constituencies. These are interest groups having little or no particular claims as organized clientele of the agencies to which their representative is appointed, but which do command the sympathetic attention of the press or constitute important communities at the electoral level. Symbolic constituencies are, in the United States, preeminently status groups and most commonly ethnic groups. Traditionally (but not entirely), ethnic groups have clustered together in the neighborhoods of America's eastern and midwestern cities, and in the party politics of these localities leaders of communal groups have demanded, and received, the recognition of nomination for or appointment to public office. This has been a common means by which parties have mobilized the loyalties, the precinct work and the votes of members of ethnic minorities, and has been identified as a device for accomplishing the assimilation of immigrant Americans into the mainstream of the American economy and society—without necessarily attenuating their communal identifications.[25]

The great advantage that representatives from symbolic constituencies bring to a cabinet is presumably the consolidation of the party loyalties of the communal groups from which they spring; the disadvantage is that they may have no great competence at or interest in doing the job at hand.[26] They may have no desire to learn the needs of their agency's clientele, or to understand the workways of the bureaucracy, or the impact of its programs, beyond the payoffs available to the cabinet official's own constituency.

3. Cabinet Building in the Carter Administration

No President is likely to pursue a pure strategy of cabinet building; rather, the strategy is typically mixed so that cabinet members may satisfy a variety of the criteria implied by the pure types mentioned above. Moreover, individual cabinet members may fit more than one category. Even so, the overall character of the mixture at any given time can be read as an expression of the claims to legitimacy made by each incumbent administration as well as of its dominant administrative style. This was certainly true of President Carter's administration, as a consideration of the seventeen cabinet-level appointments he initially made will illustrate.[27] In matters of foreign and defense policy, with the very important exception of United Nations Ambassador Andrew Young, Mr. Carter originally sought subject matter experts.[28] Cyrus Vance, Zbigniew Brzezinski, Michael Blumenthal, and Harold Brown had all put in time working in Washington for the government on problems associated with the departments they were asked to head.

In two instances Mr. Carter picked cabinet members who could be considered ambassadors from interest group constituencies. One, Bob Bergland, supervised the department whose interest group constituency was closest to Mr. Carter's own in private life, agriculture.[29] The second was the former governor of Idaho, Cecil Andrus, who brought to the Interior Department close ties with environmentalist groups.[30]

An academic labor economist, Juanita Kreps, served as the chief link between the business community and the administration: clearly not an interest group ambassador—at least not from the interest groups served by her department, but rather, widely proclaimed as a female appointee, hence a representative of a

Table 3.2 President Carter's cabinet, 1977

	Specialists	Client-oriented	Pres. Ambassad.	Washington careerist	Symbolic
State	Vance				
Treasury	Blumenthal				
Defense	Brown				
Justice			Bell		
Interior		Andrus			
Agriculture		Bergland			
Commerce					Kreps
Labor	Marshall				
HEW				Califano	
HUD				Harris	(Harris)
Transportation				Adams	
Energy				Schlesinger	
CIA			Turner		
Natl. Sec. Council	Brzezinski				
OMB			Lance		
Council Econ. Ad.	Schultze				
UN Ambassador			(Young)		Young

symbolic community.[31] Three lawyers, all Washington career-ists in one way or another, who might well have been inter-changed (as indeed one of them later was) headed the main urban departments of Housing, Transportation, and Health, Education and Welfare.[32] One of them, Patricia Roberts Harris of HUD, as a black woman, held a status as a "twofer" among symbolic interest groups that made her all but immune from dismissal, as later events were to show.[33] There were, as many people remarked, three Georgians, presumably presidential ambassadors,[34] among the top seventeen as well as one former classmate of the President's from the naval academy.[35]

Observers noted the odd resemblance between this Demo-cratic cabinet and the Republican cabinet that immediately pre-ceded it.[36] There was a curious neutrality of the Carter cabinet toward the vast stew of interest groups, both within and outside the government, that make up the traditional Democratic coa-lition. Of Mr. Carter's top seventeen appointees, how many reached into the constituencies suggested by the old New Deal voting coalition, indeed the coalition which came together to elect him?[37] Where were the representatives of the Irish, the Polish, the Jews, the Italians, the cities, the labor unions? Where indeed were the long-time active members at the grass roots of the Democratic party? Not wholly absent to be sure, but hard to find. The Carter cabinet was far stronger in symbolic than in traditional interest group representation. National Security Council Chief Brzezinski was in fact of Polish extraction, and even spoke English with a slight Polish accent. Yet it could be argued only in jest that this Columbia University professor "represented" Polish-Americans in the cabinet, unconnected as he was with the great Democratic political organizations in the eastern and midwestern cities in which Polish-Americans predominated. The same was true for Secretary of H.E.W. Joseph Califano and Italian-Americans, and so on, with only a couple of exceptions, the most significant once again undoubtedly being Andrew Young and the black community.

✳ So, perhaps the first clear signal given by President Carter in the way he constituted his administration was to proclaim a disbelief in the reality of the interest group composition of the Democratic party. He understood the need for symbolic gestures, and for satisfying those interest group demands made through the mass media, but there was, clearly, nothing in his experience of the national Democratic party—principally, by then, revealed to him by the nominating process—that confronted him with most of the varied components of the grand Democratic coalition. His own faction—the enthusiasm of his "peanut brigade" of campaign workers, and of Carter voters in primary elections—is what nominated him. Once nominated (at a national party convention paid for in full by the government) the federal government subsidized his entire general election campaign. Although it was true that his fellow-Democrats elected him President, this fact was easy to ignore, and Mr. Carter remarked on entering the White House that he "owed" his presence there to nobody.[38] ✳

His cabinet appointments, strongly weighted with can-do

technocrats, leavened by gestures to symbolic constituencies, and filled out with Georgians, proclaimed some of the implications of the President's viewpoint. Other consequences were to emerge in President Carter's dealings with Congress.

4. Getting Along with Congress

A second significant piece of evidence showing how the lessons of the process that nominated President Carter were permitted to override imperatives arising out of the post-inaugural Washington environment emerges from a consideration of President Carter's relations with Congress. These were very unpleasant.[39]

Outside observers were entitled to view Mr. Carter's inability to get along with Congress with some amazement. After all, President Carter was a middle-of-the-road Democrat, and the Congress was controlled—overwhelmingly controlled—by middle-of-the-road veterans of the Democratic party. After the election of 1976, some 292 Democrats were returned to the House of Representatives (out of 435) and 62 Democrats out of 100 sat in the Senate. The midterm election of 1978 gave the Democrats a 276 to 159 advantage in the House and 59 to 41 in the Senate. The last time an overwhelmingly Democratic Congress had coincided with a Democratic President, after the 1964 landslide election, the result had been the bumper crop of new and innovative programs of the famous 89th Congress.[40]

Times had changed on Capitol Hill since the enactment of the Great Society, however. Friends of President Carter were quick to point out that important alterations had overtaken Congress in the intervening decade and a half, making the Capitol Hill tasks of a President—any President—far more difficult. Congress had democratized its rules, for example, had endured a period of fierce antagonism with President Nixon, had created an enormous staff bureaucracy in part to wage war on the executive branch, and had undergone a drastic turnover in membership so that a majority of members could not hark back to the good old days of presidential-congressional cooperation.[41]

In the old days, it was said (the examples frequently coming from the Kennedy era of 1961–63), a President could strike a bargain with the congressional leadership, and the leadership could deliver the Congress. Committee chairmen ruled their roosts, and this meant that once a committee chairman committed himself to cooperation with the President, the President's task of assembling a majority in Congress was greatly simplified. As Lance Morrow said in *Time:*

> Congress used to operate through party discipline enforced by powerful leaders like Sam Rayburn, who in turn responded to leads from the White House. Now Congress has become a catfight of centrifugal energies, a fractured, independent crew that in its less disciplined moments approaches the opera buffa standards of the Italian Chamber of Deputies. As never before, Congressmen have narrowed their definitions of their responsibilities: they answer to their constituencies and to their special interests. Those arrayed demands do not necessarily correspond to the national good.[42]

In Mr. Carter's time, the argument continued, committee chairmen had lost their power to the chairmen of subcommittees, and subcommittee chairmanships were dispersed among the multitudes. Instead of cultivating an alliance with twenty senior Congressmen, presidential legislative liaison workers had to court 120 subcommittee chairmen, a much more complicated task.

There is a grain of truth in this argument, but no more than a grain. The "good old days" existed only during the brief span of the 89th Congress, well after Sam Rayburn had gone to his reward.[43] And the bad new days of the Carter era were structurally far more favorable to a middle-of-the-road Democratic President than anything Presidents Truman or Kennedy ever saw. Congressional reform devolved power not only downward to subcommittee chairmen but also upward to the House Democratic leadership. Mistakes, ineptitude, and presidential neglect of Congress played a far more significant role in creating the Carter administration legislative record than Carter administration apologists admit. ❋

The litany of presidential mistakes toward Congress was nearly endless: an inability to settle upon legislative priorities, a reluctance to bring Congress into the process of formulating proposals before they arrived, fully blown, on Capitol Hill, a disinclination to interact or bargain directly with Congressmen and a tendency to appeal to a mythical entity known as "the people," presumably over the heads of Congressmen, themselves elected public officials, the vast majority of whom had run well ahead of Jimmy Carter in their home districts.[44]

As two junior sub-cabinet Carter appointees recalled:

> The President sent a flotilla of major proposals to the Congress in the first eighteen months of his administration—cuts in water projects, social security finance, a comprehensive energy program, a tax rebate scheme, hospital cost containment legislation, comprehensive tax reform, welfare reform. Many of these proposals went to the tax-writing committees of the Congress: Senate Finance and House Ways and Means. And because the President had overloaded the Congress and those committees with reforms that would not command ready assent, because he was not able to marshal the administration's resources and develop political support for all the major battles that were required, and because many of his top political lieutenants were untutored in the ways of the Congress (and at the outset didn't seem to care), most of these proposals were either sunk or badly damaged. President Carter's reputation as less than skillful in domestic affairs and with the Congress was thus firmly established.[45]

President Carter's legislative liaison was in the hands of a person totally inexperienced and unknown on Capitol Hill, but this was only the beginning of the problem.[46] The Carter administration could—and eventually did—hire people more experienced in the ways of Congress to join what in time became a bloated liaison staff. For a while many of these people were housed in the White House's East Wing, physically and symbolically removed from the West Wing center of presidential

power, and only Frank Moore, their chief, ever gained much
direct access to the President.[47] The Carter administration ignored the advice of friendly predecessors to establish regular
beats for liaison personnel based on the bloc structure of Congress and instead began by assigning issue specialties to them.[48]
This meant that different liaison people would deal with the
same Congressman on different issues, and no regular relationship, no orchestration of give and take over the long haul, could
easily be established. Worse, presidential liaison people, allegedly issue specialists, were never tied into the policy formation
process in the White House and so were denied both flexibility
and credibility in dealing with Congress.

Despite repeated efforts from congressional leaders to bridge
the gap between Capitol and White House, neither President
Carter nor his closest aides who actually participated in policy-
making made informal acquaintances in Congress. It became
common coin on the Hill that Mr. Carter had conceptualized
Congress as indistinguishable from the Georgia legislature.[49]
Democrats from all parts of the political spectrum—but most
notably those from his own part—began to collect and disburse,
like children with bubble-gum cards, a fund of Jimmy Carter
stories illustrating his utter lack of interest in listening to
congressional advice, his stubbornness, his parochial insularity.
He evidently had no back-channels to Capitol Hill and wanted
none, no congressional cronies, no unofficial sources of information, indeed virtually no friends. A *New York Times* news
analysis examined the phenomenon after more than two years
of the Carter Presidency:

> The result, simply, is that he has no friends on Capitol Hill. "He
> just doesn't have that wellspring to call on," said one Southern
> Senator. "When you get in trouble, that's when you need your
> friends to come to your defense, and he just doesn't have that."[50]

For a President to "get along" with Congress and to "have
friends" there is not merely a matter of bonhomie or backslap-
ping, though superficial tokens of affability are generally ap-

preciated in the Washington world as they would be in any situation. Where there is considerable and constant turnover in the cast of characters that politicians must do business with, a pleasant disposition and a willingness to learn to do business on short acquaintance is doubly advantageous. More fundamentally, however, getting along with Congress means such things as showing respect for the institutional legitimacy of what is after all a constitutionally sanctioned branch of government, learning enough about the politics of the place to be able to draw with discernment on the talents and abilities, wisdom and good will of potential allies in shaping a reasonable policy agenda, and understanding in a non-censorious way something about the political problems and ambitions of members. Leadership by a President of an institution like Congress is certainly not precisely like the leadership of a strict hierarchy by the person at the top of the organization chart. But both sorts of leadership—especially congressional leadership—involve instilling an atmosphere of cooperation, of recognizing that credit must be spread if responsibility is to be spread, and that the morale of the troops may make a difference to overall productivity.

President Carter's difficulties on all these counts surfaced very early in his administration. A month after inauguration day the Speaker of the House told Elizabeth Drew:

> The problem with the people around Carter is that they spent so much of their time running against Washington they don't know they are now a part of Washington.[51]

And another of her sources said:

> He spent so much time in the campaign saying that he didn't owe anybody anything that nobody thinks they owe him anything.[52]

Mr. Carter's press secretary, Jody Powell, said after six months in office:

> It's the damndest thing about him . . . He went all over the country for two years asking everybody he saw to vote for him for President, but he doesn't like to call up a Congressman and ask for his support on a bill.[53]

The political resources of such a President were bound to be easily depleted, even among those, undoubtedly a great number, who wished him no particular ill. Given heavy Democratic majorities, the Speaker and the Senate Majority Leader could rally majorities in behalf of a President who could not or would not help himself, but not easily and not often. For since the rise of large congressional staffs, Congressmen no longer need to take the word of the executive branch on any controverted point if they choose not to. The congressional party can now, if it chooses to do so, chart its own course with respect to policy fully in possession of adequate intellectual fortification. The capacity to do so, however, operates at least in part independently of the inclination to do so. The development of staff capacity was a congressional response to hostilities during the presidency of Richard Nixon.[54] The use of this capacity when Congress and the Presidency were both securely in Democratic hands was a response to the presidential style of Jimmy Carter.

In order to get a sense of the internal dynamics of the Carter Congresses in relation to the Presidency some historical background is helpful. Essentially, throughout most of the last fifty years, the internal struggle of central importance to Congress has been between liberal and mainstream Democrats on one hand and a conservative coalition, encompassing conservative Southern Democrats and mainstream Republicans, on the other.[55] Franklin Roosevelt's abortive attempt in the election of 1938 to purge Congress of conservative Democrats after the failure of his Court-packing plan was an early recognition of the capacity of the conservative coalition to hamper the political plans of liberal Democratic Presidents.[56] The strength of these two grand coalitions has ebbed and flowed over the years, changing tidally with the results of biennial elections. Both sides have taken what advantages they could from internal rules of Congress pertaining especially in the Senate to freedom of debate, in the House to control over the agenda, and in both houses to seniority in committee assignments. And both have interacted strategically with the President—the conservative

5. The Crisis of Confidence, 1979

Finally, there are the lessons President Carter himself drew from the accumulating evidence of stalemate in government and his unpopularity among citizens at large as his term wore on. These too testify to the extent to which nomination politics was a model for the politics of governing in President Carter's thinking.

By the middle of the third year of his Presidency, Jimmy Carter's ratings in most public opinion polls were roughly comparable with the worst days of Harry Truman or with Richard Nixon on the eve of impeachment. In early July 1979 the *New York Times* reported that only 26 percent of Americans approved of Mr. Carter's handling of the Presidency, a slide of four points from the previous month.[64] To be sure nobody was talking about impeaching Mr. Carter, not least because he had committed no impeachable offenses. But Democrats from many points in the political spectrum were actively mounting a dump Carter movement designed to prevent his renomination, and substitute the far more popular Senator Edward Kennedy.[65] Indeed, the same *New York Times* poll showed 53 percent of Democratic respondents favoring Kennedy as the Democratic nominee as compared with only 16 percent who preferred Carter. And when Kennedy supporters were asked their next choice, more preferred Governor Jerry Brown of California than the President.[66] Republicans could take heart in the public opinion survey trial heats that showed two of their possible presidential hopefuls, Ronald Reagan and Gerald Ford, defeating Carter in an election.[67]

The President had to absorb criticism on many fronts: there was considerable inflation in the domestic economy, which economists believed could not be stemmed short of a recession; after several years of weakness against foreign currencies, the dollar continued unstable; the OPEC countries were raising the price of oil in large jumps and limiting production; a friendly regime in Iran which had supported many aspects of American diplomacy collapsed into hands that were intermittently unsteady and hostile; the price of gasoline crept toward a dollar a gallon and beyond, and sporadic shortages caused unexpected closings of gas stations, panic buying, and long lines, first in California, then further east.

David S. Broder of the *Washington Post* described Mr. Carter's response to these and to other signs of mounting difficulty for his Presidency in the early summer of 1979:

> Alone [at Camp David] with his wife, Rosalynn, Jimmy Carter sat down on the afternoon of July 4 to put his pencil to a draft of an energy speech scheduled for national television the next night . . . But between noon and 3:00 PM that Independence Day, away from his staff, Cabinet and administration, Carter decided to cancel the speech for one simple reason. He believed that neither the country nor the Congress would heed or respond to another energy speech—the fifth of his term—from him.[68]

For twelve days Mr. Carter stayed in his mountain-top retreat, leaving only twice by helicopter to sample opinions on the state of the nation from groups of private citizens: once on the back porch of a machinist's house in Carnegie, Pennsylvania, and once in the living room of a retired cattle farmer in Martinsburg, West Virginia.[69] During his twelve-day retreat, he summoned a varied cast of experts, religious leaders, labor union chiefs, selected officeholders and journalists—well over a hundred in all—to counsel with him.

Martin Schram of the *Post* reported:

> The thing that Carter and his top advisers have come to see is that the President, not just the nation, had lost the way.

> Carter found it on the mountain-top. He found it not just from listening to invited guests telling him what was wrong, but from long walks in the woods and from reading such writers as John Gardner on morale and James MacGregor Burns on leadership.

> "The President began to understand that the crisis at hand is not limited to a political crisis but [is] a leadership crisis," said one of that inner circle of advisers with him throughout his Camp David conference.[70]

Finally emerging from Camp David, he gave a nationally televised address partly on the nation's energy problem and partly about what he described as a crisis of confidence sweeping the United States.

> It is a crisis [the President said] that strikes at the very heart and soul and spirit of our national will . . .
>
> The erosion of our confidence in the future is threatening to destroy the social and political fabric of America.

Mr. Carter listed as symptoms of this crisis the following:

> For the first time in the history of our country the majority of our people believe that the next five years will be worse than the past five years.
>
> Two-thirds of our people do not even vote.
>
> The productivity of American workers is actually dropping . . .
>
> The willingness of Americans to save for the future has fallen below that of all other people in the western world . . .
>
> There is a growing disrespect for government and for churches and for schools, the news media, and other institutions.

Among the causes of the crisis, Mr. Carter identified the assassinations of John and Robert Kennedy and Martin Luther King, Jr., the lack of success of our armies in Vietnam, the "shock" of Watergate, ten years of inflation, and "a growing dependence on foreign oil." He then sounded a theme familiar to those who recalled his successful campaign for the Presidency, just three years before:

> Looking for a way out of this crisis, our people have turned to the Federal Government and found it isolated from the mainstream of the nation's life. Washington D. C. has become an island . . . a system of government that seems incapable of action.
>
> You see a Congress twisted and pulled in every direction by hundreds of well-financed and powerful special interests.
>
> You see every extreme position defended to the last vote . . . by one unyielding group or another . . .

Often you see paralysis and stagnation and drift. You don't like it
and neither do I.[71]

The next day Mr. Carter gave two further speeches, in Kan-
sas City and Detroit, both of which were well received in the
mass media, as his public opinion rating bounded upward.[72]

A Carter aide told Martin Schram: "I think we have seen
both the rebirth of the American spirit that he talks about and
the rebirth of the Carter presidency as well." And Schram
added, "In style, scope, and effort expended, that is certainly
true."[73]

There then ensued a sequence of events that astounded most
political observers. At a special White House meeting of the
cabinet on July 17, Mr. Carter gave an hour-long lecture to the
most senior members of his administration on the failings of
his Presidency, which ended with his request for the resignations of all those present.

Partial reconstructions of this meeting leaked out for the next
month.[74] A cabinet officer, recalling the unhappiness when
Richard Nixon undertook a wholesale house-cleaning of the
White House staff at the beginning of his second term, asked
whether formal resignations were necessary from officials who
serve at the pleasure of the President anyway. There was debate over whether the offers had to be made in writing or could
be made orally. At some point the President excused himself
from the meeting, leaving his trusted associate, Hamilton Jordan, the only White House staff member present, in charge.
Jordan "stood up and slapped down a large stack of 'staff evaluation forms' on the cabinet table."[75] These thirty-item forms
were to be returned in 72 hours, and were to be used in pre-
paring evaluations of subcabinet officials whose jobs it was
thereby understood were also in jeopardy.

Questions on this form, meant to be filled in by cabinet officials about their senior associates,[76] included such items as: "On
the average when does this person arrive at work? leave work?"
"How bright is this person? (on a scale of one to six)," and "To

what extent is this person focused on "accomplishing the administration's goals? Personal goals?" These two alternatives, as the form indicated, were supposed to sum to 100%.

Jordan offered to go to the President for purposes of clarification with three options for those present: no resignations, oral resignations, or written resignations. The President sent word later that day that oral resignations would do. In a conference telephone call, members of the cabinet were told by Jordan that it would be publicly announced that the offers had been made.

Later in the day it became known that Jordan had also run a meeting of senior White House officials, who were asked to follow suit. It was announced that Mr. Jordan, who already possessed the corner office in the White House's west wing that went with the job, would assume the title of White House Chief of Staff.[77]

Two cabinet officials seemed to have been the intended targets of all this activity: Secretary of Health, Education and Welfare Joseph Califano, and Secretary of the Treasury Michael Blumenthal. Three other resignations were also accepted: Attorney General Griffin Bell, by amicable prior agreement, and Energy Secretary James Schlesinger, who had previously advised the President that he thought his political usefulness was nearing its end. Transportation Secretary Brock Adams became an additional casualty when he found himself publicly at odds with White House announcements during the process itself.

No one questioned President Carter's constitutional authority to make these changes, nor were any of them made—as had been the case with President Nixon's October 1973 firing of Archibald Cox—in violation of some informal political commitment or understanding with Congress. Nevertheless the immediate reaction on Capitol Hill from Democrats and Republicans alike was overwhelmingly unfavorable.[78]

The liberal Democratic Study Group in the House of Representatives put out a parody of Hamilton Jordan's report card, in which the White House staff (instead of sub-cabinet officials) was the subject. One high-level official said that Jordan's forms "were more appropriate for a junior high school student than an executive running a $40 billion program."[79] Another said: "This will make us the laughing stock of the world. Everybody knows who is performing well in this Administration . . . If those guys in the White House don't know it, they should be fired."[80] "All over the House floor, they're shaking their heads over that one," said moderate Republican Congressman Barber Conable. "It's very destructive to morale . . . the government has damn near ground to a halt."[81] Nearly a month later a high level administration official described congressional reaction to Jack Nelson of the *Los Angeles Times* as still "savagely angry. We are in deep political trouble."[82]

Unfavorable comment was not restricted to Congress. Virtually every articulate group of Washington political observers was tapped by the newspapers for reactions, and responses ranged from puzzled to contemptuous, with only a few voices raised in the President's defense. For example, Carter supporter Irving Shapiro, chairman of the DuPont Company, said: "I'm simply baffled by this procedure. It casts a cloud over the whole administration." A high-ranking previously loyal member of Carter's own administration said: "At this point, I don't see how I could campaign for his reelection."[84]

Major newspapers printed reams of adverse comment in their news columns and editorials and editorial cartoonists had a field day. More seriously, foreign press reaction was also unfavorable, so much so that presidential press secretary Jody Powell and national security affairs adviser Zbigniew Brzezinski were moved to call in Washington-based foreign journalists in an attempt—mostly unsuccessful—to persuade them that nothing out of the ordinary had occurred.[85]

Foreign money markets made their own evaluation of the situation. There was a noticeable flight from the dollar abroad, and the price of gold floated over $300 an ounce for the first time in history. In two weeks, the dollar lost 70 percent of the ground it had gained on the West German mark since the dollar-rescue program was put into effect by the U.S. Treasury and the German Bundesbank in November 1978.[86]

The most puzzled reaction came from those who could not understand why it was necessary or prudent to ask for thirty-four resignations in order to accept a handful of them. What was characterized by the President and by his aides Hamilton Jordan and Jody Powell on national television as an "orderly, methodical" process could have easily been foreseen to produce feelings of unease in foreign capitals as well as in Washington and at least momentarily to jeopardize such important long-term administration goals as stabilization of the dollar, ratification of the SALT Treaty, and the administration's energy proposals in Congress.

Adverse comment was thus compounded of a number of elements. There were those, chiefly Republicans, who were ready to take a simple pleasure in the obvious disarray of a Democratic administration.[87] Others, chiefly Democrats, had come to admire one or more of the departing cabinet members, or disliked or distrusted many leading—and surviving—members of Mr. Carter's White House staff.[88] Equally important were the critics who fell into neither category, but consisted of those for whom the manner in which the shake-up was conducted showed an appalling lack of respect for the top management of an administration that was mostly blameless by White House standards, and a failure to anticipate the disruptive consequences caused by the wider ripples of concern that were sure to flow from the staging of such an unnecessary and unnecessarily dramatic event. One observer said: "One does not stage the entire fifth act of *Hamlet* to get rid of Laertes alone."[89]

The most sympathetic rendering of President Carter's thinking ran along the following lines: He had become genuinely distressed by the data and the analysis contained in what was described as a "voluminously dire memo" presented to him in April 1979 by his public opinion analyst Patrick Caddell.[90] As his speech indicated, these findings showed Americans to be pessimistic about the future, for themselves and for the nation. Mr. Carter felt a presidential obligation to seize the moment to lead, and felt he must put his own house in order to do so. Thus the retreat to Camp David, the wide consultations, the wholesale request for resignations to symbolize a new start. Members of the administration who had not proven themselves to be team players could be removed without excessive personal recrimination, and other, borderline cases could be put on notice that a new degree of commitment would be required of them.

It must be said that virtually nobody seems to have found this set of explanations believable. Too much other data crowded in and demanded to be taken into account, such as Mr. Carter's own low standing in the polls, the shaky empirical foundations of the Caddell analysis, the gap of three months between the delivery of Caddell's memo and Mr. Carter's decision to act on it.[91]

There was also a highly projective flavor to Mr. Carter's response, which entailed a pledge to reorganize his time so as to perform fewer merely managerial functions and to travel more out among ordinary Americans. This plan of action entirely neglected the heavily populated circle of intermediaries who are themselves organized for the purposes of sharing in the governing process and representing varied segments of the population in their relations with the government. Mr. Carter's view of "special interests" and of Congress was clearly set forth— and not for the first time—in his July 15 speech. They, the press corps and the great bureaucracies of the executive branch all together made up the "Washington community," who, Mr. Carter insisted, were out of touch with popular sentiment and hence could be ignored. The Washington press corps, in Mr. Carter's opinion, took a much dimmer view of his cabinet shake-up than the people at large, which both *Newsweek* and the *New York Times* reported, in thinly disguised indirect discourse, "fortifies his decision to hold fewer of his regular Washington press conferences and get out around the country more in the meet-the-people style of his 1976 campaign."[92] As the *Times* reported:

> Jimmy Carter reached a number of conclusions about the way he was handling his Presidency. One was that he was wasting his time, or about 40 percent of it.
>
> That is the percentage of . . . time that was committed . . . to regularly scheduled weekly meetings with budget and staff aides, department heads and the like . . .
>
> Under the new arrangement, Mr. Carter is to be free to leave the Oval Office more frequently and travel outside Washington at least once a week. He has told visitors to the White House that he intends to move around the country as much as possible in an effort to reestablish the direct contact with the public he had during the 1976 campaign.[93]

On "Meet the Press" (NBC) Hamilton Jordan was asked why the administration had proceeded in the way it had and replied that "The American people are not concerned as to exactly how it happened, but . . . with what has happened."[94]

Observers began to ask if all the thrashing about was an effort—admirable or otherwise—by the President to position himself so as to be able to run against Washington for reelection to Washington's most prominent job just as he had originally run as an outsider in 1976. Could all this turmoil merely be an attempt to create an administrative tool in the spirit of zero-base budgeting, the moral equivalent of war, and other examples of tabula rasa thinking much favored by the President[95] that would aid him in shoring up perceived political or managerial weaknesses in his administration? Questions of motive and intention were regularly confounded with questions about consequences and all sorts of answers were readily to hand. Because these answers were not always free of partisan interest and because many key items of information had to be inferred or guessed at, a fair amount of confusion remained.

Mr. Carter's own diagnosis, however, seemed clear enough. He pledged to reform himself and his Presidency by re-creating the conditions under which he was originally nominated: going out more into the country, making contact with citizens and leaving the day-to-day management of the government in the hands of Hamilton Jordan and his newly reconstructed cabinet, which to a far greater degree, he believed, would reflect the priorities and the policies of the Carter White House. This seemed to be an unequivocal statement of a belief that the central failure of the Carter administration was one of public relations, not, as so many Washington observers insisted, one of governing. This latter diagnosis of his position emphasized that in the thirty months of the Carter Presidency up to then, Mr. Carter had not learned how to get along with Congress, nor with the congeries of interest groups clustering in the nation's capital and organized to do business there.

According to this view, while Mr. Carter had correctly noted his low ratings in the public opinion surveys, their cause was not a lack of preaching and teaching from the President to the nation at large but rather reflected an accumulated sense of malaise and difficulty which were the product of Mr. Carter's own disinclination to cooperate with other political leaders in Washington. These leaders—leaders, for example, of the labor movement, leaders of Congress both in the Democratic and the Republican parties—in turn fed back to their own constituencies throughout the country their dissatisfactions, and the cumulative effect of these dissatisfactions had finally adversely affected Mr. Carter's ratings in the public opinion polls. This close paraphrase of the theory of the two-step flow of public opinion formation suggests that even though it is now possible for political leaders to reach out and influence the opinions of mass publics directly through the medium of television, over the long run people also look to leaders more proximate to themselves than the President for a sense of political orientation.[96] Thus, according to this argument, Mr. Carter's inability to win over and to learn to cooperate productively with members of Congress and leaders of interest groups—especially those near to him on the ideological spectrum—had taken their toll in the public opinion polls by an indirect route.

If this diagnosis had any merit at all then it meant that Mr. Carter had already, as he originally suspected on July 4, come perilously close to saturating his capacity to influence public opinion in his own favor directly. Thus the best method available to him to turn around his low ratings in the public opinion polls was not to travel about the United States, but to face trying to do something about his problem of getting on with the Washington community. His analysis of the situation and his pledge to remedy it pointed in exactly the opposite direction, however, and suggested that he had overlearned the lessons of the nomination process. These foretold that he would continue his nearly bankrupt strategy of neglecting if not attacking Congress and the interest groups, even those clustering around the Democratic party, and attempting to reach out directly to the people over the heads of these other political leaders in order to become a more popular President.

Even if he could become more popular by this route, it was uncertain how it would help him get greater cooperation from Congress. It was also uncertain how it would improve the prospects of the various legislative programs that he had in mind. At best a high standing in public opinion is a resource that a President may call upon in order to persuade legislators of the popularity of the overall program that he advocates. No sophisticated legislator is likely to suppose that there is a genuine one-to-one correspondence between a President's popularity and the popularity of any particular item on his agenda, but members of Congress are far more inclined to give a popular President the benefit of the doubt in considering a presidential proposal than they will a President of marginal popularity or of low popularity.

In any event a President's popularity is only one of a number of considerations which legislators generally feel that they must take into account in determining their own opinions about public policy proposals.[97] They must also concern themselves with their popularity with their own constituencies. They may have their own ideas on the merits of issues as a result of personal knowledge or experience or their access to congressional sources of information or the play of national interest groups upon them both in their constituencies and in Washington itself. Presidents can participate in orchestrating the deployment of forces upon individual members of Congress, upon their own congressional party and upon the Congress as a whole, and therefore cultivating popularity with public opinion at large is one of a number of resources and instruments available to a President who means to conduct a successful legislative program.

Yet Mr. Carter initially gave no indication of an intention to get on more happily with the Washington community. He went out of his way to speak ill of special interest groups as a general category and made no concession to the idea that some small part of the national interest might be found lurking in a corridor on Capitol Hill. Even more significantly he made no attempt to reorganize his congressional liaison operation, and although many special assistants to the President in the White House were required to proffer their resignations, not one was immediately accepted. The only material change that took place was Mr. Jordan's de jure elevation to the position of Chief of Staff.[98]

Mr. Jordan, undeniably a person in whom the President reposed great confidence, was nevertheless in very bad odor on Capitol Hill. It was said by Congressmen that Mr. Jordan was harder to reach on the telephone than the President himself.[99] The Senate Majority Leader—a Democrat in good standing—professed not to know him at all.[100] The Speaker of the House said that in the thirty months of the Carter administration he had only met Mr. Jordan twice.[101] Many other comments unfavorable to Mr. Jordan—not all of them on only slight acquaintance—also greeted the news of his elevation.

Outgoing Attorney General Griffin Bell, for example, a genuine card-carrying member of the Georgia Mafia, was reported as "telling friends . . . in a round of farewell parties that Hamilton Jordan . . . 'is not long on maturity' and might be taking on too big a job."[102]

"I am not well known and I recognize that," Mr. Jordan said

at what he described as his "debutante party," a small cocktail buffet convened on July 27, 1979—roughly two and one-half years after Jimmy Carter's inauguration—to give the Speaker and twenty members of Congress a chance to meet him. "Most Congressmen that are criticizing my elevation to Chief of Staff don't know me." Mr. Jordan continued, "That's not their fault; that's my fault. I have not made the effort to know them."[103]

All this activity constituted an open acknowledgment that the Carter Presidency was experiencing great difficulty. A question remained whether the difficulty was merely a matter of tell-tale inefficiencies, or a not-quite-tight-enough ship, or sartorial sloppiness among the White House palace guard,[104] or a spot of bad timing on Capitol Hill, or whether something more serious was involved.

Perhaps most notable in the entire episode, which in a way was the most revealing series of events in President Carter's administration, was the explicit expression by the President of his underlying assumption that the entire intermediate layer that intervenes between a President and the grass roots of the country is fundamentally dispensable. How could a President not believe that a mock execution of his entire first team would be subjected to interpretations outside his own capacity to control? Or that the clientele both of affected government agencies and of the Democratic party might not readily accept his after-the-fact reassurances that the crisis was all for the best?

It is certainly true, as Mr. Carter discovered, that a President can go on television with some regularity and even some effectiveness. But others go on television as well: news commentators, for example, who frequently talk with their sources and their friends in that intermediate layer before broadcasting their views. Congressmen, labor leaders, ethnic and communal leaders, all speak with their own voices to their own constituents. When a President is fortunate, he shares these constituents amicably with allies in his party and with associated interest groups. But only briefly and occasionally can he override the longer-term loyalties of constituents to his own benefit.

Once again, the lessons of the nomination process proved mistaken. While it was necessary to go directly to primary electorates to capture the nomination, it was imprudent to infer from success at this endeavor that direct appeals for popular support would succeed without help in a more long-term relationship. Mass persuasion over the short run of a primary election season has a chance of succeeding without elite assistance; over the longer run, however, of a presidential term of office, successful mass persuasion entails successful elite persuasion.

Toward the end of his term, President Carter gave indications that he was beginning to accept the interest group basis of the Democratic party and hence to reward the coalition that had elected him, not merely the coterie that nominated him. This change of tactics, if not of heart, could be seen, for example, in the appointments to the cabinet of a southern mayor and a western mayor, Moon Landrieu of New Orleans and Neal Goldschmidt of Portland, and of a businessman prominent in Jewish communal affairs, Philip Klutznick. Likewise, he replaced his counsel on the White House staff, Atlantan Robert Lipshutz, with Lloyd Cutler, a well-known Washington lawyer, on whom he learned to rely. But the 1980 election returns, with their accompanying public opinion analyses indicating that the major reason for the massive Democratic defection was dissatisfaction with Jimmy Carter, suggest that in finally focusing on electoral rather than nomination politics Mr. Carter woke up too late.[105] His early concession of defeat on election night, wilfully jeopardizing his running mates farther down on the ticket throughout the western states, suggested that, however well he might have learned to cooperate with his fellow Democrats, it was uncongenial to him to do so.[106]

6. Conclusion

Jimmy Carter's pathway to the Presidency was originally dictated by the rules of the game as constrained, in particular, by the reforms of 1968–72. His response was to exploit the strategic imperatives these reforms brought into being. He built a personal following and invested most of his resources in states selecting their delegates early: Iowa and New Hampshire. In both states he succeeded not in forming a broad coalition but in mobilizing a faction, emerging first in rank-order among the numerous presidential candidates who had put themselves forward.[107]

The favorable publicity generated by these early results made plausible Carter's argument that he was the logical southern alternative to George Wallace in Florida. And so by the time he met with reverses in Massachusetts a week or so later the Carter bandwagon was rolling. By the time in June that Mayor Daley was ready to put his imprimatur on the Carter candidacy, Carter had won far fewer than a majority of delegates selected up to that point: his actual total was around 38 percent.[108] Though the traditional Democratic electoral coalition voted for their largely unknown candidate, Carter entered the White House as essentially a factional, not a coalition-based President. General awareness of the factional character of President Carter's outlook was to a degree retarded by the fact that Carter was not an extremist but rather a centrist in the ideological spectrum of the Democratic party. That he was well placed to embrace a broad coalition, however, did not guarantee that he would actually do so in forming his government, and he did not do so until his campaign for reelection was nearly upon him. No doubt this suited his personal style or character. More to the point, however, was the fact that the institutional constraints upon his personal preferences were weak. It is to be expected that a public official's private preferences and characterological traits will loom particularly large when no organizational constraints, no institutional cues, are offered. And this is the nub of the problem. Nothing in Mr. Carter's prior experience as a politician, certainly nothing in his experience of the nomination process, led him to the view that he needed to come to terms with the rest of the Democratic party. Greatly overriding considerations of party unity for Carter were concerns of good government, of addressing the policy issues of the day, of finding technically sound, comprehensive solutions to problems. These in turn could be presented to Congress and sold on their merits if not to Congress directly then over the heads of Congress to the "American people".

The people, however, were not so easy to mobilize in his be-half. In part this was a matter of bad luck: during the election year of 1980 the immediate rally-round-the-flag popular re-sponse of the early days of the Iranian hostage crisis decayed into a long-drawn-out period of frustration and seeming im-potence. In part, no doubt, the two-step flow of communication from all the Washington-based intermediaries of the interest groups out across the country and from Congressmen to their constituents played a role in eventually diminishing President Carter's popularity. And finally, a certain pessimism and even grimness crept into Mr. Carter's own televised speeches, for ex-ample, on the numerous occasions when he addressed the na-tion's long-range prospects for the importation of inexpensive oil. In light of all the bad news that Mr. Carter delivered in person, over television, to the American people, it seems plau-sible to view the negativity of popular response as a triumph, rather than a failure, of presidential communication. Mr. Carter, not unlike President Nixon before him, evidently came to be-lieve that he was a beneficiary of a system of governing genu-inely free of mediation processes in the ordinary sense. He ap-peared to believe that contemporary circumstances sharply reduced the need to exhibit traditional presidential concerns with coalition building in order to govern. While both these conclusions are far from foolish deductions from the facts of genuine change in the presidential nomination process, they nevertheless proved to be off the mark. The relations between President and people are still powerfully mediated, so it seems, although by somewhat different processes and agencies than before. Presidents likewise still need interest groups and must build coalitions among them to govern successfully. This is not to suggest, however, that processes of intermediation have es-caped the consequences of political reform.

IV

Wider Consequences: Political Intermediation, Mobilization, Accountability

Reform is a process that involves more than the enactment of prohibitions and requirements. Requirements and prohibitions newly enacted in the course of reform are added to an ongoing corpus of customs and regulations, producing a pattern of incentives to which different political actors, though they may vary in their comprehension, in their vulnerabilities, and in their resources, can nevertheless be expected to respond. It is not always easy to anticipate the behavior of actors as they learn how to operate over the newly contoured terrain that reform creates. It is certain, however, that the intentions of reformers will not comprehensively determine their behavior. Thus the assessment of reforms in operation is bound to take into account at least some unanticipated activity. And sometimes the newly emergent pattern of incentives has dramatic consequences for the maintenance of the political system. We have been following two such clusters of reforms, having to do with the centralization of authority over delegate selection and the control of campaign finance.

Implicit both in reformers' conceptions of reform and in the conceptions of critics is the assumption that political actors can and do learn to change their behavior with fair rapidity in response to changed rules of the game. This applies not merely to that part of their behavior evoked by the desire to evade criminal penalties but also to strategic and tactical behavior, activities designed to take advantage of new rules and regulations and to avoid adverse impacts upon actors' plans and ambitions. Because the presidential election process is bound to be rich in implications for the ambitions of politicians, it does not seem unreasonable to wonder ahead of time how reforms will change the structure of political incentives. Yet it is apparent that in the wave of reform we have been examining only rudimentary thought was given to such matters, and that reforms emerged in a context rather inhospitable to reasoned reflection of any sort: the turmoil of 1968 and its aftermath, and the trauma of Watergate and the impeachment crisis.

Hindsight may prove to be no better, owing to the difficulties, in a complex and evolving political system, of sorting out long-run from short-run effects, manipulable from uncontrollable phenomena. Nevertheless, it seems worthwhile to make an attempt to trace the effects of party reform at least a short distance out into the political system at large. While it cannot be claimed that reforms of the party system are solely and directly responsible for widespread changes in the underlying conditions of American politics, neither are they unrelated to them. Indirectly and in interaction with more diffuse changes in political life, political reforms can be shown to contribute significantly to emerging patterns and trends of American politics that deserve close attention. Significant among these are trends affecting the institutions and practices that maintain links between the general populace and elected officials.

1. Trends in Political Intermediation

The idea of a political party as a coalition of interests and groups bound together by many sorts of ties, including the hope of electing a President, is fast becoming an anachronism. Party is increasingly a label for masses of individual voters who pick among various candidates in primary elections as they would among any alternatives marketed by the mass media. Achieving financial support through mass mailings and through the public purse has displaced in importance the mobilizing of well-heeled backers and the seeking of alliances with territorially identifiable interest groups and state party organizations. The stimulation of coverage by the mass media and the building of personal organizations state by state through the activation of volunteer workers have been replacing dependence upon party regulars and state and local party leaders. Thus, interest group activity has been changing rather than diminishing. While interest groups that are mobilized in traditional ways around the economic interests or the communal ties of their members have declined in their political influence, the fortunes of other interest groups have been greatly enhanced because the managers of the mass media have decided to smile upon them. The decision to smile reflects world views common not only among news media personnel but also among the larger groupings of well-educated persons to which they belong, and while the political consequences are unmistakable, the criteria that make for success under these changed circumstances are not easily classifiable as partisan in their content.[1] Prominent among approved interest groups are those embodying what the media of mass communications accredit as disinterested rectitude, such as Common Cause and the Ralph Nader organizations, and those speaking for interests widely perceived as historically disadvantaged such as black, Hispanic-American, and militant women's groups. These groups, frequently and, for the most part erroneously, billed as grass-roots organizations, have taken on a new weight in American politics, in some cases achieving special recognition for their clientele in party rules and in law.[2]

I do not wish to argue that groups of this sort are especially worthy or unworthy as compared with state party organizations, labor unions, farmers' groups, associations of businessmen, or other interest groups organized on traditional lines around the economic or status needs of their clientele. But many of these newer groups—the ethnically based groups are the main exceptions—come into being and are sustained by different means than traditionally organized intermediate groups. These new groups are to an unprecedented degree the creatures of the media of mass communications in that it is their power to command news coverage and to be taken seriously by the news media that in some cases brought them into prominence and in all cases sustains their political influence.[3]

For good or ill a political system having intermediation processes heavily reliant upon the mass media is the sort of political system that is emerging in the United States. This does not imply that the media are reaching directly into the homes of totally atomized individual voters. Rather, political leaders are broadcasting to publics mobilized and organized around certain principles of attentiveness and inattention, and this has implications for interest groups and their success in politics.

Two recent political events in which modern mediation processes played a part may suggest a little of how they work. One is the non-selection of John Dunlop as secretary of labor by President-elect Carter in 1976. Another is the dismissal by presidential candidate George McGovern of Senator Thomas Eagleton as vice presidential candidate on the Democratic ticket in 1972.

It was widely assumed that Dunlop had a good chance to be Jimmy Carter's secretary of labor since, like another Carter adviser, James Schlesinger, his prior association with the Ford administration had ended in an honorable departure in which his personal integrity and political astuteness had to some degree been vindicated.[4] Unlike Schlesinger, Dunlop was a Democrat. Moreover, Dunlop was known to be far and away the favored choice of George Meany and the dominant faction of organized labor for the job as their ambassador to the new administration.[5] In indicating this preference, Meany had given due regard to a norm that prescribes a measure of independence from the labor movement for the secretary. Dunlop was not himself a labor leader but a college professor and dean, an academic specialist on labor relations with a long record of practical experience as an impartial arbitrator of labor disputes.

It may well be that President Carter never intended Dunlop to have the job, but it is at least intriguing to note that the appointment was publicly opposed in only one quarter: by leaders of black and militant women's groups who believed, whether rightly or wrongly, that in his prior government service and as Dean of Arts and Sciences at Harvard, Dunlop had been unsympathetic to their aspirations.[6] One interpretation of the course of events is that in a straight fight between one set of interests, labor, and another, black groups and the women's movement, over who was to be secretary of labor, it was not the traditionally organized group that won, even though the fight was over who was to be their point of contact in an administration run by the party they traditionally favored. It is not recorded that labor exercised a comparable veto over the appointments of black citizens and women in the Carter administration. The appointments of black and female Americans to administration positions were extensively monitored in the press, however, which in due course came to refer to these two groups, with the addition of Spanish Americans and Native Americans, as virtually the only interest groups whose progress was worth tracking.[7] This reflects news decisions made by independent news specialists, but these decisions are not empty of political consequences since they serve to confer legitimacy on some groups and their political claims and to withdraw it from others, as has been happening, for example, in the case of American Jews.[8]

Another facet of contemporary political intermediation is revealed by the Eagleton case.[9] Once it was discovered by the mass media during the presidential campaign of 1972 that Senator Eagleton, the Democratic vice-presidential nominee, had not disclosed episodes of hospitalization for severe depression, it was only a matter of time before his senior colleague, Senator McGovern, had to remove him from the Democratic ticket. Why was this a foregone conclusion? Interested readers can search in vain through responsible journals of news and opinion for a serious discussion of hospitalization and recovery from mental illness as a disqualification for public office. Nor will they find

a comparison of Eagleton's life history with that of his counterpart, the Republican vice-presidential nominee, Spiro T. Agnew, who had never been institutionalized or diagnosed as
mentally distressed. In fact the news media rapidly reached a
consensus that Eagleton had to go, but so far as an outsider
could tell, it was not based on a discussion of the merits of the
case so much as on the chagrin of media people at Eagleton's
lack of candor with them and with Senator McGovern.[10] Gary
Hart, McGovern's campaign director, wrote: "There were three
possible bases for a decision on Eagleton's fate—personal, political, or factual. The decision to keep Eagleton was made on
personal grounds; the decision to remove him, on political
grounds. Both were wrong. The records, the medical evidence,
should have been the basis for a decision in either case."[11]
George McGovern, a nominee whose success depended not on
the building blocks of interest group alliances within the Democratic party, but on the support of the news media, had no
real choice but to dismiss Eagleton once the media consensus
developed. McGovern's handling of the entire episode entailed
sending messages to Eagleton by dropping hints among the
journalists covering his campaign, and Eagleton was constrained to communicate back to McGovern in much the same
fashion, a mode of communication which evidently greatly puzzled the journalists involved.[12]

   Here we can note that one characteristic of the emerging style
of political intermediation is that it is done in the sunshine. It
is easy enough for anyone who has the price of a newspaper or
access to the televised evening news to see what advice a political leader is getting from the news media. One difficulty with
such an arrangement is that when politicians must announce
themselves and their preferences on national television, they
may get locked into position before they come to understand
one another's point of view. Deliberation and negotiation, in
which mutual accommodation and mutual learning are encouraged, are hard to arrange without causing one or more public
figures embarrassment. Incidents of embarrassment in the

public record are commonly thought to be an overwhelming disadvantage at election time. And so, participants are tempted into confrontation politics and moralism in order to look good. Of course in looking good, they may to an unaccustomed degree actually be good. But there are dangers here as well as opportunities.

These dangers are clear enough: interest-group alliances and alliances with state and local party leaders can to a certain extent protect a presidential candidate against unfavorable opinions in the mass media; without these alliances a candidate or a President has no court of appeal from media disapproval and this may seriously constrain the choices available to him. To be sure, interest group and party alliances do not arise without cost or without effort. As the case of the Carter Presidency suggested, intermediation by political leaders and interest groups more proximate to voters than the President may have a long-run impact that can be adverse to a President. But there are opportunities here as well as dangers, in part because establishing alliances with cooperative intermediaries constitutes a long-run strategy for enlisting that portion of public opinion subject to their influence.

Thus while there has been a shift in intermediation processes, toward more public and less overtly partisan vehicles of communication, it is not the case that modern forms of political intermediation free political leaders from important constraints. By trading labor leaders for television news commentators as intermediaries, Presidents and presidential candidates may have achieved a kind of freedom but only at a price. The Dunlop and Eagleton cases suggest what sort of price is involved. In a large-scale society based upon appeals from leaders to followers for their votes, it is evidently inescapable that some sort of division of labor will take place in which people specialize in working for mediating institutions that are separate from leaders and followers and undertake to link them. What sort of institutions these are, what sorts of values infuse their management, what sorts of messages they spread and retard are bound to have political consequences and will influence the relations between leaders and their publics.

A sizable number of conventional notions exist about the purposes and functions of political intermediaries in large-scale political systems.[13] Intermediary groups are supposed to interpret the desires of ordinary people to leaders and to inform publics of alternatives available to them, thus tutoring their expectations about the activities of government. Intermediaries recruit and train leaders for politics, identify social problems and suggest solutions. And they conduct long-range political education, helping to form the loyalties of citizens toward the state and providing legitimacy, a provisional sort of acquiescence to the underlying political order, upon which leaders of the state can rely. Intermediary organizations teach political obligations to citizens and inform citizens of their political rights.

Traditional agents of political intermediation thus include the nuclear family, the household, and the extended family,[14] the school, primary communal groups such as exist in a work place or church or neighborhood, or a voluntary association organized for the purpose of promoting some shared interest.

It has been apparent for some time that various trends in modern society have eroded the monopoly that face-to-face and geographically localized institutions once held over the time, the attentiveness, and the loyalty of Americans. And so it should come as no surprise to learn of their decline as monopolists of political intermediation. The private automobile, the comprehensive network of roads, and the telephone have expanded the potential for individual communication enormously and have consequently attenuated the tyranny of geographical propinquity in determining the options that people have in adopting one or more organizations as their political intermediaries of choice.[15]

Television has had a somewhat different effect. Since it is not an interactive medium it has greatly increased the power of the few who are at the focus of its attention and assured that certain sorts of standardized information are readily available on a virtually universal basis. Political representation, another form of intermediation, has more and more become a specialized, even a professionalized activity.[16] Finally, the rules of politics are being rewritten to reflect all these trends and in some cases to facilitate them. National party conventions, for example, once were conducted primarily for the purpose of discovering what the delegates to them—organized primarily by their state party leaders—wanted to do. Today conventions are more frequently run according to scripts worked out by television consultants so as to maximize their advertising value to the viewing public.

Intermediaries are now heavily engaged in the various crafts of persuasion by means of mass media. In this situation direct and material interests are bound to become relatively less important as compared with symbolic interests.[17] Hence interest groups specializing in representing direct and material interests lose ground to those groups concerned with symbolic interests.

Political parties are losing whatever favored position they may once have had as prime repositories of the symbolic political loyalties of American voters. To say that political parties are in trouble is mostly to say little more than that state and local party elites have lost influence over some of the processes most important to their collective life, such as the making of political—especially presidential—nominations. Many observers claim that there has been a great burgeoning in the influence of so called single-issue interest groups, but what they are witnessing is not the proliferation of single-issue interests—which have always existed and attempted to influence the political process[18]—but rather a precipitous decline in the capacity of party elites through the control of their own institutional practices to resist, channel, accommodate, or limit the demands of these groups for extraordinary influence over the presidential nomination process.

Thus of the three major vehicles of political intermediation available to Americans—interest groups, the mass media, and political parties—all have been influenced by changes in the technology of communications available to Americans. Interest groups and parties have been significantly influenced by the mass media, and those groups and interests most dependent upon the maintenance of the structural and organizational integrity of interest groups and the parties have been the most disadvantaged by these changes.

2. The Political Mobilization of Citizens

The diminution of party loyalty in the electorate and the decline of turnout in presidential elections, insofar as these are bona fide phenomena of contemporary American politics,[19] are occurring incrementally rather than suddenly and massively. They may well be the results of changes at the elite level rather than, as reformers frequently argue, reasons for these changes.[20]

It is possible to speculate that changes in the party system might contribute in at least two ways to the modest declines observable in the political participation and party affiliations of ordinary citizens. First, in the course of discouraging coalition-building and encouraging factionalist strategies by presidential candidates, ordinary citizens may in greater numbers feel themselves and their opinions less taken account of by politicians. This phenomenon is frequently conceptualized as a distaste for extremist leadership, but the unpopularity of extremism may simply be a special case of the phenomenon of a factionalist strategy leading to the exclusion of large numbers of voters.[21] A factionalist from the center of the ideological spectrum no doubt may appeal to a larger share of the populace than an extremist; but competition for the first place votes of that larger share may be very intense, leading to tactics in which candidates seek to differentiate themselves and stake out exclusive first-choice territory. While this may capture the allegiance of a significant number of voters—presumably in the case of at least one candidate enough ultimately to win—it leaves the problem of the allegiance of those voters not attracted to the winner.

Coalition building explicitly seeks to deal with this phenomenon, and to bring large numbers of voters in under one tent. The argument here would be that neglect of this activity in the nomination process may be showing up in the mild but persistent increases in disaffection recorded in innumerable public opinion surveys and standardized measures of political participation.[22]

It is, surely, a paradox of great interest that as the education level of American adults drifts upward, at least some measures of political participation and affiliation, which at the individual level correlate positively and strongly with education, are for the general populace drifting downward.[23] In those presidential election years in which one of the major political parties nominates a political extremist there seems to be no difficulty in interpreting the result as abnormal defection and withdrawal from political activity of more moderate adherents of the party in which the blunder occurs. The increased necessity for political leaders to rely on factionalist, exclusionist strategies may simply be creating a permanent, chronic form of this same phenomenon, visible in its acute manifestation when extremists are chosen in the presidential nomination lottery which pits the leaders of many factions within a single party against one another.

A second process which may also be contributing to the chronic occurrence of depressed political participation and mobilization among ordinary Americans is the steady replacement of face-to-face, primary and geographically proximate interest groups with distant, symbolic and noninteractive mediation mechanisms. Such mechanisms may be reasonably efficient as devices for informing citizens of the date of an election and of some salient facts about candidates, but they are bound to be less comprehensively engaging to at least some ordinary voters than more personalized organizational structures.

The erosion of traditional intermediaries thus may in the long run contribute to the decay of political legitimacy within the constitutional order. This may be reflected in the palpable growth of disaffection with Presidents and in the phenomenon frequently complained of—mostly by neoconservative observers—and labeled "ungovernability," a pervasive inability of political leaders to satisfy the expectations of voters.[24]

Political reform is frequently defended as a means for decreasing the alienation of voters—and the party reforms we have discussed certainly were so described by their advocates.[25] Not enough work has been done, however, to exclude the possibility that the arrow of causation actually runs the other way: by contributing to the decommissioning of primary groups and geographically based interest groups as prime political intermediaries and by encouraging factionalist, exclusionist political tactics, reforms may be spreading the very disease that it is claimed they are curing.

3. The Subculture of the News Media

If party elites are losing influence to media elites, then it seems sensible to inquire in more detail about the sorts of performance we can expect from media elites in their new character as leading intermediaries in the American political system's presidential nomination process. This requires knowledge of the workways of the news media, many of the essentials of which have been carefully studied and are already well known.[26]

The fundamental axioms that underpin these workways are reducible to two organizational imperatives: professionalism and competitiveness. News media elites strive for professionalism, which entails establishing their own account of day-to-day reality independent from that of the politicians whom they cover. Yet of course news media reality must intersect at many points with the realities perceived by political actors and it should come as no surprise that there are frequent disagreements between the two populations. News media professionals generally perceive these disagreements as an earnest of their own professionalism and of their integrity.

Politicians occasionally take the view that journalists are attempting to create an adversary culture and consider news me-

sible.[32] Discussing the coverage of presidential campaigns, NBC broadcaster Roger Mudd says:

> Over the last 15 years, as competition has sharpened between the networks, none of us is content to let an event be an event. We have to fix it. We have to foreshorten the conclusions, hasten the end, predict before anyone else does who's going to win. We have to take an issue on our own terms and we won't let the candidate lay out the issues on his terms.[33]

Impact on political actors increases the credibility of a news organization to its customers, hence helps it compete.[34] American television viewers are used to the phenomenon of the most significant question at any presidential press conference according to CBS News being asked by the CBS reporter and so forth. Modern Presidents must be prepared to announce their intention to ask Congress to declare the same war three separate times—once for each network—if they intend to do so in response to a press conference question.

In order to be convincing purveyors of reality, if possible more convincing than the competition, journalists must get as close as they can to the sources of events. This means access to the political leaders to whom they give publicity both for themselves and their views as a quid pro quo for the proximity that lends verisimilitude to the journalists' accounts.[35]

Competitiveness thus entails snuggling up to news sources and works at cross purposes with the imperative of professionalism to maintain independence. The tensions, both institutional and personal, that result from this contradictory set of demands are endless. An elaborate code of ground rules—frequently misunderstood and violated—has grown up in Washington governing the rights of journalists to publish information they come across on social occasions, at off the record encounters, at "background" briefings, and so forth.[36]

One would think that competitiveness would lead to a strong push toward product differentiation, but this depends also upon marketing strategies. On the whole it does not work that way among the most important national news organizations.[37] Appealing to the fat part of the market, which is the marketing strategy of the major suppliers of news, rather than to specialists, entails a systematic suppression of detail and a search for instantaneous coherence, however spurious, that causes reporters and editors alike to monitor and tacitly or explicitly to collude with the competition.[38] Nobody who intends to supply mass publics with their daily ration of news can afford to be out on a limb too often, peddling what may come to be viewed as an idiosyncratic version of reality. Since the realities for a newspaper are mostly social and political realities, they depend on consensual definitions of the situation, and most news organizations most of the time willingly participate in that consensus, sometimes greatly to the advantage of undeserving politicians, sometimes greatly to their equally unmerited disadvantage.[39]

The two principles of professionalism and competitiveness thus account in a sketchy way for most if not all of the evils of the press as interpreted by critics as diverse as Spiro Agnew[40] and Daniel Patrick Moynihan, without recourse to imputations of reportorial bad faith, ugly motives, or malicious intent.[41] This is not to deny that any of these exist but only that there are better, more plausible ways to account for a larger proportion of news coverage by presuming that the product we see is the result of conventional mass marketing strategies under highly competitive circumstances and widely shared subcultural norms of professional conduct.

4. Governing Without Parties: Some Possible Results

Let us imagine ourselves in a world that looks a great deal like the United States but where more or less representative elites carry less of the burden of governing, intermediation is less a face-to-face and more a mass-marketing phenomenon and there is a greater reliance upon referenda, plebiscites, and other sorts of voting and manifestations of public opinion. These mechanisms can be characterized as enabling traditional forms of in-group mobilizing their strength, when they needed to, mostly around threats of vetoes by conservative Presidents, and the liberal group around the priorities of liberal Presidents' programs. The great resources in the hands of the conservative coalition over most of the fifty years have been the seniority of their leaders, and their tactical skill and tenacity. The great resources of the liberal group were numbers, and the claims on the Democratic side of party loyalty.

By 1960, the liberals had the numbers in the Senate, but in the House of Representatives the picture was quite different. The election of 1958 was a Democratic landslide year, sending 283 Democrats to the House.[57] Yet, as Representative Clem Miller, a liberal Democrat from northern California, pointed out at the time in one of his brilliant newsletters:

> The combination of Southern Democrats and Northern Republicans can always squeak out a majority when they want to, and they want to on a great number of significant issues . . . Actually, the Democratic party as non-Southerners define it is a minority in the House.

"There are 160 Northern Democrats and roughly 99 Southern Democrats," Miller figured:

> This includes Texas, but does not include the border states . . . which generally cancel each other out. Maryland votes against us, West Virginia with us, Missouri cancels itself out, half liberal, half Southern, and Kentucky, ambivalent, sometimes with us and sometimes against us . . . Begin with a base of 160 Northern Democratic votes. Add to it fifty percent of the (roughly 30) border state Democrats. We are always 15 to 30 votes shy. . . .[58]

So long as the conservative Democrats from the South had the option of coalescing on the floor with a mostly united Republican party, efforts to organize the Democratic party in the House by requiring greater party loyalty of such a large minority were bound to come to grief. From 1958 to 1978, however, the strength of this minority within the Democratic party in the House eroded so as to permit effective action in the Democratic caucus by the end of that period. Meanwhile, liberal Democrats became better organized through the formation of the Democratic Study Group and were better able to mobilize their big battalions as needed.[59]

A slightly different way of doing Clem Miller's arithmetic yields the twenty-year comparisons visible in Table 3.4.

Over a twenty-year period it was mostly conservative southern Democrats who lost their seats to Republicans.[60] Outside the South, Democrats, mostly liberal, replaced Republicans. So over the twenty-year span the House became more liberal overall, and this trend was accelerated within the Democratic caucus.

Table 3.4   Coalitions in the House, 1960 and 1980

	86th Congress *1959–60* *Elected 1958*	*96th Congress* *1979–80* *Elected 1978*
Democrats	280[a]	281
Republicans	152	154
Southern[b] seats	106	108
Conservative Democrats	66	47
Mainstream[c] Democrats	33[d]	31
Republicans	7	30
Non Southern Seats		
Democrats	181	203
Republicans	145	124
Democratic Caucus		
Non-South plus		
Mainstream South	214	234
Conservative South	66	47
Conservative Coalition		
Republicans plus Conservative		
Southern Democrats	218	201

[a] Three vacancies by the end of the Congress
[b] Southern seats are seats from 11 states of the old Confederacy.
[c] Mainstream Southern Democrats are those whose CQ party support scores exceed their party opposition scores by at least two to one.
[d] Includes Speaker Rayburn

Sources: *1960 Congressional Quarterly Almanac* (Washington, D.C.: Congressional Quarterly, 1960), pp. 140–41; *Congressional Quarterly Weekly Report* (January 10, 1981), pp. 82–83.

Indeed, the Democratic caucus was the engine of change within the House during the decade 1970–80. Prodded by its organized liberals, the caucus established a subcommittee bill of rights, took power from committee chairmen, deposed chairmen in historic breaches of seniority, and put the Speaker in charge of committee assignments in general and of assignments to the Rules Committee in particular.[61]

Some of these changes clearly decentralized power; but some took powers previously dispersed to committees and their chairmen and vested them in the House Democratic leadership, and especially the Speaker. And it was an organ of centralized party leadership, the Democratic caucus, that did it.

These observations must be kept in mind in evaluating the claim that Congress became less tractable than previously to leadership from a Democratic President. The twenty-year record of the institution suggested, rather, sizable gains in the numbers of regular Democratic members, and an increased potential for favorable results for any Democratic President willing to work with the congressional leadership in establishing legislative priorities and strategies. A proliferation of subcommittees meant, after all, that guidance was needed in scheduling the orderly floor consideration of what would otherwise soon become an indigestible log-jam of proposals. And with his exclusive right to make appointments to the Rules Committee, the Speaker gained the influence he needed to coordinate traffic headed for the House floor. This influence was denied all Speaker O'Neill's predecessors, reaching back to the revolt against Joseph Cannon at the turn of the century.[62]

So it will not do to argue that the undeniably significant changes in the way Congress did business were at the root of difficulties that President Carter had in mobilizing congressional support for his proposals. Congressional change was not a cause of President Carter's problems with Congress, and more generally in governing. Quite to the contrary, if anything, a hard look at Congress deepens the puzzle of Carter's difficulties. By any reasonable gauge, relations with Congress ought to have been a bright, not a dark spot in President Carter's record. And so, far from being an explanation, President Carter's difficulties with Congress themselves need explaining.

An appropriate explanation is readily to hand, for, among the side effects of changes in the presidential nomination process, as we have seen, have been sharp reductions in the number of Congressmen who participate. The numbers for the Democratic party are startling:

Table 3.5   Participation in Democratic National Conventions

	Percentage of Democratic U.S. Senators who were voting delegates or alternates	Percentage of Democratic U.S. Representatives who were voting delegates or alternates	Percentage of Democratic Governors who were voting delegates or alternates
1956	90%	33%	100%
1960	68	45	85
1964	72	46	61
1968	68	39	83
1972	36	15	80
1976	18	15	47
1980	14	15	76

For comparison, Republican National Conventions:

	Senators	U.S. Representatives	Governors
1968	55%	31%	88%
1980	63	40	74

Data were drawn from official Convention Calls for each year.

Sources: Commission on Presidential Nomination and Party Structure (Morley A. Winograd, chairman), *Openness, Participation and Party Building: Reforms for a Stronger Democratic Party* (Washington, D.C.: Democratic National Committee, January 1978); and Nelson W. Polsby, "The Democratic Nomination," in Austin Ranney (ed.), *The American Elections of 1980* (Washington, D.C.: American Enterprise Institute, 1981), p. 57. The Republican data were taken from James Ceaser, *Reforming the Reforms* (Cambridge, Mass.: Ballinger, 1982), chapter 3, footnote 18.

Any President who reads the Constitution can see how desirable it is to make common cause with allies in Congress.[63] It must be accounted a significant, indeed a massive incapacitation of party nomination processes that these processes should have operated to persuade a President otherwise to the extent they evidently did in President Carter's case.

toward state level concerns and reduced their incentives to contest with various interest groups and candidate enthusiasts for influence over the presidential nomination process. Thus centralization of power through the compliance review process in the hands of national party functionaries can lead to a weakening of party organization at the intermediate level of the state parties. Whether this in turn permits the grass roots to flourish is a matter for consideration in a later chapter.

A further consequence of the new atmosphere of regulation, professionalization, legal responsibility, and legal sanctions is the centralization of political activity within each candidate's campaign, a logical concomitant of the centralization of political authority and of criminal liability. Richard Cheney, who ran Gerald Ford's campaign in 1976, testifies eloquently on this point:

> One of the major results of the spending limitations has been to encourage the development of highly centralized campaign organizations with elaborate controls over spending. Unless a campaign develops such an organization, there is virtually no possibility that it can account for all of the funds expended or adequately comply with federal regulations. While this makes for a more efficient campaign operation, it has had the effect of choking off the kind of grass-roots activity that historically has been a part of American presidential campaigns.

> The experience of the Ford campaign in 1976 showed conclusively that it was easier to discourage grass-roots activity than to try to control and report it. In previous campaigns, it was possible to tell a local campaign or party official to go ahead with a project as long as he could raise the money to finance it. Now, federal law places a premium on actively discouraging such activity because of the danger that it could well lead to a violation of contribution or spending limits in the primary. Furthermore, in the general election, because no contributions are permitted once federal funds become available, it is even more important to discourage such activity.

> Such considerations lead to shifts in spending priorities and, therefore, campaign strategies. State-by-state primary spending limitations, the overall limitation on prenomination spending, and the requirement that none of the money raised before the con-

vention be used to promote the general election effort (which has to be totally financed with federal funds), all serve to discourage organizational activities. We found it much easier during the 1976 Ford campaign, for example, to spend money on identifiable goods and services, such as electronic media and production costs, in the general election campaign than to spend it intelligently on local and state organizational efforts. This was especially true because we had discouraged organizational activity that was not directly under our control during the primaries. The case of the Florida primary, held in March 1976, is illustrative of the difficulties posed by the new law. The Ford campaign poured significant resources into the Florida effort and won our second major victory over Governor Reagan. Within days of the election, the entire Florida operation had to be totally shut down because of the various limitations we faced. As a result, there were no resources available to keep even a symbolic operation going through the summer in preparation for the fall campaign—no headquarters facility, no phones, no paper clips, and no staff.

The same thing happened in virtually every state where we contested a primary in 1976. It was hardly surprising, then, that with only a little more than two months for the general election campaign, we found it difficult to spend money on organizational efforts at the state and local level when we had dismantled the nucleus of our organization at the end of each primary campaign. It made a lot more sense to spend it on media.

I firmly believe that the effect of the campaign finance laws in this area has been to discourage grass-roots political activity, to discourage participation, and to place a premium on strategies that rely on activities that are easily controlled and reported. Given a choice between local spontaneity and enthusiastic participation, on one hand, and control over spending, on the other, the cautious campaign manager has little choice but to opt for activities that are "controllable."[45]

The net effect on state and local party organizations of this discouragement of grass roots political activity during a presidential election year is hard to assess. At a minimum, it tends to diminish the value of state and local party leaders in their dealings with candidates, thus reinforcing trends that already have ample momentum. Further, on the assumption that presidential campaigns are a good way to build party solidarity at the grass roots, to recruit workers and to reinforce their loyalties and their commitment to the party as an organization, a consequence of political reform might well have been to encourage the atrophy of political parties at the grass roots.

Niggling restrictions of the Federal Election Commission have contributed to the drying up of voluntarism: campaign managers have had to worry, for example, whether they were liable for an assessment against the total expenditure permitted to a presidential candidate for the cost of lapel buttons bought and paid for by a local congressional candidate's campaign because the names of both the congressional and the presidential candidate appeared on it.[46] Casual observation detects the decline of the most decentralized of campaign aids: buttons, bumper stickers, and billboards. Expenditures that directly benefit the top of the ticket—television appearances, moving the candidate around by aircraft—continue to soak up lavish amounts of money, however. But cooperative expenditures, where central fund raising is used to nourish the grass roots of the party, have shriveled.

So serious was the problem thought to be that amendments to some of the restrictions on campaign expenditures were brought forward in 1979. Congress removed prohibitions against the purchase of buttons and bumper stickers for volunteer activities by state and local parties, and allowed incidental mention of presidential candidates in other candidates' literature without the mention being considered a contribution. Spending limits on volunteer activities were eased, and get-out-the-vote and some kinds of voter registration drives were allowed to party organizations without financial limit. It remained to be seen, however, whether these changes would be enough to overcome all the obstacles to local effort that had been erected by the new rules.[47]

6. Consequences for Party Competition: Third Parties

Thus far we have considered consequences of party reform for the two major political parties as organizations, from the standpoint of their internal functioning as machines for making presidential nominations and conducting election campaigns. Party reform has in addition had an impact on the party system, that is, on the relations between parties and on the ways in which they compete for public office. Presently I shall deal with the impact of reform on competition between the two major parties, but here I wish to consider briefly the effects of party reform on third parties.

There are at least three sorts of disabilities that stand in the way of the success of third parties in American national politics.[48] One is ideological. Because of the doctrinal looseness of the two major American parties, their continental reach into widely differing milieus, and their nonexistent formal criteria for membership, it is hard for a third party to get much of a toehold on ideological grounds. All popular ideologies are in some form or other generally embraced by the two major parties. The genuinely disaffected in a political system like the one prevailing in the United States are far more likely to be utterly withdrawn and unavailable for political participation than they are to be eagerly clustered in some convenient spot on the map—geographic or social—waiting for a new banner to be raised. Those inclined to participate can frequently do so on ideological terms close enough to their own to make third parties no more intrinsically attractive than one or another of the first two. By world standards the Democrats and Republicans may not cover much of the ideological spectrum, but they seem to serve their markets uncommonly well.[49]

Third, fourth, and fifth parties have from time to time emerged, and from place to place have flourished as, for example in the cases of the Liberals and Conservatives of New York. On the whole, however, minor parties have made little headway among voters. At any given time in the mid-twentieth century only a handful of officeholders at any level of government in the United States belongs to some other party than the Democratic or the Republican parties.[50]

In the second place, the bipartisan condition is facilitated by

termediation to be bypassed and hence as conducive to "direct" democracy, although, as I have tried to indicate in the discussion of the mass media as agents of intermediation, the directness of direct democracy in a very large scale society seems to me illusory. What are the consequences for government that might follow?

(1) *Crazes or manias.* We might expect an increase in the amplification of the intensity of short-term trends of opinion. Political leaders may come to believe that certain behavior is strongly demanded of them, even though these demands in fact have only weak or transitory support in the populace. In the 1950s for example it was believed that the U.S. population supported Senator Joseph McCarthy to a much greater degree than they actually did.[42] Elites on that occasion tended to interpret the movement of small straws as evidence of a big wind.[43] Their capacity to monitor short-term trends today is greatly enhanced by the growth of the use of public opinion surveys as a substitute for listening to interest group demands as formulated by their leaders and by their lobbyists. President Reagan is able, for example, to select his legislative priorities on the basis of public opinion polls made available to him on a weekly basis.[44] This is little different from President Carter's access to public opinion surveys, or his inclination to attend to them.[45]

(2) *Fads or social contagion.* Opportunities will arise for the geographic spread of sentiments, both real and imputed, from areas where they exist to areas where they do not. The enthusiastic, though uneven, epidemic of attempts to put tax limitation referenda on ballots across the country in the wake of the success of California's Proposition 13 can be interpreted in this light.[46] Real estate prices did not skyrocket everywhere in the presence of multibillion-dollar state government surpluses. However, there is no Mann Act for ideas forbidding the transportation of immature notions for immoral purposes across state lines. Rather there is the tendency for issue entrepreneurs to press their luck in one constituency after another, rather like burglars rattling all the doorknobs in the neighborhood look-

ing for weak defenses. Modest turnouts in a referendum can constitute just such a weakness.[47]

(3) *The resuscitation of ideology.* I interpret the term ideology broadly as meaning doctrines that elites invoke to capture the attention and induce the compliance of mass publics.[48] Presumably in a mass persuasion system elite politics consist in part of fights for control over the right authoritatively to interpret equivocal or incoherent events. Since most events in their uninterpreted state are somewhat ambiguous in their meaning, this is no small matter. For example, an incident of urban violence is generally an incoherent event to those at a distance from it. Does it mean that there is too much racism in society or that there are not enough police in the slums? Are looters expressing legitimate social grievances, or should they be shot? Such questions do not often have to be resolved authoritatively and incorporated into an overarching world-view in political systems dominated by representative elites. However, they must be interpreted and a social definition of such events agreed upon when more transient expressions of public opinion are the main source from which political elites must draw their entitlement to govern.

(4) *This underscores that elites do not disappear or become less significant in governing under a mass persuasion system.* They are, however, less accountable to one another and more subject to the constraints of popular fashion. They must learn to feed the mass media successfully, to cultivate different virtues, e.g. less patience of the sort employed over the bulk of his career by Richard Daley,[49] more indignation à la Ralph Nader.[50] Interest groups that organize themselves around such anachronisms as state and local party systems are bound to lose out to those that are skilled in packaging their ideas in ways that appeal to reporters and news media gatekeepers.

(5) *Heroes and bums.* Such a system runs on name recognition, on celebrity, and on typecasting. An odd similarity between elite persuasion and mass persuasion systems is the inside track both give to children of the prominent who want to

pursue political careers. Different mechanisms of recruitment are involved, however. In a mass system, name recognition is of great significance in the competition to overcome the inattentiveness of mass participants. Politicians must put enormous effort into structuring the ways in which they are presented by and to the news media, since getting caught on the wrong side of a too-visible political issue may typecast a politician and affix a black hat on him for a long time. Typecasting is, in any event, ubiquitous. Henry Jackson and Morris Udall, both liberal Democrats according to the records they have compiled over the 18 years they have overlapped in Congress, were located respectively on the far right and the far left among the Democratic presidential hopefuls of 1976.[51] This reflected dramaturgical necessities of mass persuasion politics and had only a little to do with their approach to political issues. Nevertheless it was necessary for them to collude in the scenario because their political situation demanded that they differentiate themselves and cultivate their respective factions rather than attempt to build a majority coalition.

The wider consequences of changes of this character for the actual workings of government are difficult to fathom. Two speculations at least are worth considering and both suggest an increase in certain sorts of stress in the political system.

The forces that have transformed the presidential nomination process have been far slower to affect the thousand-odd nomination processes that supply Americans with their candidates for the House and the Senate. This continuity at the level of nomination politics persists even though Congress is a greatly changed place from the way it was even a decade ago.[52] The previously moribund House Democratic caucus has become intermittently available as an instrument of majority will when that will exists. But the mobilization of that will is by no means the unchallenged prerogative of a Democratic President. Republicans, with their far narrower ideological spectrum, may find themselves better able to coordinate between President and Congress when both institutions are controlled by Republicans, but of course when a Republican President faces Democratic congressional control the mobilization of a cross-party coalition will be necessary. Congress is today better equipped than ever to find its own way without presidential guidance or cooperation into the intricacies of policy and to arrive at its own balancing of forces and priorities.

So long as elections in America are of the staggered, prescheduled, non-referendum type, and so long as nominations to Congress are decentralized, it will be difficult if not impossible for a President to attempt on a regular basis to persuade Congress by going over its head to the people. This is no substitute for the hard, frustrating, and frequently unavailing work of doing business directly with Congress. Because of the divergence that currently exists in the ways in which the President and Congress mobilize their electorates and arrive in office, we may be entering an era in which tensions and misunderstandings increase between the President and Congress, even when both are controlled by what is labeled as the same party. When one party controls the Presidency and another one or both houses of Congress, the need for carefully crafted diplomatic relations between the two branches is not lessened.

A second possible consequence of governing without the intermediation of parties and traditionally organized interest groups is a decrease in the reliance of political executives on the accumulated expertise of the permanent government. When the top of the government is dominated by client-centered political executives and executives recruited from party-oriented interest groups, bureaucrats supply technical information, policy analysis, know-how, and knowledge of programs. Other sorts of political executives erode the division of labor in which leaders of the permanent government have a distinctive place. Some cabinet officers—possibly symbolic appointees or presidential ambassadors—are liable to ignore the agencies they head altogether and will take orders with varying degrees of diligence from the White House. Others, most likely specialists and Washington careerists, may undertake policy evaluation and analysis in competition with their own agencies. Much of this activity no doubt will result in vastly improved understanding at the top of government of policy alternatives and their consequences. Moreover widespread ad hoc policy analysis at the political executive level can create over the long term a sizable number of experts outside the government who can contribute to the understanding of policy, to the consideration and selection of technically ingenious alternatives, and to ultimate public acceptance of otherwise inscrutable policy choices.

But as the comparative advantage for policy-making of being inside a government bureaucracy begins to diminish, the caliber of the agency is endangered. As agencies begin to view their nominal superiors as competitors in the provision of what they supply best—expertise—the incentives to firm up other sorts of alliances, with clientele or with Congress, increase. So, also, do incentives to depart the government altogether.[53] Thus over the long run without strenuous effort directed toward the cultivation of good will between political executives and career bureaucrats, the growth of knowledge among political executives may actually diminish the amount of knowledge available within the government.[54]

The purpose in elaborating these hypotheses is not to make the claim that these sorts of outcomes are the natural and direct result of party reform. Rather, they are the possible results of other forces working in the political system when parties fail as mechanisms of intermediation and other devices fill in the spaces left by the shrinkage of parties. If parties do not mediate between President and Congress, if parties do not provide the basis for the formation of a governing coalition that orchestrates the activities of the executive branch, if parties do less in the way of organizing mass-elite relations, what alternatives are readily available to take up the slack? These are the questions I have been addressing. The chain of causation implied in this discussion is that party reform has weakened parties, and in that sense has nourished alternatives to party. These alternatives—the mass media, interest groups favored by the news me-

dia, presidential candidates and Presidents only loosely attached to their parties—have grown in importance for a great
variety of reasons, most of which are beyond the scope of the
present inquiry. Thus our exploration of significant change in
the body politic focuses not upon the proliferation of bacteria,
many of which might well have flourished anyway, but on the
weakened condition of the host, which has provided avenues of
attack for functional alternatives to parties.

5. Accountability

An interesting problem of social control that emerges from these
reflections has to do with establishing accountability to the en-
during values of a democratic society in elites that gain power
in systems of mass persuasion. In the system of multiple elites
evolved under the U.S. Constitution, accountability has been
maintained mostly by means of the checks and balances explicitly built into the machinery of government and by means of a
party system that structures the alternatives for electoral choice.
In such a system elites monitor one another. What sorts of
mechanisms provide checks and balances for newly emerging
centers of power that are taking the place of parties in the presidential nomination process, such as those which control the
mass media? It is no doubt too early in the development of the
new system of intermediation to give a definitive answer. One
traditional response—that the mass-marketed news media
monitor one another by virtue of their freedom to publish and
their multiplicity—has some long-run merit. The needs of the
American system of news manufacture and supply to arrive at
shared and consensual views on many issues work against the
effectiveness of this norm, however, and suggest that the news
media are more effective in establishing certified views than in
providing access to a diversity of voices. Diversity in publishing
and broadcasting in any event implies differentiated, diverse,
and small audiences and does not address the issue of access to
the large audience of basic news consumers. The resistance of

the major news media to such innocuous monitoring and corrective devices as independent, non-governmental press councils is well known, as is their disinclination to admit error. Finally, there is the problem of the increasing consolidation of ownership of newspapers. A more responsible consideration of this cluster of problems is long overdue.

To what extent do newer methods of intermediation perform the full range of social functions that earlier fell to the old? It is in this case also too early, or perhaps too difficult, to say. Clearly, political education continues apace. Demands continue to be made upon the political system in the name of citizens and blocs of citizens. The government seems to enjoy more than enough legitimacy to get its routine work accomplished without difficulty. If there are any nagging doubts about the newer forms of political intermediation, they surround the issue of the accountability of elites. But on this issue many traditionally organized political intermediaries are also vulnerable. To what extent did George Meany represent his rank and file? And how did he know? We can suspect, without really knowing, that on one great set of issues, civil rights, at least as it had to do with access to blue collar jobs and neighborhoods, labor union leadership was far in advance of the attitudes of their rank and file. Whether they were or not, the rather sluggish methods of accountability that have prevailed in the labor movement permitted labor leaders to lead on this issue more or less with impunity.

The accountability of the leaders of the newer interest groups, such as Common Cause or the Ralph Nader organizations, to the people in whose behalf they ostensibly speak, or even to their paid-up members may be even more tenuous. Indeed, of the eighty-three "public interest" groups studied by Jeffrey Berry, who seems to be the only scholar to have investigated the question, 30 percent had no members at all, and consisted only of lobbyists. Of the rest, Berry says flatly,

> If "democracy" is taken to indicate that constituents have a formal opportunity to select their leaders, . . . public interest groups are not democratic [but] quite oligarchic in nature.[55]

> Fifty-seven percent (33 out of 58) of the public interest member-
> ship groups have no structure that ostensibly elicits and considers
> membership opinion.[56]

The capacity of such groups to deliver the votes of the people they organize directly must at the least be highly questionable. In any event, the numbers involved are quite small.[57] The
real clients of new style interest groups are news media managers. So long as newspaper, magazine, and television people
believe in the rectitude of Ralph Nader, and others similarly
situated, and defer to them and their judgments, and give them
publicity, politicians will feel obliged to defer to them as well.
And leaders of these sorts of interest groups can continue to
claim to be authoritative interpreters of the desires of people
at the grass roots.

It will no doubt come as a disappointment to some observers
that current trends in political intermediation do not seem to
provide for greater accountability and hence greater openness
and democracy in some larger sense. In fact it can be argued
that groups equally deserving as the ones that have gained
ground have lost ground because of their propensity to organize along more traditional communal or face-to-face lines. In
particular the groups traditionally served by city machines, geographically compact and ethnically homogeneous neighborhood groups, for example, may well be suffering greatly.
Women with a history of activism in political parties may be at
a disadvantage compared with women with a history of activism
in the women's movement. This is a complicated business, leading as it eventually may to distinctions between nominal members of disadvantaged groups (e.g., women) and authorized
members (e.g., women active in the women's movement).[58] Life,
as Presidents increasingly have occasion to remind us, is unfair
and illustrations of that uncomfortable maxim can be found in
the field of political intermediation as readily as in any other.

The newer methods of intermediation operate unevenly in
the political system. They have far more to do with the elec-

tions of Presidents or governors of large states where mass publics can be efficiently mobilized and party leaders are relatively weak than with nominations and elections to Congress. They involve the manipulation of attitudes that may be tenaciously held as well as those that are more ephemeral, and they evoke loyalties that are probably mostly nontransferable. For these reasons one must sharply question whether it makes sense for any President to believe, as Jimmy Carter evidently did, that the type of intermediation that got him nominated and elected is adequate to the formation of a governing coalition.

For the purposes of governing, alliances with relevant factions and blocs in Congress and with national interest groups not necessarily organized on the new principles, are bound at a minimum to prove useful. Efforts to ignore, bypass, or run roughshod over such groups by appealing over their heads to the people, are doomed on at least two counts. First, the appeal to public opinion itself is likely to fail because of the fickleness and lability of mass public attitudes on most issues, and because of the nontransferability of a President's popularity, when the President is popular, to the objects of a President's desires. One week a President may be riding high in the news media because of a couple of stunning congressional victories; the next week an adverse reaction on Wall Street can jeopardize the rest of his program. Second, even if by some unusual combination of circumstances, public opinion does for once yield to a President's entreaties, the effects may or may not reach Congress or influence congressional disposition of an issue. Members of Congress, after all, have their own constituencies and their own means of reaching them, and they may find themselves ill-disposed toward a President who prefers to deal indirectly with them through what they may interpret as coercion rather than face to face and in a spirit of mutual accommodation.

It may be entirely feasible for a President to live according to the dictates of a strategy that is concerned exclusively with his own renomination and reelection if he wants nothing of Congress and nothing from traditional interest groups. But if a President means to do more than hold onto office, he will have to face the pockets of pluralism that remain in the political system and somehow deal with them. If Common Cause and other reformers succeed in their efforts to reduce the capacity of Congressmen to facilitate their own reelections by attenuating their privileged access to publics in their home districts,[59] it may well be true in some future time that Presidents will be able to get their way on matters of public policy by direct appeal to public opinion. At the moment, however, checks and balances preclude this under ordinary circumstances.

Thus traditional interest groups based on geography and economic self-interest still exercise meaningful influence in Congress. So, with a few exceptions, do state and local party organizations, in the shrinking number of places where these retain their traditional strength. In the presidential nomination process, however, these groups have lost ground to groups more approved of by the mass media and organized on different principles, where interest group leaders reach their own constituencies by means of media-based publicity rather than through some sort of internal structure of communications, whether communal or corporate. The enormous growth of the influence of the news media over the presidential nomination process has led Presidents and their professional political consultants more and more to believe that a high level of public approval is the central resource needed to govern and that the attainment and maintenance of high popularity is relatively unconstraining as compared with the constraints of bargaining with interest groups. It is not required that Presidents entertain such beliefs, but it is not necessary to give these beliefs up (when Presidents hold them) in order to succeed in manipulating the nomination process to their advantage. These systemic changes consequently were not merely to be found at the root of President Carter's difficulties in governing; difficulties of this sort will in time come to be seen less as idiosyncracies of the Carter administration than as realities to be confronted by any administration.

V

Political Reform
and Democratic Values

1. Primaries and Participation: Some Problems

The confusions of the historical moment that stimulated the reforms we have been considering do not permit a straightforward assessment of the goals and motives of those most responsible for their promotion. Certainly among the ideas animating the drive for reform, however, were thoughts that the presidential selection process could be improved by making it possible for more people to participate. Consequently a set of guidelines having as a proximate consequence the opening of delegate selection to a series of primary elections could be defended, at a minimum, as in some sense contributing to the democratization of presidential nominations: where previously only a handful of party leaders may have selected delegates to the national party convention, now millions of voters have a part in the process. In no case has the advent of primaries reduced the number of people involved. Observers have been ready on these grounds alone to argue that whatever else the party reforms may or may not have accomplished, they have surely opened up a process that was sorely in need of democratization.[1]

Table 5.1 Comparison of Democratic primary electorate and Democratic general electorate, 1976. (Percentages of voters)

State	Less than high school education		Black		Over age 65		College degree or beyond		Income over $20,000/yr.	
	Primary	General	Primary	General	Primary	General	Primary	General	Primary	General
California	11	27	12	15	9	19	34	17	35	23
Florida	13	30	8	14	23	28	28	17	26	16
Illinois	19	34	15	16	8	17	23	6	25	21
Indiana	21	40	10	11	7	24	13	6	17	11
Massachusetts	12	19	2	3	10	18	36	22	24	24
Michigan	20	30	11	22	11	17	20	10	16	17
New Hampshire	11	18	—	—	6	13	38	18	15	14
New Jersey	12	41	17	26	9	16	35	14	37	19
New York	15	31	15	20	15	14	32	19	32	16
Ohio	15	32	11	17	7	19	25	10	23	1?
Oregon	19	18	n.a.	n.a.	23	13	23	20	15	23
Pennsylvania	17	32	8	15	9	15	23	15	20	9
Wisconsin	18	25	3	7	13	19	22	15	n.a.	n.a.

Note: n.a. signifies data are not available. Dash signifies less than one percent.

Source: Democratic Party, Commission on Presidential Nomination and Party Structure, "Openness, Participation and Party Building: Reforms for a Stronger Democratic Party," Washington, D.C., January 25, 1978, pp. 11–13.

Two venerable lines of argument in political science suggest that this accomplishment may be illusory. The first has to do with the sorts of participants who dominate primary electorates. The second has to do with the formal properties of choice in primary elections as they are run in the United States, in which outcomes are produced by aggregating the first—and only the first—preferences of voters who spread their selections over a broad field of contenders.

Because primary elections have long been a feature of American state politics, there is a considerable history to the argument establishing the first point. As V. O. Key, Jr., one of the ablest of those who have studied the matter says, "The American political tradition caps decisions made by popular vote with a resplendent halo of legitimacy." Yet the chapter of Key's book of which this is the first sentence is titled: "Participation in Primaries: The Illusion of Popular Rule."[2] Key shows that for the large number of state primaries which he examined, in several states and over a number of different elections, "the effective primary constituency" is often "a caricature of the entire party following."[3]

Key's major findings—that state primary electorates were unrepresentative of the state electorate, and that candidates frequently needed to mobilize only very small numbers of voters to win—are confirmed for more recent national primary elections, notably by work of Austin Ranney, James I. Lengle, and the Democratic party's own post-1976 rules-examining body, the Winograd Commission.[4] Table 5.1 gives Winograd Commission findings comparing selected characteristics of Democratic primary electorates with Democratic voters in the 1976 election for 13 states.

Consistently, and not only in the case of 1976, those voters lower down on the socioeconomic scale are disproportionately missing from primary electorates. Lengle's work shows in addition that socioeconomic differences are associated with ideological differences. As people gain in education they are predisposed to identify themselves as more ideologically extreme.

This suggests that a lack of demographic representativeness in a primary electorate may produce significantly different results in the types of candidates chosen to lead the party. Direct tests of this inference among California Democrats in 1968 and 1972 strongly sustain the notion that candidates are perceived differently and supported differently by voters differently situated along the socioeconomic spectrum. Similarly, differences occur in their views about the importance of different issues.[5]

The better-off voters who vote in primary elections are thus, in their hundreds of thousands, in a sense stuffing the ballot box much in the manner of the fans who vote for their favorite players in the election that from time to time determines who will play in organized baseball's all star game, as Richard Schier's inspired analogy illustrates:

> In 1970, baseball Commissioner Bowie Kuhn announced his intention "to give the game back to the fans" by permitting them to pick the players, this despite two earlier periods of experimentation with this method of selection. In 1957, spirited balloting by Cincinnati fans elected seven Reds to take the field along with Stan Musial as the starting lineup. (Managers chose the pitchers and reserves.) After this debacle player selection was restored to the players, managers and coaches until Commissioner Kuhn revived participatory democracy in 1970.

> The repetitive access to the balloting enjoyed by fans in Los Angeles, Philadelphia and Cincinnati—cities with huge ballpark attendance—gives them an advantage similar to that with which the news media's attention to the first primary endows the whims of New Hampshire voters. Neither in baseball nor in politics has the ideal of one-man, one-vote been realized. . . .

> Two years in a row, American League fans elected an outfield in which none of the three players were comfortable in center field. This same problem plagued the Democrats in 1972. . . .[6]

> Criticisms of these two processes are strikingly parallel: An activist minority can impose its choice on the more apathetic majority; good candidates may be overlooked or left out; certain localities occupy a strategic position that gives their residents a disproportionate influence; and the length of the process makes timing an element of great significance.

We have the word of a member of the McGovern commission on party structure and delegate selection that the new rules "were consciously designed to maximize participation by persons who are enthusiastic for a particular aspirant in the year of the convention." That they have succeeded is not in doubt as the nominations of both George McGovern and Jimmy Carter testify. But the experiences of these two gentlemen also suggest that this enthusiasm may wane quickly.[7]

In spite of the supposed democratization of the selection process, and the increase in the number of women and black delegates, those delegates actually chosen to be present at Democratic conventions do not appear to differ greatly in their socioeconomic status from delegates chosen by old party elites. As Haynes Johnson of the *Washington Post* said of the delegates to the 1972 Democratic convention that ratified the selection of George McGovern: "Whatever else is new in American politics this year, the old ingredients of money and education and class still dominate the process.[8] A *Post* questionnaire sampling about half the delegates turned up 39 percent as holders of postgraduate university degrees. In the general population about 4 percent had done some graduate work. Income figures were:

Table 5.2 Economic standing of delegates selected under new rules

Annual income	1972 Democratic delegates (Post survey)	Nationally (U.S. Census)
under $5,000	6%	18%
$5–9,999	10	32
$10–14,999	20	27
$15–25,000	31	18
over $25,000	31	5

Source: Haynes Johnson, "Portrait of the New Delegate," *Washington Post* (July 8, 1972).

What has changed is that candidates have gained and state party leaders have lost the right to designate who the delegates shall be. The numbers of designees available to the various candidates are increasingly prescribed by the results of primaries, which allocate each state's entitlement in different proportions to different candidates. In picking their delegates, candidates must adhere to whatever rules the national parties have imposed about the demographic characteristics of delegations. In practice this has meant that Democratic conventions have in-

Table 5.3   Socio-economic standing of 1972 Democratic minority delegates

Education (years):

	Hispanics (n = 53)	Blacks (n = 162)	American Indians (n = 45)	For comparison: General Population
0–8	2.0%	1.2%	0.0%	24.8%
9–12	9.4	14.2	20.0	52.2
13–15	37.7	30.9	26.7	10.9
16+	50.9	53.7	53.3	12.1
	100.0	100.0	100.0	100.0

Income ($1000, per annum):

	Hispanics (n = 58)	Blacks (n = 176)	American Indians (n = 50)	For comparison: General Population
less than 10	19.0%	25.1%	20.0%	43.6%
10–14.9	41.4	27.8	30.0	26.1
15 or more	39.6	47.1	50.0	30.3
	100.0	100.0	100.0	100.0

Occupation:

	Hispanics (n = 54)	Blacks (n = 165)	American Indians (n = 50)	For comparison: General population
professional, technical	40.7%	52.7%	32.0%	8.8%
management	11.2	15.8	20.0	6.2
clerical	7.4	4.8	10.0	10.9
student	24.1	12.7	8.0	5.7
housewife	5.6	4.2	12.0	27.6
unemployed	1.9	1.8	4.0	3.7
other	9.1	8.0	14.0	37.1
	100.0	100.0	100.0	100.0

Source: *The 1972 Convention Delegate Study* (ICPSR #7287), made available by the Inter-University Consortium for Political and Social Research.

creasingly "represented" categories of people previously "underrepresented"—usually with high-status, well-educated, and well-off members of the groups in question, as Table 5.3 shows.

The second sort of distortion which primary elections promote is harder to describe. It rests on the seemingly intractable fact that once the number of alternatives available to an electorate rises above two, and so long as only the first choices of voters are counted, there is a nontrivial likelihood that the plurality winner of such an election will turn out to be unwanted by a majority. The process provides no method for achieving a more acceptable result.[9]

The problem to which this possibility points is one of finding a method for expressing accurately the widely spread sentiments of voters in the result of an election in which there can be only one winner. If out of all possible alternatives there is one choice that is overwhelmingly popular then of course this problem does not arise. Frequently, however, there is no such popular solution, and the voting population has a complex structure of preferences. Among the elements of complexity it is possible to identify such phenomena as cycling, or an inability to determine a majority choice.

No clear first choice of a majority emerges for any candidate when successive pair-wise comparisons yield the result of candidate A beating B, B beating C, and C beating A. In theory, this cycling phenomenon happens whenever the pattern of preferences among three or more voters is distributed among three or more candidates in a manner approximating the following:

Voter	1	2	3
Preference	A	B	C
Rank	B	C	A
	C	A	B

Given the large array of alternatives frequently present in a primary election and the large number of voters, it is easy to imagine a structure of preferences which would actually result in cycling if successive pair-wise comparisons were permitted to occur. In practice, however, primaries do not permit the full array of voters' preferences to be expressed. Only first choices are given. Not only does this risk failure to produce a winner actually preferred by a majority, but it also suppresses information which it is necessary for voters to have in order to adapt their own views to the spread of preferences, perhaps by voting strategically so as to concert on satisfactory even though not first-choice candidates. So in practice when the structure of preferences in the electorate is such that there is actually no spontaneous, clear first choice, primary elections conceal this fact without necessarily producing the same winner as would emerge if more information about voters' preferences were to be disclosed to those doing the choosing.

A significant implication is that when sentiment is spread among many possible choices the results of primary elections are quite likely to be far more responsive to formal properties of the choice-making situation—which of all possible pair-wise comparisons happens to be first in sequence, for example, or how many options are available to voters in a given primary election—than to the underlying structure of preferences in the voting population.

Even if aggregating the responses of large numbers of voters spread among large numbers of alternatives were not a problem, eliciting an accurate expression of individual voter preferences from first choices alone would be. First choices disclose only a minimum about which among the array of alternative candidates might be satisfactory and which unsatisfactory. A version of this issue has been called the "intensity" problem, in which it is proposed as a desideratum of a decision-making process to be able to register how strongly voters feel for or against a given candidate.[10] Many voters may feel more strongly about which among the possibilities presented to them are unsatisfactory than satisfactory. This can in principle be discovered by a device known as approval voting, in which voters are permitted to vote for as many candidates as they like—but only once for each candidate meeting their approval.[11] American primary elections do not employ approval voting, however.

Some voters may feel strongly about their first choice but indifferent thereafter. If passions run high but choices are spread around, it is likely that the ultimate winner will be unpopular and, depending on the confidence of voters in the choice mechanism that produced him, possibly even damaged in his overall acceptability. This is arguably one reason why sharply contested primary elections sometimes lead to losses in the general election.[12] My argument is simply that this can in part be a result of the mechanism of choice.

What is missing in the relatively automated processes of choice involved in the simple allocation of securely pledged delegates, allocated according to the results of a ballot in which first choices only are allowed, are devices for arranging compromises. Second choice candidates enjoying widespread approval are unable to get into a game in which only first choices are counted. This becomes a problem because not all first choice candidates of some voters are minimally acceptable to other voters—conceivably even to large numbers of voters to whom the party wants to appeal in the general election. Processes of deliberation ought in principle to be able to smooth out some of the difficulties that arise when a plurality first choice candidate causes divisions of this sort in the party electorate. Primary elections do not deal with the problem at all, leaving it to fester until the general election.[13]

In summary, then, it can be shown that a candidate selection process heavily reliant on primary elections fails to meet a number of tests that it would be desirable for this sort of decision-making process to meet:

(1) It cannot be relied upon to identify a candidate who would beat each of the others in pair-wise comparisons. Successive pair-wise comparisons are not, in general, what primaries do. More characteristic of early primaries is a large number of entries. Sometimes there is in fact no candidate who

would beat all the others in pair-wise comparison, but even when this is true the sequence of primaries and other formal properties of the system dictate the result, producing what in effect may well be the wrong winner.[14]

(2) Even if primaries produce a clear winner, as, stimulated by the needs of the news media for a coherent and clear result, they usually do, that winner may be less effective than some other satisfactory candidate might have been in winning a general election.

(3) Primaries do not register second choices, intensities of feeling, or anathemas, all valuable information about the structure of voters' preferences in forestalling premature closure on the wrong choice.

(4) If primaries succeed in reflecting the choices of any population, it is not a population fully or accurately reflective of the party electorate, or the general electorate.

V. O. Key says:

> The small size of the blocs of voters necessary to win nominations has a most significant consequence for the nature of the party . . . The direct communion of potential candidates with small groups of voters places enormous difficulties in the way of those party leaders disposed to work beyond the primaries to the general election and to put forward the most appealing slate. Individual politicians with a grasp on a small bloc of voters which can be turned into a primary victory are difficult to discipline or to bargain with. The support of even a weak personal organization, the loyalties and admiration of an ethnic group, a wide acquaintance within a religious group, simple notoriety achieved in a variety of ways, an alliance with an influential newspaper—these and a variety of other elements may create power within the narrow circle of people who share control in the politics of the direct primary.[15]

All these considerations bear on the capacity of the political parties to perform the function of nominating presidential candidates in a manner that reflects a consensus of some population that by ordinary criteria of democratic theory ought to have the right to nominate. Because the system that primaries largely replaced was also flawed in its fulfillment of precepts of democratic theory, observers and participants may well differ about which system overall is better. My purpose here is merely to indicate that the matter turns out to be a closer question than is commonly believed to be the case.

Thus, I do not conclude that primaries should be discarded because they are only illusorily democratic. Rather, I suggest that democratic theory presents a mixed verdict with respect to primaries as a device for revealing and executing the popular will, and that not all versions of democratic theory make primaries so desirable as to bar the examination of a system dominated by primaries from the standpoint of its practical consequences.

2. Other Criteria: Peer Review and Deliberation

Such great stress has been put on the desirability of increased participation in the presidential nomination process that other possible desiderata have been neglected. It is well, however, to consider a few other possibilities. The design of a presidential selection process might, after all, in the abstract reflect a number of values associated with democratic government. From time to time a wide variety of practical mechanisms have been employed or proposed, and all have weaknesses. For example:

(1) Selection of the nominee by the party's congressional caucus. This process neglects the interests of those parts of the country in which the party is weak, and which fail to return members of Congress for the party in question. It biases the choice toward candidates known by, favorably known by, and perhaps especially accessible to members of Congress, themselves an elite group focused to a far greater degree today on Washington and its politics than was the case when the congressional caucus actually selected the nominee.

(2) Selection by a national primary. This process would pre-

sumably favor whatever candidates were well known to citizens at large and who could, for whatever reasons, mobilize a strong factional following. In a large field of
candidates, as a national primary would surely attract, the
two surviving to the run-off would presumably be the two
with the most tenacious hold on the largest factions, but
this might produce a set of alternatives deeply disapproved
of by many—conceivably even a majority—of the party's
voters.

In some respects, these two mechanisms represent polar alternatives, whose weaknesses are complementary. The caucus
fails to represent enough legitimate interests in the population,
and thus is too narrow; the primary, while in theory broadly
participatory, is in fact a lottery without the capacity to deliberate, which in consequence is liable to set at naught the participation of most party voters.

What criteria ought a presidential selection process to meet?
Two technical desiderata immediately suggest themselves:

(1) The process has to be able to meet deadlines imposed by
    the need to campaign before the general election takes
    place, and so it cannot be so elaborate as to come to no
    timely conclusion.

(2) And of course it must succeed in picking a candidate. It
    cannot result in a tie, or in an expression of indifference as
    among several alternatives.

To these, we might add two desiderata of a broad political
character:

(3) The process should do as little as possible to harm the sub-
    sequent chances of the party's candidate in the general
    election, or the party's capacity to field and elect candidates
    thereafter.

(4) It should select candidates who are likely to be able to exe-
    cute the duties and responsibilities of the office of Presi-
    dent with some exceptional degree of distinction.

Thus, simultaneously, the process should be in some sense good for the party, good for the system of competition between the parties, good for the Presidency, and good for the successful maintenance, more generally, of democratic government in the United States.

There seems to be little controversy about any of these as abstractly desirable criteria. Moreover, the system both as currently and as recently constituted does fulfill the technical criteria without great difficulty—though not without complaints associated with the allegedly too-early start of the election season. With respect to the next two criteria a number of practical problems have arisen owing to disagreement over proper instruments.

Consider the proper role of popular participation in the nomination process. In 1968 it could have been argued—indeed it was argued, most strenuously—that bars to full and-timely participation by rank and file members of the Democratic party caused disaffection that drastically harmed the party's capacity to contest the presidential election. Yet, after the party passed through a series of reforms, greatly enhancing participation in the selections of 1972 through 1980 the Democratic party was, evidently, even more incapacitated than before from contesting the general election.

Thus enhanced participation is no longer as popular as it once was as the sole criterion by which a party nomination process can be evaluated. At least two other criteria have been added to the list: peer review and deliberation. In some accounts these criteria are interchanged, but for our purposes it may be useful to distinguish them.

Peer review is a criterion which entails the mobilization within the party of a capacity to assess the qualities of candidates for public office according to such dimensions as intelligence, sobriety of judgment, intellectual flexibility, ability to work well with others, willingness to learn from experience, detailed personal knowledge of government, and other personal characteristics which can best be revealed through personal acquaintance. Whereas the participation criterion contemplates increasing the legitimacy of the nominee within the party by involving large numbers of people in the choice process, the criterion of peer review seeks to increase the confidence of voters in the capacities of the nominee actually to execute the office of the Presidency effectively. Since the sort of information involved in peer review is never likely to be spread widely in the population at large, the building of this criterion into the process of candidate selection presumably entails an enlarged role for experienced politicians, who have a long-run stake in the party and who may also have the means of informing themselves in detail about the abilities in non-public situations of candidates for public office.

This information, it is rightly pointed out, was fully available to the political leaders who entered a smoke-filled room to pick Warren G. Harding. Politicians have been known actually to prefer lesser to better candidates, to act from motives other than the purely disinterested, and to be grossly mistaken in their judgments. All these considerations argue the wisdom of restraining the criterion of review by fallible and self-interested peers from becoming the sole method controlling the selection of candidates. They do not, however, rebut the proposition that there are some things that Presidents must do that people exposed to candidates only through the intermediation of the news media are unable to inform themselves about. And so while mistakes and misapplications are bound to occur in peer review as with any process, the alternative of providing no means for the assessment of potential Presidents by peers seems less desirable. Without the potentiality—or perhaps the threat—of peer review the incentives for prospective candidates to maximize name recognition and minimize public service—to cultivate the show horse rather than the work horse style—would become overwhelming. This would be true for the idealistic and the cynical alike. Connoisseurs of the process by which the dominance of the criterion of participation takes its toll on the public service of candidates can, if they like, watch the way in which absenteeism on key legislative roll calls among Senators running for President and members of Congress running for the Senate has spread to earlier and earlier periods in the run-up to elections.

If having the good opinion of colleagues and others intimately connected with government and politics means little or nothing to a candidate's chances for advancement, the nomination process then works at cross-purposes with the process of governing, which relies so heavily on accountability among elites. This may lead, in the first place, to inferior government, as persons unable to pass muster with their peers occasionally prove to be popularly attractive. In the second place, it may contribute to popular disaffection with government, as complaints about ineffective on-job performance filter down from Washington and interest group elites into the constituencies.

Deliberation as a characteristic of a presidential selection process should be considered separately from peer review, because it is not the peers of candidates alone who should, or who do deliberate. I take this criterion by which a choice process is evaluated to mean, simply, that the devices for aggregating individual preferences into collective choices maintain some capacity for receiving, manipulating and responding to a wider range of information than the first choices of participants.

The opposite of deliberation in this conception is, I suppose, automation, and the outcome that deliberation is supposed to ward off is a situation in which the formal properties of the choice process—the sequential order in which decisions are scheduled, the particular set of alternatives available to a given set of choosers, the number of decisions to be made on a given day—impose a result. It is no secret that the processes through which human interaction and communication are facilitated and impeded have a powerful role to play in determining the outcomes that are permitted to emerge. The criterion of deliberation simply highlights this fact and rates as more satisfactory procedures in which choosers can explore their own preference structures and those of other relevant actors, can avoid out-

comes weakly preferred by small majorities and strongly disliked by large minorities, can juxtapose a number of different
sets of alternatives before settling on a collective choice.

While maximizing deliberation may sound like a plea for the
resuscitation of meaningful national party conventions, practical observers of political trends will caution that conventions
may come so late in the nomination process as to be beyond
redemption. Communication by means of mass media coverage
of early events in the nomination process is now so efficient
and so swift that it is simply impractical for party delegates to
wait until they assemble face to face in a grand conclave to discover what they are thinking. This may well be true; consequently the criterion of deliberativeness, if it is to be applied at
all, must be applied to the process as a whole. We must ask to
what extent, and by what means, sensitivity to the varied concerns of legitimate participants in the choice process can be
maintained and closure on a nominee having widespread support achieved.

The need to devise a choice process which gives weight to
more than one value almost certainly requires some diversity
or mixture of mechanisms. It is probably too simple to associate
primaries exclusively with participation, party leaders and
leader-dominated caucuses with peer review and interaction
between or mixtures among delegates chosen by different
mechanisms with deliberation. As I have attempted to show,
primaries are imperfect mechanisms for participation; as the
notorious smoke-filled room suggests, peer review is imperfectly
accomplished by party bosses; and serious presidential selection
by face to face interaction among large numbers of party leaders at national conventions seems an irretrievably nostalgic
proposition.

It seems worthwhile, nevertheless, to examine a few proposals that have bubbled to the surface of debate about party reform in order to gain some sense of the range of practical possibilities for achieving varying approximations of success in
meeting criteria like the three we have explored.

3. Some Practical Proposals

Over the last decade a large number of practical proposals to improve the presidential nomination and election process have been given some attention. Some old chestnuts, like the abolition of the electoral college, have not been much discussed in connection with the nomination process, although by the logic expounded in Chapter Two it is at least arguable that abolition would draw more candidates into the election sweepstakes, and fewer of them would accept national party nomination as definitive. Pressure would build to rectify the financial advantages now legally conferred on the major parties in favor of a larger, ever more serious cadre of independent candidacies, and the capacity of the parties to channel preferences would, no doubt, suffer further reverses.

Within the parties themselves, conversation has mostly focused upon strengthening rather than weakening the influence of party in the nomination process. Many suggestions have been made, at least six of which seem worth discussing.

A. *Windows.* An unexpectedly vehement body of opinion has developed among party leaders—including leaders in the vanguard of the last round of reform—on the subject of primary elections.[16] Complaints have largely been made about excessive expenditures of money, time, and energy, about a process that stretches out too long, about how the early primaries totally dominate the process and obliterate the significance of later ones in spite of the incapacity of any small cluster of states to "represent" all the rest, never mind tiny New Hampshire with its elderly population, its large French-speaking minority, its backward economy, and its lack of state-wide communication other than the wildly idiosyncratic *Manchester Union-Leader.*

Yet the morning after the New Hampshire primary, politicians complain, something snaps into place on the NBC Today show that no amount of hard work in Massachusetts or New York or California can seem to rebut.[17] The proposal to force delegate selection—by primary or otherwise—into a shorter time period, a "window" of perhaps three to five months, is an attempt to meet this problem.[18] If three, or seven, or twelve states all selected their delegates on the same early day, it is supposed that the resulting challenge to the television networks' capacities for sorting signal from noise would keep a few more candidacies alive a little longer. The state-by-state party processes of delegate selection could be allowed a little more leeway to proceed unmolested by media-induced bandwagons and a little power would have been snatched away from the news media and vested in the state parties.

On the other hand, it might not work that way, and the overwhelming need for reportorial coherence might simply mean that the first trial heat, consisting of several states, and hence a more legitimate test than New Hampshire alone, would totally overshadow the rest. Soon, all states would clamor for early entry[19] and by swift increments a national primary would be the de facto result with its overwhelming reliance on participation to the exclusion of all other values.

If the proposal works as its proponents hope, there are still problems. Lone Ranger challenges such as the one Senator Eugene McCarthy launched in 1968 would be far more difficult if it had to be expensively conducted in several, conceivably widely scattered, states all at the same time. So the real losers in such a scheme might be long-shot candidates, and the real winners the pre-primary favorites. Insofar as pre-primary favoritism can still be conferred by the good opinion of the mass media, their powers would be unimpaired. Practically speaking, however, the news media, before the various straw polls and primaries on which they peg their coverage are held, tend to "take seriously" candidates who are well regarded by virtue of peer reputations among heavyweight national politicians. So the adoption of the window plan may enhance peer review in the process, would hurt the prospects of an effective protest being mounted through the primaries, and therefore would likely as not aid mainstream and centrist candidacies.

B. *Reserved seats at the convention.* A method for reintroducing peer review, and perhaps deliberation, into the national party convention might be to reserve delegate seats for various public or party officials.[20] In the most common version of this proposal these officials would not be required to commit themselves to some candidate in advance, as virtually all other delegates now generally do. If the proportion of uncommitted to committed delegates is high enough, presumably these uncommitted officials would be in a position to take the lead in turning the convention into a genuinely deliberative body, in which the criterion of peer review also would be given due regard. Much, therefore, depends upon the ratio of uncommitted to committed delegates. It is difficult to specify a threshold number in advance of some accumulated experience. Below the threshold, ex-officio delegates would almost certainly refuse to hold out against the favored candidate of the bulk of committed delegates. Public and party officials must, after all, work with the presidential candidate and certainly with the president of their party. Moreover, the elected officials among them have their own election and reelection to worry about and are unlikely to be interested in quixotic gestures. It seems improbable that either party will soon try to send to the national convention a contingent of uncommitted elected and party officials large enough to provide cover for a deliberative process at the convention that can afford to be seen to thwart the desires of delegates selected in the ordinary way. For these reasons, what appears at first blush to be a means for reasserting the values of peer review and deliberation promises in practice to be ineffective.

The definition of democracy as increased participation measured simply by numbers of participants is straightforward and appealing to many commentators in the mass media. Moreover it has the incidental effect of increasing the influence in the process of the mass media, which are best at reaching large numbers of people regardless of their affiliations or commitments to party organizations. Thus a political analysis of the process of party reform, and of recurrent episodes of reconsideration of reform, would suggest that insofar as the conceptions of democracy and fair play most commonly entertained by news media commentators are invoked, they come in on the side of the post-1968 wave of changes, which "opened up" the process, "democratized" it, and provided for greater participation.[21]

Within the political parties, the fundamental division of interests is between presidential candidates and their agents on the one hand, and state parties and their leaders on the other. It is in the interests of prospective presidential candidates for state delegations to be relatively permeable to their influence, for decisions about the identities of delegates to be made in highly visible processes, for commitments to candidates to come early in the selection process. It is in the interests of state parties and their leaders to maintain their influence over the composition of delegations to the national conventions, to remain neutral as among possible candidates until they can see which way the wind is blowing and arrange for appropriate access for the benefit of the state party.

This division of interests seldom results in a clear-cut debate over the legitimacy of the two sides: whether prospective presidential candidates and their minions ought to dominate party reform commissions, whether state party leaders ought to be the people represented on party decision-making bodies. Good politicians in the American tradition do not seek confrontations on issues of this kind. Nevertheless, this fundamental issue—the issue of who the President-selecting party is and ought to be—pervades the politics of party reform and needs clarification.

Opinion within the Republican party is far less divided than among the Democrats on this issue, principally because the most popular Republican presidential candidates and the most influential state party leaders have typically not been far apart on political issues during the 1960s and 70s. Among the Democrats, however, the rejection of state party leaders turned out to be the structurally significant consequence of the attack from within the party on Lyndon Johnson and his war policies. It has proven difficult to dislodge presidential candidates from their position of influence and to reassert the legitimacy of state party leaders. This, certainly, is one way to read the pulling and hauling that has taken place in the several Democratic party re-reform commissions—Mikulski, Winograd, Hunt—over the entitlement of state party leaders and elected politicians to get a free ride as uncommitted delegates to national party conventions. Uncommitted delegates are scarcely what prospective presidential candidates want, and so the candidates and their agents on reform commissions battle to minimize their numbers. Until the numbers of delegates uncommitted for one reason or another are large enough to return to the national party convention a genuine decision-making function in the presidential selection process, the submergence of state parties and their leaders, and the dominance of presidential candidates and their agents will continue.

C. *Binding or unbinding delegates.* Party rulemakers have tinkered with various formulas for requiring delegates to vote for the candidate they agreed to support during the process that selected them, or, contrariwise, not requiring that delegates do so. Much of this discussion, as I have mentioned, has been difficult to follow owing to the general failure to sort out the underlying question of why various delegates are present at the convention in the first place. In most states "delegates for" various candidates are apportioned to candidates on the basis of the candidate's proportion of the primary vote. The delegates themselves are sometimes picked by candidate managers after it is determined how many bodies are needed, and then these slots are filled; sometimes they are picked beforehand, and run "committed" to candidates of their choice. In the case of the Democrats, at large and post-primary delegate vacancies are filled according to the complex rules of demographic identity that are now written into party law. By such straightforward means black delegates for George Wallace can be sent to national conventions.

Insofar as delegates come into convention as designated representatives of the candidates who selected them, whether the convention itself acts to bind them or omits to do so seems immaterial. Insofar as delegates represent various interest groups in some sort of alliance with candidates it may be to the candidates' advantage—though surely not much to their advantage—to bind them by convention rule. If delegates were, as they increasingly are not, authentic representatives of state party organizations, then of course the flexibility of a lack of commitment might be of benefit to them in case no candidate came into the convention with a majority of committed delegates. But even if a delegation consisted of nothing but state party loyalists, it is hard to see how it could claim the right to maneuver freely if it had made a commitment to a candidate as a condition of its selection by a state party caucus or primary.

The issue, in short, cannot be settled at the convention but only at the state level where the original bargain between candidates and delegates is sealed. This is the case, at least, in theory. The legal niceties on this issue are not materially clarified by what seems to be a current Supreme Court view that whatever takes place at a national convention is subject in the first instance to national party rules rather than state law.[22] As a political matter the binding of delegates seems almost an irrelevancy given the methods by which they are most commonly chosen.

D. *Increasing allowable financial contributions.* As inflation proceeds apace, the limitations to which givers of political money are restricted means that contributions can buy less and less. Independently collected and expended funds which escape regulation take on greater importance. The capacity of parties to conduct their own business declines. Thus a general consensus has developed favoring the setting of contribution limitations at some higher level. The advantages of dispensing altogether with these limitations, as well as limitations on expenditures, is less often discussed, even though the case for no limits at all seems uncomplicated and compelling.

Public finance of elections serves two clear purposes. It encourages political competition by helping serious major party candidates get into the race, and it provides a framework for the disclosure of receipts and expenditures of money in political campaigns. Limitations on contributions and expenditures are, at best, attempts to equalize the financial resources available in primaries to various candidates. They have failed to do so. Rich candidates can and do outspend poor ones because so much of the personal funds of candidates are beyond the reach of regulation.[23] And well-publicized candidates can generally raise more money in small contributions than badly publicized ones. Independent expenditures cannot be regulated, but since candidates and parties can be, the influence of independent political operators increases at the expense of parties and candidates. Monitoring of expenditures and contributions creates great amounts of regulatory business and requires defensive measures by candidates which detracts from their central tasks of campaigning.

The original justifications for limitations consisted mostly of gossip and hearsay about the alleged susceptibility of candidates for the Presidency or electorates to be bought.[24] The persistence of these beliefs makes it highly unlikely that expenditure or contribution limitations will be abolished. More likely they will be adjusted upward, but the structure of regulations will remain and the power of organizations outside the reach of regulation will continue to grow.

E. *Abolition of cross-over primaries.* In a few states, it is possible for voters to vote in the primary of their choice without making a prior declaration of party membership. A decision of the Supreme Court places firmly in the hands of the national party the right to exclude delegates chosen by an electorate contaminated in this fashion.[25] No doubt national parties will be tempted to exercise this right. The effects on any given presidential race will be utterly trivial. National parties can, however, with impunity inflict needless embarrassment upon the state party of a state such as Wisconsin, which maintains a cross-

over primary as a survival of its progressive political heritage.
The national party that hastens first to do this—it will probably
be the Democrats, who joyfully did battle with the state of Wisconsin in the Supreme Court—undoubtedly will suffer marginal losses in popularity in the state.[26] This sort of reform provides a pristine example of an excellent principle pointlessly—
indeed fatuously—pursued. It gives a bad name to reform.

F. *Primaries detached from delegate selection.* A final suggestion
dramatically cuts the Gordian knot that the primaries have tied
around the nomination process and proposes that states be permitted to select their delegates by whatever means they choose,
but that they be required to run an advisory or beauty contest
primary. Thus the voters of each state would have a chance to
express their views to their respective state delegations, but state
delegations would retain the right to maneuver as they pleased.
This proposal leaves open the issue of delegate commitments
to candidates, though presumably it does not favor them. The
actual prevention of prior commitments could be effected only
if the delegate selection process were insulated in ways that
McGovern guidelines make difficult. This proposal also provides for a restriction on the scope of participation while increasing the amount of voting. It seems unlikely to be enacted,
in the first place because many states have primary elections
that actually select delegates as a legitimate part of their customary political practices. The main losers if this proposal were
enacted would undoubtedly be the candidates, since they would
have to sweep advisory primaries in a fashion approximated in
1952 by Dwight Eisenhower in Minnesota in order to carve out
something like the sort of autonomy from state party leaders
that they presently enjoy. It is, of course, an attenuation of that
autonomy that is at the heart of this proposal and that com-
mends it to its advocates.

4. On Turning Back the Clock: Are Parties Recoverable?

Nobody knows with certainty whether any amount of tinkering
with the presidential nomination process will in the end do the

slightest good. The most common responses to attempts to re-
start the engine of party in presidential nominations are asser-
tions about the irreversibility of events. In such discussions
metaphors about the futility of turning back the clock, returning the genie to the bottle and toothpaste to the tube abound.

It therefore seems desirable to explore the assumption, implicit in much of this book, that political parties are worth the
trouble we have been taking over them, that they are institutions whose functions are so vital as to make their preservation
and vigor a matter of legitimate concern. It is certainly the case
that much of what political parties have accomplished in the
past is now done, on the whole with greater evenhandedness,
efficiency, and dignity by other means. Welfare systems, for example, see to the indigent and disadvantaged without imposing
quid pro quo restraints on the political attitudes or voting behavior of recipients. Civil service systems at the municipal, state,
and federal levels show a capacity for recruiting job holders
according to expected quality of job performance to a degree
never contemplated in most patronage systems. Schemes for
competitive bidding on service contracts save taxpayers large
amounts of money over the sweetheart deals that Plunkitt of
Tammany Hall once described as "honest graft."[27]

So, undeniably, the range of activities that political parties
once undertook to perform has shrunk steadily. This general
shrinkage of the scope of party activity is not a phenomenon
one associates with the transformations of the post-1968 era.
The professionalization of public service has been going on at
least since the assassination of President Garfield in 1881.
Plunkitt's phillipics against the civil service were uttered at the
turn of the century.[28] Modern institutions of welfare are on the
whole in the United States a much more recent phenomenon,
but it is in any case unlikely that even the most robust partisan
of strong local parties would wish the return of the indigent
populace to dependency upon gifts of food from their precinct
captains. Nostalgia, in short, will not do as a foundation for
public policy, and especially since there can be so little grounds
for regret in the changes that have taken place.

On what basis, then, can political parties be recommended for a continuing role in the nomination process? Perhaps two: no better institutions have evolved to conduct nominating politics, and, second, the tasks parties still perform are both essential to harmonize with the presidential nomination process and crucial for the proper general functioning of the political system. Parties are organizations that, when they are functioning, mobilize voters, coordinate the activities of leaders, and by recruiting candidates and sponsoring political campaigns, provide some linkage between the two levels of politics. These typical intermediary activities can in part be performed by interest groups and by the mass media, but none of these tasks is central to the lives of interest groups and to the mass media as organizations. If either type of organization actually found itself stuck with the ongoing responsibility of performing classic party functions it would soon either disintegrate, reshape itself, or grow ancillary structures. Demands for access and accountability from unfamiliar sources would have to be met and dealt with, and in many cases acceded to, to avert electoral defeat. For, exclusive, narrow, and hierarchical as various state and local parties may be, seen from the perspective of the nation as a whole, American political parties are broadly based and highly diversified structures when compared with any interest group or cluster of interest groups. They are able to generate policy on a very wide range of topics, and to provide a legitimate forum for stalemate on topics where there is disagreement. The capacity of parties to gather and process information about human wants and demands nation-wide is impressive even when compared with the wire services and the television networks, and their capacity to evaluate wants and demands and select among them in some coherent and organizationally defensible fashion greatly exceeds that of any of the news media.

Given the formidable needs for coordinated political activity required in the face of the constitutional separation of powers, of the federal structure of the nation; of its geographic reach, of the heterogeneity of section, race, ethnicity, occupation, and economic condition that characterizes the American population, it is fair to say that parties still have work to do and were they not to exist, something very like them would have to be invented. Consequently recommendations concerning the organizational design and worries about the organizational performance of parties have some considerable point. It is by no means clear that the revival of organizational integrity among political parties entails turning back the clock to conditions more hospitable to their organizational survival; potentially hospitable conditions exist today and seem likely to continue to exist so long as leaders continue to be elected by popular vote and legislatures meet in the fifty states and in Washington. Presidents, governors, and mayors will continue to have the need for voters who elect them and the legislators on whom they must rely organized in some fashion. Political party seems as good a name as any to give to the organizations that undertake these tasks.

Thus what is at issue is not the survival of basic party functions so much as the thoughtful design of organizations to perform those functions in as effective a fashion as possible. What seems to have happened, looked at in a very broad overview is simply that an organization that works best when it has been highly decentralized has been significantly centralized in its powers and operations.

Historically, this centralization process can be interpreted as the last poisonous gift of the American institution of slavery. Slavery discredited all the decentralized organizations that fed on it and protected it and its successors. As late as 1964 a transparently racist state delegation from Mississippi was sent to the Democratic national convention, representatives of the dying politics of intimidation and denial of the right to vote on racial grounds.[29] Because the rest of the Democratic party for all sorts of reasons could not countenance that, justifications had to be found and systematically argued on general principles to the effect that the national convention had the power to keep its own house in order and to enforce rules of decency upon its

component parts, the state parties. The same general principles, asserting the simple right of the whole to regulate the part,
can serve equally well to forbid the innocuous Wisconsin cross-
over primary.

There is nothing incoherent in constitutional doctrines which
proclaim an institution capable of asserting centralized standards in one matter, and likewise in another. So further appeal
in the Wisconsin case, if one should be forthcoming, cannot
stand on constitutional grounds, but must on prudential
grounds. As a matter of prudence, not jurisprudence, the national conventions, their rules committees, and the reform and
re-reform commissions which seem so readily to be adopted by
party bureaucrats as creatures of the conventions, should be
reluctant to impose any standards at all on the parties of the
several states. Racism, that ugly legacy of slavery, should be the
great and obvious exception. Where racism survives in the conduct of local party business the representatives of all the other
state parties should on prudential grounds exercise the power
the courts have given to them to take whatever measures are
needed to assure fair, equitable, and race-blind political participation. On prudential grounds all other interventions into state
and local politics, all other attempts to make uniform the political cultures of widely separated, historically distinct entities,
ought to be resisted. The prudential grounds are these: state
and local parties that root in local soil have the best chance of
surviving and prospering, of winning elections and recruiting
good candidates, and bringing to the national nominating process the authentic voices of the people of the several states.
These voices deserve to be heard, and it cannot be assumed
that the formulas that work in eliciting these voices in a place
like California also will work in the same way in Louisiana or
Vermont or Ohio.

If central conceptions of justice and equity should not entirely determine the contributions that state parties make to
presidential nominations, what should? Even in places where
local patronage organizations still flourish, it does not seem unreasonable to conclude that representation at national party

conventions should follow the social contours that influence the ways in which local party effort is organized. States that are nonpartisan in spirit will rely more heavily on middle-class volunteer workers, and this spirit ought freely to be permitted to emerge at national party conventions as well. Interest groups at the local and state level ought to be given incentives for involving themselves in alliances with local and state parties. State and local parties can be greatly strengthened in their state and local political efforts by such alliances, and these alliances can be further facilitated by the assurance that state and local parties—not deals directly with presidential candidates—will form the basis for participation in the presidential nominating process.

In some states, to be sure, where state and local parties are weak, such deals with national candidates will continue to be made. The strongest overall design, the design that best helps nominees to get elected and Presidents to govern, is that of the mixed system: state conventions dominated by party bosses where party bosses survive and actually coordinate local political effort; interest group dominance of presidential nominations where interest groups finance and staff campaigns; and primary elections where parties are weak or where the norms of civic participation so dictate.

Do mixed systems necessarily produce better candidates? In most respects the question is unanswerable, but not, perhaps in one. Mixed systems by expressing the varied political cultures of the far-flung United States provide a better education to prospective candidates than any more uniform alternative choice process. Candidates who must come to terms with the realities of American politics in all their variety and complexity are better suited to governing America than those for whom such an education is unavailable or unattainable. Mixed systems may pick a different winner than more uniform processes in a given presidential year or they may not. What they can be assured of doing year in and year out is placing within each candidate's grasp a more enlightened understanding of what it takes to govern.

Notes

Preface

1. For a list of some of them see Nelson W. Polsby, "Contemporary Transformations of American Politics: Thoughts on the Research Agendas of Political Scientists," *Political Science Quarterly* 96 (Winter 1981–82), pp. 551–70.
2. *Presidential Elections: Strategies of American Electoral Politics* (New York: Scribner, 1964, 1968, 1971, 1976, 1980).
3. Byron E. Shafer, "The Party Reformed," Ph.D. dissertation, University of California, Berkeley, 1979; to be published as *The Quiet Revolution: Reform Politics in the Democratic Party, 1968–1972* (New York: Russell Sage Foundation, forthcoming).
4. "Presidential Cabinet Making: Lessons for the Political System" (Bloomington, Indiana: The Poynter Center, June 1977) and *Political Science Quarterly* 93 (Spring 1978), pp. 15–25; "Coalition and Faction in American Politics: An Institutional View," in S. M. Lipset (ed.), *Emerging Coalitions in American Politics* (San Francisco: Institute for Contemporary Studies, 1978), pp. 103–23, and Lipset (ed.), *Party Coalitions in the 1980s* (San Francisco: Institute for Contemporary Studies, 1981), pp. 153–78; "Interest Groups and the Presidency: Trends in Political Intermediation in America," in Walter Dean Burnham and Martha Wagner Weinberg (eds.), *American Politics and Public Policy* (Cambridge, Mass.: MIT Press, 1978), pp. 41–52; "The News Media as an Alternative to Party in the Presidential Selection Process," in Robert A. Goldwin (ed.), *Political Parties in the Eighties* (Washington, D.C.: American Enter-

prise Institute, 1980), pp. 50–66; and "Party Reform and the Conduct of the Presidency," in James Sterling Young (ed.), *Problems and Prospects for Presidential Leadership in the 1980's* (Lanham, Maryland: University Press of America, forthcoming).

Introduction

1. In 1980, for example, that bellwether of American liberal journalism, Tom Wicker of the *New York Times,* said of the two candidates of the major parties:

   Think of that: an incumbent President whose record of ineptitude stands unmatched since Warren G. Harding and whose campaign is based on foreign policy crises largely of his own making; or a 69-year-old ex-Governor twice rejected by his own party, with no foreign policy, national security or Congressional experience.

   "Getting Down to Cases," *New York Times* (March 16, 1980). As is frequently the case, Mr. Wicker was not alone. A sampling of complaints reaching wide audiences might include: Albert R. Hunt, "The Process Is Out of Kilter," *Wall Street Journal* (November 10, 1980); Cyrus R. Vance, "Reforming the Electoral Reforms," *New York Times Magazine* (February 22, 1981), pp. 16ff; Adam Clymer, "Poll Finds Reagan-Carter Choice Unsatisfactory to Half of Public," *New York Times* (April 18, 1980); Donald C. Bacon, "What's Wrong with the Way Americans Pick a President?," *U. S. News and World Report* (March 31, 1980), p. 35; Richard Reeves, "When Reform Backfires," *Esquire* (March 1980), pp. 8, 11; "Is This Any Way To Pick a President?," *Newsweek* (October 15, 1979), pp. 69–70, 79; and Terry Sanford, *A Danger of Democracy: The Presidential Nominating Process* (Boulder, Colo.: Westview Press, 1981).

2. Carter and Reagan's only competitors are Grover Cleveland (elected in 1884) and Woodrow Wilson (elected in 1912), neither of whom served in national government before becoming President. All thirty-five other Presidents had at least some prior national service to their credit, and for most that service was extensive.

3. Even so, by mass criteria both major party candidates were uniquely unpopular in 1980. For the first time, a University of Michigan survey recorded that both major party candidates were on balance viewed unfavorably by the mass electorate. See Arthur H. Miller and Martin P. Wattenberg, "Policy and Performance: Voting in the 1980 Election," delivered at the 1981 Annual Meeting of the American Political Science Association (pp. 5–6, figure 1).

4. See Alan L. Otten, "Western Europe Is Less Than Thrilled by Carter-Reagan Choice in U.S. Vote," *Wall Street Journal* (June 25, 1980). Among the European expressions of what Otten characterized as "near horror" about the 1980 presidential choice were these: "*Le Monde* asks: 'How can the most powerful democracy in the world find itself reduced to a choice between candidates of so little weight?'" and, from a British journalist, "'We give our actors knighthoods, but we don't make them prime minister.'" Anthony King says: "All over Europe in the autumn of 1980, wherever people met to talk politics, there was only one topic of conversation: How on earth had a great country like the United States, filled with talented men and women, managed to land itself with two such second- (or was it third- ?) rate presidential candidates as Jimmy Carter and Ronald Reagan?" "How Not To Select Presidential Candadates: A View from Europe," in Austin Ranney (ed.), *The American Elections of 1980* (Washington, D.C.: American Enterprise Institute, 1981), pp. 303–28.

5. How presidential campaigns are financed I take to be a fundamental issue of party finance, even though, strictly speaking, it is candidates for public office, not party organizations per se, that are raising and spending most of the money with which we shall be concerned.

Chapter I: The Party Reforms and How They Grew

1. A thorough account of the presidential selection process in 1952 is contained in Paul T. David, Malcolm C. Moos, and Ralph M. Goldman, *Presidential Nominating Politics in 1952*, 5 volumes (Baltimore: Johns Hopkins University Press, 1954). See especially, Volume 1, *The National Story*.

2. See Mary Earhart Dillon, *Wendell Willkie* (Philadelphia: Lippincott, 1952), pp. 311–35.

3. See Jules Abels, *Out of the Jaws of Victory* (New York: Holt, 1959), pp. 57–61; and Irwin Ross, *The Loneliest Campaign* (New York: New American Library, 1968), pp. 47–53.

4. *The National Story*, pp. 31–33.

5. He won in California, Illinois, Maryland, Massachusetts, Nebraska, New Hampshire, New Jersey, Ohio, Oregon, Pennsylvania, South Dakota, and Wisconsin. He entered 14 out of the available 16 primaries, and won 12 of them (*The National Story*, pp. 55–56).

6. *Ibid.*, p. 65.

7. *Ibid.*, pp. 150–55.

8. President Truman discusses his views of the various candidates in *Years of Trial and Hope, 1946–1952* (Garden City, N.Y.: Doubleday, 1956), pp. 490–97.

9. A group of labor leaders representing both the AFL and CIO met with the 74-year-old Barkley at breakfast on the day before the convention and announced, with regret, that they could not support him because of his age (*The National Story*, p. 117).

10. This very complex business is described in *The National Story*, pp. 136–49; in John Bartlow Martin, *Adlai Stevenson of Illinois* (Garden City, N.Y.: Doubleday, 1976), pp. 593–95; and in Jack Arvey, as told to John Madigan, "The Reluctant Candidate," *The Reporter* (November 24, 1953), pp. 19–26.

11. See Martin, *Adlai Stevenson*, pp. 597–98; *The National Story*, pp. 151, 154.

12. Martin, *Adlai Stevenson*, pp. 513–604, is exhaustive on Stevenson's hesitations.

13. See V. O. Key, Jr., *Politics, Parties, and Pressure Groups*, 5th edition (New York: Crowell, 1964), pp. 375–94; Louise Overacker, *The Presidential Primary* (New York: Macmillan, 1926); Paul T. David, Ralph M. Goldman, and Richard C. Bain, *The Politics of National Party Conventions* (Washington, D.C.: Brookings Institution, 1960), p. 249.

14. Joseph Bruce Gorman, *Kefauver: A Political Biography* (New York: Oxford University Press, 1971), pp. 80–85.

15. Charles A. H. Thomson reports that an unpublished NBC survey of television viewers of the 1952 Democratic Convention in the New York area showed only Kefauver supporters responding that television was the most important news medium (ahead of newspapers) in helping them make up their minds. *Television and Presidential Politics* (Washington, D.C.: Brookings Institution, 1956), pp. 47–48. Other evidence of Kefauver's high and favorable visibility (this time among television viewers in southern Ohio) is found in, Members of the Department of Marketing, Miami University, Oxford, Ohio, *The Influence of Television in the Election of 1952* (Oxford, Ohio: Oxford Research Associates Inc., December 1954), p. 22.

16. Gorman, *Kefauver*, p. 88.

17. *Ibid.*, p. 91.

18. *Ibid.*, p. 91. This comparison is all the more remarkable in view of the fact that a local team, the Yankees, played in this series, beating the Philadelphia Phillies four games to none.

19. *Ibid.*, p. 87.
20. *Ibid.*, p. 92.
21. *Ibid.*, p. 92. See also G. D. Wiebe, "Responses to the Televised Kefauver Hearings," *Public Opinion Quarterly* 16 (Summer 1952): "The routine life of [New York] city was substantially altered as people interrupted normal pursuits to sit and watch the parade of local corruption and bribery that was unfolded on their television screens" (p. 180).
22. Gorman, *Kefauver,* p. 106.
23. Republican leaders in 1952 would have been fortunate to have had available Herbert H. Hyman and Paul B. Sheatsley's, "The Political Appeal of President Eisenhower," *Public Opinion Quarterly* 19 (1955–56), pp. 26–39. Such evidence as the Minnesota primary proved to be equally effective for their purposes.
24. An attempt to codify textbook rules of the nomination process as of 1960 is Nelson W. Polsby, "Decision-making at the National Conventions," *Western Political Quarterly* 13 (September 1960), pp. 609–19, esp. 616.
25. Theodore H. White, *The Making of the President 1960* (New York: Atheneum, 1961), p. 87.
26. For accounts of the Smith-Hoover contest of 1928, see Ruth C. Silva, *Rum, Religion, and Votes: 1928 Re-examined* (University Park: Pennsylvania State University Press, 1962); and Allan J. Lichtman, *Prejudice and the Old Politics* (Chapel Hill: University of North Carolina Press, 1979).
27. White, *1960,* p. 85.
28. *Ibid.*, pp. 97–114; and Harry W. Ernst, *The Primary That Made a President: West Virginia, 1960* (New York: Holt, 1962).
29. See Ithiel de Sola Pool, Robert P. Abelson, and Samuel Popkin, *Candidates, Issues and Strategies* (Cambridge, Mass.: MIT Press, 1964), pp. 68, 117–18; Philip Converse, Angus Campbell, Warren E. Miller, and Donald Stokes, "Stability and Change in 1960: A Reinstating Election," *American Political Science Review* 55 (June 1961), pp. 269–80; and Philip Converse, "Religion and Politics in the 1960 Election" in Angus Campbell (ed.), *Elections in the Political Order* (New York: Wiley, 1967), pp. 96–124.
30. Aaron Wildavsky, "What Can I Do? Ohio Delegates View the Democratic Convention," in Paul Tillett (ed.), *Inside Politics: The National Conventions, 1960* (Dobbs Ferry, N.Y.: Oceana, 1962), pp. 112–31. DiSalle tells the story somewhat differently in his autobiography, *Second Choice* (New York: Hawthorn Books, 1966), pp. 197–202.

31. V. O. Key, Jr., *Politics, Parties, and Pressure Groups,* p. 403.

32. "Six-month U.S. Toll at 9557," *New York Times* (July 4, 1968); and Joseph B. Treaster, "Fresh Fighting Reported at DMZ: American Combat Deaths Pass the 30,000 Mark," *New York Times* (December 13, 1968). At the end of March 1968, according to President Johnson, 525,000 American military personnel were in Vietnam. See Lyndon B. Johnson, *The Vantage Point: Perspectives of the Presidency 1963–1969* (New York: Holt, 1971), p. 436.

33. *Statistical Abstract of the U.S. 1973* (Washington, D.C.: U.S. Government Printing Office, 1973), p. 148.

34. See Theodore H. White, *The Making of the President 1968* (New York: Atheneum, 1969), pp. 259–63, 271.

35. See Lewis Chester, Godfrey Hodgson, and Bruce Page, *An American Melodrama* (New York: Viking, 1969), pp. 21–31.

36. See Gallup polls for January 21, 1968, February 18, 1968, March 10, 1968. Also John E. Mueller, *War, Presidents, and Public Opinion* (New York: John Wiley, 1973).

37. See David Halberstam, "The Man Who Ran Against Lyndon Johnson," *Harper's* (December 1968), pp. 47–66.

38. Among the people approached by Lowenstein who gave the matter some consideration were John Kenneth Galbraith, Senator Robert Kennedy, Senator George McGovern, and Representative Don Edwards. See Jules Witcover, *Eighty-five Days* (New York: G.P. Putnam's Sons, 1969), pp. 27–29; David Halberstam, *The Unfinished Odyssey of Robert Kennedy* (New York: Random House, 1968), pp. 3–19; Jeremy Larner, *Nobody Knows* (New York: Macmillan, 1970), pp. 17–22.

39. See Eugene McCarthy, *The Year of the People* (Garden City, N.Y.: Doubleday, 1969), pp. 89, 294–95. See also Arthur Herzog, *McCarthy for President* (New York: Viking Press, 1969), pp. 75–99.

40. A leading McCarthy campaigner wrote: "When the votes were tallied, I was somewhat surprised that a full 48 percent of the voters liked LBJ enough to write in his name. But since all the newscasters said that our 42 percent was a great victory for McCarthy, we were ecstatic" (Ben Stavis, *We Were the Campaign* (Boston: Beacon, 1969), p. 26).

41. Witcover, *Eighty-five Days,* pp. 15–44; Halberstam, *Unfinished Odyssey,* pp. 3–67.

42. Quoted in Halberstam, *Unfinished Odyssey,* p. 67. The illegitimacy of a Kennedy dynasty was by no means conceded by those favorable to Kennedy. See, for example, Theodore White's incredulity at the hostility Kennedy encountered as he "tried to enter on his inheritance" (*1968,* p. 151).

43. See Halberstam, *Unfinished Odyssey.*
44. Lyndon B. Johnson, *The Vantage Point,* p. 435. See also *Congressional Quarterly Weekly Report* (April 5, 1968), pp. 731–34.
45. Narrative accounts now available on 1968 are deficient in their coverage of Humphrey and his camp. See, however, Meg Greenfield, "Hubert Humphrey in 1968," *The Reporter* (June 13, 1968), pp. 19–24; Hubert H. Humphrey, *The Education of a Public Man* (Garden City, N.Y.: Doubleday, 1976). Notably unfriendly to Humphrey are the discussions in Arthur M. Schlesinger, Jr., *Robert Kennedy and His Times* (New York: Ballantine Books, 1978); and Chester, Hodgson, and Page, *An American Melodrama,* esp. pp. 142–55. And, mesmerized as always by the Kennedys, is Theodore White, *1968.*
46. Humphrey, *Education,* p. 368.
47. *Ibid.,* p. 371. See also *Newsweek* (June 3, 1968), pp. 28–29.
48. Contrast the attitude of the *New Republic* in 1964 and 1968. In 1964 the *New Republic* said:

> With Humphrey as Vice President, the Senate will have a presiding officer who knows every nerve and muscle of that body; the President will have a traveling emissary welcome abroad because he is interested in the problems of others and unafraid of change; and the President will have too a collaborator who shares his hope that this good society can become "a great society" ["Johnson-Humphrey," *New Republic* (August 8, 1964), p. 4].

In 1968:

> The editors of this journal are among those who have applauded Hubert Humphrey's energetic and good-humored championship of the underdog for over two decades. We do not gladly turn against him now. If the clock could be turned back, we would turn it back. It can't be done. The Vice President is trapped in a desperate situation for which he is only partly responsible. But he is trapped. He could break out of it, but only by following Lyndon Johnson, removing himself from the race and turning his party free. . . . The fires burning in the hamlets of Vietnam and in the ghettos of our cities illuminate a face of America we would rather not see. The Vice President's complicity is inescapable; that is his tragedy ["Calling All Delegates," *New Republic* (July 27, 1968), pp. 3–4].

In *Me and Ralph* (Washington, D.C.: New Republic, 1976), p. 1, David Sanford paints a portrait of the management of the *New Republic* as of 1968 that will probably not surprise its readers:

> I remember very well the snowy night [in 1968] when I delivered galley proofs of a *New Republic* lead editorial exhorting Eugene McCarthy to run for President, to the home of Gilbert Harrison, then the magazine's owner. When I knocked at the door I was greeted by three children, Mrs. Harrison, and a yellow Labrador retriever. The youngest son called out, "Daddy, your friend is here," and in a second or two I saw Gil Harrison, bounding up the stairs from the basement with a look of great expectation on his

face that was dashed when he saw me. "Oh, Dave, it's you," he said with a faint air of disdain. As I stood in Harrison's book-lined study, still in my galoshes, the friend he was really expecting arrived at the door. It was Gene McCarthy, there to read the proofs.

49. Gallup poll, April 28, 1968.
50. Gallup poll, May 15, 1968.
51. The Gallup Report News Release, June 2, 1968, "Humphrey Choice of Local Democratic Leaders."
52. *Newsweek* (June 3, 1968), p. 28.
53. "Robert Kennedy's Chances: What a Survey Shows," *U.S. News and World Report* (June 3, 1968), pp. 48–49.
54. Kennedy ended the year having won primaries in the District of Columbia, Indiana, Nebraska, California, and South Dakota, receiving 30.6 percent of all the votes cast in primaries in 1968. McCarthy got 38.7 percent of all the votes cast in primaries, winning in Wisconsin, Pennsylvania, Massachusetts, Oregon, New Jersey, and Illinois. The remainder of the votes cast in primaries was widely scattered: 8.9 percent for unpledged delegates, 7.3 percent for Senator Stephen Young of Ohio, 5.1 percent for President Johnson, 3.2 percent for Governor Roger Branigan of Indiana, and so on. A convenient source is the Congressional Quarterly publication *Presidential Elections Since 1789* (Washington, D.C., 1975).
55. Richard Tuck, "Teddy We Hardly Know Ye," *Washington Post* (November 11, 1979).
56. See Jack Newfield, *Robert Kennedy: A Memoir* (New York: Dutton, 1969); Halberstam, *Unfinished Odyssey;* Schlesinger, *Robert Kennedy and His Times.* Also Richard Harwood, "The Robert F. Kennedy Legacy," *Washington Post* (June 6, 1969); Ronald Steel, *Walter Lippmann and the American Century* (Boston: Little, Brown, 1980), p. 587; Jules Witcover, *Eighty-five Days*, pp. 335–37.
57. Witcover, *Eighty-five Days*, pp. 322–23.
58. Humphrey, *Education of a Public Man*, p. 373.
59. See Stephen MacDonald, "Hovering Doves: If Humphrey Is Picked, Peace Movement Could Get Violent," *Wall Street Journal* (August 28, 1968); Meg Greenfield, "The Hyperbole of the McCarthy Supporters," *Washington Post* (July 28, 1968).
60. The Hughes Commission grew out of a meeting of the Connecticut State "McCarthy for President" Steering Committee, held in West Hartford on June 23, 1968. The participants in the meeting were unhappy about the outcome of the previous day's Connecticut state Democratic convention, where McCarthy supporters had

taken only 9 of the state's 44 delegate positions, even though the Connecticut delegation had been selected legally, and the number of McCarthy delegates was proportional to the number of McCarthy's supporters (200 out of 960) at the convention. The McCarthy group decided to assemble a formally neutral commission that could document their claims that, even if selection processes across the country were legal, they were neither fair nor democratic.

It was decided that for the commission to have its desired effect it would have to appear neutral and representative. After a great number of problems in securing members, the commission was constituted. It was composed of a chairman who was a McCarthy backer amenable to party reform (Gov. Harold Hughes of Iowa), a vice-chairman from the Humphrey camp (Rep. Donald Fraser), a black leader (Georgia state senator Julian Bond), a woman (columnist Doris Fleeson Kimball), a Kennedy supporter (California attorney Fred Dutton), and two well-known writers on political and legal subjects, Professor Alexander Bickel of the Yale Law School, a Kennedy supporter, and Harry Ashmore, formerly the executive editor of the Little Rock *Arkansas Gazette,* who had become an officer of the Center for the Study of Democratic Institutions in Santa Barbara, California, a McCarthy supporter.

The staff consisted mostly of Connecticut McCarthy campaigners. For example, Geoffrey Cowan, a Connecticut McCarthy delegate coordinator, became the associate staff director. He arranged with William M. Johnson, II, a small publisher who supported McCarthy, to contribute $10,000 in exchange for rights to publish the reports and whatever else might be written.

Tom Alder was selected as the commission staff director since Cowan seemed too visibly political, given his position in the McCarthy campaign. Alder had been less involved in the Democratic race because he was trying to start a fourth party to the left of the Democrats. The rest of the staff was composed of five McCarthy supporters, a Kennedy backer, and six persons who were unattached.

The staff had less than six weeks to assemble a report. On August 4, the co-chairman of the Connecticut McCarthy campaign, Anne Wexler, and Hughes publicly announced the creation of the commission. The commission met only once, on August 13. All the commissioners but Ashmore attended. At this meeting, commissioners made their only collective contribution to the commission report, agreeing to most of its staff's proposals.

Only two of these proposals caused the commissioners to balk. One was the staff's plan to abolish winner-take-all primaries. Dutton, of California, a winner-take-all state, objected. Second, the commission refused to do away with all state party conventions, as the staff also recommended even for those which could be considered "participatory." Fraser saved the latter.

The report, written by the staff, remained critical of the winner-take-all primary and the participatory convention, although in the end it was not recommended that they be abolished. The report recommended the representation of minority opinion at all levels of decision making, by ending use of the unit rule and winner-take-all elections. Public participation in the selection process was to be promoted, preferably through proportional primaries.

See Byron E. Shafer, "The Party Reformed," Ph.D. dissertation, University of California, Berkeley, 1979, pp. 8–64; to be published as *The Quiet Revolution: Reform Politics in the Democratic Party, 1968–1972* (New York: Russell Sage Foundation, forthcoming); Richard G. Stearns, "The Presidential Nominating Process in the United States: The Constitution of the Democratic National Convention," Ph.D. dissertation, Oxford University, 1971, pp. 25–39; and Commission on the Democratic Selection of Presidential Nominees, *The Democratic Choice* (Washington, D.C., 1968).

61. *The Democratic Choice,* pp. 22, 31, 33.
62. See Alan L. Otten, "Still the Boss: Many Detect LBJ's Touch in Convention Planning," *Wall Street Journal* (August 20, 1968); Laurence Stern, "HHH Sought To Shift Site of Convention," *Washington Post* (December 3, 1968); White, *1968,* pp. 338–39.
63. See "C.B.S. Man Is Attacked on Floor of the Convention," *New York Times* (August 28, 1968); "Guards Halt Delegate Till He Discards Paper," *ibid.;* Tom Wicker, "Victor Gets 1,761: Vote Taken Amid Boos for Chicago Police Tactics in Street," *ibid.* (August 29, 1968); Wallace Turner, "New York Delegate Dragged from Hall by Police," *ibid.;* "Scorn Expressed in Papers Abroad: Police and Security Actions in Chicago Assailed," *ibid.*
64. See Norman C. Miller, "Celebrity Delegates at Democratic Parley Get No VIP Handling," *Wall Street Journal* (August 28, 1968); White, *1968,* pp. 284–85; Chester, Hodgson, and Page, *An American Melodrama,* pp. 581–91.
65. The foregoing quotations are from *Rights in Conflict,* a report submitted by Daniel Walker, director of the Chicago study team, to the National Commission on the Causes and Prevention of Violence (New York: Dutton, 1968), pp. 1, 3–4, 50.

66. "In the Jungle," *New York Review of Books* (September 26, 1968), pp. 11–13. At this time, the *New York Review* was widely regarded as the most influential publication in the United States among intellectuals, according to a study of the subject by Charles Kadushin, *The American Intellectual Elite* (Boston: Little, Brown, 1974). For other reports on the Democratic convention, see Tom Wicker, "America Was Radicalized," *New York Times Magazine* (August 24, 1969), pp. 27ff.; Norman Mailer, "Miami Beach and Chicago," *Harper's* (November 1968), pp. 41–130; Elia Kazan, "Political Passion Play: Act II," *New York* (September 23, 1968).

67. White, *1968*, p. 302. See also, Stewart Alsop, "Can Humphrey Win?," *Newsweek* (September 9, 1968); Richard A. Pride and Barbara Richards, "Denigration of Authority? Television News Coverage of the Student Movement," *The Journal of Politics* 36 (August 1974), pp. 637–60.

Literary critic Elizabeth Hardwick offered the following mellow retrospective about a month later for the readers of the *New York Review of Books:*

> Wednesday night, during the siege of the Hilton, when the police mercilessly beat young men before the eyes of everyone, you could hear the timid but determined voices of "concerned" women calling out, "What are the charges against that young man?" Or, "Stop, please, Sir, you are killing him!" The mention of the instruments of law and order sent the police into a wild rage and for a moment they stopped beating demonstrators and turned to threaten the frightened suburbans. During the raid on the McCarthy Headquarters, a girl in tears asked, "What are the grounds?" The police answered, "Coffee grounds." With this lawlessness of the Law, misery fell from the sky. Suppose, you found yourself wondering, *they* should take over! "I have been a life-long Democrat," people kept whispering in bewilderment. Few had realized until Chicago how great a ruin Johnson and his war in Vietnam had brought down upon our country.

This article was decorated with a David Levine cartoon showing Humphrey in a policeman's helmet, holding a truncheon. Ms. Hardwick continues:

> Hubert Humphrey is an altogether embarrassing figure, with his dyed black hair and glowing television makeup. He creates a sense of false energy—like an MC on an afternoon show. The present Democratic leadership appears to be divided between bullies and cowards and Humphrey asks us to take our chances on the coward. You will find me less dangerous, he seems to be trying to assure us.

> The Vice President has many words and he uses them over and over. "I am the Captain of the team," he says. Many of the choice sentences of his acceptance speech had been the choice remarks of his appearance before the California delegation. (Peace and freedom do not come cheaply, my

friends.) He brought forth Winston Churchill and St. Francis of Assisi—one strong and one humble—and topped the embarrassment of the first by the second. He is always frantically smiling; repose is a rapid fade to sentiment. In between, where feeling and person would lodge, there is simply nothing. He does not seem in touch. Empty smiles, a wound-up toy. Nothing in him inspires confidence. He cannot allow himself to be distracted by events. The entire convention appeared to intrude upon his smiles. Nothing has happened since the Thirties: that is his message, that is the real Humphrey, now, "Captain of the team."

Elizabeth Hardwick, "Chicago," *New York Review of Books* (September 26, 1968), pp. 5–7.

68. Described in Hubert H. Humphrey, *Education of a Public Man*, pp. 383–94. See also, Louis Harris, "Conventions: Nixon Gained, HHH Was Hurt," *Washington Post* (October 3, 1968). McCarthy delegate John Kenneth Galbraith reminisces:

. . . There are times when one must be completely adamant, and this was one. The war was the transcendent issue. Compromise would not only have cost us the confidence of our own supporters, it would have provided sanction for those saying the war must go on. A firm stand would require Humphrey to move toward our position during the campaign.

A Life in Our Times (New York: Ballantine, 1981), p. 503.

69. *Congressional Quarterly Weekly Report* (August 30, 1968), p. 2287.

70. The chairman, Senator George McGovern of South Dakota, had become a candidate for President in 1968 after Robert Kennedy was assassinated, and was credited with keeping some of Kennedy's supporters engaged in practical politics. He endorsed his old neighbor Humphrey after the nomination and campaigned enthusiastically for him. Donald Fraser, member of Congress from Minneapolis, was vice-chairman and when McGovern became a 1972 Presidential candidate succeeded to the chairmanship.

71. See "Democrats Name Two Reform Groups," *New York Times* (February 9, 1969).

72. Commission on Party Structure and Delegate Selection to the Democratic National Committee, *Mandate for Reform* (Washington, D.C., April 1970).

73. These claims were fortified by a legal opinion by Democratic party general counsel Joseph Califano and by subsequent directives from national chairman Lawrence O'Brien. See Stearns, "The Presidential Nominating Process," pp. 36–38.

74. The full text of the guidelines is given in an appendix to this chapter.

75. *Mandate for Reform*, p. 34.

76. Shafer, "The Party Reformed," pp. 323–25.

77. *Ibid.*, pp. 324–25.

78. *Mandate for Reform,* p. 34.
79. See, however, for a thorough reconstruction, Shafer, "The Party Reformed."
80. *Cousins v. Wigoda* 419 *U.S.* 477 (1975). In this case the exclusion of duly certified delegates from Illinois by the credentials committee of the 1972 Democratic convention was upheld. The delegates had been slated by the Daley machine.
81. Excellent reviews of the field up to 1971 may be found in Alexander Heard, *The Costs of Democracy* (Chapel Hill: University of North Carolina Press, 1960), pp. 344–55; and Herbert E. Alexander, *Money in Politics* (Washington, D.C.: Public Affairs Press, 1972), pp. 183–251.
82. Frederick C. Mosher *et al., Watergate* (New York: Basic Books, 1974), p. 87.
83. See Nelson W. Polsby, "Policy Initiation in the American Political System," in I. L. Horowitz (ed.), *The Use and Abuse of Social Science* (New Brunswick, N.J.: Transaction Books, 1971), pp. 296–308; and Polsby, *Political Innovation in America: The Politics of Policy Initiation* (forthcoming: esp. Chap. 5).
84. A good part of this history remains to be written. For an overview see Frank J. Munger and Richard F. Fenno, Jr., *National Politics and Federal Aid to Education* (Syracuse, N.Y.: Syracuse University Press, 1962). See also Ted Bryant, "Carl Elliott: His Legislation Helped Millions Go to College," *Birmingham Post-Herald* (May 24, 1982).
85. P.L. 93–443 (October 15, 1974).
86. These limits were $1,000 for individuals, $5,000 for political committees, and $10,000 (per House candidate) and $20,000 (per Senate candidate) for political parties.
87. See P.L. 93-443, sec. 204.
88. The plaintiff first in alphabetical order was the conservative Senator from New York, James Buckley, who sued the Secretary of the Senate, Francis Valeo. Thus the case entered the law books as *Buckley et al. v. Valeo* 424 *U.S.* 1 (1976).
89. First amendment issues raised by this case are given an exceptionally clear and convincing exposition in Daniel D. Polsby, *"Buckley v. Valeo:* The Special Nature of Political Speech," *Supreme Court Review 1976* (Chicago: University of Chicago Press, 1977), pp. 1–44.
90. P.L. 94-283.
91. To $20,000 per year.
92. To $5,000 per year.
93. A good overview of the new law and its immediate impact from

several perspectives is Michael J. Malbin (ed.), *Parties, Interest Groups, and Campaign Finance Laws* (Washington, D.C.: American Enterprise Institute, 1980). See also Herbert E. Alexander and Brian A. Haggerty, *The Federal Election Campaign Act After a Decade of Political Reforms* (Los Angeles: Citizens' Research Foundation, 1981); and Gary R. Orren, "Presidential Campaign Finance: Its Impact and Future," *Commonsense* 4 (Number 2, 1981), pp. 50–66.

Chapter II: Consequences for Political Parties

1. See Everett Carll Ladd, Jr., " 'Reform' Is Wrecking the U.S. Party System," *Fortune* (November 1977), pp. 177–88; Jeane Jordan Kirkpatrick, *Dismantling the Parties: Reflections on Party Reform and Party Decomposition* (Washington, D.C.: American Enterprise Institute, 1979); Terry Sanford, *A Danger of Democracy* (Boulder, Colo.: Westview Press, 1981); Austin Ranney, *The Federalization of Presidential Primaries* (Washington, D.C.: American Enterprise Institute, 1978); Ranney, *Curing the Mischiefs of Faction* (Berkeley: University of California Press, 1975); Cyrus R. Vance, "Reforming the Electoral Reforms," *New York Times Magazine* (February 22, 1981), pp. 16, 62–69; James W. Ceaser, *Reforming the Reforms* (Cambridge, Mass.: Ballinger, 1982).

2. See William J. Crotty, *Decision for the Democrats* (Baltimore: Johns Hopkins University Press, 1978), pp. 254–73; Kenneth A. Bode and Carol F. Casey, "Party Reform: Revisionism Revised," in Robert A. Goldwin (ed.), *Political Parties in the Eighties* (Washington, D.C.: American Enterprise Institute, 1980), pp. 3–19; Charles Longley, "National Party Reform and the Presidential Primaries," prepared for delivery at the 1981 Annual Meeting of the Mid-West Political Science Association, April 15–19, 1981, Cincinnati. Bode was director of research of the McGovern Commission; Casey was a member of its research staff; and Longley was a summer intern on the staff of the Commission.

3. See John F. Bibby, "Party Renewal in the National Republican Party," in Gerald M. Pomper (ed.), *Party Renewal in America* (New York: Praeger, 1980), pp. 102–15.

4. McGovern campaign official Richard G. Stearns argued in 1972 that the shift in this burden was not intended by the McGovern Commission but arose as a consequence of a subsequent interpretation of guideline requirements in an exchange of letters "in late 1971 between [Democratic] party chairman Lawrence O'Brien and Rep. Donald Fraser of Minnesota, McGovern's successor as chairman of the reform commission. In these memoranda, Fraser out-

lined, and O'Brien assented to, a ruling that made a deficient percentage of minorities, women, or young persons *prima facie* evidence of discrimination, thereby making any delegation on which these groups were underrepresented susceptible to challenge . . . As a result, the convention was confronted with an unprecedented number of credentials challenges, many of them frivolous . . ." (Richard G. Stearns, "Reforming the Democrats' Reforms," *Washington Post Outlook,* December 3, 1972).

5. "Democratic Rules Reform Having Impact on '72 Race," *New York Times* (June 10, 1972). See also Apple, "Primaries: Change Is Profound," *New York Times* (February 10, 1972); Norman C. Miller, "Democrats' New Rules for Picking Delegates Add to '72 Uncertainty," *Wall Street Journal* (January 19, 1972).

6. Of course, in the case of Illinois this proved to be optimistic in 1972. See Stearns, "Reforming the Reforms."

7. Bode and Casey, "Party Reform: Revisionism Revised."

8. *Ibid.,* p. 17.

9. *Ibid.,* p. 10.

10. Report of the Commission on Presidential Nomination and Party Structure (Morley A. Winograd, chairman), *Openness, Participation, and Party Building: Reforms for a Stronger Democratic Party* (Washington, D.C.: Democratic National Committee, January 1978), p. 24.

11. Evidently subsidies do encourage candidacies. The creation of a state subsidy for gubernatorial election campaigns in New Jersey drew a record-breaking number of hopefuls out of the woodwork—twenty-one in all. See Larry Light, "Large Primary Field for New Jersey Governor," *Congressional Quarterly Weekly Report* (May 16, 1981), pp. 861–62.

12. F. Christopher Arterton, "Campaign Organizations Confront the Media-Political Environment," in James David Barber (ed.), *Race for the Presidency* (Englewood Cliffs, N.J.: Prentice-Hall, 1978), pp. 13–14.

13. "Democratic Rules Reform Having Impact on '72 Race," *New York Times* (June 10, 1972).

14. Systematic study of news coverage also shows a pattern highlighting early decisions, as the study based on 1980 data by Michael Robinson and Margaret Sheehan demonstrates. *Over the Wire and on TV* (New York: Russell Sage, forthcoming).

15. "TV's Newest Program: 'The Presidential Nominations Game,' " *Public Opinion* 1 (May–June 1978), pp. 41–46.

16. P.L. 93-443, Section 101 (b) (1): "Except as otherwise provided . . . no person shall make contributions to any candidate with

respect to any election for Federal office which, in the aggregate, exceed $1,000." See also Joel L. Fleishman, "Freedom of Speech and Equality of Political Opportunity: The Constitutionality of the Federal Election Campaign Act of 1971," *The North Carolina Law Review* 51 (January 1973), pp. 389–483; Fleishman, "Public Financing of Election Campaigns: Constitutional Constraints on Steps Toward Equality of Political Influence of Citizens," *ibid.*, 52 (December 1973), pp. 349–416; Michael Gartner, "Campaign Financing: A Dubious Law," *Wall Street Journal* (April 5, 1972).

17. Official Federal Election Commission figures for all 1980 prenomination presidential campaigns show the following distributions of sources of funding:

Table 2.3 Prenomination campaigns, 1980 sources of funding

	Percent of total contributions
Individual contributions	56.5%
Federal matching funds	23.5
Loans	12.3
Refunds	5.0
Political Action Committees	1.2
Other	1.5
	100.0%

	Individual contributions
Less than $500	55.4%
$500–$749	13.0
$750 or more	31.6
	100.0%

Source: Federal Election Commission, *FEC Reports on Financial Activity 1979–1980, Final Report, Presidential Prenomination Campaigns* (Washington, D.C.: Federal Election Commission, October 1981), pp. 1–5.

18. See James I. Lengle, *Representation and Presidential Primaries: The Democratic Party in the Post Reform Era* (Westport, Conn.: Greenwood, 1981), p. 83; Arlen J. Large, "All Those Candidates—Is It a Joke?," *Wall Street Journal* (January 28, 1972).

19. Mark Alan Siegel, "Toward a More Responsible Democratic Party: The Politics of Reform," Ph.D. dissertation, Northwestern University, June 1972, p. 237. Not until 1976, however, were all dele-

gates selected in the state primary. In 1968, 123 delegates had been selected in the June 18 primary, and 65 at-large delegates were selected at the June 28 state Democratic committee meeting. In 1972, 248 delegates were selected in the June 20 primary, and only 28 at-large delegates were selected at the June 24 state committee meeting. In 1976, all 274 delegates were selected in the April 6 state primary election (*Congressional Quarterly Weekly Report* (August 23, 1968), p. 225; (June 24, 1972), p. 1513; and (July 10, 1976), p. 1797).

20. Ranney, *The Federalization of Presidential Primaries*, pp. 2–3.
21. Defenders and critics of the contemporary nomination process are agreed on this point. See Everett Carll Ladd, Jr., *Where Have All the Voters Gone?* (New York: Norton, 1978); Crotty, *Decision for the Democrats;* Ranney, *The Federalization of Presidential Primaries*.
22. The compatibility of this discussion with David Truman's classic treatment of groups in the political process will no doubt be apparent. See Truman, *The Governmental Process* (New York: Knopf, 1951).
23. See Madison, *The Federalist #10* (New York: Modern Library, 1937), pp. 53–62. This is no place to quibble with James Madison, but it does seem that in *Federalist* 10 Madison does not foresee what has in fact occurred: that the constitutional machinery he and his colleagues devised mitigates the effects of faction by requiring factions to enter into coalitions.
24. See V. O. Key, Jr., *Southern Politics* (New York: Knopf, 1950), pp. 259–61; O. Douglas Weeks, "Texas: Land of Conservative Experience," in William C. Havard (ed.), *The Changing Politics of the South* (Baton Rouge: Louisiana State University Press, 1972), pp. 201–30, esp. pp. 212ff.; Eugene W. Jones, Joe E. Ericson, Lyle C. Brown, Robert S. Trotter, Jr., *Practicing Texas Politics* (Boston: Houghton Mifflin, 1974), pp. 74–81.
25. See Duane Lockard, *New England State Politics* (Princeton: Princeton University Press, 1959), pp. 228–319; Joseph I. Lieberman, *The Power Broker* (Boston: Houghton Mifflin, 1966); Joseph P. Lyford, *Candidate,* Eagleton Institute Case #9 (New York: McGraw-Hill, 1960).
26. These are not fictional numbers. Jimmy Carter won 22,875 votes in the 1976 New Hampshire primary, giving him 29.4% of the vote. Morris Udall was second with 23.9% of the vote, or 18,594 votes. One percent of the vote equaled 778 votes. In the 1972 Democratic primary, 1% of the vote equaled 888 votes, and in 1968, 550 votes. For the Republicans the numbers were somewhat

higher: 1040 votes equaled 1% in 1968, 1171 votes in 1972, and 1083 in 1976.

27. Here, for example, is a description of Jimmy Carter's 1976 strategy: "In the simplest terms, the strategy was to show well in the Iowa precinct caucuses on January 19, to stimulate press interest in Carter, and then to spend as much money as could be raised and borrowed—from friendly Atlanta banks and Georgia business interests—to win the New Hampshire and Florida primaries. Despite innumerable reports of Carter master plans and organizational genius, there was no plan and precious little organization after the Florida vote on March 9. The Carters gambled that their early victories would generate fundraising, organizational, and press 'momentum'—the political cliché used to describe what is happening when no one is sure," (Richard Reeves, *Convention* (New York: Harcourt Brace Jovanovich, 1977), p. 180).

Joel McCleary, Carter's national finance director told F. Christopher Arterton: "We had no structure after Florida; we had planned only for the short haul. After Florida, it was all NBC, CBS and the *New York Times*" (Arterton, "Campaign Organizations Confront the Media-Political Environment," in Barber (ed.), *Race for the Presidency*, p. 7).

Hamilton Jordan, in his famous August 4, 1974, memorandum laying out a strategic program for prospective candidate Jimmy Carter wrote:

The prospect of a crowded field coupled with the new proportional representation rule does not permit much flexibility. . . . No serious candidate will have the luxury of picking or choosing among the early primaries. To pursue such a strategy would cost that candidate delegate votes and increase the possibility of being lost in the crowd. I think we have to assume that everybody will be running in the first five or six primaries. A crowded field enhances the possibility of several inconclusive primaries with four or five candidates separated by only a few percentage points. Such a muddled picture will not continue for long as the press will begin to make "winners" of some and "losers" of others. The intense press coverage which naturally focuses on the early primaries plus the decent time intervals which separate the March and mid-April primaries dictates a serious effort in all of the first five primaries. Our "public" strategy would probably be that Florida was the first and real test of the Carter campaign and that New Hampshire would just be a warmup. In fact, a strong, surprise showing in New Hampshire should be our goal which would have tremendous impact on successive primaries. Our minimal goal in these early primaries would be to gain acceptance as a serious and viable candidate, demonstrate that Wallace is vulnerable and that Carter can appeal to the "Wallace" constituency, and show through our campaign a contrasting style and appeal. Our minimal goal would dictate at least a second-place showing in New Hampshire and Florida and respectable showings in Wisconsin, Rhode Island, and Illinois. Our national goals (which I think are highly attainable) would be to win New Hampshire and/or Florida outright, make strong showings in the other three early primary states and beat Wallace. [Martin Schram, *Running for President* (New York: Pocket Books, 1976), pp. 261–62.]

See also Jules Witcover, *Marathon* (New York: Viking Press, 1977). A strategy of differentiation and factional mobilization worked to Lyndon Johnson's advantage in his first election to the House of Representatives, in 1937, as Rowland Evans and Robert Novak describe in *Lyndon B. Johnson: The Exercise of Power* (New York: New American Library, 1966), pp. 7–8.

28. "Democratic Reforms: They Work," *Wall Street Journal* (May 16, 1972).

29. Jack W. Germond and Jules Witcover, *Blue Smoke and Mirrors* (New York: Viking, 1981), p. 96.

30. F. Christopher Arterton, "Campaign Organizations Confront the Media-Political Environment," in Barber (ed.), *Race for the Presidency*, p. 17.

31. Perhaps tradition or the herd insinct among journalists also plays a part; otherwise it is hard to explain the disparity in the coverage of the February 26 primaries in New Hampshire and Minnesota.

32. In 1980, for example, only 9 percent of all uncommitted delegates sent to the Democratic National Convention were selected in primary states and 62 percent of the uncommitted Republicans were from primary states. The numbers of uncommitteds in both cases were very small: 116.1 out of 3,311 Democratic delegates; 101 out of 1,994 Republicans. See Jonathan Moore (ed.), *The Campaign for President* (Cambridge, Mass.: Ballinger, 1981), p. 278.

33. For an early discussion of this phenomenon, see Stanley Kelley, *Professional Public Relations and Political Power* (Baltimore: Johns Hopkins University Press, 1956). See also, Larry J. Sabato, *The Rise of Political Consultants: New Ways of Winning Elections* (New York: Basic Books, 1981).

34. As Fred Barbash and Bill Curry, "Campaign '80: In FEC Maze, Auditors Supplant 'Fat Cats'," *Washington Post* (June 14, 1979) report:

At the George Bush for President headquarters in Houston, a 255-page manual of Federal Election Commission rules and regulations is called "The Bible." It holds all of man's accumulated knowledge on how to get eligible and stay eligible for federal matching presidential campaign funds.

If the manual is "The Bible," the Bush headquarters building itself is a temple to the FEC rules and regulations. The fund-raising operation is segregated on the fifth floor—because fund-raising expenses, including the rent, are to be segregated for FEC campaign expenditure reporting. The operation devoted to winning Texas '80 delegates to the 1980 Republican convention is confined to the third floor—because the state-by-state expenditures must be carefully controlled to avoid exceeding FEC limitations. The national political operation of the Bush campaign is handled separately on the second floor, to avoid commingling it with the other segregated expenditures. . . .

The campaigns have become more like businesses—centralized, heavily regulated, and loaded with accountants—with what many 1980 presidential campaign strategists foresee as a sharp decline in the potential for grass-roots participation and state-by-state flexibility. . . .

Officials from the various campaigns estimate that compliance—accountants to keep the records, computers to check them, copiers to copy them, and lawyers to interpret and (sometimes) get around them—will cost at least $1.5 million per campaign up to the time of the nomination conventions. "By the time the FEC comes in to audit us," said Stan Huckaby, head of an accounting firm that has been retained by Sen. Howard Baker's campaign, "we will have audited ourselves three times. There will be a manual check before it goes into the computer, a check by the computer and another check when it comes out.". . .

As a result, the accountants are likely to have expanded roles in campaign planning. "Before the law," said Huckaby, "the last person they wanted in a room before making a decision was an accountant. Now, the accountant is essential."

35. As Richard B. Cheney, who ran the Ford 1976 campaign rather sardonically put it, compliance with the law may mean a candidate is "better equipped to serve as director of the Office of Management and Budget than President" (Rhodes Cook, "Public Financing Alters Presidential Politics," *Congressional Quarterly Weekly Report* (October 6, 1979), p. 2228).

36. There is, for instance, the great example of Les Biffle, the Democratic secretary of the Senate in the 1950s, who went about the country during the 1948 campaign claiming he was a vacationing chicken farmer in order to take soundings of public opinion. Such a venture would today be regarded as unsystematic (*New York Times* (August 1, 1948), p. 49).

37. Joel Kotkin and Paul Grabowicz, "The New Star Trek: Cashing In on Politics," *Washington Post Outlook* (February 25, 1979):

Prominent among the emerging powers is a strange new breed of Hollywood movie stars and rock singers—not issue-advocates of the Robert Redford, Shirley MacLaine or Marlon Brando variety, but a group whose political talent is simply to raise more campaign cash in a night than others might lure in a year. Indeed, the new group fittingly cares far more about personalities than about issues, if it thinks about issues at all. . . . The growing trek of such stars to political campaigns derives, in large part, from 1974 changes in federal election laws that limited individual campaign contributions to $1,000. "The stars can contribute their services without being deemed as having gone over the $1,000 limit," observes Gray Davis, [Jerry] Brown's chief of staff and manager of his 1978 reelection. "Entertainers can attract contributions, particularly smaller ones, which would otherwise not be available to a candidate," Davis says. "People go to one of our concerts basically to see the Eagles perform. Frankly, we'd have trouble getting one-fifth the people there just to see Jerry.

Michele Willens, "The Hollywood-Washington Connection," *California Journal* (August 1979), pp. 265–68, reports:

In 1976, Jimmy Carter's lack-luster campaign was born again, thanks to a concert by the Allman Brothers. Jerry Brown's brief run for the presidency that same year was substantially funded—about 40 percent—by the entertainment industry.

See also Morton Mintz, "Defeat of PAC Restraints Could Cost Democrats the House in 1982," *Washington Post* (December 25, 1980); Dennis Farney, "A Modern Machine: How Savvy Matt Reese, a Political Consultant, Gets Out Winning Vote," *Wall Street Journal* (March 23, 1972); Theodore H. White, "The Making of the President Ain't What It Used To Be," *Life* (February 1980), pp. 66–80.

38. An example of these efforts would be the requirement that state delegations represent candidates who win even small amounts of support, as the Democrats put into their 1974 (Mikulski Commission) reforms. See David S. Broder, "New Democratic Rules: First Ballot Victory Unlikely," *Washington Post* (March 31, 1974).

39. See the comments of the professional political managers of a large number of 1980 candidates on this point in Jonathan Moore (ed.), *The Campaign for President*, pp. 1–50.

40. In 1980 the Democrats and Republicans together selected 5305 delegates of which exactly 217.1 came to either convention unpledged.

41. In 1976 the Republicans had a disagreement over pledged delegates and in 1980 repealed their requirement that delegates stay committed. Democrats are likely to do the same in 1984.

42. This may have cost the Democrats a seat in Congress at their next opportunity after the 1980 election. The first special Congressional election of the 97th Congress, occasioned by the death of Republican incumbent Tennyson Guyer, was held in June 1981 in the conservative 4th district of Ohio. Even though he was denied any help from the national Democratic party, as required by the resolution banning assistance to candidates refusing to back the ERA, the Democratic candidate, Dale Locker, came within 378 votes of winning the seat (Oxley, R, 41,904 (50.2%); Locker, D, 41,526 (49.8%)). Locker had voted against ERA as a state legislator, and personal convictions aside, must have known that advocating the ERA in the small towns of western Ohio would hurt

him more than national party aid could help. The resolution made it necessary for the party to withhold its aid regardless of the chance of victory.

43. In the Democratic case the rule is given in McGovern guideline 4(c): requiring state parties to "conduct the entire process of delegate selection in a timely manner, i.e., within the calendar year of the convention." In the Republican case the guideline is contained in Rule 31(o):

> No delegate shall be deemed eligible to participate in any district or state convention, the purpose of which is to elect delegates to the said national convention, who were elected prior to the date of issuance of the call of such national convention unless this rule be inconsistent with the law of the state.

The call is usually issued late in the year preceding the convention.

44. In *Cousins v. Wigoda* 419 *U.S.* 417 (1975) and *Democratic Party of U.S. v. La Follette* 67 *L. Ed. 2d* 82 (1981).

45. Richard B. Cheney, "The Law's Impact on Presidential and Congressional Election Campaigns," in Michael J. Malbin (ed.), *Parties, Interest Groups and Campaign Finance Laws* (Washington, D.C.: American Enterprise Institute, 1980), pp. 240–41. See also Bill Keller and Irwin B. Arieff, "As Campaign Costs Sky-Rocket, Lobbyists Take Growing Role in Washington Fund-Raisers," *Congressional Quarterly Weekly Report* (May 17, 1980), pp. 1333–46.

46. During the 1976 presidential election campaign the FEC spent much time and energy deciding three seemingly trivial cases. The judgment receiving the most publicity concerned a campaign button paid for by Rep. Edward Koch's (D-N.Y.) election committee. The button, which featured Koch's name along with Carter and Mondale, was feared by the committee to constitute a contribution to the Carter campaign. The FEC ruled, in a letter to the committee, that the button would not be considered such a contribution.

The FEC dealt with the same basic issue in two other cases. The FEC allowed Rep. Douglas Walgren (D-Pa.) to distribute a brochure containing a picture of the Congressman with Carter without counting it as a contribution to the Carter campaign. Representative Parren J. Mitchell (D-Md.) was not allowed to use an advertisement picturing him with Carter, Mondale, and Senate candidate Paul Sarbanes. The FEC published no reason for the different outcomes.

Michael J. Malbin, "After Surviving Its First Election Year, FEC Is Wary of the Future," *National Journal* (March 26, 1977), pp.

469–73. See also "The Koch Quandary and Other Matters," *ibid.*, p. 471.

47. P.L. 96-187. See Charles W. Hucker, "Congress Fine Tunes Campaign Law," *Congressional Quarterly Weekly Report* (January 5, 1980), p. 31. For an early assessment giving mixed notices, see Xandra Kayden, "Parties and the 1980 Presidential Election," in *Financing Presidential Campaigns* (mimeo), (Institute of Politics, John F. Kennedy School of Government, Harvard University, January 1982), Chapter 6.

48. A monographic treatment of the entire subject is Daniel A. Mazmanian, *Third Parties in Presidential Politics* (Washington, D.C.: Brookings Institution, 1974).

49. *Ibid.*, p. 5, and *Congressional Quarterly* provide useful data on third party presidential voting:

Table 2.7   Third parties in presidential elections receiving more than one percent of the popular vote, 1828–1980

Year	Party	Percentage of total votes cast
1832	Anti-Mason	7.8
1844	Liberty	2.3
1848	Free Soil	10.1
1852	Free Soil	4.9
1856	Whig-American	21.5
1860	Southern Democratic	18.1
	Constitutional Union	12.6
1880	Greenback	3.3
1884	Greenback	1.7
	Prohibition	1.5
1888	Prohibition	2.2
	Union Labor	1.3
1892	Populist	8.5
	Prohibition	2.3
1900	Prohibition	1.5
1904	Socialist	3.0
	Prohibition	1.9
1908	Socialist	2.8
	Prohibition	1.7
1912	Progressive*	27.4
	Socialist	6.0
1916	Socialist	3.2
	Prohibition	1.2
1920	Socialist	3.4

Table 2.7   *(continued)*

Year	Party	Percentage of total votes cast
1924	Progressive	16.6
1932	Socialist	2.2
1936	Union	2.0
1948	States' Rights Democratic	2.4
	Progressive	2.4
1968	American Independent	13.5
1972	American	1.4
1976	Independent (McCarthy)	1.0
1980	Independent (Anderson)	7.0
	Libertarian	1.0

*The vote for the Republican party was 23.2 percent, making the vote of the short-lived Progressive party the second highest of the election.

Sources: Robert A. Diamond (ed.), *Presidential Elections Since 1789* (Washington, D.C.: Congressional Quarterly, Inc., 1975), pp. 65–99; *Congressional Quarterly Weekly Report* (November 6, 1976), p. 3118; and *ibid.* (November 8, 1980), p. 3299. See also Daniel A. Mazmanian, *Third Parties in Presidential Politics* (Washington, D.C.: Brookings Institution, 1974).

50. This can be illustrated with figures for elected officeholders at the state level.

Table 2.8   Proportion of state officials that are either Democrats or Republicans

	Dem	Rep	State legislators % Major party	Others*	%
1959	4813	2510	96.7	250	3.3
1969	4284	3126	96.7	254	3.3
1977	5022	2348	98.3	127	1.7

	Dem	Rep	State executives % Major party	Others*	%
1959	339	96	89.7	50	10.3
1969	236	179	98.1	8	1.9
1977	242	123	97.9	8	2.1

*Other includes minor parties and non-partisan offfices

Sources: Council of State Governments, *The Book of the States*, Supplement I, 1959, Supplement I, 1969, *State Elective Officials and the Legislature, 1977*.

In some local jurisdictions, party designations are forbidden by law to candidates for public office.

51. See Douglas Rae, *The Political Consequences of Election Laws* (New Haven: Yale University Press, 1971).

52. P.L. 93-443, P.L. 94-283. See Stephen E. Gottlieb, "Putting Meaning into the Right of Association: The Job of Political Parties" (mimeo, presented at the American Bar Association's Wingspread Conference on the Presidential Selection Process, Racine, Wis., July 16–18, 1981), pp. 47–53.

53. P.L. 93-443, sec. 9008. See Gottlieb, "Putting Meaning into the Right of Association."

54. See Nicholas Zapple, "Historical Evolution of Section 315," in Austin Ranney (ed.), *The Past and Future of Presidential Debates* (Washington, D.C.: American Enterprise Institute, 1979), pp. 56–74.

55. See Joel Fleishman, "Freedom of Speech"; see also American Bar Association, Special Committee on Election Reform, *Symposium on Campaign Financing Regulation,* Tiburon, Calif., April 25–27, 1975, pp. 5–13; Daniel D. Polsby, *"Buckley v. Valeo:* The Special Nature of Political Speech," *Supreme Court Review* (1976), pp. 1–43; Frank Lynn, "Millionaires Drop Lobbying Unit; Change Laid to Fear of Publicity," *New York Times* (November 19, 1971).

56. On the Anderson campaign, see Dom Bonafede, "Can John Anderson Succeed Where Teddy Roosevelt Failed?" *National Journal* (May 17, 1980), pp. 806–10; Rhodes Cook, "High Hurdles for the Anderson Campaign," *Congressional Quarterly Weekly Report* (May 17, 1980), pp. 1315–18, and "Alternative Party Candidates May Have Substantial Impact on 1980 Presidential Election," *ibid.* (October 18, 1980), pp. 3143–49.

57. Table 2.9 compares the two parties in size.

Table 2.9 Trends in political affiliation: Size of the two parties

	Republican	*Democratic*	*Independent*
1937	34%	50%	16%
1940	38	42	20
1944	39	41	20
1949	32	48	20
1952	34	41	25
1960	30	47	23
1964	25	53	22

Table 2.9   *(continued)*

	Republican	*Democratic*	*Independent*
1968	27	46	27
1972	28	43	29
1975	22	45	33
1980 (Apr–Jun)	23	47	30
1980 (Oct–Dec)	26	43	31

Source: *The Gallup Opinion Index,* Report No. 183 (December 1980), p. 64.

On the issue of cohesion there are considerable data comparing Democrats and Republicans on a variety of issues but a full-blown examination of the proposition that Democrats are, on the whole, more dispersed in their political attitudes than Republicans does not seem to have been conducted.

One simple measure of dispersion, the standard deviation, when applied to Democratic and Republican respondents to the 1972 University of Michigan Center for Political Studies election study on twelve issues spanning a wide gamut of concerns showed Democrats more dispersed on all twelve, as Table 2.10 indicates:

Table 2.10   Dispersion of attitudes comparing Democrats and Republicans across a seven-point scale, 1972

	Standard deviation	
Issue	*Democrats*	*Republicans*
1. Liberal/Conservative Self-Identification	1.281	1.134
2. Government Aid to Minorities	2.079	1.752
3. Rights of the Accused	2.169	2.011
4. Women's Equality	2.286	2.227
5. Government Fight Air Pollution	1.921	1.879
6. Government Health Insurance	2.445	2.291
7. Busing for Integration	1.893	1.196
8. Legalize Marijuana	2.249	1.989
9. Government Action on Inflation	1.549	1.492
10. Vietnam Withdrawal	1.922	1.798
11. Progressive Income Tax	2.390	2.231
12. Government Job Guarantees	2.064	1.818

Source: Center for Political Studies, University of Michigan

The differences in the numbers do not look enormous, but it should be remembered that the dispersion of the entire populations of Democrats and Republicans can only occur over a range of seven points for each, and consequently small differences in standard deviations do signify differences that deserve to be taken seriously.

Rough confirmation of the overall conclusion is provided by a CBS News/*New York Times* survey in the spring of 1981 on ten different issues. Here rank and file Democrats were less dispersed than Republicans on four issues (Equal Rights Amendment, Allow Abortions with Doctor's Consent, Government Spending on Job Programs, Aid to the Arts) and more dispersed on six (Government Spending on Military-Defense, and on Food Stamps, Reagan's Tax Cut, Prayer Amendment, Government Regulation of Business). See Martin Plissner and Warren Mitofsky, "Political Elites," *Public Opinion,* October/November 1981, 49.

In general, dispersion among Democrats, cohesion among Republicans, appear to be what politicians and journalists have commonly believed about the two parties over the last generation or so. An example of this sort of sentiment is expressed in Dean Acheson, *A Democrat Looks at His Party* (New York: Harper, 1955), pp. 23–27:

From the very beginning, the Democratic party has been broadly based . . . It has been the party of the many . . . They have many interests, many points of view, many purposes to accomplish . . . It is this multiplicity of interests which . . . is the principal clue in understanding the vitality and endurance of the Democratic party. The economic base and the principal interest of the Republican party is business . . . Here lies the significant difference between the parties, the single-interest party against the many-interest party.

This conclusion in its general outline does not seem to be a matter of much partisan controversy. John Bibby, an active Republican political scientist, has recently referred to the "intense ideological faction within the more ideologically homogeneous GOP, the conservatives" ("Party Renewal in the National Republican Party," in Pomper (ed.), *Party Renewal in America,* p. 106), and Charles O. Jones, in his excellent book *The Republican Party in American Politics* (New York: Macmillan, 1965), chafes only slightly at the party-of-business label (p. 3) while firmly identifying the Republicans as the smaller, minority party. See also Gallup Report no. 194 (November 1981), pp. 29–45, which shows Democrats greatly outnumbering Republicans (45 percent to 27 percent). The Democratic party is also identified by Gallup survey respondents as favoring farmers, skilled workers, unskilled workers, labor union members, blacks, small business people, women, unemployed people, young people, retired people and "the average citizen." The Republicans were identified as better for upper income people, corporation executives, professional and business people, and (narrowly) white collar workers.

The plausibility of the claim that the two parties are indeed different is greatly strengthened by elite studies such as David R. Mayhew's *Party Loyalty Among Congressmen: The Difference Between Democrats and Republicans 1947–1962* (Cambridge, Mass: Harvard University Press, 1966). Mayhew's conclusion is that the Republicans in the House during the period he studied adhered to a policy of ideological cohesion and commitment to conservative principles, voting against their party colleagues who pursued purely district interests on individual issues. The Democrats, on the other hand, voted in favor of the entire range of particular interests put forward by their various factions, and maintained a broadly "inclusive" coalition.

Table 2.11 gives recent information on the House of Representatives, and shows Democrats far more dispersed across the available ideological alternatives than Republicans:

Table 2.11   Ideological divisions in the House, 86th Congress, 1st Session (1959) and 95th Congress, 1st Session (1977)

	Democrats		*Republicans*	
86th Congress				
Liberals	51%	(142)	4%	(6)
Moderates	13	(37)	15	(23)
Conservatives	36	(102)	81	(124)
95th Congress				
Liberals	50%	(145)	1%	(2)
Moderates	30	(86)	20	(29)
Conservatives	20	(57)	79	(115)

Source: Lawrence C. Dodd and Bruce I. Oppenheimer, "The House in Transition: Change and Consolidation," in Dodd and Oppenheimer (eds.), *Congress Reconsidered* (Washington, D.C.: Congressional Quarterly, 1981), p. 35.

Finally, a recent study of political elites by CBS News shows a less dramatic, but generally consistent pattern:

Table 2.12 Distributions of Democrats and Republicans by ideology

	Rank and file		National committee members		1980 National convention delegates	
	Dem.	*Rep.*	*Dem.*	*Rep.*	*Dem.*	*Rep.*
Liberal	24%	11%	36%	1%	46%	2%
Moderate	42	33	51	31	42	36
Conservative	29	51	4	63	6	58

Source: Martin Plissner and Warren Mitofsky, "Political Elites," *Public Opinion* (October/November 1981), pp. 47–48.

On the ten issues covered in the CBS poll, Democratic National Committee members were more dispersed in their opinions than Republican National Committee members on all issues except the School Prayer Amendment, E.R.A., and Abortions with Doctor's Consent (Plissner and Mitofsky, Table III, p. 49).

58. See Hugh A. Bone, *Party Committees and National Politics* (Seattle: University of Washington Press, 1958); Cornelius P. Cotter and Bernard C. Hennessy, *Politics Without Power* (New York: Atherton Press, 1964); John F. Bibby, "Party Renewal in the National Republican Party," in Pomper (ed.), *Party Renewal in America;* and Cornelius P. Cotter and John F. Bibby, "Institutional Development of Parties and the Thesis of Party Decline," *Political Science Quarterly* 95 (Spring 1980), pp. 1–27.

59. See Thomas E. Mann and Norman J. Ornstein, "The Republican Surge in Congress," in Ranney (ed.), *The American Elections of 1980*, pp. 263–302, esp. pp. 263–67; John F. Bibby, "Party Renewal in the National Republican Party," in Pomper (ed.), *Party Renewal in America;* Cotter and Bibby, "Institutional Development of Parties and the Thesis of Party Decline," esp. pp. 18–19.

60. Compare, for evidence, the disparities between party identifications as monitored by public opinion surveys and party presidential vote:

Table 2.13 Party identification compared with party
presidential vote

	Dem. % of party ID	Dem. % of pres. vote	Difference	Rep. % of party ID	Rep. % of pres. vote	Difference
1968	55	43	−12	33	43	+10
1972	51	38	−13	34	61	+27
1976	52	50	−02	33	48	+15
1980	52	41	−11	33	51	+18

Source: Center for Political Studies, University of Michigan. (Independent leaners included with the party toward which they lean.)

61. This notion is argued at length in Nelson W. Polsby, "What If Robert Kennedy Had Not Been Assassinated in 1968," in Polsby (ed.), *What If? Explorations in Social Science Fiction* (Lexington, Mass: Lewis Publishing Co., forthcoming).

62. Much evidence on this point can be found in Jeane Kirkpatrick, "Representation in the American National Conventions: The Case of 1972," *British Journal of Political Science* 5 (July 1975), pp. 265–322. In 1972, even delegates to the Republican National Convention were more representative of the views of rank-and-file Democrats than were McGovern delegates to the Democratic convention (Tables 9–10, pp. 304–5).

63. See Table 2.9 above.

64. On the reasons for defection: one year in recent history, 1952, seems to have featured more Republican "pull" than Democratic "push," for defecting Democrats. See Herbert H. Hyman and Paul B. Sheatsley, "The Political Appeal of President Eisenhower," *Public Opinion Quarterly* 1 (Winter 1955–56), pp. 26–39. For the elections since 1968, most defecting Democrats appear to have been more at odds with the Democratic candidate than pleased with the Republican alternative. For 1972, see Jeane Kirkpatrick, "Representation in the American National Conventions: The Case of 1972"; Arthur H. Miller, Warren E. Miller, Alden S. Raine, and Thad A. Brown, "A Majority Party in Disarray: Policy Polarization in the 1972 Election," *American Political Science Review* 70 (September 1976), pp. 73–78; George Gallup, "Democratic Defections Expected To Shatter Voting Patterns," *Washington Post* (October 19, 1972); Haynes Johnson, "Vital Bloc Breaks Democratic Ties," *Washington Post* (October 8, 1972); Richard Harwood, " 'Ethnics' Alienated by Forces of Change," *Washington Post* (October 9, 1972).

For 1980, see Adam Clymer, "The Democrats Look For New Ideas, and Jobs," *New York Times* (November 9, 1980); Clymer, "Displeasure with Carter Turned Many to Reagan," *ibid.;* and especially William Schneider, "The November 4 Vote for President: What Did It Mean?" in Ranney (ed.), *The American Elections of 1980,* pp. 212–62.

65. See Everett Carll Ladd, Jr., "The Brittle Mandate: Electoral Dealignment and the 1980 Presidential Election," *Political Science Quarterly* 96 (Spring 1981), pp. 1–25; also Adam Clymer, "Displeasure with Carter Turned Many to Reagan"; and data in *Public Opinion* (December/January 1981), p. 43; Arthur Miller, "What Mandate? What Realignment?" *Washington Post Outlook* (June 28, 1981); Louis Harris, "No Mandate for a Switch on Social Questions Seen," *Washington Post* (December 4, 1980); George Skelton, "Conservative Mandate for Reagan Contains Limits," *Los Angeles Times* (November 20, 1980); *Public Opinion* (December/January 1981), pp. 24–25.

66. See Table 2.9 above.

67. In 1980, as in the previous fifteen congressional elections, more people voted for Democratic than for Republican House candidates. The popular vote for House candidates in 1980 was 51 percent Democratic, 48 percent Republican (*Public Opinion* (December/January), p. 24). Even after the 1980 elections, Democrats controlled almost twice the number of state legislative houses nationwide (63/34), and far more Democrats than Republicans sat as members of state legislatures. The figures are: Democratic members, 4,497; Republican members, 2,918 (*ibid.,* p. 25). And although the Republicans won more senatorial elections in 1980 this result was achieved without a Republican landslide in the popular vote. Without counting votes cast for the unopposed Democratic Senator from Louisiana, Russell Long, almost 3 million more people voted for Democratic candidates for the Senate than voted for Republicans. Republicans won 21 out of the 33 Senate seats up for a decision in 1980, but mostly by small margins. Of the fifteen races where the winner won by the biggest margins, nine were won by Democrats. See Nelson W. Polsby, "Party Realignment in the 1980 Election," *Yale Review* (Fall 1982).

68. Chicago Mayor Richard J. Daley, who had been ejected as a delegate from the Democratic convention of 1972, even though he and his slate had won their places in the Illinois primary, gave his last hurrah in 1976 when far in advance of the convention he threw in the towel and endorsed Jimmy Carter. On June 8, 1976,

when Carter had 38 percent of the delegates then allocated, Mayor Daley said, "This man, Carter, has fought in every primary, and if he wins in Ohio, he'll walk in under his own power." See Jules Witcover, *Marathon*, p. 349. Carter won in Ohio but on the same day lost in New Jersey and California. The final primary elections of June 9 gave Carter 39 percent of the total delegates. The remaining 61 percent were widely spread, including an uncommitted 18 percent. See Donald R. Matthews, "Winnowing," in J. D. Barber (ed.), *Race for the Presidency*, p. 72, Table 3.

Chapter III: Consequences for Governing

1. Two good overviews giving twentieth-century historical background on cabinet selection up to the Eisenhower administration are Richard F. Fenno, Jr., *The President's Cabinet* (Cambridge, Mass.: Harvard University Press, 1959) and Laurin L. Henry, *Presidential Transitions* (Washington, D.C.: Brookings Institution, 1960).

2. Neither, in Carter's case, did his campaign rhetoric. See Jack Knott and Aaron Wildavsky, "Jimmy Carter's Theory of Governing," *The Wilson Quarterly* 1 (Winter 1977), pp. 49–67, for an excellent preview of the concerns of the Carter presidency based on his campaign rhetoric.

3. For an account of the collective activities of the cabinet in Eisenhower's first term see Robert L. Donovan, *Eisenhower: The Inside Story* (New York: Harper, 1956).

4. Douglass Cater, "A New Style, a New Tempo," *The Reporter* (March 16, 1961), pp. 28–30.

5. A number of important issues are involved in the appointment of an attorney general, including the management of criminal indictments, appointments to the judiciary, and oversight of the activities of the FBI. Some of these issues cut unusually close to the political interests of Presidents, a fact that was not lost on Kennedy so soon after the difficulties, small-scale scandals, and embarrassments that had necessitated an appointment of a special prosecutor and the replacement of one attorney general in the Truman administration. See Cabell Phillips, *The Truman Presidency* (New York: Macmillan, 1966), pp. 403–14; and Jules Abels, *The Truman Scandals* (Chicago: Henry Regnery Co., 1956). For an account of Robert Kennedy's performance as attorney general see Victor Navasky, *Kennedy Justice* (New York: Atheneum, 1971). Other relevant works on John Kennedy and his cabinet include Adam Yarmolinsky, "The Kennedy Talent Hunt," *The Reporter*

(June 8, 1961), pp. 22–25, and Richard F. Fenno, Jr., "The Cabinet: Index to the Kennedy Way," *New York Times Magazine* (April 23, 1962), pp. 13ff.

6. An account of President Nixon's administrative goals and activities early in his Presidency is contained in Rowland Evans and Robert Novak, *Nixon in the White House: The Frustration of Power* (New York: Random House, 1971). It is useful to contrast Richard Nathan's *The Plot That Failed: Nixon and the Administrative Presidency* (New York: John Wiley, 1975), written from the perspective of later events.

7. On Nixon's first reorganization, see Evans and Novak, *Nixon in the White House*, pp. 237–41.

8. On Nixon and labor, see the following more or less representative news stories: Richard J. Levine, "Labor Taking a Tougher Line with Nixon," *Wall Street Journal* (February 20, 1970); Byron E. Calame, "Nixon-Labor Rift: Back to Normal," *ibid.* (August 24, 1971); "Nixon and the Unions: Can the 'Honeymoon' Last?," *U.S. News & World Report* (April 21, 1969), pp. 82–84; "Unions Open Fire on Nixon over Jobs, Civil Rights," *ibid.* (March 9, 1970), pp. 69–70; "George Meany Cuts His Ties with the White House," *ibid.* (September 10, 1973), pp. 78–79; "Meany Steps Up His War on Richard Nixon," *ibid.* (October 29, 1973), pp. 90–91; James M. Naughton, "President Asks Labor's Support; Reception Is Cool," *New York Times* (November 20, 1971); Philip Shabecoff, "Leader of Labor Declares Nixon Sought Incident," *ibid.* (November 23, 1971); Shabecoff, "Union Chiefs See New Meany Role," *ibid.* (November 24, 1971); Naughton, "Nixon Focusing on Meany as Likely Campaign Target," *ibid.* (November 25, 1971); George Meany, "Labor and Nixon," *The American Federationist* (December 1971), pp. 2–8; Meany, "A Dark Shadow of Shame over the Spirit of America," *ibid.* (November 1973), pp. 2–6. See also Peter Brennan's *Current Biography* entry, 1973, pp. 59–62.

9. On Nixon and the scientific community, see, for example, Daniel S. Greenberg, "Science Under Nixon: Influence Has Declined in National Affairs," *Science* 169 (September 11, 1970), pp. 1056–57. Greenberg says (p. 1056): "The scientific presence in Washington that grew up after World War II was never so potent as alarmed political traditionalists made it out to be; nor was it ever so unheeded and abused as many scientists made it out to be. But a look into science's Washington outposts after 2 years' absence quickly confirmed my impression that, however powerful the community may once have been in national affairs, 20 months under Nixon have inflicted upon it a gigantic loss of influence,

visibility, and confidence. . . . [T]here is little to suggest that the
President accords scientific activity any special or privileged role
in national life, and there is a good deal to suggest that the President, as well as many of his closest advisers, regard the scientific
community as having succeeded in making unwarranted claims on
national resources and political sympathy." See also "Nixon on
Science," *ibid.* 174 (October 29, 1971), p. 477; "White House Presents Vapid Technology Plan," *ibid.* 175 (March 24, 1972), p. 1343;
"Congress Holds Down NSF Budget; Nixon Vetoes HEW Bill,"
ibid. 177 (September 1, 1972), p. 775; "OMB: Hand in the Till or
on the Tiller?," *ibid.* 179 (March 2, 1973), p. 879; and Deborah
Shapley, "White House Science: Hail and Farewell," *ibid.* 179
(March 30, 1973). On Nixon and education, see "Battle Looms
over Funds for Education," *The Chronicle of Higher Education* 4
(January 26, 1970); and Cheryl M. Fields, "Nixon's Legislative
Plans Called Little Help to Colleges," *ibid.* 4 (May 18, 1970).

10. The tip of the iceberg was revealed in a story in the normally
prosaic, civil service routine-oriented *Federal Times,* Inderjit Badh-
wan, "Government-wide Patronage Deals" (September 25, 1974).
See also *Documents Relating to Political Influence in Personnel Actions
at the Department of Housing and Urban Development,* published by
the Subcommittee on Manpower and Civil Service of the House
of Representatives Committee on Post Office and Civil Service,
December 12, 1974 (Washington, D.C.: U.S. Government Printing
Office, 1974), and Dom Bonafede, "Nixon Personnel Staff Works
To Restructure Federal Policies," *National Journal* (November 12,
1971), pp. 2440–48. On July 19, 1973, the *Washington Post* published a list of 94 persons formerly employed in Mr. Nixon's 1972
campaign effort or on the White House staff who had been de-
ployed out into cabinet departments or regulatory agencies. This
was characterized as a "partial list." Additional discussion of the
public administration problems of the Nixon Presidency together
with documentation, is contained in Subcommittee on Manpower
and Civil Service, *Final Report on Violations and Abuses of Merit Principles in Federal Employment* (Washington, D.C.: U.S. House of Representatives Committee on Post Office and Civil Service, December 30, 1976). See also Richard Nathan, *The Plot That Failed.*

11. For a famous discussion of the theory underlying this view see
Woodrow Wilson, *Congressional Government* (New York: Meridian,
1956; first published 1885).

12. See Lou Cannon, "OEO Chief Savors Shutdown," *Washington Post*
(February 4, 1973); Jules Witcover, "OEO Dismantlers Proceed

with Speed, Zeal: Fear, Rumors Plague Staff," *Washington Post* (February 17, 1973); and Austin Scott, "Plans To Neutralize Hill Revealed," *ibid.*

13. See in general, Richard P. Nathan, Allen D. Manvel, Susannah E. Calkins, and associates, *Monitoring Revenue Sharing* (Washington, D.C.: Brookings Institution, 1975); and Charles L. Schultze, Edward R. Fried, Alice M. Rivlin, and Nancy H. Teeters, *Setting National Priorities: The 1972 Budget* (Washington, D.C.: Brookings Institution, 1971), pp. 134–57.

14. ". . . the growth of the Executive Office of the President was relatively constant, until the late 1960s when the annual growth rate doubled; . . . with the advent of the Nixon Administration the growth rate increased almost 400% over the last part of the Johnson Administration" (U.S. House of Representatives, Committee on Post Office and Civil Service, *A Report on the Growth of the Executive Office of the President, 1955–1973* (Washington, D.C.: Government Printing Office, 1972), p. 3). See also Evans and Novak, *Nixon in the White House,* pp. 237–41. On impoundment, see Louis Fisher, *Presidential Spending Power* (Princeton: Princeton University Press, 1975), pp. 147–74, 175–201. In a January 31, 1973, news conference, Nixon claimed "the constitutional right for the President of the United States to impound funds . . . is absolutely clear . . . I will not spend money if the Congress overspends, and I will not be for programs that will raise the taxes and put a bigger burden on the already overburdened American taxpayer" ("Transcript of the President's News Conference on Foreign and Domestic Matters," *New York Times,* February 1, 1973).

15. The press release proclaiming the reorganization is dated January 5, 1973, to coincide with the beginning of Mr. Nixon's second term. Useful background material is contained in *Papers Relating to the President's Departmental Reorganization Program: A Reference Compilation* (Washington, D.C.: Government Printing Office, 1972). The reorganization plan never took effect.

16. For an expansion of this point, see Nelson W. Polsby, *Political Promises* (New York: Oxford University Press, 1974), pp. 6–14.

17. As the author of the *Federalist* 51—either Hamilton or Madison—put the matter: "To what expedient, then, shall we finally resort, for maintaining in practice the necessary partition of power among the several departments, as laid down in the Constitution? . . . [B]y so contriving the interior structure of the government as that its several constituent parts may, by their mutual relations, be the means of keeping each other in their proper places." For more

modern accounts see Richard E. Neustadt, *Presidential Power* (New York: Wiley, 1980); E. Pendleton Herring, *The Politics of Democracy* (New York: Holt, 1940); and Herbert Agar, *The Price of Union* (Boston: Houghton Mifflin, 1950).

18. Leader of this fashion, as of so many, was Arthur Schlesinger, Jr., *The Imperial Presidency* (Boston: Houghton Mifflin, 1973), p. 405. See also Theodore Sorenson, *Watchmen in the Night* (Cambridge, Mass.: MIT Press, 1975).

19. See Herbert Y. Schandler, *The Unmaking of a Presidency: Lyndon Johnson and Vietnam* (Princeton, N.J.: Princeton University Press, 1977), pp. 256–65, and Clark Clifford, "Vietnam Reappraised: The Personal History of One Man's View and How It Evolved," *Foreign Affairs* 47 (July 1969), pp. 601–22.

20. Perhaps the most remarkable modern exception is Lawrence O'Brien of Springfield, Massachusetts, who began his Washington career as John F. Kennedy's chief of legislative liaison and stayed on to become postmaster general under Lyndon Johnson and do two stints as chairman of the Democratic National Committee. His metamorphosis from JFK's patronage assistant and ambassador to Capitol Hill to Washington careerist got him in great trouble with other Kennedy loyalists. O'Brien says: "My decision to stay [in the Johnson White House] came at about the time that . . . others of the Kennedy team were leaving the government, and there was some bitterness at my staying. . . . I knew that some of them hated my guts for staying with Lyndon Johnson" (Lawrence F. O'Brien, *No Final Victories* (Garden City, N.Y.: Doubleday, 1974), p. 180).

21. Safire, *Before the Fall* (Garden City, N.Y.: Doubleday, 1975), pp. 250–62.

22. John Pierson, "The Job Is Demanding, But the Little Extras Ease a President's Lot," *Wall Street Journal* (April 4, 1969).

23. Bob Woodward and Carl Bernstein, *The Final Days* (New York: Simon and Schuster, 1976), p. 344, describe a scene in the White House on August 2, 1974: "The air conditioner was on high and, as usual, a fire was burning in the fireplace." Washington summers are not noted for their brisk weather.

24. See Richard E. Neustadt, *Presidential Power* (New York: John Wiley, 1980).

25. See Raymond E. Wolfinger, "Why Political Machines Have Not Withered Away and Other Revisionist Thoughts," *Journal of Politics* 34 (May 1972), pp. 365–98; Milton L. Rakove, *Don't Make No Waves—Don't Back No Losers* (Bloomington: Indiana University Press, 1975); and Fred I. Greenstein, *The American Party System and*

the American People (Englewood Cliffs, N.J.: Prentice-Hall, 1963).

26. Richard F. Fenno, Jr., *The President's Cabinet* (Cambridge, Mass.: Harvard University Press, 1959), is especially good at exploring the problem of competence versus other values in cabinet formation.

27. Biographical material on the Carter cabinet can be found in the *Congressional Quarterly* publication *President Carter* (Washington, D.C.: Congressional Quarterly, April 1977), pp. 22–43, and in *Current Biography* under alphabetical listings for 1977, except for Zbigniew Brzezinski, 1970, pp. 53–55; Patricia Harris, 1965, pp. 189–91; James Schlesinger, 1973, pp. 379–81; Charles L. Schultze, 1970, pp. 379–81; and Stansfield Turner, 1978, pp. 431–34. General commentary on President Carter's cabinet-building activity includes David Cohen, "Carter Has a Clear Field in Filling Jobs," *Los Angeles Times* (November 12, 1976); Karen Elliott House, "Seek and Ye Shall Find: Well Maybe Not So in Carter's Regime," *Wall Street Journal* (February 2, 1977); Alan L. Otten, "Politics & People: First Notices," *Wall Street Journal* (February 17, 1977); Leslie H. Gelb, "Carter Finding Few Outsiders," *New York Times* (December 15, 1976); Helen Dewar and Hobart Rowen, "Carter in No Hurry on Cabinet Selections," *Washington Post* (December 5, 1976); and Bruce Adams and Kathryn Kavanagh-Baran, *Promise and Performance* (Lexington, Mass.: Lexington Books, 1979).

28. See Laurence Stern, "Young: 'Point Man' for New Policy," *Washington Post* (March 13, 1977); William Greider, "Trilateralists To Abound in Carter's White House," *Washington Post* (January 16, 1977); Alan Baron, "Special Report: Carter's Foreign Policy Appointments," *The Baron Report* (January 25, 1977).

29. Bergland grew up on a Minnesota farm and graduated from the University of Minnesota School of Agriculture. He was a field representative for the Minnesota Farmers' Union before buying a farm of his own in 1950. During the 1960s he was a regional official of the Department of Agriculture's Agricultural Stabilization and Conservation Service. In 1970 he was elected to Congress and served on the House Agriculture Committee.

30. See Margot Hornblower, "A New Breed Shakes Old Order at Interior Dept.," *Washington Post* (April 3, 1977).

31. President Carter seems to have been determined to give this particular position to a woman. Mrs. Kreps was appointed after Jane Cahill Pfeiffer turned the job down.

32. Patricia Roberts Harris, Brock Adams, and Joseph Califano.

33. See Joseph Califano, *Governing America* (New York: Simon and

Schuster, 1981). Mrs. Harris replaced Califano as Secretary of Health, Education and Welfare. Califano quotes President Carter at the time of the shake-up that removed him from office and sent Mrs. Harris to HEW as telling a cabinet meeting to evaluate all the assistant secretaries in their departments and "get rid of all those who are incompetent except minorities and women" (p. 431). See also Herman Nickel, "Carter's Cactus Flower at HUD," *Fortune* (November 6, 1978), pp. 110–13.

34. Bert Lance, budget director; Griffin Bell, attorney general; and Andrew Young, ambassador to the U.N. Each returned to Georgia following his tour of duty with the Carter administration.

35. Admiral Stansfield Turner, CIA director.

36. See Jack Nelson, "Cabinet Choices Disappoint Some of Carter's Backers," *Los Angeles Times* (December 26, 1976); Edward Walsh, "Costanza Defends Carter on Recruitment of Women," *Washington Post* (January 28, 1977); Fred L. Zimmerman, "Carter's Cabinet: A Johnsonian Mix of Old Faces," *Wall Street Journal* (December 27, 1976); Edward Walsh, "Financial Data Are Released for Cabinet, Four Aides," *Washington Post* (February 26, 1977); David S. Broder, "No New 'Generation of Leaders'," *Washington Post* (December 24, 1976); Roger Morris, "Jimmy Carter's Ruling Class," *Harper's* (October 1977); Adams and Kavanagh-Baran, *Promise and Performance.*

37. As Robert Axelrod demonstrated in his "1976 Update," *American Political Science Review* 72 (June 1978), pp. 622–24, to his valuable "Where the Votes Come From" series, which began in the *American Political Science Review* 66 (March 1972), pp. 11–20. Axelrod says (p. 622), "For the Democrats, the New Deal coalition made a comeback in 1976. . . . The Democrats got a majority of the votes from each of the six diverse minorities which make up their traditional coalition: the poor, blacks, union families, Catholics, southerners, and city dwellers."

38. See Elizabeth Drew, "Our Far-Flung Correspondents: Settling In," *The New Yorker* (February 28, 1977), pp. 82–88.

39. News accounts of the extraordinary relations between President Carter and Congress are legion, and can be found for each year of his incumbency, as this sampling will attest: *1976:* Richard Harwood, "Gaffes, Strategy Errors Whittled Carter's Big Lead," *Washington Post* (November 4, 1976); *1977:* Martin Tolchin, "Byrd, Hinting Strained Relations, Says Carter Fails To Seek Advice," *New York Times* (January 27, 1977); Elizabeth Drew, "Settling In"; Dennis Farney, "Jimmy Carter and the Insiders," *Wall Street Jour-*

nal (April 11, 1977); Norman C. Miller, "Carter Not Playing by the Unwritten Rules of the Game," *Wall Street Journal* (April 22, 1977); Adam Clymer, "Carter's Woes with Congress," *New York Times* (June 2, 1977); Graham Hovey, "Congress and Foreign Policy: Snags in Both Houses Indicate Administration Is Not Handling Legislative Relations Properly," *New York Times* (June 22, 1977); *1978:* "His Mood at Mid-Term," *Newsweek* (August 28, 1978), pp. 20–21. *1979:* Meg Greenfield, "What Carter Thinks He's Doing," *Newsweek* (February 26, 1979), p. 100; Steven V. Roberts, "Carter, at Midterm, Is Still 'Outsider' to Many in Congress," *New York Times* (March 7, 1979); Martin Schram, "Carter's Chief Opponent in '80 Campaign May Be Congress," *Washington Post* (May 21, 1979); Steven V. Roberts, "Carter and the Congress: Doubt and Distrust Prevail," *New York Times* (August 5, 1979); Martin Tolchin, "Slow Improvement Is Seen in White House Relations with Congress," *New York Times* (November 26, 1979); *1980:* Jack Anderson, "The Gang That Thought Mineta Was Italian," *Washington Post* (May 25, 1980); Albert R. Hunt, "Carter's Congressional Record," *Wall Street Journal* (September 2, 1980); Irwin B. Arieff, "President Remains an Outsider: Carter-Congress Relations Still Strained Despite Gains," *Congressional Quarterly* (October 11, 1980), pp. 3095–3102.

The tenor of these public stories was amply confirmed in private conversation by members of Congress, notably by members ideologically in overwhelming agreement with the President. An excellent overview of Jimmy Carter's difficulties with the Washington community and especially Congress is Haynes Johnson's *In the Absence of Power* (New York: Viking, 1980). See also Betty Glad, *Jimmy Carter: In Search of the Great White House* (New York: Norton, 1980), for example, p. 420.

40. As the authoritative *CQ Almanac* said:

> [T]he first session of the 89th, starting early and working late, . . . passed more major legislation than most Congresses pass in two sessions. The scope of the legislation was even more impressive than the number of major new laws. Measures which, taken alone, would have crowned the achievements of any Congress, were enacted in a seemingly endless stream.
>
> The pace of the session was so breathless as to cause a major revision of the image, widely prevalent in preceding years, of Congress as structurally incapable of swift decision, prone to frustrate demands for progress. The change was due to three primary factors not always present in past years: The decisive Democratic majorities elected in 1964, the personal leadership of President Johnson, and the shaping of legislation to obtain maximum political support in Congress.

"Congress 1965—The Year in Review," *Congressional Quarterly Almanac* 21 (Washington, D.C.: Congressional Quarterly, 1965), p. 65.

41. See Norman J. Ornstein, Robert L. Peabody, and David W. Rohde, "The Contemporary Senate: Into the 1980s," in Lawrence C. Dodd and Bruce I. Oppenheimer (eds.), *Congress Reconsidered* (Washington, D.C.: Congressional Quarterly Press, 1981), pp. 13–30; and Norman J. Ornstein and David W. Rohde, "Shifting Forces, Changing Rules, and Political Outcomes: The Impact of Congressional Change on Four House Committees," in Robert L. Peabody and Nelson W. Polsby (eds.), *New Perspectives on the House of Representatives*, 3rd edition (Chicago: Rand McNally, 1977), pp. 186–269.

42. Lance Morrow, "A Cry for Leadership," *Time* (August 6, 1979), p. 25. For similar sentiments, see "A More Independent-Minded Institution: House, Senate Chiefs Attempt To Lead a Changed Congress," *Congressional Quarterly* (September 13, 1980), pp. 2695–2700.

43. Rayburn died November 16, 1961. During the 89th Congress, which lasted from January 1965 to December 1967, the Speaker was John W. McCormack of Massachusetts.

44. As Table 3.3 shows:

Table 3.3 Presidential strength in congressional districts, 1960–76

Year	Number of districts carried by President[a]	President's vote compared with vote for his party's successful house candidates		
		President ran ahead	President ran behind	
1960	204 (Kennedy)	22	243	(Democrats)
1964	375 (Johnson)	134[b]	158[b]	(Democrats)
1972	377 (Nixon)	104	88	(Republicans)
1976	220 (Carter)	22	270	(Democrats)

[a] Refers to the winning presidential candidate in each election.
[b] Does not include two districts where the percentage of the total district vote won by House members equaled the percentage of the total district vote won by the President.

Sources: Compiled from information in the *Congressional Quarterly Weekly Report*, Vol. 36 (April 22, 1978), p. 972; and *1967 Congressional Quarterly Almanac*.

This table is adapted from John F. Bibby, Thomas E. Mann, Norman J. Ornstein, *Vital Statistics on Congress, 1980* (Washington, D.C.: American Enterprise Institute, 1980), p. 20.

See also Hedrick Smith, "Congress and Carter: An Uneasy Adjustment," *New York Times* (February 18, 1977); David S. Broder, "Kirbo Expects Carter To Have 'Problem' on Hill," *Washington Post* (February 22, 1977).

45. Ben W. Heineman, Jr., and Curtis A. Hessler, *Memorandum for the President* (New York: Random House, 1980), p. xix.

46. See Eric L. Davis, "Legislative Reform and the Decline of Presidential Influence on Capitol Hill," *British Journal of Political Science* 9 (October 1979), pp. 465–79.

47. On access to Carter, see Eric L. Davis, "Legislative Liaison in the Carter Administration," *Political Science Quarterly* 95 (Summer 1979), pp. 287–301. See also Spencer Rich, "Shakedown Cruise: Carter's Hill Liaison Had Rough Sailing But Frank Moore Sees Smoother Seas," *Washington Post* (February 25, 1977).

48. Davis, "Legislative Liaison," pp. 288–89.

49. As Haynes Johnson recounts: "One day in December 1976, in Plains, Tip O'Neill told Carter: 'Mr. President, I want you to understand something. Some of the brightest men in America are in this Congress of the United States. Don't make the mistake of underestimating them. They've been there for years, and on any specific piece of legislation they know why every comma, every semicolon, every period is there. We want to work together, but I have a feeling you are underestimating the feeling of Congress and you could have some trouble.' Carter instantly replied: 'I'll handle them just as I handled the Georgia legislature. Whenever I had problems with the Georgia legislature I took the problems to the people of Georgia'" (*In the Absence of Power* (New York: Viking, 1980), p. 22).

50. Steven V. Roberts, "Carter Discord with Congress: President Is Apparently Seeking To Ease Strains," *New York Times* (June 5, 1979; See also Edward Walsh, " 'The Buck Stops Here': Carter Relishes Truman's Slogan," *Washington Post* (April 25, 1977); David S. Broder, "Why Carter Is Hanging Tough," *Washington Post* (April 2, 1977); Lou Cannon, "Shakedown Cruise for Carter, Hill: The Independent Democrats," *Washington Post* (May 23, 1977).

51. Elizabeth Drew, "Settling In," p. 86.

52. *Ibid.*, p. 87.

53. James T. Wooten, "Carter Gains in Confidence—And Gets a Few Lessons in the Limits of Presidential Power," *New York Times* (July 23, 1977).

54. See Charles O. Jones, "Congress and the Presidency," in Thomas

E. Mann and Norman J. Ornstein (eds.), *The New Congress* (Washington, D.C.: American Enterprise Institute, 1981), pp. 223–49 (esp. pp. 229–37).

55. See John F. Manley, "The Conservative Coalition in Congress," *American Behavioral Scientist* 17 (November-December 1973), pp. 223–47; James T. Patterson, *Congressional Conservatism and the New Deal* (Lexington: University of Kentucky Press, 1967).

56. See Jasper B. Shannon, "Presidential Politics in the South: 1938," *The Journal of Politics* 1 (May and August 1939), pp. 146–70, 278–300.

57. See Richard Bolling, *House Out of Order* (New York: E. P. Dutton, 1965), pp. 58–61; Neil MacNeil, *Forge of Democracy* (New York: McKay, 1963); and Mark F. Ferber, "The Formation of the Democratic Study Group," in Nelson W. Polsby (ed.), *Congressional Behavior* (New York: Random House, 1971), pp. 249–69.

58. Clem Miller, *Member of the House,* edited, with additional text by John W. Baker (New York: Scribner, 1962), pp. 123–24.

59. On the growth of the Democratic Study Group and its effectiveness, see Kenneth Kofmehl, "Institutionalization of a Voting Bloc," *Western Political Quarterly* 17 (June 1964), pp. 256–72; and Roger H. Davidson, "Subcommittee Government: New Channels for Policy Making," in Thomas E. Mann and Norman J. Ornstein (eds.), *The New Congress,* pp. 99–133, esp. pp. 107, 128–29.

60. Wolfinger and Arsenau show that it was mostly done through the filling of vacancies rather than through contested elections. Raymond E. Wolfinger and Robert B. Arsenau, "Partisan Change in the South, 1952–1976," in Louis Maisel and Joseph Cooper (eds.), *Sage Electoral Studies Yearbook,* vol. 4: *Political Parties: Development and Decay* (Beverly Hills: Sage Publications, 1978), pp. 179–210. See also Lawrence C. Dodd and Bruce I. Oppenheimer, "The House in Transition: Change and Consolidation," in Dodd and Oppenheimer (eds.), *Congress Reconsidered* (Washington, D.C.: Congressional Quarterly Press, 1981), pp. 31–61.

61. Ornstein and Rohde, "Shifting Forces, Changing Rules, and Political Outcomes."

62. On the revolt against Cannon, see Blair Bolles, *Tyrant from Illinois: Uncle Joe Cannon's Experiment with Personal Power* (New York: Norton, 1951); and Charles O. Jones, "Joseph G. Cannon and Howard W. Smith: An Essay on the Limits of Leadership in the House of Representatives," *The Journal of Politics* 30 (August 1968), pp. 617–46.

63. For example: Article I, Section 1, places all legislative powers in

the hands of Congress; Article I, Sections 2 and 3, gives the right of impeachment to the House of Representatives and allows the Senate to try all impeachments; Article I, Section 7, allows Congress to override a presidential veto of a bill; Article I, Section 8, among other powers, gives Congress the right to set and collect taxes and other revenues; and Article II, Section 3, allows the President to recommend legislation to Congress for its consideration.

64. Adam Clymer, "Carter's Standing Drops to New Low in Times-CBS Poll," *New York Times* (June 10, 1979); Jurek Martin, "Carter's Precarious Path to the Summit," *Financial Times* (London) (June 15, 1979), p. 22; Barry Sussman, "Poll: Carter Holding Strength," *Washington Post* (June 17, 1979); Hedrick Smith, "Carter Rating Falls in Gas Crisis; Intimates Fearful on Re-election," *New York Times* (June 29, 1979); Adam Clymer, "Gas Lack Helps Drop Carter to 26% in Poll," *New York Times* (July 13, 1979).

65. By August 1979 seven independent committees, in as many states, had registered with the Federal Election Commission to promote the Kennedy presidential candidacy. Kennedy formally disavowed them all ("Money and the Non-Candidate," *National Journal* (August 4, 1979), p. 1286). In Gallup poll trial heats Kennedy was running far better than Carter against selected Republican candidates. See the summary of results released by the Gallup poll on August 20, 1979. See also Timothy D. Schellhardt, "Criticizing Carter: Many Interest Groups Believe the President Has Let Them Down; Draft-Kennedy Move Gains," *Wall Street Journal* (June 28, 1979); Joseph F. Sullivan, "Jersey Democratic Chiefs Voicing Doubts on Cater," *New York Times* (May 29, 1979); Bill Peterson and Edward Walsh, "O'Neill Fuels Speculation on Kennedy," *Washington Post* (September 11, 1979); Adam Clymer, "Move Grows at Capitol To Urge Carter To Shun Race," *New York Times* (September 13, 1979); T. R. Reid, "Kennedy," in Richard Harwood (ed.), *The Pursuit of the Presidency* (New York: Berkley, 1981), pp. 65–66.

66. Clymer, "Carter's Standing Drops."

67. The Gallup poll summary released on August 20, 1979, showed Carter beating Reagan or Ford all through 1978, but starting at the end of June 1979 and from then onward, Ford or Reagan beat Carter.

68. David S. Broder, "Carter Seeking Oratory To Move an Entire Nation," *Washington Post* (July 14, 1979), p. A1.

69. Edward Walsh, "President Seeks Advice of More Private Citizens," *Washington Post* (July 14, 1979), p. A8.

70. Martin Schram, "Carter: Back on the Track and Eager To Retake the Lead," *Washington Post* (July 17, 1979).

71. The text of President Carter's speech is printed verbatim in the *New York Times* (July 17, 1979), p. A15, and *Congressional Quarterly Weekly Report* 37 (July 21, 1979), pp. 1470–72.

72. The texts of these speeches are given in *Congressional Quarterly Weekly Report* 37 (July 21, 1979), pp. 1472–79. On Monday, July 16, one day after the President's televised speech, a New York Times–CBS News telephone national sample survey disclosed a jump of eleven points in the number of respondents approving of Mr. Carter's "handling of his job." See Adam Clymer, "Speech Lifts Carter Rating to 37%; Public Agrees on Confidence Crisis," *New York Times* (July 18, 1979). Among those who listened to Mr. Carter's speech, 49% said they had "greater faith in President Carter's leadership" and 45% said "no." Among respondents who had had not heard the speech, only 26% said "yes" and 60% said "no."

73. Schram, "Back on the Track," July 17, 1979.

74. The most detailed and coherent recounting of these events was Elizabeth Drew, "Phase: In Search of a Definition," *The New Yorker* (August 27, 1979), pp. 45–73. I rely also upon contemporary accounts in the *New York Times, Los Angeles Times, Washington Post, Wall Street Journal, Time, Newsweek, National Journal,* and *Congressional Quarterly Weekly Report.* See in addition Joseph A. Califano, *Governing America* (New York: Simon and Schuster, 1981), pp. 425–48.

75. Terence Smith, "President Replaces Three Cabinet Secretaries: Bell, Blumenthal and Califano," *New York Times* (July 20, 1979); See also "The White House Report Card," *San Francisco Chronicle* (July 20, 1979).

76. Originally it was intended that all officials making more than $25,000 a year were to be rated until somebody pointed out to Jordan that in the Defense Department alone that involved several hundred people. Jordan retreated to requiring filled-out forms on assistant secretaries and above.

77. See Martin Schram, "Today Was the Day Hamilton Jordan Took Charge," *Washington Post* (July 18, 1979).

78. See Hedrick Smith, "Jackson Decries Cabinet Upheaval and Says Kennedy Will Run in '80," *New York Times* (July 25, 1979); Frank Lynn, "Top Democrats Disturbed by Resignations of Cabinet," *New*

York Times (July 20, 1979); "Resignation Reaction in Congress: 'Rebirth,' 'Nuts'," *Los Angeles Times* (July 18, 1979); "Cabinet Reorganization Drew Mixed Reviews," *President Carter 1979* (Washington, D.C.: Congressional Quarterly Press, 1980), pp. 5–9.

79. Steven V. Roberts, "Capital Turmoil Saddens and Confuses U.S. Aides," *New York Times* (July 21, 1979).

80. Robert Shogan, "Carter Reevaluating Hundreds of Officials," *Los Angeles Times* (July 19, 1979).

81. Mary Russell, "On the Hill One Step Forward for Carter—and One Back," *Washington Post* (July 20, 1979).

82. Jack Nelson, "Carter Shuffles Staff: Georgia Circle Intact," *Los Angeles Times* (August 11, 1979), p. 2. One congressional subcommittee chairman said of Carter's attacks on Congress: "He's trying to save himself, and it could help him, but it won't help him with his programs up here," (Steven V. Roberts, "Carter and the Congress: Doubt and Distrust Prevail," *New York Times* (August 5, 1979), p. E2).

83. James M. Perry and Albert R. Hunt, "Capital Confusion: Carter's Shakeup Stirs Tension and Disarray—Just as He Tries to Lead," *Wall Street Journal* (July 20, 1979).

84. Roberts, "Carter and the Congress" (August 5, 1979).

85. Robert D. Hershey, Jr., "Press Abroad Is Critical of Cabinet Shuffle in U.S.," *New York Times* (July 23, 1979); Jim Hoagland, "Nothing Has Changed, Carter Aides Tell Foreign Reporters," *Washington Post* (July 26, 1979).

There was a great deal of unfavorable foreign press reaction printed in the main American newspapers. A sample: "There is no longer any doubt about it—Carter has stopped governing and has started the election campaign" (a West German paper quoted in Clayton Fritchey, "A Kennedy Surrogate," *Washington Post,* July 30, 1979).

The foreign policy expert for the West German opposition party CDU, Alois Mertes, said trust in America has declined because it "cannot be decided or come about by praying. It rather has to grow from inner conviction and must root in credibility," (Michael Getler, "West Germany Says Carter's Moves Threaten NATO," *Washington Post,* July 27, 1979).

Alberto Rouchey, writing in *Corriere della Sera,* said: "The indecisiveness of the 39th President, together with his inability to hide his lack of decision has become the subject of accurate and merciless analysis"; *Die Zeit* criticized the firings as incomprehensible. "Incomprehensible because, after all, he hired those he is now firing. He has poorly coordinated and inadequately led them. And isn't he himself the very 'Washington' he now criticizes?" (Both in Robert D. Hershey, Jr., "Press Abroad Is Critical of Cabinet Shuffle in U.S." *New York Times,* July 23, 1979.)

Time said: ". . . Carter's handling of the mass firings caused Europeans to cluck in wonder. A high ranking West German Foreign Ministry official asked: 'Is this serious, or is this just a great religious exercise for the soul?' "

"Oslo's middle-roading daily *Verdens Gang* called the Washington situation a 'circus' and a 'balancing act without a safety net.' "

"Concluded London's conservative *Daily Mail:* 'to revive his personal standing with voters before the next presidential election looks more like a narcissistic charade than a national crusade.' "

"*The Economist* suggested that Carter's efforts would not be successful, 'unless there is some understanding of how the world works and some readiness to eschew symbolism and appearances and go instead after the substance of the problems.' "

"One money trader in Milan summed it up as follows: 'When Carter speaks, the dollar plummets' " ("Slumping to a New Low Abroad," *Time* (July 30, 1979), pp. 23–24).

86. Michael Getler, "Carter's Shakeup Worries West Germans," *Washington Post* (July 21, 1979); Hobart Rowen, "Resignation Offer Shocking Abroad," *Washington Post* (July 19, 1979).

87. Republican reactions included the following:

"If somebody told me that Anastazio Somoza had just been named to replace Harold Brown as Secretary of Defense," Rep. Guy Vander Jagt (R-Mich.) said to a colleague on the House floor in the early afternoon, "I'd run out to see if it was on the news ticker in the lobby" (David S. Broder and Ward Sinclair, "A Political Skylab Hits the Capital," *Washington Post,* July 20, 1979).

Senator Lowell Weicker: "I think the President is nuts. This is just a continuation of the scapegoat operation. It is the President, not his Cabinet, that the American people have lost confidence in" ("Resignation Reaction in Congress: 'Rebirth,' 'Nuts'," *Los Angeles Times,* July 18, 1979).

Senate Republican Whip Ted Stevens, said: "Some of us are seriously worried that he might be approaching some sort of mental problem. He ought to take a rest" ("Carter's Great Purge," *Time* (July 30, 1979), pp. 10–16).

88. Democratic responses included the following:

Senator Abraham Ribicoff of Connecticut "described the mass resignation as 'a very foolish move.' He added: 'There's no justification for blanket resignations. The President should know how good a member of his Cabinet or staff is'" (Frank Lynn, "Top Democrats Disturbed by Resignation of Cabinet," *New York Times,* July 20, 1979).

House Majority Whip John Brademas: "He's like a football player who's behind in the game, then catches the ball and is breaking through to daylight, when he suddenly runs out of bounds" (Mary Russell, "On the Hill: One Step Forward for Carter—and One Back," *Washington Post,* July 20, 1979). "Rep. William Ford (D-Mich.), chairman of an Education and Labor subcommittee, said the actions were 'disastrous' for a higher education bill he [Carter] is working on" (*ibid.*).

"Said Tim Hagen, the Cleveland area Democratic Party chairman: 'In baseball, you fire the manager. Here they are asking the players to quit.' Sniped the Massachusetts Democratic Party chairman, Chester Atkins: 'The mouse that roared is still a rodent.' " "Said Democratic Congressman Charles Wilson of Texas: 'Good grief! They're cutting down the biggest trees and keeping the monkeys' " ("Carter's Great Purge," *Time* (July 30, 1979), pp. 10–16).

"David Obey of Wisconsin called the dismissals 'a victory for mediocrity—a dunderheaded performance' and warned that they would weaken President Carter's chances of renomination" (Hedrick Smith, "Dismissals Taken as Pre-Campaign Move by Carter," *New York Times,* July 20, 1979).

89. "The Cabinetmaker Selects His New Timber," *The Economist* (July 28, 1979), pp. 39–43.

90. See Tom Morgenthau with James Doyle, "The Mood of a Nation," *Newsweek* (August 6, 1979), pp. 26–27.

91. Caddell's data were of the following sort: In a national opinion survey, people were asked to rate the state of the country and the state of their own lives five years ago, today, and five years from now, on a scale of one to ten. Because what "the state of" the country and one's own life are supposed to mean is intentionally left unspecified, so as to evoke whatever is salient to respondents, this scale is regarded as a generalized, self-administered measurement of optimism-pessimism. Caddell's data showed a decline in expectations of the future. It is unclear how responses were aggregated to arrive at this conclusion or what inferences might sensibly be drawn from it. Needless to say, Caddell's analysis was not widely shared among public opinion analysts, as *Newsweek* discovered: "Says one opinion expert, the University of Michigan's F.

Thomas Juster: 'My instinct is that it's an exaggerated story. It just doesn't make any sense' "(p. 26).

"Political scientist Warren Miller also at the University of Michigan, says the degree of voter alienation has been 'grossly overinterpreted.' 'There is no massive and personal disaffection from society—or government,' Miller says. Instead, he adds, 'there is clear dissatisfaction with the Carter Presidency' " ('The Mood of a Nation," *Newsweek* (August 6, 1979), p. 27). See also Patrick H. Caddell, "Crisis Of Confidence I: Trapped in a Downward Spiral," *Public Opinion* 2 (October/November 1979), pp. 2–7; Warren E. Miller, "Crisis of Confdence II: Misreading the Public Pulse," *ibid.*, pp. 9–15.

92. Thomas M. DeFrank, "How Carter Sees It," *Newsweek* (July 30, 1979), p. 25. See also Terence Smith, "On Carter and the Washington Press Corps," *New York Times* (August 2, 1979).

93. Terence Smith, "Reporter's Notebook: At the White House Jeans Are Passé and Neckties De Rigueur," *New York Times* (July 27, 1979).

94. See Charles Mohr, "Jordan Says Carter Will Widen His Circle of Advisers," *New York Times* (July 23, 1979).

95. See Knott and Wildavsky, "Jimmy Carter's Theory of Governing."

96. See Elihu Katz and Paul F. Lazarsfeld, *Personal Influence* (Glencoe, Ill.: Free Press, 1955).

97. The literature on opinion formation among members of Congress is by now voluminous. See John W. Kingdon, *Congressmen's Voting Decisions* (New York: Harper & Row, 1973); Aage R. Clausen, *How Congressmen Decide* (New York: St. Martin's Press, 1973); Donald R. Matthews and James A. Stimson, *Yeas and Nays: Normal Decision Making in the U.S. House of Representatives* (New York: John Wiley, 1975); Lewis Anthony Dexter, "What Do Congressmen Hear?," in Nelson W. Polsby (ed.), *Congressional Behavior* (New York: Random House, 1971), pp. 28–41; and Dexter, *The Sociology and Politics of Congress* (Chicago: Rand McNally, 1969).

98. Dom Bonafede, "White House Report: The Fallout from Camp David—Only Minor White House Changes," *National Journal* (November 10, 1979), pp. 1893–97.

99. Joseph Califano claims that in his 2½ years as secretary of H.E.W. he had spent only two hours with Jordan and that Jordan seldom returned the telephone calls of members of the cabinet (*Governing America*, p. 441).

100. " 'I'm sure I've met him,' Senate Majority Leader Robert Byrd loftily remarked last week. 'But I've never had a conversation

with him' " ("Here Comes Mr. Jordan," *Time* (July 30, 1979), p. 22).

101. James M. Perry, "Capitol Kept in Suspense as Carter Mulls Resignation Offers of Top Aides, Cabinet," *Wall Street Journal* (July 19, 1979).

102. "Bell, Departing, Is Given President's Warm Praise" *New York Times* (August 5, 1979), p. 42.

103. "Jordan's 'Beautiful' But Who's Jerdun?" *New York Times* (July 28, 1979).

One immediate addition in White House staffing was the employment on the senior staff of Hedley Donovan, the recently retired editor-in-chief of Time Inc. publications, early Carter boosters. It was not made clear what Mr. Donovan's responsibilities would be, nor did it ever become clear in the months after, but it could not escape the notice of observers that Mr. Donovan's predominant expertise and life experience were as a New York-based executive of a national news publication. Administration spokesmen insisted that Mr. Donovan's job would be substantive, connected neither with public relations nor politics. The announcement of his employment was greeted with fulsome approbation by *Time* magazine (August 6, 1979), pp. 20–21. Said *Time:* "Donovan expresses himself with conviction and candor. His sound, unruffled judgment . . . has been one of his great strengths." See also John Osborne, "Hedley the Don," *The New Republic* (January 26, 1980), pp. 9–10.

104. Terence Smith, "At the White House Jeans Are Passé," *New York Times* (July 27, 1979)

105. According to the CBS News/ *New York Times* exit poll on November 4, 1980, the Democratic defection rate was 25 percent. See Adam Clymer, "The Democrats Look for New Ideas, and Jobs," *New York Times* (November 9, 1980); and Clymer, "Displeasure with Carter Turned Many to Reagan," *ibid.* William Schneider writes: "Former Carter supporters were four times as likely as former Ford supporters to report that they "sat out" the 1980 presidential election. Abstention siphoned off even more Democratic voters than did defection to other candidates. The result was that Carter was able to hold on to only a little more than a third of those who had given him his scanty majority four years earlier, while Reagan retained two-thirds of the former Ford voters . . . . The 1980 election was essentially a referendum on the Carter administration. . . ." (Schneider, "The November 4 Vote for President: What Did It Mean?," in Ranney (ed.), *The American*

Elections of 1980) pp. 212–62.) See also Nelson W. Polsby, "Party Realignment in the 1980 Election," *Yale Review* (Fall 1982).

106. See Kenneth Reich, "State Democrats Bitter on Carter's Early Concession," *Los Angeles Times* (November 5, 1980); William Endicott, "Anti-Carter Vote Seen in State Races," *ibid.* (November 6, 1980); Roger Smith, "Early Concession Costly: State Party Leaders Sure Carter 'Paralyzed' Effort," *ibid.* (November 7, 1980); John Fogarty, "Carter Saw No Harm in Conceding Early," *San Francisco Chronicle* (November 7, 1980); and John Balzar, "Demos Hurt by Early TV Vote Report," *ibid.* (March 11, 1981); Jack W. Germond and Jules Witcover, *Blue Smoke and Mirrors* (New York: Viking, 1981), pp. 314–15.

107. The actual results in the Iowa precinct caucuses on January 19, 1976, were: Uncommitted 38.5; Carter 29.1; Bayh 11.4; Harris 9.0; Udall 5.8; Shriver 3.1; Jackson 1.1; the rest less than 1%. In the New Hampshire primary of February 24, 1976, the results were: Carter 29.4, Udall 23.9, Bayh 16.2, Harris 11.4, Shriver, 8.7, Humphrey (write-ins) 5.6, Wallace (write-ins) 1.4, Jackson (write-ins) 1.4, Ellen MacCormick, 1.3 (*Congressional Quarterly Weekly Report* (February 28, 1976), p. 459; and *ibid.* (July 10, 1976), p. 1810).

108. See Nelson W. Polsby, "The Democratic Nomination," in Ranney (ed.), *The American Elections of 1980,* pp. 37–60.

Chapter IV: Wider Consequences

1. If there is a tendency, the consensus seems to be that it is "liberal." Half of the Washington reporters in Stephen Hess's sample said they thought there was a political bias in the Washington news corps, and of these, 96 percent said the bias was liberal in its direction. Most Washington reporters identified themselves as something other than liberal, however. See Stephen Hess, *The Washington Reporters* (Washington, D.C.: Brookings Institution, 1981), pp. 87ff. Another recent survey of the political and social opinions of influential U.S. journalists places them as predominantly liberal, as favoring welfare and capitalism, as well-educated and unalienated. See S. Robert Lichter and Stanley Rothman, "Media and Business Elites," *Public Opinion* (October/November 1981), pp. 42–46, 59–60.

2. When the McGovern Commission adopted guideline A-2, designed to encourage national convention representation of "minority groups, young people and women in reasonable relation-

ship to their presence in the population . . ." it was not explicit about which groups qualified as minorities. The Commission report, *Mandate for Reform,* only documented what was regarded as disproportionate absence of black delegates (pp. 26–27). No other minority groups were discussed. The *Delegate Selection Rules for the 1980 Democratic National Convention* (Washington, D.C.: Democratic National Committee, June 9, 1978) cited the need for state parties to develop and submit Affirmative Action Programs for women, blacks, Hispanics, and Native Americans (p. 7, rule 6A). The Commission on Presidential Nomination and Party Structure (Morley Winograd, chairman) likewise referred to a "particular concern for minority groups, Native Americans, women, and youth, in the delegate selection process," in its recommended delegate selection rules (*Openness, Participation and Party Building: Reforms for a Stronger Democratic Party* (Washington, D.C.: Democratic National Committee, January 25, 1978), pp. 96–97, rule 18). And contained in the 1974 Mikulski Commission report was the following affirmative action rule: "In order to encourage full participation by all Democrats, with particular concern for minority groups, native Americans, women and youth, in the delegate selection process and in all party affairs, the national and state Democratic Parties shall adopt and implement affirmative action programs" (*Congressional Quarterly Weekly Report* (March 9, 1974), p. 607).

3. An interesting case in point is a group on the national political scene that has only recently been given much media visibility: the physically handicapped. The processes of deliberation leading up to the proclamation of sweeping guidelines concerning provision for the handicapped of access to public facilities by the Secretary of HEW, Joseph Califano, were greatly hastened by televised demonstrations and, according to Califano's account, by Califano's fears of lurid, unfavorable headlines (see *Governing America* (New York: Simon and Schuster, 1981), pp. 258–62). It may be instructive for a reader to compare the justifications given therein with those of Jacobus tenBroek in "The Right To Live in the World: The Disabled in the Law of Torts," *California Law Review* 54 (May 1966), pp. 841–919.

4. See the essay on Dunlop in *Current Biography 1951,* pp. 173–74; and the account of the appointment of Ray Marshall, who got the job in the Carter administration in *Current Biography 1977,* p. 287; also Bruce Adams and Kathryn Kavanagh-Baran, *Promise and Performance* (Lexington, Mass.: Lexington Books, 1979), pp. 38–39, 42.

5. "Some Snags in the Stretch," *Time* (December 27, 1976), p. 6:

". . . Carter aides asked AFL-CIO officials to suggest alternatives to Dunlop who would be acceptable to labor boss George Meany. Back came the word: 'His first, second, third and fourth choices are Dunlop.' " Lane Kirkland, AFL-CIO secretary-treasurer said: "He comes as close to being the indispensable man as there is" (Edward Cowan, "Labor Leader Says Economy Needs Permanent Tax Cut of $25 Billion," *New York Times,* December 14, 1976).

6. Eileen Shanahan, "17 Groups Seek a Labor Secretary Committed To Fight Discrimination," *New York Times* (December 11, 1976); Tom Wicker, "The Dunlop Signal," *New York Times* (December 14, 1976); "The Cabinet Problem," *New York Times* (December 20, 1976). See also Robert G. Kaiser, "Women Lobby for Role in Carter Camp," *Washington Post* (December 5, 1976).

7. See Adams and Kavanagh-Baran, *Promise and Performance;* see also Nancy Hicks, "Feminists Critical of Carter on Jobs," *New York Times* (February 8, 1977); Edward Walsh, "Costanza Defends Carter on Recruitment of Women," *Washington Post* (January 28, 1977); "Carter Appointments: 13% Are Women, 11% Are Black," *Washington Post* (June 19, 1977).

8. See, for example, Charles McC. Mathias, Jr., "Ethnic Groups and Foreign Policy," *Foreign Affairs* (Summer 1981), pp. 975–98, for criticism of Jewish influence in foreign affairs.

9. See Theodore H. White, *The Making of the President 1972* (New York: Atheneum, 1973), pp. 263–80; Gordon L. Weil, *The Long Shot* (New York: Norton, 1973), pp. 156–94; Timothy Crouse, *The Boys on the Bus* (New York: Random House, 1973), pp. 325–33; Gary Hart, *Right from the Start* (New York: Quadrangle, 1973), pp. 250–54, 256–65; and Douglas E. Kneeland, "Behind Eagleton's Withdrawal: A Tale Of Confusion and Division," *New York Times* (August 2, 1972).

10. In addition to several editorials, the *Washington Post* provided a summary description of press opinion. Twenty-three newspapers in their survey commented adversely and ten (including the *Post* itself) called for Eagleton's withdrawal from the ticket. Among the others seeking Eagleton's withdrawal were the *New York Times, Los Angeles Times, Baltimore Sun,* and *Newsday.* The *New York Post* was quoted as saying: "In this year of great national decision . . . [Eagleton] had disqualified himself by his apparent act of conceal-ment . . ." (Jack Fuller, "Editorials Are Mixed on Eagleton," *Washington Post,* July 28, 1972). See also *Washington Post* editorials on July 27, 29, 31, and August 2, 1972.

11. Hart, *Right from the Start,* p. 265.

12. See Timothy Crouse, *The Boys on the Bus,* pp. 320–33. One might

compare this episode with Dwight Eisenhower's handling of the disclosure of the Nixon fund, which jeopardized Richard Nixon's place on the Republican ticket in 1952. There was considerable pressure from the newspapers—notably the *New York Herald Tribune*—on Nixon to withdraw, but Nixon's famous television speech—the Checkers speech—presumably saved him from disgrace. In addition, several political friends and allies of General Eisenhower seem to have played important roles in determining the outcome, whereas accounts of the Eagleton episode give the impression that McGovern was more or less on his own. See Earl Mazo and Stephen Hess, *Nixon: A Political Portrait* (New York: Popular Library, 1968), pp. 76–125.

13. Alexis de Tocqueville, *Democracy in America* (New York: Knopf Vintage, 1956) is a classic statement. More modern discussions include David B. Truman, *The Governmental Process* (New York: Knopf, 1971); and Robert H. Salisbury, "Interest Groups," in Fred I. Greenstein and Nelson W. Polsby (eds.), *Handbook of Political Science* (Reading, Mass.: Addison-Wesley, 1975), vol. 4, pp. 171–228.

14. Indications of changes in the average size of American nuclear families—from 4.11 in 1930 to 2.73 in 1981—have important political consequences. For a rough estimate of the decline of primary group intermediation and the rise of intermediation through the mass media, compare these numbers with those on the number of television sets per household in 1950 (.101) and 1979 (1.67), and average viewing per day in 1950 (4.6 hours) and 1980 (6.3 hours). Bureau of Census, *Statistical Abstract of U.S. 1979* (Washington, D.C., 1979).

15. There are a number of indices that show how technology has multiplied the options of individual Americans to engage in communication with one another over long distances. Note, for example, the following:

Table 4.1 Increased capabilities for long-distance interaction among Americans

	1920	1950	1978
Auto registrations (thousands)	9,239	48,567	117,100
Telephones in use (millions)	13	43	169
Domestic airways passenger miles (billions)		8	182.7

Source: *Statistical Abstract 1979*, pp. 581–82, 642, 667.

16. See Nelson W. Polsby, "Legislatures," in Greenstein and Polsby (eds.), *Handbook of Political Science,* vol. 5, pp. 257–319.

17. Among the writers interested in the ways in which social incentives shape organizational and political behavior and who have dealt in detail with problems similar to this one I particularly recommend James Q. Wilson. See his *The Amateur Democrat* (Chicago: University of Chicago Press, 1966) and *Political Organizations* (New York: Basic Books, 1973), esp. chapter 3.

18. Examples of such interests in American political history abound: abolitionism and the temperance movement are two of the most famous. Among the classic studies of single issue interest groups in the twentieth century are E. E. Schattschneider, *Politics, Pressures and the Tariff* (New York: Prentice-Hall, 1935); Peter H. Odegard, *Pressure Politics: The Story of the Anti-Saloon League* (New York: Columbia University Press, 1928); Clement E. Vose, *Constitutional Change* (Lexington, Mass.: Lexington Books, 1972), esp. pp. 69–137; and Raymond Bauer, Ithiel de Sola Pool, and Lewis Anthony Dexter, *American Business and Public Policy* (New York: Atherton, 1963).

19. The best single summary I have seen on the turnout question is Richard Brody, "The Puzzle of Political Participation in America," in Anthony King (ed.), *The New American Political System* (Washington, D.C.: American Enterprise Institute, 1978), pp. 287–324. See also William J. Crotty and Gary C. Jacobson, *American Parties in Decline* (Boston: Little, Brown 1980).

20. A particularly vigorous argument to this effect is made by Byron Shafer in his unpublished paper "Reform and Alienation: The Decline of Intermediation in the Politics of Presidential Selection" (mimeo, Russell Sage Foundation, 1981).

21. For example consider some of the seemingly disparate findings in Jack Dennis's important article "Trends in Public Support for the American Political System," *British Journal of Political Science* 5 (April 1975), pp. 187–230. Dennis reports that the numbers of people were on the increase who said:

(1) Parties "make a difference" and are ideologically distinguishable

(2) Divided government is preferable

(3) Parties were less interested in what respondents thought, less controllable by citizens

(4) They had personally campaigned or donated money to politics.

These findings—and especially when taken together—are compatible with distaste for and worry about political extremism. So are the trend lines on many of Dennis's indicators of public support that break downward with the 1964 "choice not an echo" presidential election (see his figure 2.). See also Norman H. Nie, Sidney Verba, and John R. Petrocik, *The Changing American Voter* (Cambridge, Mass.: Harvard University Press, 1976).

22. A good summary is Jacob Citrin's "The Alienated Voter," *Taxing and Spending* (October–November 1978), pp. 7–11. See also Arthur H. Miller, "Political Issues and Trust in Government," *American Political Science Review* 68 (September 1974), pp. 951–72; and Jack Citrin, "Comment: The Political Relevance of Trust in Government," *ibid.*, pp. 973–88.

23. This is true, for example, of the propensity of voters to turn out and vote, but not true, as Dennis ("Trends in Public Support") shows, of the willingness to give money or to campaign. See Richard Brody, "The Puzzle of Political Participation."

24. See Samuel P. Huntington, "The Democratic Distemper," *The Public Interest* 41 (Fall 1975), pp. 9–38; Aaron Wildavsky, "The Past and Future Presidency," *ibid.*, pp. 56–76; and Wildavsky, "Government and the People," *Commentary* 56 (August 1973), pp. 25–32.

25. The Hughes Commission wrote: "A convention of delegates selected by party officials is open to the same criticism as direct appointment of delegates to the National Convention—party officials do not necessarily represent the party membership on issues of presidential politics. The Commission's study indicates that over 600 delegates to the 1968 Convention were selected by processes which have included no means of voter participation since 1966" (Commission on the Democratic Selection of Presidential Nominees, *The Democratic Choice* (Washington, D.C., 1968), p. 24). See also William J. Crotty, *Decision for the Democrats* (Baltimore: Johns Hopkins University Press, 1978), pp. 254–57.

26. The locus classicus is Bernard C. Cohen, *The Press and Foreign Policy* (Princeton: Princeton University Press, 1963). Further explorations of themes first identified by Cohen can be found in a series of Harvard doctoral dissertations, e.g., Edward Jay Epstein, *News from Nowhere* (New York: Random House, 1973); Leon Sigal, *Reporters and Officials* (Lexington, Mass: D. C. Heath, 1973); and Paul Weaver, "The Metropolitan Newspaper as a Political Institution," P.h.D. dissertation, 1969; Paul Weaver, "How the *Times* Is Slanted Down the Middle," *New York* (July 1, 1968), pp. 32–36. See also Herbert J. Gans, *Deciding What's News* (New York: Vintage Books, 1980).

27. The phrase "adversary culture" is Lionel Trilling's and comes from his discussion of modernism in literature in *Beyond Culture,* (New York: Viking, 1965), pp. xii ff. It was pressed into service in the present context by Daniel Patrick Moynihan in "The Presidency and the Press," *Commentary* 51 (March 1971), p. 43 (reprinted in Moynihan, *Coping* (New York: Random House, 1973), pp. 318–20). See also Joseph Kraft, "The Imperial Media," *Commentary* (May 1981), pp. 36–47; Max M. Kampelman, "The Power of the Press: A Problem for Our Democracy," *Policy Review* 6 (Fall 1978), pp. 7–39; and Michael Schudson, *Discovering the News* (New York: Basic Books, 1978), pp. 176ff. The essental text on "radical chic" is Tom Wolfe, "Radical Chic," pp. 3–94 of *Radical Chic and Mau-Mauing the Flak Catchers* (New York: Farrar, Straus, and Giroux, 1970).

28. Lichter and Rothman, *op. cit.,* give evidence of liberalism but not of much radicalism in the attitudes of their influential news media respondents.

29. See Paul H. Weaver, "Captives of Melodrama" *New York Times Magazine* (August 29, 1976), pp. 6, 48, 50–51, 54, 56–57; Thomas E. Patterson, *The Mass Media Election: How Americans Choose Their President* (New York: Praeger, 1980).

30. Robert G. Kaiser described some of these in the course of his reports on the television coverage of the 1980 election for the *Washington Post.* His conclusion on October 10: "There are three stock formats for the basic television news report on the 1980 campaign. Format One might be called 'Charge-Countercharge' . . . Format Two is . . . a day in the candidate's life on the road . . . Format Three is the handicapper's report from one of the major racetracks, an evaluation of the horse race in one of the big states" ("T.V. on the Trail: A Three-Course Menu for Fluff"). Similar comments have been made about print journalism. See Paul Weaver, "The Politics of a News Story," in Harry M. Clor (ed.), *The Mass Media and Modern Democracy* (Chicago: Rand McNally, 1974), pp. 85–112. Weaver's view of the components of the typical news story is summarized by Schudson (p. 185), as follows:

> . . . The bias is toward statements of fact which are observable and unambiguous; toward broad, categorical vocabulary—"say" rather than "shout" or "insist"; toward impersonal narrative style and "inverted pyramid" organization which force a presentation of facts with "as little evocation of their real-world context" as possible; toward conflicts rather than less dramatic happenings; toward "events" rather than processes.

Cohen, *The Press and Foreign Policy,* comes to similar conclusions.

31. The *Post*'s ombudsman in 1981, Bill Green, wrote: "There is no question about the pressures and competition in the *Washington*

Post's newsroom. They are powerful. Some people flourish, others get crushed. It is major-league journalism. 'Hardball' as [*Post* Executive Editor] Ben Bradlee describes it. The troubling question is whether pressure on the staff distorts the news published in the paper" ("The Pressures: Heat and the Achievers Both Have a Tendency to Rise," *Washington Post*, April 19, 1981).

32. See Daniel Machalba, "UPI Struggles as It Loses Ground to AP, Other News Services," *Wall Street Journal* (July 11, 1979).

33. "Reporters Appraise Campaign Roles," *New York Times* (February 1, 1982).

34. The belief by news organizations that impact on political actors is important constitutes at least one explanation for the odd spectacle of the *Los Angeles Times* taking out full-page ads in the *New York Times* and *Washington Post* in order to display notable instances of its political coverage to audiences it does not ordinarily have. See also David Halberstam, *The Powers That Be* (New York: Dell, 1979), pp. 548–49, 1006.

35. Here is an unself-consciously comic example of the process at work: "The United States finds it hard to understand why King Hussein . . . joined the outcry against Camp David. . . . But there are reasons for the policy from the Jordanian viewpoint. They were explained by me by Hussein's articulate brother, Crown Prince Hassan—the King is abroad—and by high officials" (Anthony Lewis, "At Home Abroad: When Friends Fall Out," *New York Times* (April 16, 1979), p. A17).

36. The ground rules—"Lindley rules"—which define the mutual expectations of reporters and news sources under "off the record," "deep background," "background," and "on the record" circumstances were codified by Ernest K. Lindley of *Newsweek*. See William J. Small, *Political Power and the Press* (New York: Norton, 1972), pp. 178–79. A *New York Times* reporter, commenting on quotations embarrassing to Budget Director David Stockman in the August 1981 *Atlantic Monthly* said: "In Washington, editors frequently meet socially with government officials and other people in the news to talk informally about public affairs. Such meetings do not generally produce news articles directly, but may encourage an editor to assign a reporter to pursue on the record what an editor has been told off the record" (Jonathan Friendly, "Post Allowed Editor to Scoop Newspaper," *New York Times* (November 13, 1981), p. 39). See, in general, Lou Cannon, *Reporting: An Inside View* (Sacramento: California Journal Press, 1977); Joseph Alsop and Stewart Alsop, *The Reporter's Trade* (New York: Reynal, 1958); William L. Rivers, *The Opinionmakers* (Boston: Beacon Press, 1965),

especially pp. 34–39; and Robert Pierpoint, *At the White House* (New York: Putnam, 1981).

37. In the field of national news, the most important general news organizations are the three television networks, the two wire services, the two big news magazines, and the handful of big newspapers owning their own national syndication services, principally the *New York Times* and the *Washington Post–Los Angeles Times*. For evidence of heavy dependence on wire service coverage of national and political news by local newspapers scattered all across the United States, see Michael J. Robinson and Margaret H. Sheehan, *Over the Wire and on TV* (New York: Russell Sage, 1982), chapter 2.

Wire service reports frequently dominate the production of news in the first place, according to the observations by Timothy Crouse of political campaign reporting in 1972. See *The Boys on the Bus* (New York: Random House, 1972), p. 22: "Most reporters . . . followed the wire service men whenever possible. Nobody made a secret of running with the wires; it was an accepted practice."

Readers will recognize that differentiated marketing strategies, aiming mostly at businessmen, are at work for otherwise important news organizations like the *Wall Street Journal* and *U.S. News and World Report,* for whom deductions from the axiom of competitiveness must be suitably modified. Stephen Hess, *The Washington Reporters* (Washington, D.C.: Brookings Institution, 1981), p. 140, gives a list of "influential" news media similar to the one above, based on his interviews with Washington reporters, and their reading and listening habits, subtracting the *Los Angeles Times* and including the now-defunct *Washington Star*, the *Wall Street Journal,* and *U.S. News and World Report.*

38. See Bernard C. Cohen, *The Press and Foreign Policy*, pp. 58ff.

39. A theory of the underlying process of social definition and its consequences was worked out years ago in some detail by W. I. Thomas. See Edmund H. Volkart (ed.), *Social Behavior and Personality: Contributions of W. I. Thomas to Theory and Social Research* (New York: Social Science Research Council, 1951).

40. Vice President Agnew's famous contribution to media criticism ("nattering nabobs of negativity" and so on) was a single speech given on November 13, 1969, in Des Moines, Iowa, before a meeting of the Midwest Republican Conference. It was written by Pat Buchanan and had President Nixon's prior approval. See Evans and Novak, *Nixon in the White House: The Frustration of Power* (New York: Random House, 1971), pp. 315–17. Other, more measured complaints about news media treatment of President Nixon be-

fore Watergate are contained in James Keogh, *President Nixon and the Press* (New York: Funk and Wagnalls, 1972).

41. A complementary view from another part of the ideological spectrum, that concentration of the ownership of newspapers in unworthy hands leads to inaccurate or malicious news coverage, seems to me about equally limited in its explanatory power, especially as far as national news coverage is concerned. It cannot be ruled out in some circumstances—e.g., for many decades in Los Angeles (see David Halberstam, *The Powers That Be,*. p. 167), in Wilmington, Delaware (see Ben H. Bagdikian, *The Effete Conspiracy*, New York: Harper & Row, 1972, pp. 69–79), or Manchester, New Hampshire (see Eric Veblen, *The Manchester Union Leader in New Hampshire Elections*, Hanover, New Hampshire: University Press of New England, 1975)—but will not cover as many cases or constraints upon outcomes as the normal exercise of professionalism under competitive conditions such as I am describing.

42. See Nelson W. Polsby, "Toward an Explanation of McCarthyism," *Political Studies* 8 (October 1960), pp. 250–71.

43. As a fine recent book on McCarthy's press coverage documents. See Edwin R. Bayley, *Joe McCarthy and the Press* (Madison: University of Wisconsin Press, 1981).

44. "Wirthlin is a regular visitor at the White House. In one two-week period early this month, he said, he had two private meetings with the president. Sometimes he meets with Mr. and Mrs. Reagan together. He also has private sessions with the senior presidential aides, and with the secretary of state, Alexander M. Haig, Jr." (Robert G. Kaiser, "White House Pulse-Taking," *Washington Post*, February 24, 1982). See also B. Drummond Ayres, Jr., "G.O.P Keeps Tabs on Nation's Mood," *New York Times* (November 16, 1981); and Dom Bonafede, "As Pollster to the President, Wirthlin Is Where the Action Is," *National Journal* (December 12, 1981), pp. 2184–88.

45. See Wendell Rawls, Jr., "Carter's Poll-Taker Seems To Voice 1980 Catchwords," *New York Times* (August 14, 1979); E. J. Dionne, Jr., "Polls, Once Scorned, Gain New Esteem," *New York Times* (April 5, 1980); E. J. Dionne, Jr., "The Business of the Pollsters," *New York Times* (June 29, 1980).

46. Patricia Meisol, "Searching for a Cure for the Proposition 13 Epidemic," *National Journal* (August 26, 1978), pp. 1362–65. ". . . voters in eight states and some counties will be confronted with ballot proposals on Nov. 7 that would limit taxing or spending or both. Three of them—in Idaho, Michigan and Oregon—are lifted almost verbatim from the constitutional amendment that Califor-

nia voters approved overwhelmingly on June 6" (p. 1362). The others were in Arizona, Colorado, Nebraska, South Dakota, and Texas.

47. As James S. Coleman's work has documented. See *Community Conflict* (Glencoe, Ill.: Free Press, 1957), p. 19.

48. This follows the usage of Frederick M. Watkins. See Watkins, *The Age of Ideology: Political Thought, 1750 to the Present* (Englewood Cliffs, N.J.: Prentice-Hall, 1965).

49. See, for example, Edward C. Banfield, *Political Influence*, (New York: Free Press of Glencoe, 1961).

50. See, for example, David Sanford, *Me and Ralph* (Washington: New Republic Book Co., 1976).

51. *Congressional Quarterly* keeps annual account of interest group ratings of Congressmen according to their recorded votes on issues of interest to them. Americans for Democratic Action and the AFL-CIO Committee on Political Education maintain, roughly speaking, left-wing score-cards; Americans for Constitutional Action is, more or less, right-wing.

Table 4.2   Voting records of Senator Jackson and Representative Udall

| Year | ADA | | COPE | | ACA | |
	Jackson	Udall	Jackson	Udall	Jackson	Udall
1961–2	100	100	100	80	3	18
1963–4	82	88	73	82	6	7
1965–6	80	82	100	0	11	8
1967	69	93	100	100	0	4
1968	57	92	100	100	12	0
1969	78	67	100	80	14	0
1970	56	76	100	83	24	0
1971	56	81	100	82	27	4
1972	40	100	100	100	38	0
1973	55	84	100	82	21	8
1974	62	65	82	100	11	8
1975	61	47	90	92	8	13

Each score is the percentage of selected votes on which Jackson or Udall agreed with the given organization's position. The appropriate votes and scores are calculated by the interest groups and compiled by *Congressional Quarterly*. A high score indicates agreement between Udall or Jackson and the organization. A traditional liberal Democrat would be expected to receive high ADA and COPE scores and low marks on the ACA scale. More specific information on the scoring is in *Congressional Quarterly Weekly Report* (March 21, 1981), p. 516.

Source: *Congressional Quarterly*.

52. See Norman J. Ornstein, "The House and the Senate in a New Congress," in Thomas E. Mann and Ornstein (eds.), *The New Congress* (Washington, D.C.: American Enterprise Institute, 1981), pp. 363–83. Also Norman J. Ornstein (ed.), *Congress in Change* (New York: Praeger, 1975).

53. For a general discussion of tensions between political executives and the permanent government, see Hugh Heclo, *A Government of Strangers* (Washington, D.C.: Brookings Institution, 1977).

54. Data on resignations of senior officials is highly suggestive. "About 95 percent of top bureaucrats reaching retirement age—those between 55 and 59 with 30 years of federal experience—are deciding to leave, compared with about 18 percent in 1978, the General Accounting Office (GAO) reports" (p. 1296). William J. Lanouette, "SES: From Civil Service Showpiece to Incipient Failure in Two Years," *National Journal* (July 18, 1981), pp. 1296–99. This trend may be variously attributed to the deleterious effects of the pay cap on senior civil servants coupled with an uncommonly generous pension program—both conditions which obtained in only slightly diminished degree in 1978—or to the governmental reforms of the Carter administration, which effectively deprived senior civil servants of tenure in office.

55. Jeffrey M. Berry, *Lobbying for the People: The Political Behavior of Public Interest Groups* (Princeton: Princeton University Press, 1977), p. 186.

56. *Ibid.*, p. 188.

57. To mention only some of the largest: The Sierra Club has approximately 270,000 members nationally, Common Cause 225,000, Environmental Defense Fund 47,000, Natural Resources Defense Council 40,000, and Friends of the Earth 25,000.

58. William Cavala, "Changing the Rules Changes the Game: Party Reform and the 1972 California Delegation to the Democratic National Convention," *American Political Science Review* 68 (March 1974), pp. 27–42, is an early discussion of some of these issues in the context of delegate selection politics. On the difficulties of nominal versus authorized membership in a politically significant group, see, for example, the unpublished "Testimony of Lilia Molina Before the National Democratic Committee's Commission on Presidential Nominations" (mimeographed, Democratic National Committee, October 16, 1981). Ms. Molina was concerned about Hispanic members of the California delegation to the 1980 Democratic National Convention, and, among other observations, pointed out: "(1) Jim Costa, listed as Hispanic, is of Portuguese

ancestry, and even though technically Hispanic, does not identify
with the majority Hispanic group in California: Chicanos; (2) Louis
Papan, listed as Hispanic, is of Greek Ancestry; and (3) Houston
B. Quick, listed as Hispanic, was not listed as such by the California Democratic Party" (p. 2).

59. By attacking Congressional use of the frank, for example. See
Common Cause, et al. v. William F. Bolger, et al. Civil Action No.
1887-73 in the United States District Court for the District of Columbia. See also the programmatic suggestions and accompanying
discussion in an article by two Common Cause officials, David
Cohen and Wendy Wolff, "Freeing Congress from the Special Interest State: A Public Interest Agenda for the 1980's," *Harvard
Journal on Legislation* 17 (Spring 1980), pp. 253–93.

Chapter V: Political Reform and Democratic Values

1. See Kenneth A. Bode and Carol F. Casey, "Party Reform: Revisionism Revisited," in Robert A. Goldwin (ed.), *Political Parties in
the Eighties* (Washington, D.C.: American Enterprise Institute,
1980), pp. 3–19; Donald M. Fraser, "Democratizing the Democratic Party," *ibid.,* pp. 116–32; William J. Crotty, *Decision for the
Democrats* (Baltimore: Johns Hopkins University Press, 1978); De-
metrios Caraley et al., "American Political Institutions after Watergate—A Discussion," *Political Science Quarterly* 89 (Winter 1974–
75), pp. 713–49; Charles Longley, "National Party Reform and
the Presidential Primaries," prepared for delivery at the 1981 Annual Meeting of the Mid-West Political Science Association, April
15–19, 1981, Cincinnati; Norman C. Miller, "Democratic Reforms: They Work," *Wall Street Journal* (May 16, 1972); David S.
Broder, "From the Grass Roots Up," *Washington Post* (January 23,
1980); Broder, *The Party's Over* (New York: Harper & Row, 1972),
pp. 230–32.

2. V. O. Key, Jr., *American State Politics* (New York: Knopf, 1956), p.
133.

3. *Ibid.* p. 152.

4. See Austin Ranney, *The Federalization of Presidential Primaries*
(Washington, D.C.: American Enterprise Institute, 1978); and
Ranney, *Curing the Mischiefs of Faction* (Berkeley: University of
California Press, 1975); James I. Lengle, *Representation and Presi-
dential Primaries: The Democratic Party in the Post Reform Era* (West-
port, Conn.: Greenwood, 1981); Commission on Presidential
Nomination and Party Structure (Morley Winograd, chairman),

Openness, Participation and Party Building: Reforms for a Stronger Democratic Party (Washington D.C.: Democratic National Committee, January 25, 1978).

5. Lengle, *Representation and Presidential Primaries.*
6. Richard F. Schier, "Take Me Out to the Pol Game," *New York Times* (July 17, 1979).
7. *Ibid.*
8. Haynes Johnson, "Portrait of the New Delegate," *Washington Post* (July 8, 1972). Most studies of the "representativeness" of delegates stress delegates' political attitudes rather than their social standing. See, for example, Jeane Kirkpatrick, *The New Presidential Elite* (New York: Russell Sage Foundation, 1976); Mark Stern, Sandra Guest, Roger Handberg, William Maddox, "Party Reform and Party Change," presented at Mid-West Political Science Association Meeting, April 15–19, 1981, Cincinnati; Barbara G. Farah, "Convention Delegates: Party Reform and the Representativeness of Party Elites, 1972–1980," prepared for delivery at the 1981 Annual Meeting of the American Political Science Association, New York, September 3–6, 1981.
9. A good introductory discussion of some of the issues involved in what has become an enormous and very esoteric literature is Dennis C. Mueller, *Public Choice* (Cambridge: Cambridge University Press, 1979), especially pp. 19–67.
10. Perhaps the most famous discussion of this problem in the literature of political science is contained in Robert A. Dahl, *A Preface to Democratic Theory* (Chicago: University of Chicago Press, 1956), pp. 90–119. See also John D. May, "Up with Dick Daley," *Intellectual Digest* (March 1973), pp. 85–87.
11. See Steven J. Brams and Peter C. Fishburn, "Approval Voting," *American Political Science Review* 72 (September 1978), pp. 831–47; Brams, *The Presidential Election Game* (New Haven: Yale University Press, 1978), pp. 193–229; and Brams, "Approval Voting: A Practical Reform for Multicandidate Elections," *National Civic Review* 68 (November 1979), pp. 549–53, 560. As with any automated process, there are problems associated with approval voting in that its proponents are probably wrong in thinking such a system guarantees that centrists or moderates would be favored. Moderates win under approval voting only if voters who favor extremist candidates also cast their votes for moderates. But if centrist voters, being moderate, find a wide range of alternatives acceptable and ideological voters meanwhile bullet-vote, an extremist candidate could end up the winner.

12. See James I. Lengle, "Divisive Presidential Primaries and Party Electoral Prospects, 1932–1976," *American Politics Quarterly* 8 (July 1980), pp. 261–78; Robert A. Bernstein, "Divisive Primaries Do Hurt: U.S. Senate Races, 1956–1972," *American Political Science Review* 71 (June 1977), pp. 540–45; Andrew Hacker, "Does a 'Divisive' Primary Harm a Candidate's Election Chances?" *American Political Science Review* 59 (March 1965), pp. 105–10; Donald Johnson and James Gibson, "The Divisive Primary Revisited: Party Activists in Iowa," *American Political Science Review* 68 (March 1974), pp. 67–77.

13. The most pertinent historical example of this problem at work is no doubt the nomination of Senator George McGovern by the Democrats in 1972. It was not delegates from primaries alone who selected McGovern as the nominee. The primaries did, however, reveal a pattern of preferences within the party that, while selecting McGovern, foreshadowed his landslide defeat. Brokerage mechanisms at the national convention were not available to deal with the impending disaster. See Vermont Royster, "Can McGovern Overcome the Odds?" *Wall Street Journal* (July 13, 1972); Fred L. Zimmerman, "Unhappy Days: A Mood of Bitterness Deepens at Convention as Squabbles Drag On," *Wall Street Journal* (July 11, 1972); Arlen J. Large, "Divided Democrats: Party Likely To Emerge from Its Convention with Severe Wounds," *Wall Street Journal* (July 10, 1972); George Gallup, "No Democrat Shows Ability To Attract Votes Like Nixon," *Washington Post* (July 2, 1972); Jude Wanniski, "The McGovernites and Darwin's Law," *Wall Street Journal* (July 10, 1972); Arlen J. Large, "And Now McGovern Must Seek To Charm Another Constituency," *Wall Street Journal* (June 8, 1972); David S. Broder, "The Splintered Majority," *Washington Post* (July 9, 1972); Frank Lynn, "State Democratic Factions Fail To Unite on McGovern," *New York Times* (October 8, 1972); Ronald Sullivan, "Lag in Student-Vote Drive Laid to McGovern's Staff," *New York Times* (October 2, 1972); Jack Rosenthal, "Yankelovich Says Polls May Create a Bandwagon," *New York Times* (October 6, 1972). At its first opportunity following the 1972 debacle the Democratic party once again tinkered with its rules for delegate selection under the aegis of a new commission headed by Representative Barbara Mikulski. The Mikulski rules abolished winner-take-all primaries and encouraged proportional representation in caucuses and conventions in an attempt to keep in the running strong candidates who did not win early primaries but made a respectable showing. See David S. Broder, "New Democratic Rules: First-Ballot Victory Unlikely," *Washington Post* (March

31, 1974). The effort has proven unsuccessful. Early delegate commitments stimulated by news media coverage of early decisions seem to have prevailed, and the role of the national convention has remained vestigial. Thus the problem of aggregation described in the text remains.

14. The "right winner" in this example would *either* be (1) the winner of all pair-wise comparisons, if such a candidate exists or (2) if there is no such winner, the candidate who emerges after a process in which delegates are allowed to deliberate, change their preferences for strategic purposes, and respond to the views of other delegates.

15. Key, *American State Politics,* pp. 144–45.

16. See, for example, Donald Fraser, "Democratizing the Democratic Party."

17. See Michael J. Robinson, "TV's Newest Program: 'The Presidential Nominations Game,'" *Public Opinion* 1 (May–June 1978), pp. 41–46; Michael J. Robinson and Karen A. McPherson, "Television News Coverage before the 1976 New Hampshire Primary: The Focus of Network Journalism," *Journal of Broadcasting* 21 (Spring 1977), pp. 177–86; Michael J. Robinson and Karen A. McPherson, "The Early Presidential Campaign on Network Television," in A. Casebier and J. J. Casebier (eds.), *Social Responsibilities of the Mass Media* (Washington, D.C.: University Press of America, 1978), pp. 5–41.

18. This was suggested both by the Democratic party's post-1976 Winograd Commission and its post-1980 Hunt Commission. In both cases exceptions were given to the states of Iowa and New Hampshire.

19. As indeed they already do, given the overwhelming influence of early results on later alternatives. *Congressional Quarterly Weekly Report* (December 26, 1981), p. 2567 shows:

Table 5.4 States seek early primaries

	1968		1972		1976		1980	
Democratic Primaries								
February to early April	2	(12%)	4	(17%)	8	(27%)	13	(37%)
Late April to June 1	10	(59%)	14	(61%)	19	(63%)	14	(40%)
Rest of June	5	(29%)	5	(22%)	3	(10%)	8	(23%)
	17	(100%)	23	(100%)	30	(100%)	35	(100%)

Table 5.4   *(continued)*

	1968		1972		1976		1980	
Republican Primaries								
February to early								
April	2	(13%)	4	(17%)	7	(25%)	11	(34%)
Late April to								
June 1	9	(56%)	13	(57%)	18	(64%)	13	(41%)
Rest of June	5	(31%)	6	(26%)	3	(11%)	8	(25%)
	16	(100%)	23	(100%)	28	(100%)	32	(100%)

Source: *Congressional Quarterly.*

20. This also was a proposal of the Democratic party's Hunt Commission.
21. See Richard L. Rubin, *Press, Party and Presidency* (New York: Norton, 1981), pp. 191–96. "Not only was [television journalists'] affirmation of primaries clear from the vastly disproportionate air time given primaries compared to other selection methods, but also numerous phrases attributing inherent democratic values to primaries appeared, sprinkled liberally throughout network news" (p. 193).
22. *Cousins v. Wigoda* 419 *U.S.* 477 (1975); *Democratic Party of U.S. v. La Follette* 67 *L. ED.2d* 82 (1981).
23. There is a $50,000 expenditure limit on candidates and their immediate families for those presidential candidates accepting public funding according to the 1976 amendments. Thus, according to P.L. 94-283, Section 305: ". . . no candidate shall knowingly make expenditures from his personal funds, or the personal funds of his immediate family, in connection with his campaign for nomination for election to the office of President in excess of, in the agregate, $50,000." See also *Buckley et al. v. Valeo* 424 U.S. 1 (1976).
24. There was evidence, of course, of political contributions by politically interested persons and groups, and of the already illegal collection of funds. Readers will judge for themselves the plausibility of the inferences constructed of these materials by the District of Columbia Circuit Court in *Buckley v. Valeo* 519 F.2nd 821 (D.C. Circuit, 1975) and the Supreme Court in *Buckley et al. v. Valeo.* The Circuit Court opinion gives excellent guidance through the evidence on this point in the legislative record. A brilliant defense of the Circuit Court's position is Harold Leventhal, "Courts and Political Thickets," *Columbia Law Review* 77 (April 1977), pp. 345–87. Leventhal, a former treasurer of the Democratic party, is

thought to have been the judge of the District of Columbia Circuit most influential in writing the per curium—unsigned—opinion of the Circuit Court. A consideration of the constitutional issues raised by *Buckley v. Valeo* less indulgent to the view of the D.C. Circuit is Daniel D. Polsby, *"Buckley v. Valeo:* The Special Nature of Political Speech," *Supreme Court Review 1976* (Chicago: University of Chicago Press, 1977), pp. 1–44.

25. *Democratic Party of U.S. v. La Follette.*

26. See the careful analysis of this and related issues by one of Wisconsin's foremost political scientists, Leon D. Epstein, "Party Confederations and Political Nationalization," prepared for the conference on the Continuing Legacy of the Articles of Confederation, Center for the Study of Federalism, Temple University, Philadelphia, August 30–September 2, 1981.

27. William L. Riordan, *Plunkitt of Tammany Hall* (New York: Dutton, 1963) (first printed 1905), pp. 3–6.

28. *Ibid.,* pp. 11–16 and *passim.*

29. A good brief account of the response of the national convention is Richard H. Rovere, "Letter from Washington," *The New Yorker* (October 16, 1965), pp. 233–44. See also Lester M. Salamon and Stephen Van Evera, "Fear, Apathy, and Discrimination: A Test of Three Explanations of Political Participation," *American Political Science Review* 67 (December 1973), pp. 1288–1306; and Fraser, "Democratizing the Democratic Party."

Index

255

Security and Liberty

Restriction by Stealth

Kate Moss
Wolverhampton University, UK

Preface by Martin Gill

Foreword by Ken Pease
University of Loughborough, UK

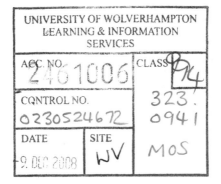

palgrave
macmillan

First published 2009 by
PALGRAVE MACMILLAN

Palgrave Macmillan in the UK is an imprint of Macmillan Publishers Limited, registered in England, company number 785998, of Houndmills, Basingstoke, Hampshire RG21 6XS.

Palgrave Macmillan in the US is a division of St Martin's Press LLC, 175 Fifth Avenue, New York, NY 10010.

Palgrave Macmillan is the global academic imprint of the above companies and has companies and representatives throughout the world.

Palgrave® and Macmillan® are registered trademarks in the United States, the United Kingdom, Europe and other countries.

ISBN-13: 978-0-230-52467-5   hardback
ISBN-10: 0-230-52467-2   hardback

This book is printed on paper suitable for recycling and made from fully managed and sustained forest sources. Logging, pulping and manufacturing processes are expected to conform to the environmental regulations of the country of origin.

A catalogue record for this book is available from the British Library.

Library of Congress Cataloging-in-Publication Data

Moss, Kate, 1965–
    Security and liberty : restriction by stealth / Kate Moss ; preface
    by Ken Pease.
        p. cm.
    Includes bibliographical references.
    ISBN 978-0-230-52467-5 (alk. paper)
        1. Civil rights–Great Britain. 2. National security–Great Britain.
    3. Civil rights–United States. 4. National security–United States.
    I. Title.
    JC599.G7M67 2009
    323.0941–dc22   2008030092

Printed and bound in Great Britain by
CPI Antony Rowe, Chippenham and Eastbourne

For my greatest achievements – my children,
Gemma and Christopher.

Contents

Acknowledgements

I would like to thank Professor Ken Pease for having the conversation with me that led to the idea for this book and for his huge encouragement throughout, which as always, has been inspirational.

Many thanks both to Professor Ken Pease and Professor Herschel Prins for taking the time to proof read every chapter and make incredibly sensible comments on all of my drafts. I am very fortunate to be able to call on such eminent help.

Many thanks also go to Professor Martin Gill for his encouragement throughout; from listening to my idea about the book, to reading and commenting on the final draft.

Thanks also to Gemma Moss who helped to demystify Garland and to postgraduate students Kamara Heron and David Knight, whose work on detention without trial and football hooliganism, provided valuable material for chapters four and five.

Thanks to 'Billy' – you know who you are–for your help with chapter six.

I am very grateful to Olivia Middleton at Palgrave Macmillan, who has been both encouraging and patient.

Thanks also to my husband 'Brooksie' who is always supremely supportive.

Finally my thanks to the School of Legal Studies, Wolverhampton University who have been instrumental in facilitating this work, and in particular to Brian Mitchell, Martin Cartwright and my best chum Rowland Hughes. The drinks are on me again boys!

Preface

The Crime Prevention and Security Management Series

This new Series seeks to develop new insights on security and crime prevention. There are a variety of ways of achieving this, by, for example, producing new research or developing new theories or re-evaluating old ones. What Kate Moss does in this book is question the value and appropriateness of using legislation to control crime. More than that, she seeks to bring what has been a neglected subject to the forefront of academic debate.

For Kate, the heavy emphasis by New Labour on using legislation to facilitate crime control has passed with relatively little academic evaluation, and this book is where she starts to make amends. She discusses the restrictions imposed on people by the criminalising of behaviour that in many cases had long been held to be reasonable; the difficulty created by the different types of legislation that has been passed in providing appropriate protection for citizens; the movement away from policing by consent and the augmentation of powers for the police not matched by sufficient safeguards to protect people's civil liberties.

She illustrates her case with examples that are varied, for example, the strategies of detention without trial, football banning orders and attempts to secure the borders. She discusses how previously 'normal' behaviours have been restricted and longstanding civil liberties compromised or eroded. Her essential point is that more laws do not make crime less likely, indeed they often make it more common.

As you will read, Kate does not mince her words. She invites readers to recognise the changing political landscape in providing security and preventing crime. She does not disguise her disappointment at the stance of criminology and criminologists. For her, crime control has lost direction, legislation has been based on perceived risks rather than real ones. As a consequence what has emerged is a legislative framework that is heavy handed and disproportionate. It is also counterproductive and beyond being unnecessary, and an infringement of basic human rights, it can, she argues actually work in the interests of offenders including terrorists.

Not everyone will agree with Kate, and some no doubt will strongly disagree, but few will surely deny that this is an area which merits more attention. In this way, we ignore her at our peril.

Martin Gill

Foreword

Cane toads are a huge problem for Australian wildlife and agriculture. Citizens are encouraged to catch and kill them. The humane way of killing cane toads is to freeze them gradually.[1] Apparently the toads suffer no discomfort as their body temperature falls. After 48 hours, they are frozen solid. If things happen gradually, people, like cane toads, don't really notice. When I first became interested in crime in the early 1970s, ideas in the ascendant included the strict circumscription of behaviour properly criminalized, and the corresponding circumscription of the discretion properly exercised by judicial and paroling authorities. George Jackson[2] was the tragic poster boy for the second of these trends. For those for whom this is pre-history, the basic facts of Jackson's life and death merit re-telling. Jackson's robbery of a petrol station earned him a 'one year to life' sentence in 1959. His intransigence at parole hearings meant that he was still imprisoned eleven years later, when with two other prisoners he was charged with murdering a guard. Later the same year, Jackson's seventeen year old brother Jonathan was shot dead in an attempt to free him. A year later, George Jackson himself was killed by a prison guard. While there are many strands to the story, it is certain that had a determinate sentence been imposed, based upon the seriousness of Jackson's initial offence, his release would have come long before the bloody events of 1970 and 1971. Jackson's fate, resulting not from his crime but from his refusal to 'fake reformed' was one of the contributing factors leading to the development of mechanisms to rein in discretion in sentencing and parole decisions – on both sides of the Atlantic.

If, when the notions of due process and just deserts held sway, anyone had predicted that a generation later Guantánamo Bay would be filled with untried people and flights of extraordinary rendition exported prisoners to places convenient for their torture, they would have been thought insane. That the UK Parliament is now haggling not about the principle of detention without trial but how many weeks and months

---

[1]http://www.agric.wa.gov.au/content/pw/vp/toad/canetoad_welfare.htm (accessed 12th May 2008)
[2]http://www.spartacus.schoolnet.co.uk/USACjacksonG.htm (accessed 14th May 2008)

such detention would be allowed to last, is breathtaking. But like the freezing cane toad, we seem largely oblivious to what is happening.

Kate Moss sets the birthplace of this book in a lunchtime meeting between us. I remember it well, a fact which reflects the admirable speed with which Kate has completed it, and the passionate enthusiasm for the idea which we both felt. The resulting book is more nuanced and wide-ranging than our lunchtime rant. Kate deals with a range of aspects of the creeping power of the executive, some less dramatic than others, all of them important elements of burgeoning fear-driven law and practice. She notes the unfeasibility of widespread use of the Human Rights Act 1998 by individuals as a bulwark against the oppressive use of state power. She analyses the increasing over-reach of the criminal law, and the constitutional arrangements which have facilitated this. She places the Devlin-Hart debate about the legislation of morality in a modern context. The chapter addressing detention without trial is perhaps the most depressing in the book for an old-style liberal, closely followed by her discussion of privacy issues.

Jeffrey Rosen (2004) has cogently argued how security and civil liberties can co-exist in a post September 11th world. As for Rosen, fear of terrorism is a motif of Kate Moss' book, sometimes explicit, sometimes implicit. The oft-asked question concerns the point at which this fear allows state power to be ramped up to the point at which a terrorist's work is done for him and the homeland now inhabited ceases to be the homeland whose security was sought. Kate's canvas is broad, showing how a cast of mind can spawn legislation and practice over a wide range only tenuously associated with terrorism. I am touched that she invited me to write this foreword, and hope the book proves as influential as it deserves to be.

Ken Pease
14th May 2008

Rosen, J. (2004) *The Naked Crowd: Reclaiming Security and Freedom in an Anxious Age*. New York: Random House.

1
The Retreat from Liberty

Introduction

Writing in March 2006, Martin Bright, political editor for the New Statesman commented that the current British government has a mania for legislation. Citing a response from Home Office Minister Baroness Scotland to a question posed by Lord Tebbitt, he suggested that since 1997, and according to the latest Home Office information, over four hundred forms of behaviour, previously legal, are now illegal, thanks to a plethora of legislation passed presumably under the banner of the need for security and crime reduction. Some of this avalanche of legislation would not be well known, such as those offences created by the Elections and Referendums Act 2000. Some are arguably the result of a recognition that the law must continue to play 'catch up' with those criminals who avail themselves of advances in technology. In these cases, offences created by the Sexual Offences Act 2003 such as grooming and downloading internet child pornography have a place, as do good examples of ground breaking legislation such as the Crime and Disorder Act 1998, the Human Rights Act 1998 and the Freedom of Information Act 2000. However, according to Bright (2006):[1]

> This government has a mania for legislation. Since 1997 it has introduced no fewer than 11 education bills to tinker around the edges of our bewildering school and university system. The genuine improvements that have taken place, especially in primary schools, have been the result of targeted investment and an improvement in the morale

---

[1]www.newstatesman.com/200603200004

of the teaching profession. If anything, new legislation has hampered this process. In other areas this fetish is more pronounced. According to the Home Office, there are now 404 forms of behaviour that were legal when the Labour government came to power and which are now outlawed. Some of these offences, such as 'grooming' by paedophiles on the internet or the downloading of child pornography, recognise that the law must adapt to changing technology. But can all the 402 other offences really be necessary?

So is this true? Does the present government really have a mania for legislation and if so, what is the explanation for this? Moreover, should we be worried about it? My reason for writing this book came out of a long – some might say rather protracted – interest in one particular aspect of the Crime and Disorder Act 1998 (hereinafter referred to as CDA) – namely section 17. I had become interested in this as a result of a brief conversation with my long time friend Ken Pease. The CDA was rightly viewed by most academics at that time as being a far reaching, radical and innovative piece of legislation which had emanated from the 1991 Morgan Report, albeit in a rather more sanitised version than had been suggested in the 1991 report. Nonetheless, aspects of it for criminologists like Ken were of interest since for the first time it (amongst other things) placed some statutory responsibility for crime reduction on local authorities alongside the police. It had been widely suggested that the responsibility for crime reduction should not solely lie with the police as the long accepted primary crime prevention agents, but should be spread more widely amongst other agencies and – although of course the CDA did not legislate for this – amongst the general public. This was what section 17 – by legislating to make statutory the duty to consider crime prevention in 'all decision making processes' – did. His interest in this was therefore not surprising and I suppose, given that he found himself that day in a Law School talking to me, it is also not surprising that the conversation came round to what the implications of this move might be.

So it was that our interest in this area grew and subsequently gave rise to a number of academic publications based on our research of the area carried out amongst various police forces and local authorities.[2] The main thrust of my personal interest in section 17 became the fact that

---

[2]See for example Moss & Pease (1999); Bullock, Moss & Smith (2000); Moss & Seddon (2001); Moss & Ardley (2007); Cockfield & Moss 2002; Moss (2003) and Moss & Stephens (eds) (2006).

whilst it statutorily obliged local authorities to do all that they reasonably could to prevent crime and disorder in their areas, it quickly became clear to me that this duty did not extend to central government. Not a problem you might think, until of course as a lawyer, you start to look at the legal loopholes or practical anomalies that this might create.

Further examination of the application of this section of the CDA, and the instances where local authorities and police forces, hard pressed by crime and disorder issues, had tried to use it to alleviate the crime and disorder problems in their areas created by attractive nuisances such as those associated with the burgeoning late night economy and developers wishing to cash in on this, soon demonstrated something to me. This was the fact that although the purpose of section 17 had been emphasised by central government as being an 'enabler' for crime reduction, when it was actually used by local authorities to try to resist contentious planning applications by pub and nightclub developers, and these rejected applications had subsequently gone to appeal, the Planning Inspectorate had something interesting to say. Namely that since they were an arm of central government and therefore not bound by the criteria laid out in section 17, they would not support local authorities' positions on appeal where they were specifically based on section 17.

I have written about these cases in the literature previously cited but back to the point in hand. Why did this pre-empt my interest in writing a book like this? I suppose because it drew my attention first to the problems of legislating to reduce crime and whether this was a) possible and b) a good way of doing it in the first place. Second, in thinking about these aspects I became aware of just how much legislation *had* actually been passed in the last ten years under New Labour and I began to question just why there had been so much. This is where this book begins, with three questions which I shall seek to answer. First, what evidence is there for the veritable deluge of legislation which has reached the statute books over the last ten years and what are the reasons for this? I shall attempt to give some examples of this – primarily in the sense of an overview of all the ways in which I believe we are currently criminalised by more and more legislation, but moreover by all the associated ways in which, over quite a short space of time, we have, in various other stealthy ways had our essential civil liberties restricted. This presents a veritable cornucopia of possibilities and it quickly became clear to me that in order to produce something coherent some choices had to be made. My choice therefore was that having given an overview of the evidence for restriction through legislation and other related means, that my second task was to highlight some particularly interesting areas in which to concentrate this argument and to present to the reader some detailed examples which in my view demonstrate the point I am trying to make. This approach links well to the theme of this series of books in security and risk management because my aim, in line with the theme of the books, is to generate a new insight on crime reduction. My final aim is to ask, is legislating to reduce crime a really good idea, or are there better ways of doing it and if so, what are these and why are they better? In other words, why might it be wrong to over legislate and what sort of societies could be produced from a propensity to over legislate?

The evidence – an overview

Bright (2006) is obviously not the only person who has commented recently on what could easily be described as a 'deluge' of criminal justice and associated legislation – not to mention Government Directives – which have filtered down on the unsuspecting public over the last ten to 15 years. Arguably much of this has been prompted by what could be described as 'knee jerk' reactions to social problems. Prins (2007:190) comments that:

> It is as though our political leaders think that all social problems can be resolved through the statute book. Many of these statutes have been ill-thought-through, over-complicated and highly unlikely to achieve the aims expected of them.....The most noticeable and worrying development is the political desire for a 'quick fix'....as though our leaders are singularly unable to tolerate ambiguity and uncertainty. This produces a state of rhetoric over reality.

It is important to remember the context in which this propensity for legislating arises. Specifically it appears at least in part to have been a result of the government's manifesto commitment in 1997 to be 'tough on crime, tough on the causes of crime.' A commitment which they themselves would doubtless argue has been successful since undoubtedly they have made a huge financial investment in this idea. The government would doubtless also argue that the figures and the facts speak for themselves. The chances of being a victim of crime are at their lowest for 20 years, the official crime rate has fallen by 35 per cent since 1997 and the government is very close to meeting its target of a 15 per cent reduction in crime in the five years to 2007–2008. The number of people's homes being broken into and the number of cars being stolen or damaged has also reduced dramatically in line with national targets. There has been less success with violent crimes, such as homicide and robbery. However, success is also claimed in other areas. This includes a reduction in the number of unfounded asylum claims, meeting the target on bringing more offenders to justice and being above target in relation to the number of problem drug users entering treatment programmes.

Even given these alleged successes, the Home Office has had one of the most challenging and difficult times in its 250 year history. This included a capability review which found that the Home Office approach to leadership and strategy was the worst of all Whitehall departments and a series of crises which saw three successive Home Secretaries over a period of only 18 months. These crises include the increase in the prison population which is currently, for the first time over 80 thousand; an increase in the number of dangerous prisoners escaping from open prisons[3] and an admission that they are unaware of the number of foreign offenders in the country. This period has culminated with the most radical change since the Home Office was first created in 1782. With almost immediate effect the department has lost its responsibility for the prison service (which it has held since 1823) and the probation service. We are now told that their focus will shift towards tackling the threat of terrorism, alongside taking on responsibility for the police service, for crime reduction, immigration and asylum, and identity and passports.

Legislation has been a key part of the Home Office's approach. One of the first (and generally well received) pieces of legislation was the Crime and Disorder Act 1998 which put crime and disorder reduction partnerships on a statutory footing with the requirement to undertake a crime audit and set targets within a three year strategy. Not all legislation has been as positively received. Since 1997 the Home Office has produced over 60 bills and during the ten years in office has created over 3,000 new offences. For example, a sixth immigration bill, an eighth terrorism bill, and a twenty third justice bill. Attempts to deal with the challenges have not been convincing. The introduction of policies and programmes and a greater focus on operational performance have been almost as relentless as the legislative drive but there have been inconsistencies. The rationalisation of police force structures and the democratisation of policing, which was a real promise of the police reform programme introduced by former Home Secretary Charles Clark, appear now to be very much on the back burner. Efforts to deal with the difficulties of immigration and asylum have centred on the creation of an arms-length executive agency

---

[3]Berry, J. (2006) *The Guardian* UK News Section, May 6th, page 7.

– something that was previously resisted – and after efforts made to create the National Offender Management Service it will now move to the Ministry of Justice.

In summary, the last ten years has been a real challenge. Substantial financial investment by the Government has resulted in increased resources but the claimed successes remain untested and the reputation of the Home Office is at an all time low. At the same time one must surely assume that the investment in criminal justice cannot and will not continue. The pledge to be 'tough on crime and tough on the causes of crime' arguably remains elusive (although the Government would doubtless disagree) and in the midst of all this rhetoric and media hype about crime, what appears to have been forgotten is what we may have given up in order to achieve these modest reductions. The evidence appears clear, that more legislation which criminalises more behaviour has indeed reached the statute books during the last ten years than ever before. The question is, does more law reduce more and more crime? Surely the reverse is true, that more law merely criminalises more and more behaviour? So what is the evidence for this and has this impacted our essential rights and liberties as citizens? Moreover, does this represent a new form of social control – a point which epitomises the theme of this series of books and which will be taken up in more detail in Chapter 2.

A question of rights and liberties?

What are our rights and liberties currently in the UK? The Human Rights Act 1998 (HRA) gave legal effect in the UK to certain fundamental rights and freedoms which were originally contained in the European Convention on Human Rights (ECHR). Sixteen basic rights were taken from the European Convention on Human Rights. These rights not only affect matters of life and death like freedom from torture and killing but also affect rights in everyday life: what individuals can say and do, their beliefs, right to a fair trial and many other similar basic entitlements. The rights include:

- right to life
- prohibition of torture
- prohibition of slavery and forced labour
- right to liberty and security
- right to a fair trial
- no punishment without law

- right to respect for private and family life
- freedom of thought, conscience and religion
- freedom of expression
- freedom of assembly and association
- right to marry
- prohibition of discrimination
- protection of property
- right to education
- right to free elections
- abolition of the death penalty

But how does the Human Rights Act 1998 work in practice? The HRA is said to give 'greater effect' to Convention Rights in two main ways: First by making it clear that as far as possible the courts in this country should interpret the law in a way that is compatible with Convention rights. Second, it places an obligation on public authorities to act compatibly with Convention rights. The HRA also gives people the right to take court proceedings if they think that their Convention rights have been breached or are going to be. Parliament makes laws but it is the courts that have to interpret them. The HRA makes it clear that when they are interpreting legislation the courts must do so in a way which does not lead to people's Convention rights being breached. Moreover, the courts are now under a duty to develop the common law – the law which has been developed through decisions of the courts themselves – in a way that is compatible with Convention rights. But what happens if the Courts cannot read the law compatibly? If the law is an Act of Parliament, the courts have no choice but to apply the law as it is, even though it breaches Convention rights. However, the higher courts (the High Court, the Court of Appeal and the House of Lords) have the power to make what is called a 'declaration of incompatibility'. This is a statement that the courts consider that a particular law breaches Convention rights. It is meant to encourage Parliament to amend the law, but the courts cannot force the Government or Parliament to amend the law if they do not want to.

Added to this a lot of law is not set out in Acts of Parliament but rather in secondary legislation. Secondary legislation is law made under the authority of an Act of Parliament. Rather than set out detailed provisions in an Act of Parliament, Parliament will frequently give the power to make detailed laws to a government minister. The Act of Parliament will give the minister the power to make law but the law itself will be set out in regulations or orders. For example, most social security law is set out in regulations rather than in Acts of Parliament. Where the courts find that an item of secondary legislation is incompatible with Convention rights, they have the power to strike the law down or not to apply it. This applies to all courts, not just the higher ones. The only circumstance where this is not possible is where the secondary legislation merely repeats a requirement of an Act of Parliament.

The HRA also requires public authorities to act in a way that does not breach Convention rights. The HRA does not define the term public authority, but it is clear that bodies like the police, local councils and government departments and agencies are all public authorities. Private individuals and bodies will not be public authorities for the purposes of the HRA unless they are performing a public function. So, for example, a private security company that has a contract with the Government to transport prisoners to and from court will be a public authority for the purposes of the HRA (and therefore under a duty to respect Convention rights) when it is transporting prisoners but will not be when it is guarding private property under a contract with a private business. The issue of whether a person or body is a public authority for the purposes of the HRA can be very difficult to determine. As there is no definition of a public authority in the HRA this is something that the courts have to decide on.

If an individual thinks therefore that his/her Human Rights have been breached what can s/he do about it? Someone who believes that a public authority has breached their Convention rights, or is proposing to, can bring court proceedings against the public authority. A person can also raise a breach of their Convention rights as a defence in any court proceedings against them. In either case the person must be a 'victim' of the breach or potential breach, that is, someone who is directly affected by it, (this is a requirement that has its origins in ECHR case law). Generally, a person bringing court proceedings against a public authority under the HRA will be seeking a declaration that the public authority has breached their Convention rights or is proposing to do so. If the breach is continuing they will also want an order that the public authority should stop acting in a way that breaches their Convention rights. They may also seek compensation, although the courts have made it clear that it is not always appropriate for them to award this.

When someone brings proceedings against a public authority for breach of their Convention rights, the public authority may be able to defend itself by saying that it had no choice but to act in the way that it did because it was required to do so by an Act of Parliament. Where this happens the most the person bringing the case may hope to achieve is a declaration of incompatibility. In most cases the appropriate court proceedings to bring against a public authority under the HRA will be an application for judicial review. Court rules require an application for judicial review to be brought 'promptly' and in any event within three months of the decision or action being challenged. Where someone does not make an application for judicial review there is a one year time limit for starting proceedings.

What about proceedings against private individuals or bodies? Private bodies and individuals are not required by the HRA to respect Convention rights, therefore it is not possible to take proceedings under the HRA against them. Theoretically this does not mean that the HRA will not have an effect on court proceedings between private bodies or individuals since the courts themselves are public authorities under the HRA and are also required to interpret existing laws and to develop them in a way that is compatible with Convention rights. However, how likely is all of this to actually take place? It is suggested not very since to take a case in any of the ways so described would be a very lengthy and costly process. The majority of people would simply not be able to afford such a course of action and such cases would be unlikely to attract legal aid. The fact remains therefore that although these so called rights are now enshrined in law, access to them is another matter entirely.

Thus it is that our rights are enshrined in a little used and inaccessible piece of legislation, recourse to which rarely happens. In stark contrast to this, laws restraining or restricting behaviour of various types are many and varied and arguably we have seen a growth in such laws which have most recently been passed on the basis of their necessity to combat diverse problems ranging from anti social behaviour to terrorism. The British Government has long debated the issue of liberties and rights but in spite of legislation such as the ECHR, and the HRA 1998 it would appear that individuals are becoming less tolerant on the one hand and yet more formally restricted on the other. Why is this? Maybe the States' move to impose more formal restrictions on citizens is having an effect on people's attitudes to free speech. Maybe the more we are told we should be restricted in the name of the protection of our security, then the more paranoid we become and therefore the less tolerant we become because we are all so afraid of subversion and what that might mean. Take for example two recent examples. In August 2006 two Muslims were asked to disembark from a plane because of the concerns of other passengers and in April 2006 in Paris a car deliberately ploughed into crowd of protesting students.[4] Terrorism has doubtless had an impact upon these sorts of occurrences and consequently upon the way in which people view their security and the way in which they are told they should be responding to this. Media influences about issues such as terrorism, violent crime, victimisation and even health risks such as the risk of dying from avian flu are all reported in such a way as to instil unnecessary moral panics into the general population – this same condition being so ably reported by Cohen (2002).

It appears that individuals are being made to feel they are more at risk, they therefore accept what the Government says about needing more legislative restraints on behaviour and movement and therefore the general acquiescence that is required to push more and more legislation through on the back of this is readily available and plays right into the hands of a government who seeks to enforce the social control of the state by these means arguably more than any other government ever has. It is possible to make this point by reviewing just a few of the ways in which our privacy is compromised. A good example is CCTV in town centres – most notably a type recently suggested by the police and supported by some local councils – which is capable of monitoring conversation in the street using high powered microphones. These devices are already being used and it has been reported in the media that there is interest in having more installed in London before the 2012 Olympic Games. However, this suggestion lends weight to the debate that Britain is becoming a 'surveillance society.' A report in *The Times* recently (based on the work of Norris & Armstrong, 1999) highlighted that there are more than 4.2 million CCTV cameras, with the average person being filmed more than 300 times a day. The addition of microphones takes surveillance into uncharted territory. However, the same article also reported that laws in Holland actually limit the recording of the sounds to short bursts and that the implementation of such technology would depend on the privacy laws of the country involved. It is interesting to speculate on how severe the legal obstacles in Britain would be to the implementation of these sorts of devices and also on what the general public would think is a reasonable use of technology. There would also doubtless be issues surrounding police resources and their capacity to deal with matters arising out of this technology. Two further pertinent points in relation to this debate is that the work of Gill, Bryan & Allan (2007) suggests that the public like

---

[4]www.dailymail.co.uk/pages/live/articles/news/news.html?in_article_id=401419&i n_page_id=1770 and http://news.bbc.co.uk/1/hi/world/europe/ 4888182.stm

CCTV but they assume that it works, when the evidence for this is not that good. Similarly the work of Gill, Little, Spriggs & Collins (2006/07) and Gill & Loveday (2003) demonstrates that for some offenders, CCTV represents merely another problem to be managed.

What about the prospect of ID cards? An interesting debate has ensued regarding the crime prevention possibilities of this move as against the possible infringements of privacy, no doubt and understandably sensitive for those who can remember how the Third Reich were able to identify Jews during the Holocaust. What about the fact that our mobile phone calls can be monitored through a process whereby the hardware locates a signal which leaves a trace that the police can and do access for investigative purposes? In London, the use of 'Oyster' travel cards permits the charting of people's travel on public transport and let's not forget that emails sent and received at work can be electronically scanned to ensure that they are, amongst other things, appropriate. Tracing mobile phone calls is also relatively easy. It appears that we may use these forms of control more than anyone else. For example, the Germans have constitutional protections that limit such data gathering far more effectively than in Britain. Anecdotally, whilst speaking to a German police officer at an information sharing conference recently I was surprised to hear of the restrictions which exist on the reporting of crime there – the police being unable to report in the media, suspects as being for example either white, black or Asian. So should the British addiction to surveillance be a cause of concern? Is our privacy being invaded, are we being over controlled or restricted and do we have little control over who collects information? It is relevant to look at some examples of current restrictions.

Are we free to speak?

'Everyone has the right to freedom of opinion and expression; this right includes freedom to hold opinions without interference and to seek, receive and impart information and ideas through any media and regardless of frontiers.'

Article 19, Universal Declaration of Human Rights

Freedom of expression and opinion is a foundation without which many other basic human rights cannot be enjoyed. Allowing people to publicly investigate and report on human rights abuses makes it much harder for those responsible for them to hide behind a veil of silence and ignorance. Similarly freedom of expression makes a valuable contribution to other key areas of concern – good governance, rule of law and democracy. The media has a vital role in scrutinising and evaluating the actions of Government, forcing them to manage resources and set policies in a transparent and equitable way. And without journalists having the right to report on court cases and legal judgements, it would be much harder to guarantee an independent and fair judicial process. Finally, the ability to hold, exchange and challenge the opinions of yourself and others is a necessary component of a functioning democracy.

Governments have a duty to eliminate barriers to freedom of expression and information, and to create an environment in which free speech and free media flourish. Media professionals should be able to work freely without fear of intimidation, violence or imprisonment. Sadly, there are still many countries around the world in which Governments stifle dissent and criticism or fail to prevent other groups from targeting the media. A free and independent media requires governments to provide a fair and transparent regulatory environment, an equitable distribution of broadcasting frequencies and opportunities for all sections of society to access and contribute to the media.

How is freedom of expression currently being upheld in the UK? Freedom of expression covers a number of issues all of which cannot be discussed here. However, of relevance to this chapter is the issue of freedom of speech in relation to religion, which has been a topic of some recent debate both legally and within the media (*The Times*, 3rd February 2006).[5] In June 2005 the UK Government unveiled controversial plans to make incitement to religious hatred illegal. It was claimed that the new offence would give equal protection to all faiths, although it should be remembered that Jews and Sikhs are already covered by race hate laws which give them full protection from incitement because the courts regard them as distinct races. Christians, Muslims and others have not been given the same protection because it is said that they do not constitute a single ethnic block. Northern Ireland has its own laws to deal with sectarian discrimination between Protestants and Catholics. The proposed law was designed to cover words or behaviour intended or likely to stir up religious hatred and would create a new offence of incitement to religious hatred, applying to comments made in public or in the media, as well as through written material. Unsurprisingly this move by the Government proved to be controversial. Oppo-

---

[5]www.timesonline.co.uk/tol/comment/letters/article725454.ece

nents claimed that it would stifle free speech whilst Ministers claimed that the new law would not affect 'criticism, commentary or ridicule of faiths'.

Religious hatred was primarily defined in the Racial and Religious Hatred Bill as 'hatred against a group of persons defined by reference to religious belief or lack of religious belief' – showing it would also have covered atheists. The maximum penalty for anybody convicted of the proposed offence would have been seven years imprisonment but the Attorney General would also have been able to veto any prosecutions. The new offence was designed to stop hatred being whipped up against people because of their religion – not just their race – banning people from intentionally using threatening words or behaviour to stir up hatred against somebody because of what they believe. There are already Europe-wide regulations banning religious discrimination in the workplace, whilst the Human Rights Act incorporated the concept of religious freedom into British law. Judges can also impose higher sentences if religion is a motive for a crime – such as an arson attack on a place of worship.

Early in 2006, the primary version of this Bill was defeated in the Commons, it being widely viewed as a measure which was both unnecessary and a dangerous infringement of free speech. At this point it was clear that some amendments would have to be made if the bill were to be passed subsequently. The final version of the law contains specific freedom of speech safeguards aimed at ensuring people can only be found guilty if they intend to stir up hatred. A ban would apparently only be relevant to 'threatening' words and behaviour, not things which were merely critical, abusive or insulting.

Having been passed after amendment, this new law gives us cause to think about some of the issues. Its opponents argued amongst other things that it would seriously undermine freedom of speech since religion, unlike race, is a matter of personal choice and therefore appropriate for open debate. Added to this, aggravated crimes against religious groups were already protected through existing legislation, so arguably to enact further laws would merely stifle religious debate and feed an increasing climate of censorship. Whilst the Muslim Council of Britain welcomed the move, arguing that the courts had already extended such protection to Sikh and Jewish people, it was also debated that to protect some groups but not others contravened European human rights law and therefore was not a protection of faith, but a protection of those who are attached to a particular identity marker. It is also true that similar laws in Australia had stirred up tensions between different religious groups. Some

British Muslims believed religions must be allowed to criticise each other, and that the proposed new law could open a Pandora's Box of prosecutions between faiths.

In amongst all of this, we can ask what happened to free speech? What has happened to one's right to have an opinion? No one would argue that society should discredit and disregard hate speech, but how much further does this particular example of legislation go? Writing in the *Guardian* at the time of the final vote, Polly Toynbee stated (2006):

> What's at stake here is the right to be insulting and cause offence. Many Muslim groups think it will protect their religious sensitivities – and so it will, by shifting the cultural balance away from free speech towards a sanctimonious right to feel offended. It puts religious belief into a sacred compound protected by legal razor-wire from robust mockery or public abuse. In this inquisition of a bill, religion will become a minefield, a no-go area in the world of ideas. Before you speak or write, ask yourself not only if you intend to abuse and insult, but if you are 'reckless' about any insult that may unwittingly be caused to someone somewhere? Expect the degree of insult people feel to tighten a little more each year under case law. It is already happening under employment law with certain kinds of harassment; if someone says they feel harassed, then lawyers warn no other evidence is required.

Clearly if you want to eradicate something from society, then making it illegal is a sure fire winning way of doing that. After all, our prisons are empty, all drivers obey speed limits, nobody gets murdered, drugs are a thing of the past and who has heard of anybody being burgled? Even for those who welcomed a change in the law to protect faith communities from 'religious hate crime'; the statute should clearly have allowed for both theological and secular disagreement, but legislative drafting – at all times a very imprecise science – does not allow for this common sense approach. Arguably without very clear definitions there is a real danger of opportunistic abuse. Could those intolerant to the opinions and beliefs of others assume 'victim' status and pursue legal action? The cynic might say how long will it be before a law is passed making all insults of any kind illegal? What sort of society would we be living in then? Certainly not one where the right to freedom of speech and expression prevails – at one time something which the UK might have considered one of the cornerstones of its (albeit uncodified) Constitution. More worrying has this move, along with others which will also be discussed in this chapter, signaled a move by the government towards the exploitation of public indifference to the essentials of a free society? More and more it might be construed that controversial views are, to cite Wolf (2006) 'classified as "unacceptable" or "inappropriate" by a host of interest groups.'

It is interesting to note at this point that the huge debate which raged after the publication of Danish caricatures of the prophet Mohammed in a Norwegian newspaper occurred almost concurrently with the final readings of this legislation. What began almost certainly as a foolish prank subsequently became the subject of a serious debate about freedom of expression both for the media and for the general population. Of course, this debate does not simply revolve around the presence or absence of total freedom – none of us is totally free, nor perhaps should we expect to be in terms of what we say or do. Most of us live in societies where arguably we sacrifice aspects of freedom in order to live together in harmony. A paradigm much associated with Rousseau's idea of the social contract. Such is, or should be our compromise. But what it does revolve around is the equitable application of such principles amongst diverse populations. Whilst arguably wrong to publish insulting cartoons of the prophet, it must be similarly wrong for those so insulted to issue forth with placards calling for the beheading of those who perpetrated the insult. If this is not similarly insulting, then it surely implies an inequality of behaviour and treatment on behalf of those who have been insulted. Be insulted by all means, but who so insulted can claim the right to death for the perpetrator of the insult? It's not even as if Christianity or any other faith for that matter has never been the subject of ridicule or insult. Readers may not recall beheadings being called for historically in relation to Monty Python's Life of Brian or Shakespeare's less than generous portrayal of the character Shylock in the Merchant of Venice. Similarly such protestations have not been made contemporaneously in relation to the artwork of Gilbert and George. Of course, freedom of speech should not be used to vilify any religious figure but similarly restricting it could be dangerous particularly for minorities.

Problems of freedom of expression or free speech are not of course confined to religion, although this is probably one of the more sensitive areas in which to have this particular debate. Early in 2007, this issue came to the fore once again in relation to the cash for honours inquiry concerning whether Downing Street had offered honours for loans. Interestingly as the almost year long inquiry drew to a close the

Attorney General[6] sought to gain an injunction to prevent the BBC from reporting a story that revealed why the cash for honours inquiry had allegedly widened into one about the perversion of justice. Writing under the headline 'Police set to gag media as honours enquiry end' *The Times* (March 5 2007) reported that:

> this was not the first time lawyers were consulted over a possible injunction. Scotland Yard was prepared to seek an injunction if the media discovered that Tony Blair had been interviewed by detectives for a second time between January 26, when the interview took place and February 1, the day after Lord Levy, the Prime Minister's chief fund raiser, was re-arrested.

Although details of these injunctions have never been made public it was also reported in the media that their terms were very restrictive. This demonstrates how it is possible for politicians to severely restrict the media's right to free expression in relation to political issues, the reasoning used in this case being that the leaking of such information may jeopardise any subsequent trial. The gagging nature of this episode was mirrored somewhat in the subsequent decision of the Foreign Office to discontinue valedictory dispatches as a direct result of that given by retiring British Ambassador Sir Ivor Roberts in which he accused Labour of damaging British interests by ignoring expert advice. Writing in the *Times* (September 24, 2007) Christopher Morgan reported that:

> The valedictory dispatch has become an institution over the centuries, giving a diplomat license to speak at the end of his career. But Robert's polemic, written this month, so angered the government that within hours, Sir Peter Ricketts, the permanent under secretary at the Foreign Office, withdrew the right of retiring ambassadors to pen a swan song.

Roberts' frank dispatch was not the first of its kind. Perhaps most famous was that of Sir Nicolas Henderson who commented on Britain's decline to a 'second tier power' in 1979. However, it is interesting to note the apparently less tolerant line that has been taken in response to Roberts' dispatch as a worrying trend in favour of gagging those who may not agree with government policy.

---

[6]A political appointment from the ranks of the government of the day and supposedly able to wear two hats – one being political and the other supposedly a-political.

Perhaps more worrying still is the recent pushing through of a Private Members Bill in May 2007 which is designed to exclude Members of Parliament from freedom of information laws.[7] If this finds its way to the statute book in due course, it will limit voters' rights to information about both MP's pay and other perks such as travelling expenses. The Private Member's Bill, which was introduced by Conservative MP David Maclean, has been justified as being required to protect correspondence between MP's and their constituents. However, it is already the case that such correspondence is exempt under existing law. It has been suggested that the real effect of the Bill would be to do two particular things. First, to prevent the disclosure of detailed information about MPs' expenses claims and Parliament's spending and second, to allow MPs to lobby public authorities in secret, knowing that this could not be subsequently disclosed under the Act. In effect, it basically means that MP's who support this do not believe that they should have to comply with existing Freedom of Information legislation – but why should they not? Arguably this would neither be proportional, nor fair, since similar safeguards for constituents already exist.

So are we free to speak? From these examples only if we are non controversial, do not have a view or only have one which fits in nicely with current politics. Do we feel free to speak? Perhaps less and less. These examples perhaps show us something else. That self censorship prevails more and more and we have to ask ourselves why? Perhaps because in today's society the most prolific form of censorship is fear and that fear is increasingly a result of being restricted in ways we never imagined. For example who would have thought that you would not be able to defend your property against unwanted intruders? The next example demonstrates how this restriction on our liberty to defend ourselves against attack works.

A strange case of self defence?

Anyone familiar with British law will be aware of the vexing and infuriating fact that the law protects property more robustly than it does people. In relation to protecting your property as a homeowner, things could not be more bizarre than the way in which the law now treats this issue. Putting up barbed wire could easily be considered by a British Judge to be unreasonable on the basis that you owe your burglar a duty

---

[7]http://www.publications.parliament.uk/pa/pabills/200607/freedom_of_information_amendment.htm

of care not to injure him whilst he is attempting to burgle your property. In fact, defend your property in any way at all and you may be exposing yourself to serious risk. The restriction of behaviour by the interpretation of law goes beyond the erosion of the liberty of the innocent to a new dimension – that of protecting the offender as if s/he was a victim.

Take for example the case of 76 year old Ted Newbery, whose allotment had in 1986, been the subject of numerous attacks. Mr Newbery decided to retaliate and in the process shot and wounded one of two men who were trying to break into his shed. Although Mr Newbery was acquitted of wounding he was then sued for damages and ordered to pay one of the burglars £4,000. Stung by the public outcry which followed this ruling, the Judge in question Mr Justice Rougier defended his decision by saying that Mr Newbery should have turned on his light or fired a warning shot instead so that the burglars ran away. It does appear ill-conceived however to suggest that a 76 year old man who had been the subject of repeated attacks against his property, and on this occasion, besieged in a lonely hut by two younger men who were proved to have said that they 'would have him' should have thought about whether he owed them a duty of care under the circumstances.

Hitchens (2003:173) cites Brian Mackenzie (in his previous role as chairman of the Police Superintendents Association), now Lord Mackenzie of Framwellgate as responding to cases such as this in the following way:

> If you tell the man in the street that someone broke into someone's house and was assaulted by the homeowner they are going to say it serves them right. In my view, possible attack is the occupational hazard for the burglar. He is liable to be clobbered if he is caught. That is his own misfortune.....We shouldn't be arresting victims, rushing them down to the police station and charging them. As officers we should be applying the test of what the man in street would think reasonable.

Hitchens (*op cit*) goes on to comment however that this view was not – and probably still isn't – shared by Lord Mackenzie's [then] superiors whom he adds are probably more interested in the theories of social control and negotiation as taught as Bramshill. In fact it was the Occupiers Liability Act 1984 which allowed Ted Newbery to be sued in this way. It also allowed ninety three year old Ruby Barber to be ordered by her local council to remove barbed wire from her property which she had spent £450 on having installed after becoming the frequent target of burglars. She was eventually allowed to keep it, but only because she agreed to erect a notice on the wire which stated that it both posed a danger and that she would accept liability for any injury that a prospective burglar might sustain whilst climbing onto her property. These examples would suggest that in the UK, there is a very particular attitude towards the use of force, namely that protecting your property is tantamount to 'taking the law into your own hands' but does this attitude prevail elsewhere?

In the USA the law reflects a different attitude towards the use of force. It would appear that in many American states, a householder is entitled to defend himself and these states have specific laws which uphold a citizens' right to protect his/her property. The principle known as 'defence of habitation' is a widely recognised one in American law and even allows for the use of deadly force if a homeowner can prove that s/he reasonably believes that someone is trying to enter the home using force or violence. This differs from the UK version where the use of 'reasonable force' is judged by others.

What makes it all possible?

The first possibility is the insecurity that people are constantly persuaded that they should feel. Insecurity is a powerful motive and perhaps explains why the general public appear more and more willing to acquiesce to greater restrictions on their liberty. Take for example CCTV. A recent Home Office evaluation of the effectiveness of town centre CCTV (Gill & Spriggs 2005) found that at best it only had a modest impact on suppressing crime and that offenders are not necessarily put off by CCTV. It also revealed that those who installed CCTV had little appreciation of what the systems were meant to achieve and failed to evaluate their effectiveness once in place. What local authorities were doing was responding to public demand, often from traders fearful that CCTV in neighbouring towns was taking consumers away from their outlets. Shoppers do not fear CCTV. On the contrary, they welcome it. What they fear is the anonymity of the town centre crowd. So the need to allay insecurity may be one reason which lies at the core of the governments' ability over the last ten years to legislate to put measures like this in place. Hailed not as a restriction or an infringement of liberty, but as a boost to 'reassurance policing' it may not achieve much in deterring or detecting crime, but members of the public feel reassured by a conspicuous presence.

Such is the normalisation of being watched – having our details verified over the telephone and being asked impertinent questions by, for example credit card companies – that we are beginning to fail to recognise the greater insidiousness that is taking place within our society. Credit card companies do a lot more than they say. For instance, they make profits by selling information that they acquire when we purchase goods. That information is assembled and analysed so that marketing is targeted at those most likely to be responsive to it. Amazon knows the books you read, Tesco knows what you like to eat. Information about lifestyles and habits are constantly gained from consumption patterns and is now such a sophisticated process that it is an academic discipline with its own name – geodemographics.

What else makes this sort of intrusion into our daily lives possible? Waddington (2007) says that intelligent snooping, but called 'Intelligence-led policing' is viewed in a positive light by the public because they feel that interventions are sometimes necessary and probably more focused than they actually are. He goes on to comment that (2007:2):

> When anti-terrorist police raiding premises in Forest Gate accidentally shot an innocent man and found nothing incriminating, protesters demanded that police intelligence should be improved. Responding to such a demand can only mean that police would need to know more about those they suspect of terrorism before they act. Such snooping will not only be directed at those who turn out to be terrorists, but also against others upon whom suspicion alights only to be extinguished by further surveillance. It is not only when specific individuals are suspected that the demand for intelligence-led policing is loudly heard. It is also there when sections of the population disproportionately receive the unwelcome attention of police officers. Notably, it is the disproportionate use of stop and search against ethnic minorities that is raised in this connection. But here civil libertarians find themselves in a quandary: in order for stop and search to be targeted at those most likely to be engaged in criminality it requires more, not less, surveillance.

Added to this is the simple fact that the public actually demand measures such as increased surveillance, usually after a terrible (albeit very rare) crime such as the Soham murders. The subsequent inquiry by Sir Michael Bichard (2004) found the Humberside Police wanting over its record keeping, and advised the creation of a national police intelligence database, capable of exchanging information with social services. The problem here – and which is referred to by Waddington (*op cit*) – is that he rightly says Huntley had never been convicted, so any information held by Humberside Police and Hull Social Services could arguably have not been relied upon. He claims that the Bichard Inquiry never proved that any of the information concerning Ian Huntley made him in any way different from thousands of men who have consensual sexual relations with underage girls. The Bichard Inquiry advised that a national database would be better than other public sector ones but why should any information which comes to the police and which is indiscriminately loaded into a nationwide database be any better than anything which has gone before? Waddington (*ibid*) rightly says that there is no evidence that expense and intrusion into privacy will prevent future murders. Indeed the only evidence in this area currently[8] suggests that for formal data sharing to be effective, it should be highly focused and of maximum relevance to the crime reductive purpose to be achieved. As succinctly put by Waddington (2007:3):

And where was Liberty that self-appointed guardian of our civil liberties when all this was being proposed? Its evidence to the Bichard Inquiry confined itself to lamely challenging the suggestion, made by the chief constable of Humberside Police, that the Data Protection Act 1998 forbade the retention of information about Huntley's nefarious past. Had Liberty been true to its own principles, it should have celebrated and defended the zealous adherence to privacy demonstrated by Humberside Police. But in the fevered atmosphere that surrounded the Soham murders and Bichard Inquiry, that would have taken courage. When faced with two horrific murders, Liberty colluded with the public demand that such horror must not be allowed to happen again. And that is precisely how the surveillance society expands. It is not foisted on an unwilling public, but actively and loudly demanded when the costs of anonymity are brought brutally to public attention. The battle between privacy and surveillance is uneven. Set against the convenience and reassurance offered by surveillance and the outrage prompted by horrors such as the Soham murders, concerns about privacy are easily subordinated. Scandals, such as the miscarriages of justice that provoked a criminal justice crisis during the 1980s, swung the balance in favour of civil liberties. However, it is difficult to imagine what might propel privacy up the policy agenda. No one dies from invasions of privacy. Public attention is always likely to be

---

[8]See Moss & Ardley (2007); Moss & Pease (2004) and Brookes, Moss & Pease (2003).

fleeting and criticism muted, even when newspaper staff bug Royal phone calls.

More relevant perhaps is that the general public simply don't appreciate how lives are being changed – arguably not for the better – by greater and greater restrictions, most of which have found their way onto the statute books of this, a country which once prided itself on being the bastion of free speech and expression. The next chapter will explore some of the ways in which this has been made possible.

2
Constitutional Origins of Erosion

In this chapter I will advance the idea that there are a number of constitutional factors unique to the UK which have enabled a greater degree of social control to proliferate during the last ten years. Specifically it is my assertion that the nature of the parliamentary system – characterised as it is by flexibility; *ad hoc* rule making; legislation driven by personal and social trends; a lack of formal or entrenched procedures for enacting amending or repealing legislation and knee jerk responses to social and cultural changes in the last decade – has enabled the government of the past decade to erode the essential liberties of individuals whilst at the same time ratcheting up the numerous ways in which behaviour can be deemed to be criminal through multiple pieces of legislation.

What we know today as the British Constitution is underpinned by some momentous laws. For example, Magna Carta, the little known or understood, but still existing common law, and of course the English Bill of Rights a modern form of which campaigners have demanded noisily, seemingly unaware that this was not a new idea. What has also underpinned British democracy (until recently) is its *laissez faire* approach to these issues, citizens being firm in the belief that one could go out into the street in the UK and do or say anything unless it was specifically prohibited by law. This was our basic freedom, our civil liberty, unencroached upon by governmental forces. That was until the moral panic set in. It is true that there were some increases in crime up to the point in 1997 at which new Labour came to government, but nothing to write home about. But it was a great vote winner – the promise to be 'tough on crime, tough on the causes of crime.' What it *did* achieve was to persuade the public at large – helped in no small part by the media – that we were suffering a huge crime wave driven by social deprivation and that action must be taken.

Once in power, new Labour swiftly set about adapting the legal system to one which now resembles something more repressive. Notable examples of this include further augmentation of existing prevention of terrorism legislation by David Blunkett[1] and the overt contempt for civil liberties shown by Tony Blair in relation to mandatory drug testing and collection of DNA samples for all arrestees whether subsequently proved guilty or innocent. What new Labour has been able to achieve in the last decade however would arguably not have been possible had it not been for the fact that the rot must have set in rather earlier than this. Where do the origins of the systematic erosion of our liberty have their roots?

Notions of liberty and security

Within the evolved constitution of the UK arguably the erosion of liberties and the potential to over legislate is possible because of the inherently flexible nature of the British Constitution and its reliance on procedures and practices which are non-statutory in nature. This makes it difficult for courts to question those procedures and practices whilst at the same time they can be used by ministers to act in ways which are against the basic principles of civil liberty.

Our fundamental notions of liberty and security in the UK have their roots in the gradual evolutionary process of the constitution itself. Much of this constitution is flexible and lacking formality and is based in many ways upon residual and almost ethereal powers which have their roots in the Divine Right of Kings which was passed to Parliament after the so called 'Glorious Revolution'. In order to understand how our basic liberties have altered in significant ways, it is important to establish the principles of the British Constitution at the outset and to explain what our original liberties and freedoms are based upon. This will enable us to see exactly how they have changed recently.

The British Constitution is unique mainly because of the rules it contains and the way in which they have evolved over a long period of time. To understand this better it is necessary to outline the characteristics of the constitution and to explain how historical events have helped to shape and mould it into what it is today. Our fundamental liberties and freedoms, as citizens of this constitution are an integral part of this. The British constitution is not written in a basic document or even a group of documents although much of it is written down in various pieces of legislation, policy documents and other constitutional writings. It is often said

---

[1] Including measures which would breach the age old right of *habeas corpus*.

that the UK does not have a constitution because it is not written into a single underpinning document and it is this which sometimes confuses the debate about this aspect. This interpretation became rather fashionable after the American War of Independence when the US decided to establish a framework for their government in a single document. They called this their constitution and ever since some writers have argued that this is the only possible meaning of this word. This is very misleading and even worse, countries are sometimes distinguished by reference to those that are considered to have a written constitution and those that do not. The eminent constitutional writer Munro (1999) says quite rightly that this is an unhappy distinction and in reality those countries who claim to have written constitutions merely have short documents which provide a framework. A better distinction to make would be to say that some countries have some important rules enshrined in a particular document which is then thought to have special sanctity whilst others have a constitution with many sources, none having more special recognition than any others. This would be a more accurate description of the British Constitution which is certainly characterised by its historically innate flexibility. The UK has not (like the US) experienced a major civil war or revolution. Jennings (1959:8) commented that:

> ...the British Constitution has not been made but grown...it has been constantly added to, patched and reconstructed...but it has never been razed to the ground and rebuilt on new foundations.

This is a good way to describe the constitution but it should at the same time be remembered that Parliament did rebel against Charles I and experiment with a republican government for a short time thereafter. This experiment failed, Cromwell actually preferring what Munro (1999) calls civil legality, to the nakedness of the military sword; he took office as Lord Protector in 1653, under a document called 'the Instrument of Government'. This was followed by another called 'the Humble Petition and Advice'. Cromwell died soon after this and there was a return to the monarchy (the Restoration). So apart from this one brief time in history there has never been one document of greater importance than any other.

Characteristics of the UK Constitution

The UK Constitution is often referred to as flexible in the sense that it does not have difficult procedures for changing laws. Most can be altered using the same procedures that were used for passing them in the first place. It is also flexible in the sense that as each parliament succeeds its predecessor, it is an accepted fact that each new parliament can repeal or pass any legislation it sees fit and therefore no earlier parliament can bind its successor. The case most famously cited in support of this is *Ellen Street Estates v Minister of Health [1934] 1 KB 590* which concerned a conflict between two statutory provisions concerning the assessment of compensation following a compulsory purchase of land. The question for the Court of Appeal was which of the two provisions should take effect.

This is an interesting fact when considering the possibilities for legislating and the relative lack of constraint which can be brought to bear upon the British government in relation to this. Arguably this is one factor which has helped the present government over the last decade to legislate freely on a plethora of different issues. The only necessity has been to justify it. This they have done on the basis of rising crime rates and the increased need for security. Whether either of these reasons is fact or convenient fiction remains to be seen.

The UK is unitary and not federal because the UK Parliament is considered to be the supreme legislative body. It is monarchical in the sense that although the functions of the monarch are in the main ceremonial, the sovereign is still considered to be the Head of State and succession to the throne is hereditary. The constitution is also considered to be bicameral because there are two Houses of Parliament: the House of Lords, still constituted mainly on a hereditary basis (although calls have long been made for this to be changed) and the House of Commons to which members of Parliament are elected. This of course is the focus of political attention. The House of Commons has what is known as executive dominance which basically means that because of the way in which political parties are elected, the winning party which then forms a government is normally able to command support for practically any measures that it wishes to adopt. This is an important point in relation to this issue of over legislating and one to which I shall be returning later. The UK constitution is also characterised by its civil service which administers all governmental decisions. Civil servants are considered to be non-political and cannot be members of Parliament.

There are three organs of government – the Executive, the Legislature and the Judiciary. The Executive consists of the Prime Minister and the Cabinet. The Legislature comprises the two Houses of Parliament which together make the laws of the country. The House of Commons is elected by universal suffrage and members of the House of Lords are either appointed by the government of the day (if they can lend the government enough money) or they inherit their seat. The Judiciary is the third organ of government and comprises Judges and the courts and through the age old notion of the separation of powers are deemed to be formally separate from the government. The Judiciary is supposed to interpret and apply the law which Parliament makes and to keep the government within the limits of its powers. Since 1973 it has also had to interpret European Community law. Although Judges are appointed by the Executive, they are supposed to be independent of both the executive and the legislature and it is this independence which is customarily referred to as the separation of powers.

The UK constitution is also of course characterised by the notion of parliamentary sovereignty whereby Parliament is the supreme legislative body and has the ability to enact or repeal any law on any subject whatsoever. It is also incapable of binding itself or its predecessors and it is this characteristic more than any other which really sets the UK constitution apart.

Finally the historical avoidance of formalised rules and regulations is also steeped in history and this again makes it odd that of late, there appears to have been a backlash against this traditionally constitutional way of doing things and a move towards over regulation within a constitution which has always sought to avoid this phenomenon. Two very good examples of this avoidance historically are the use of the Royal Prerogative and the reliance on constitutional conventions. It is pertinent to mention this here to demonstrate how little the government seeks self regulation but during the last decade has sought to over regulate its citizens. The inherent way in which the machinery of government operates serves to reinforce the flexibility that characterises the British government. Arguably it is this flexibility which in part has made it possible for the current government to enact so many different pieces of legislation relatively freely and without recourse to special procedures. The UK Parliament is evolutionary in nature and the very process of this evolution has produced a system which whilst characterised by debate – which is a positive feature – is also characterised by it lack of recourse to legal rules and procedures much of the time. To demonstrate this it is necessary to highlight some of the non-legal rules of the constitution. So what are conventions and the Royal Prerogative?

Non-legal rules of the constitution

Uniquely the workings of the British constitution are characterised not just by accepted legal rules but also by non-legal rules which are commonly called conventions. These are not laws in the strict sense, but are rules which have been adopted by virtue of their long use. Their origins are historic and although non-legal their significance should not be underestimated. They have often originated in very casual circumstances and one very good example of this is the convention that the Prime Minister of the day visits the monarch alone. This convention was not always the case. After the First World War, it was usual for the Prime Minister and the whole of the Cabinet to make this regular visit to the monarch. However, Lloyd George, then PM, did not care for this too much. He therefore forbade his Cabinet to accompany him on these visits and it is now a convention that the PM makes this visit alone.

The fact that conventions are not legal rules but merely accepted ways of doing things is an interesting feature of the flexibility of government operation. This inherent flexibility and almost ethereal quality of some of the procedures of Parliament have been commented on by many writers. Notably Munro (1987:35) has said that:

> Many matters which are of interest to students of the British Constitution are not matters of law at all. Nobody need be surprised by this, other than a few lawyers who naively imagine that law is what makes the world go round.

DeSmith (1998) describes convention as a form of political behaviour which might be regarded as obligatory, whilst Wheare (1951) called them rules which are no more than a description of usual practice. So how can they be illustrated? Consider giving Royal Assent to legislation. Could it ever be refused? It was 1708 when it was last refused on the occasion when Queen Anne would not approve the Scottish Militia Bill, but it is generally accepted to be a convention that it would normally never be refused. Consider the office of Prime Minister. It is a convention. No law says that we either have to have a Prime Minister or describes how we should choose one. It is convention which dictates that the sovereign invites one person to head the government, although the office itself is mentioned in other statutes such as the Chequers Estates Act 1917. Consider the fact that by law the sovereign may dismiss the Prime Minister and the cabinet if she wishes. It is merely a convention that she would not do so. It is also a convention that the sovereign chooses the person best able to command a majority in the House of Commons. In recent times where one party generally has an absolute majority there is in fact no real choice. Ministerial responsibility itself is nothing more than convention, but what is meant by this? Ministers are of course responsible for the general conduct of the government, not only in terms of personal acts but also in terms of the department they are in charge of. Praise for success is interchangeable with blame for failure and if misconduct is serious, this can of course result in resignation. There have been some famous examples of this such as the resignation in 1982 from the Foreign Office of Lord Carrington after the invasion of the Falklands, where criticism was made of the Government's failure to anticipate the crisis. Similarly Leon Brittan and Michael Hestletine both resigned in 1986 over the Westland Affair where the Department of Trade and Industry were held responsible for leaking advice they had received from the Solicitor General. More recently, prominent figures such as Edwina Currie, Peter Mandelson and Ron Davies have resigned over issues referred to as either personal political errors or private indiscretions. Indisputably, conventions have been, and still are important but their power to control or hold accountable the machinery of government can only be matched by their potential flexibility. Their potential to hold ministers accountable is a positive feature but since individual ministers often drive legislation and policy on the back of their own interests, are they sufficient to quell the possible misuse of power or to prevent ministers from acting in anything other than the public interest? This really depends on how, if this issue arose, the Judiciary might interpret the use or application of conventions and this, in large part is to do with whether they can be considered equal to legal rules or not. If so, they may well act as one of the checks and balances on the actions of parliament.

Jennings (1940) famously stimulated debate amongst his students by claiming that laws and conventions were one and the same and pointed to some similarities between them. First, he claimed that the acceptance of both law and convention were determined by general acquiescence. Second he said that the major conventions were as firmly fixed as laws and could probably be cited with as much precision as laws. Third, he said that they often overlapped in subject matter and finally that laws may not necessarily be any more certain than some conventions. Dicey (1915) however stated that law and conventions must be differentiated and said that this could be done on the basis that laws would be enforced by the courts whereas conventions would not be. But is this strictly true – are all laws court enforced? Dicey (1915) implies that they are but the answer to this must be no in a strict sense. It might however be true to say that laws have a susceptibility to court enforcement and this may have been what he meant. So, it follows that when rules are not strictly legal rules, the courts will not respond to them in quite the same way as they do law, and consequently case law on this area does appear to bear this out.

The most oft and famously cited case on the role and place of conventions is the case of *Attorney-General v Jonathan Cape Ltd [1976] QB 752*, also known as the 'Crossman Diaries Case'. Richard Crossman was a Cabinet Minister who kept a political diary with a view to its publication. After his death in 1974, his executors decided to publish the diaries in book form with extracts in the *Sunday Times*. The Attorney General (hereinafter referred to as AG) sought an injunction to prevent publication on the basis of collective ministerial responsibility which meant that ministers were, by convention, obliged to preserve Cabinet secrecy. Deliberating on the case, the Lord Chief Justice (Lord Widgery) accepted that a true convention was an obligation founded in conscience only and that if this was the only argument upon which the AG based his case, then he could not uphold it. The AG however, did have another strand to his case and this was based on the law of breach of confidence. Lord Widgery admitted that cabinet proceedings *could* be protected by the law of confidence but *only* for a limited period of time. In this case, publication of the diaries ten years after the events had taken place was not objectionable. What this case demonstrates is that the courts will not provide a remedy simply because there has been breach of a convention so although many acts can be undertaken on the basis of convention, possible misuse of such will not give rise to legal intervention unless that breach is covered by existing law. It is possible in certain circumstances for a convention to be enacted as law. For example section 4 of the Statute of Westminster 1931 provided that no future Act of Parliament was to extend or be deemed to extend to a Dominion as part of its law unless the consent of that Dominion was expressly declared in that Statute. This did not precisely reproduce an existing convention which was operating but did incorporate it in a modified form. Legislation in 1998 on devolution also provided some interesting examples of decisions concerning conventions. Some existing conventions, such as the role of the Prime Minister in recommending the appointment of the Lord President of the Court of Session in Scotland were placed on a statutory basis and became part of the Scotland Act 1998.

Conventions represent therefore a rather *ad hoc* approach to certain kinds of decision making within Parliament. There are those who advocate that this approach is preferable because it is responsive and adaptable to changing ideas and circumstances, but this does not take account of the fact that it also allows for lack of certainty over ministerial decision making as well as a lack of authoritative judicial certainty at times when this might well be required. This is one example of the flexibility which prevails within the British Constitution and which provides some context for the way in which it is possible for decision making and legislation, based on the ideas and interests of individuals to prevail perhaps without the most stringent scrutiny and as knee jerk responses to the 'moral panics' of the day (see Cohen, 2002). The Dangerous Dogs Act 1991 provides one excellent example of this.[2]

Prerogative powers

A further set of peculiar powers of parliament is exemplified in the exercise of the Royal Prerogative and where these originate are also relevant. This power is what is known as a residue which is deemed to have been left over from the Divine Right of medieval Kings and Queens. Munro (1987:256) describes it as:

'Those attributes belonging to the crown which are derived from common law not statute and which still survive.' And further that it nature requires examination so that 'we may see what sort of creature we are dealing with.'

Prerogatives consist of legal attributes, not just matters of convention, tradition or practice and in some cases the courts *will* recognise prerogatives and even enforce them. It would be rational to imagine that the prerogative was only composed of powers but this is not strictly the case. They also afford some rights and immunities; for example, the right to treasure trove is a Royal Prerogative as is the Crown's immunity from suit. Parliament can diminish the prerogative or get rid of it entirely by

---

[2]The issue of pit bulls and other dangerous dogs being kept illegally in Britain was highlighted by the death of the five-year-old girl, Ellie Lawrenson who died of severe head and neck injuries after being mauled at her grandmother's house in St Helens, Merseyside. The dog was a pit bull terrier-type breed. Subsequently the Dangerous Dogs Act 1991 banned the breeding and sale or exchange of four breeds: pit bull terriers, Japanese tosas, the dogo argentinos, and the fila brasileiros. Cross-breeds of those dogs are also covered by the law which says that owners of 'dogs known as a pit bull terriers' must have them neutered, muzzled and on a lead in public. If a dog injures someone, the owner can be jailed for up to two years. A dog classed as 'dangerously out of control in a public place' may be destroyed. The owner can be fined and imprisoned for up to six months.

enacting a statute but it cannot enlarge it. For example in *BBC v Johns [1965] 1 All ER 923* Lord Diplock stated that it was:

> 350 years and a civil war too late for the Queen's courts to broaden the prerogative. The limits within which the executive may impose obligations or restraints on citizens of the UK without any statutory authority are now well settled and incapable of extension.

In spite of this, the importance of the prerogative and the ways in which it can, and has been used, should not be underestimated. As such it represents yet another example of the way in which decision making within Parliament can be carried out without recourse to formal rules, on an *ad hoc* basis and often without recourse to the courts of law who may, due to either the notion of separation of powers or judicial deference seek not to give judgement on particular actions in what are considered non-justiciable cases. This arguably works against liberty rather than for it and it is worth detailing some of the ways in which this has already occurred.

The range of parliamentary issues that come within the scope of the prerogative may, to the non-lawyer, seem startling and is well put by Munro (1987:160):

> The prerogatives that remain are relics. But they are not unimportant relics. The conduct of foreign affairs is carried on mainly by reliance on the prerogative, as are the control, organisation and disposition of the armed forces. It is also by virtue of the prerogative that Parliament is summoned, prorogued and dissolved and under it that Royal Assent is given to Bills.

Dicey (1915) had gone further than this since he said that it covered every act of parliament which the executive government could do, without needing (or indeed having) an Act of Parliament. One example of this can be found in *R v Criminal Injuries Compensation Board ex parte Lain [1967] 2 All ER 770* where the compensation scheme which was set up in 1964 without statutory authority, to make ex gratia payments to the victims of crimes was said, by Chief Justice Lord Parker, to be established under the prerogative.

The historical significance to this far reaching power is important. Medieval Kings and Queens were really like feudal landlords as well as heads of their kingdoms. They had property rights, advantages and immunities in litigation and some less well defined powers which they were supposed to use for the good of their subjects. Much of the time, forces of personality – particularly the Tudor monarchs – rather than constitutional factors dictated the exercise of power. They did exercise their powers fully – you might even say vigorously – and within certain limits the Crown could supplement the law by proclamations. By the end of the reign of Elizabeth I however, who had not got on with her Parliament quite as well as some of her predecessors, disagreements were becoming more frequent and broke down completely in the 17th century. The exercise of the Royal Prerogative was one of the central issues of the crisis since it implied that in many respects the King was above the ordinary law of the land. It was inevitable that this would come to a head. The main question parliamentarians wanted resolved was whether Kings were answerable to law in any respect at all or were they answerable to God alone? It is at this point that cases such as the Prohibitions del Roy 1607 and the Case of Proclamations 1611 are often cited by lawyers as demonstrating how some of the prerogative powers were taken away from the King and vested in Parliament. For example in the former, the court held that the King had lost his prerogative power to judge disputes between citizens and in the latter, it was decided that the King could no longer create new laws by proclamation using the prerogative.

These cases should not however be viewed in isolation because they only represent certain crisis points against a backcloth of political drama in which Charles I tried to dispense with Parliament leading to rebellion and James II subsequently occupied the throne of an albeit limited monarchy. Around this time, more of the existing prerogatives were declared illegal and the revolution provided a framework for some constitutional principles to be established more firmly. These include the supremacy of Parliament, the notion that prerogatives were not above the law and that title to the throne was founded in parliamentary enactment. All these things are historically of great significance but what of the prerogative today? Parliament sought to control it historically but what controls – if any – operate in relation to it today?

Effective control?

Both Dicey (1915) and Bagehot (1928) appreciated something which another great constitutional writer, Blackstone (1979) did not. This was that most of the prerogatives which had been solely vested in the monarch were, towards the end of the 18th and 19th centuries, being exercised by the leaders of Parliament and not by the monarch. This happened gradually and notably through the operation of convention because certain political events began to happen with such regularity as to make them matters of convention. For example, the beginnings of the party system; the greater dependence of the monarch on parliament; the growth of the House of Commons and regular Cabinet meetings not attended by the monarch. Not all of these happened at once but they slowly became settled practices and doctrines to the extent that by their virtue we can now say that we have a limited monarchy and Cabinet government. So why is it still referred to as the Royal Prerogative? Well, readers may ask, what's in a name? Whilst most prerogatives are now exercised by government ministers, this does not mean that the monarch hasn't any prerogatives left at all. Sometimes the sovereign is involved in the exercise of the prerogative in a formal capacity. For example under the prerogative of mercy the royal pardon remains with the monarch although in practice it would be exercised by the Home Secretary of the day. The sovereign does exercise some prerogatives where personal choice is still evident. The granting of some honours is amongst these. However in most cases where prerogative powers still remain, they are by convention, not used. For example, the power to dismiss the Prime Minister, his Cabinet, the Government and Parliament.

Modern governments have retained the prerogative in large part rather than getting rid of it or placing it on a statutory footing. The reason for this is obviously because it is useful to have at your disposal broad, discretionary powers like these so that in certain circumstances it is possible to act in particular ways without having to go through formally approved channels. This is not to say that such powers cannot be placed on the statute books if it is thought to be desirable. In 1914 and 1939, the prerogatives to wage war were put on a statutory footing because as Viscount Radcliffe said in *Burmah Oil v Lord Advocate [1965] AC 75:*

> extreme actions ought to receive explicit parliamentary approval.

In spite of this it has been far more common for the government not to expressly repeal the prerogative, but instead to seek to hold it in abeyance – that is to suspend it – in case they ever want to use it again. In cases like this, where a statute and a prerogative appear to co-exist, the worry is that the government will choose whichever version of the power suits it best at the time or which produces a more favourable result for them. So how do the courts respond to this exercise of discretionary power? The best example of this situation is the case of *Attorney General v De Keyser's Royal Hotel [1920] AC 508*. During the 1914–1918 war the plaintiff's hotel was requisitioned for use by the Flying Corps under the Defence of the Realm Acts 1914–1917. This statute expressly included a provision for providing statutory compensation. Not wishing to pay up later, the government tried to argue that the hotel had actually been requisitioned under the royal prerogative, for which no compensation was payable or at best only an ex gratia amount. The court however ruled that possession had indeed taken place under the statutory power therefore compensation was payable according to this.

This case might well give the impression that the royal prerogative is always subject to review by the courts. Indeed if this were so, there could not be much argument against it. However De Keyser's Royal Hotel provides a pretty straightforward example of the exercise of the power which the courts had no difficulty in judging. They have not found other decisions regarding its exercise quite as easy as we shall discover. In terms of political accountability, which takes place through the supervision of Parliament it is important to note how this can occur. Usually any exercise by a minister of a prerogative can be questioned in Parliament by debate, but how effective is this? In reality the amount of time for such debate is restricted and often comes after legislative government business has been discussed. This process is often hindered by lack of information and tends to be retrospective – that is – the government negotiates and reaches a decision and then the House of Commons can pass a judgement on it. Such difficulties hinder the proper scrutiny of its exercise and the tendency also to give political answers to questions (that is, no answer at all) adds to this. In addition, some issues are no-go areas. For example operational defence matters, details of arms sales and military assistance to other countries are all matters about which questions will not be answered because there are said to be precedents which justify this. The end result of this is that parliamentary control of these peculiar and significant powers is extremely limited.

Judicial control?

Are the courts in any better position to control ministers' use of such powers? Originally courts claimed that they had the authority to determine the existence and extent of prerogative powers and had done so ever since the Case of Proclamations 1611. So what is the courts general response to those who question the validity of the exercise of such powers as the prerogative – particularly when such exercise could be claimed to be an infringement of a person's basic civil liberties or personal freedoms? The most oft cited case in respect of this, and one which demonstrates well the precarious balance between security and liberty is that of *Chandler v DPP [1964] 3 All ER 142 HL*. This case concerned Chandler and others who conspired to enter a Defence Air establishment called Weatherfield Air Base which was leased to the Americans. They did this because nuclear weapons were stationed on the base including aircraft armed with nuclear missiles on permanent stand by under a (then) current defence policy. Under the Official Secrets Act 1911 (s1) it was an offence for anyone to be in, or in the vicinity of, a prohibited place 'for any purpose prejudicial to the interests of the state.' Chandler and his friends fulfilled this criterion by conspiring to break in (they did not actually break in) and protest against the use of aircraft carrying nuclear weapons. On appeal, the House of Lords held that Chandler could not bring evidence at his trial to show that his purpose was not prejudicial to the safety and interests of the State. He wanted to bring evidence that his acts were actually beneficial because he wanted to prove that the UK needed unilateral nuclear disarmament. The court however held that he could not bring this evidence because the safety of the State quite clearly involved defence and the defence of the realm, as cited in the case of *R v Hampden [1637] 3 St Tr 825,* was a matter for the Crown alone. Similarly the use and disposition of the armed forces was a matter for the Crown and the Crown alone under the prerogative. The court held that the government was the sole judge of what is best for the safety and interests of the State, and as such it would be incompetent for the court to hear evidence with the intention that the court should decide if nuclear disarmament was best for the State or not. In so doing, the court was basically saying that whilst they will look to see if a prerogative exists or not, and will say – if they deem there isn't one – that the Crown is acting unlawfully, if they judge that there *is* a prerogative, they will refuse to question its exercise. This case demonstrates quite clearly that the courts are limited in passing judgement on the actions of the government in such situations and will not even take evidence from citizens in respect of such issues.

Lest the reader should imagine that perhaps this case is a singular instance, there have been many others. For example, the case of *Laker Airways v Department of Trade [1977] QB 643.* Freddie Laker wanted to introduce competition in passenger travel across the Atlantic. Under the Civil Aviation Act 1982 (CAA) the Civil Aviation Authority is empowered to grant licenses to run an air service. As a result, Laker bought wide-bodied jets and trained crews to operate them. He required a license from the US Aeronautical Board but they could not grant such a license unless the British Government designated Laker as an approved carrier in accordance with the Bermuda Agreement 1946 (an international agreement which had the status of a treaty). At first the UK government did indeed designate Laker's Sky Train as a designated carrier but before the US had time to grant a permit, the Secretary of State for Trade asked the Civil Aviation Authority to revoke Laker's license because he said there had been a change of policy. He then published a White Paper under the CAA setting out the new policy for airline regulations. This included the criterion that only one airline could operate on any one given route. Laker of course wanted to see competition, which under the terms of the CAA was justified since the Act said clearly that there always ought to be more than one airline on any one given route. So he sought a declaration from the court that the Secretary of State was acting unlawfully because the change of policy suggested in the White Paper conflicted directly with the statute. The Secretary of State claimed that he had been acting not under the statute but under the prerogative powers granted to him as a minister, and as such this was unreviewable by the courts. In reality the minister was actually trying to use these powers to circumvent statutory procedure. It is therefore interesting to note what the court had to say regarding this.

Judging the case, Lord Roskill felt that the statute gave a citizen such as Laker rights to a hearing. He was also prepared on this occasion to say that the Crown had acted wrongly:

> I do not see why a prerogative power should have survived the passing of an Act unfettered so as to enable the Crown to achieve by the back door that which cannot lawfully be achieved by entry through the front door.

In a reference to the previous case of De Keyser (*ibid*) he said that it would be meaningless for Parliament to impose restrictions and limitations on the exercise of statutory powers if the Crown is free at its own pleasure to disregard these provisions. Thus the prerogative could be seen not so much as abolished, repealed or restricted, but fettered. Lord Justice Lawton agreed that although there was no express mention of the prerogative in the statute, the Secretary of State could not lawfully use the Crown's prerogative powers to take away the statutory rights of citizens. Therefore, by necessary implication, the prerogative is restricted in its use by the Civil Aviation Act 1982. This case demonstrates that in certain limited circumstances, the courts will express the view that a minister's exercise of such powers is unlawful, but apparently only when an existing Act of Parliament covers the same, or similar ground to that of such a power. At this point they do not hold that ministers' actions are necessarily unlawful, but that the importance of the statute, for the time being at least, outweighs the importance of the prerogative powers. However, this does not mean that the power is abolished but held in abeyance, or in this case described as fettered until such time as it may be required in the future. It is possible therefore to say that statutes may occasionally limit the exercise of ministers' powers in limited circumstances. There are however other situations, arguably of greater importance where the courts will not review the exercise of these powers at all. The case of *CCSU v Minister for the Civil Service [1985] 3 All ER 935* is one such example.

One of the prerogatives is the employment and dismissal of civil servants and the laying down of conditions of service. In the mid-1980's at the Government's Communications base at Cheltenham – known as GCHQ – crown employees were occupied in monitoring all the communication and satellite communications coming into the country, 24 hours a day. This was considered vital for the defence of the realm at that time. Until 1982 it was never publicly known that GCHQ at Cheltenham existed but when Geoffrey Prime was prosecuted under the Official Secrets Act 1911, it was revealed that he worked there. At this time the Civil Service (most of whose members belong to a trade union) had been in dispute with the government and caused a great deal of disruption in its various branches. Cheltenham was expected to join in the strikes and the working to rule. The Minister for the Civil Service at that time[3] then announced that under the Royal Prerogative, Crown employees would no longer be allowed membership of a trade union. There had been no consultation and no warning before this announcement. This was a major upheaval for people at Cheltenham and the unions objected that they had not been consulted. There was no obligation under the prerogative that they should be consulted, however at common law, a doctrine of consultation has been developed and for executive powers, the law has developed the notion that no one can have a detrimental decision made about them without having been heard and being able to put their own side of the case. This is not a statutory right but the development, by law, of the right to a fair hearing. The trade unions claimed that

---

[3][Then] Prime Minister, Margaret Thatcher.

under this doctrine – no less clear than the prerogative itself – they had a right to be consulted and put their view before a decision was made. They claimed that the exercise of the prerogative by the government was affected by the common law rule of a fair hearing and challenged the government's exercise of the prerogative as being void and invalid. This was the same sort of challenge which had not been allowed previously in Chandler and it is interesting to note the judgement of the court in this case. Their Lordships said that the reason that the principle of the prerogative could not be reviewed by the courts was that in relation to many of the important prerogative powers such as control of the armed forces or foreign policy, the courts were not a suitable place for a decision. They commented that the prerogative powers challenged in this case were those which concerned the conditions of recruitment to the civil service and on the face of it there was no particular reason why this should be immune from review. However, they also commented that the employee did not have any right to be consulted although s/he did have a reasonable expectation that there would be consultation and as such it could be said that *prima facie* the Crown had acted unlawfully. However the reason given by the Crown for making this decision in relation to its employees was on the basis of national security and this they said outweighed the reasonable right to a hearing. On this basis the court went back to its traditional stance and said they were therefore not prepared to review the prerogative with regard to national security and the decision of the minister stood as being legal.

What does this tell us about the ability of government ministers to exercise these doctrines in relation to the civil liberties of individuals? It tells us that you can be told you are not allowed to demonstrate against nuclear warfare, that you can be prevented from joining a trade union, that your basic rights as an employee can therefore be infringed, that you have no right to a fair hearing to dispute government action in such cases and that the courts will not even judge your case even if you do bring one – that is, if you have enough money to do so. This is the basis of the democracy in which we all currently live. A democracy based on events which took place nearly 800 years ago when King John was held to account by a group of rebel barons who demanded a charter of liberties to protect England from his unfair and erratic behaviour. It was at this point in history that we could say that the principle of a higher power than the sovereign was first established. This higher power became known as the rule of law and was enshrined in Magna Carta, sometimes described as the most potent symbol of freedom under the law in western civilisation. Yet if you visit the field in which this momentous event is said to have taken place you will find no English commemoration. What you will see is a monument erected by the American Bar Association and a John F Kennedy memorial garden and you might well ask yourself why? For the simple reason that whilst the Americans have sought to commemorate the Magna Carta as being the basis, some 500 years later, of their American Bill of Rights, the British have sought not to mark this place at all. This is the same country where hundreds of laws, technically still in force make it illegal to carry a bag of soot along the road in Congleton; to meet the Queen without wearing socks; to flag down a London taxi if you have the plague and which also makes it entirely legal to shoot a Welshman with a bow and arrow in Chester, as long as it is after midnight. All of these rather amusing laws have come about, and are still enforceable precisely because of the way in which the British constitution operates. We can laugh at such things because they are not serious and would probably never be enforced. They simply linger as a result of a system which never expressly repeals anything, however ludicrous. More worrying are the laws which have more recently passed onto our statute books specifically from the current government and which directly limit exactly those rights which were said to have been enshrined by Magna Carta. These are the current laws which make it illegal to eat a cake iced with the words 'freedom of speech' on it; which also make it an offence to stand peacefully in the street holding a placard up with 'not aloud' on it.

Perhaps things could be worse. There are aspects of government that are healthy such as the idea of Parliamentary debate, although the quality, the nature and the length of time given over to such is often questionable. It is important however to note that this is the background against which all governmental and ministerial action takes place. The judgements made in the cases highlighted in this chapter – and these examples represent only a small proportion of those which could have been cited – *have* not, and no doubt *will* not prevent ministers from continually trying to push out the boundaries of not just the legislative process, but also the exercise of discretionary powers such as the prerogative, even if it conflicts with statute. In the process, many citizens have found (and probably will find in the future) their civil liberties infringed and even find themselves embroiled in long drawn out and expensive legal battles in an effort merely to restate the basic human rights that they thought they had under our so called democracy.

What do these examples demonstrate about the way in which parliament operates and the wide legislative and discretionary powers that they have at their disposal? First it tells us that judicial or political checks and balances are only of limited value and do not operate within matters of high policy. These will obviously be the most serious cases where arguably, the courts *should* be called upon to decide whether parliament has acted legally or not. Second, some of these powers are deliberately not expressly repealed or put on a statutory footing because they are more useful to the State in their current malleable state. Usually held in abeyance, or merely temporarily fettered, as so described by Roskill LJ in Laker Airways (*ibid*), this inherent flexibility of both conventions and the prerogative is demonstrably a vehicle by which successive ministers have tried to control the behaviours or actions of people in various ways ranging from sitting on a runway – arguably peacefully protesting against nuclear war – to arguing against business monopolies (something which the Monopolies and Mergers Commission currently actively seeks to scrutinise) through to having the right to join a trade union. These trends, which have their basis in the deep rooted evolutionary processes of British Government, have helped to make it possible for individual ministers, and sometimes the government as a whole to act in ways which unfairly restrict the liberty of citizens. Although it is possible to argue that if wronged, every citizen has the right to redress through the courts; this fails to recognise the severe constraints which access to justice has for citizens of the UK and how such ordinary people can possibly, even if they do have the right, fund expensive law suits against the government. Added to this there have recently been some uncomfortable trends in relation to such rights of access to justice. For example, a recent suggestion that proposed legal reforms being considered by the government could mean that thousands of petty criminals would never even get their day in court. A scheme under consideration early in 2007 saw Lord Falconer, the Lord Chancellor together with the Solicitor General making plans for people arrested for shoplifting, theft and criminal damage to have their sentences decided not by magistrates but by a prosecutor in consultation with the police. Obviously this move – if sanctioned – would cut legal aid bills for magistrates' court cases and might speed up the snail-like pace of the British court system, but it could also find ordinary people pressured – by the vast machinery of the legal system – to plead guilty in order to qualify for this method of sentencing. Added to this are current fears expressed by the Law Lords over further proposed government anti-terror measures. Whilst it is true that MP's have willingly given the government and the security forces extraordinary powers – including the detention of suspects for long periods of time without charge, of which more is in a later chapter – it is also true that it remains Parliament's responsibility to protect the rights of its citizens where necessary. Writing in the *Mail* on Sunday (October 15, 2006) regarding the Special Immigration Appeals Commissions role in hearing cases of those detained on the grounds of national security, Lord Woolf, former Lord Chief Justice cautioned against the use of secret courts to deal with terrorist suspects, calling them 'an affront to our liberty.' He also called for courts to be allowed to rule on the lawfulness of any government proposal that might seriously affect the rights of the individual in order that they might be able to provide advisory declarations on the lawfulness of any measure thus proposed.

The European perspective

It is relevant at this point to ask whether the protection of individuals' human rights and personal freedoms in the UK have been better served since the enactment of both the European Convention on Human Rights and the Human Rights Act 1998. The Convention took effect in 1953 and was essentially brought about to avoid the abuses of human rights that had taken place in World War II. It does not form part of the law of the European Community, but was developed to act as a separate system of jurisprudence with its own institutions and procedures. Although it does not form part of UK law, there has been an expectation that the UK would not legislate directly contrary to what the convention laid down. The articles of the Convention provide for the observance of a number of fundamental rights including freedom of expression, freedom of thought conscience and religion, the right to life, the right to security and liberty prohibition from torture, inhuman or degrading treatment or punishment and the right to a fair trial.

Initially, the Convention imposed what could be described as 'negative obligations' on a member state. This means that it has identified a number of human rights with which member states should not interfere. It appears that this has developed into what could be termed as a theory of state obligation. This means that member states have to do more than just be seen to comply with obligations. This is demonstrated well in the case of *Plattform 'Artze fur das Leben' v Austria* [1991] 13 EHRR 204 where the court said it was not sufficient just to allow marches and demonstrations, but that the state should take positive steps to make sure people could do this without interference from others. The Convention was not intended to set rigid or inflexible rules but to allow member states some discretion in relation to how they would interpret and apply the Convention in a national context. The reason for this is to reduce the possibility of tensions between member states and the European Court which could then lead to a lack of consensus. The idea is rather to achieve maximum compliance from all parties about the general standards that the Convention sets. For this reason there is said to be a 'margin of appreciation' regarding the extent of member states compliance which depends on the nature of the right in question and on the situation in which it arises. Each case therefore is judged on its own merits.

The case of *Handyside v UK [1979–80] 1 EHRR 737* for example establishes that member states will be allowed more flexibility to decide issues in relation to public morality. Alongside this, the doctrine of proportionality also exists which is a way of testing whether member states actions are compatible with Convention standards. If a member state says that they acted in a legitimate way regarding the public interest, the European Court will then ask whether the action taken was proportionate to the aims pursued and whether the reasons given are relevant and sufficient. This can be demonstrated by the case of *Bowman v UK* Bowman v UK [1998] 26 EHRR 1 in which the applicant distributed literature in the 1997 elections about the views of the main candidates on abortion. She was taken to court under section 75 of the Representation of the People Act 1983 because she had spent more than the £5 which was designated under the Act. She took her case to the European Court under Article 10 of the Convention claiming that it was her right to freedom of expression. The court held that although some legitimate limit on expenditure was right, to ensure fairness between candidates, section 75 imposed an unnecessarily severe restriction on the dissemination of opinions and that this was particularly odd when national publicity campaigns had no restrictions on them whatsoever. Therefore they held that there had indeed been a violation of Article 10.

Issues of torture and derogation

We could deduce from this, since the advent of the Convention and its subsequent implementation into UK law following the enactment of the Human Rights Act 1998, that personal rights and liberties now have more stringent safeguards in respect of them. However, this does not take into account two other factors, namely the differing interpretations by the courts of what such articles mean in practice, nor does it acknowledge the possibility that under Article 15, a contracting state may derogate from any of the articles which interfere with the rights protected in the convention 'in times of war or other public emergency threatening the nation.' It should be noted that this does not apply to Articles 2, 3, 4 or 7, which are non-derogable. An interesting example of the problem that interpretation of the articles can produce is the case of *Ireland v UK [1979–80] 2 EHRR 25* which was brought under Article 3, the prohibition from torture, inhuman or degrading treatment or punishment. The case concerned interrogation techniques used against IRA suspects under the internment operations in 1971. The suspects had been hooded and forced to lean against a wall on their finger tips and tip toes whilst being subject to white noise and continuous questioning. If they fell they were beaten. All were deprived of food, water and sleep. However, this was not held to be torture under the terms of Article 3 and this shows that there is a very tough test as to what constitutes torture.

In terms of the issue of derogation, perhaps the best examples of this are the cases of *A and others v Secretary of State for the Home Department*; and *X and another v Secretary of State for the Home Department [2004] UKHL 56, HL*. This case concerned the UK governments reaction to the terrorist attacks in the United States on September 11, 2001 when they subsequently introduced Part 4 of the Anti-terrorism, Crime and Security Act 2001 (ACSA). The extended power enabled the detention of foreign nationals against whom no action was being taken with a view to deporting them. It was clear from the outset that this power might be inconsistent with Article 5(1) of the Convention for the Protection of Human Rights which guaranteed a person's right to liberty. In order therefore to get around this problem the UK government made the Human Rights Act 1998 (Designated Derogation) Order 2001, by way of a statutory instrument (SI 2001/3644), which would enable them to derogate from their obligations under Art 5(1) on the basis that a public emergency threatening the life of the nation (within the meaning of Art 15(1) of the convention) existed in the United Kingdom. The appellants were non-UK nationals certified and detained as suspected international terrorists by the Home Secretary under Part 4 of the ACSA 2001. None had been the subject of any criminal charge and in none of their cases was a criminal trial in prospect. They all challenged the lawfulness of their detention contending that such detention was inconsistent with obligations binding on the United Kingdom under the convention, (which had been given domestic effect by the Human Rights Act 1998) and that the United Kingdom was not legally entitled to derogate from those obligations because this was incompatible with the convention.

They appealed to the Special Immigration Appeals Commission (SIAC), which allowed their appeals on the ground that the 2001 Order and the ACSA 2001 were discriminatory because they allowed only suspected terrorists who were non-nationals to be detained. That decision however was then reversed by the Court of Appeal who held (but only by a majority of one) that the appellants had shown no ground strong enough to warrant displacing the Secretary of State's decision that there was a 'public emergency threatening the life of the nation' within the meaning of Art 15(1). The court also commented that great weight should be given to the judgment of the Secretary of State, his colleagues and Parliament on the question, because they had been called on to exercise a pre-eminently political judgment.

This case demonstrates that in spite of the European Convention and the Human Rights Act 1998 theoretically preserving the rights of indviduals in serious cases affecting their civil liberties, both the power to interpret and to derogate from these obligations, can work to undermine those rights and have indeed done so in these sorts of situations. The question to be asked therefore is how effective are these sorts of safeguards if they can so easily be dismissed in situations which arguably they were designed to safeguard?

Legislative restrictions in the UK

Aside from the European context it should be remembered that there are a plethora of legislative restrictions upon the rights of individuals in the UK, to assemble, to protest and in doing so, to take advantage of their right to freedom of expression. Within the UK, the ability to freely express oneself and the tolerance of public protest has evolved as a mark of a free and democratic society. Prior to the Human Rights Act 1998 there were no positive rights to do so, but merely an understanding that one could do as one wished, as long as it was not directly prohibited by law. Prior to the enactment of various laws restricting the right to freedom of expression, protest and assembly, two views appeared to proliferate regarding this fundamental right. First, the liberal view, as expressed in cases such as *Beatty v Gilbanks [1882] 9 QBD 308* and *Redmond v Bate [1999] All ER 864*. In this case, members of the Salvation Army were charged with a breach of the peace when they continued to hold a meting which had attracted a large crowd. The court held that there was no principle in English law that allowed a person to be punished if his own lawful actions resulted in another acting unlawfully. In the latter case, the defendants were preaching on the steps of Wakefield Cathedral when bystanders began to shout at them. The defendants were arrested by the police for obstruction as they feared a breach of the peace would occur but the court acquitted them because the police should have arrested the bystanders rather than the preachers. Second, it has also been the case that in some instances a more authoritarian approach has been taken by the courts. For example, in *Kent v Metropolitan Police Commissioner [1981] The Times, 15 May,* the Commissioner had issued a ban on all processions after the Brixton riots. The extent of the ban was such that it covered an area of 786 square miles. Members of CND, who wished to plan a march in the area tried to get this decision judicially reviewed on the basis that it was irrational but the court refused to interfere with the police exercise of discretion in this case.

Currently, whilst there are few restrictions on the right to join or form organisations – unless (according to the Terrorism Act 2000) they promote or are engaged in violence or acts of terrorism – from the 1980s there was a substantial codification of the laws relating to public order in the UK through legislation such as the Highways Act 1980, the Public Order Act 1986, the Criminal Justice and Public Order Act 1994, the Police Act 1996, the Protection from Harassment Act 1997, the Crime and Disorder Act 1998, the Racial and Religious Hatred Act 2005 and the Serious Organised Crime and Police Act 2005. In all I have cited some eight individual pieces of legislation which now determine what can be lawfully expressed, where, to whom, by whom and under what circumstances. Proscriptions about the use of the highway, what constitutes a rave, and what amounts to public disorder, be it in the form of a riot, an affray, violent disorder, causing fear or the provocation of violence, or harassment alarm or distress to someone is all now enshrined by statute. We now also have the possibility of racially motivated offences, the offences of racial and religious hatred and most recently sections 132–138 of the Serious Organised Crime and Police Act 2005 have said that no protests can take place 'in the vicinity of Parliament' – whatever that means. Marches and processions can be banned outright – and this means a blanket ban, since it does not allow for specific marches or processions to be banned but rather bans categories of such. Besides all of this, the common law is still in existence which means that a breach of the peace – arguably the vaguest offence still in existence – is still possible even without legislation. Arguably the concept of breach of the peace could be seen as being so vague that it could actually legitimise the arrest of protestors in what might otherwise be deemed to be a lawful protest.

It must be true to say that the interpretation of these sorts of offences by the courts, has, in the main erred on the side of the authoritarian approach. However, more recently there have been one or two victories for civil liberties and freedom of expression with more liberal interpretations. For example, in the case of *DPP v Jones [1999] 2 AC 240 HL* the appellants were taking part in a peaceful and non-obstructive assembly which had gathered on the roadside grass verge next to the perimeter fence at Stonehenge. This area was subject to an order under section 14(1) of the Public Order Act 1986 which prohibited 'trespassory assemblies' and the appellants were duly charged and convicted of this offence in both the Magistrates Court and later the Divisional Court who commented that a peaceful assembly such as this, taking place on the public highway, did indeed exceed the limits of the public's rights of access. However, on appeal to the House of Lords it seems that sense prevailed since they were deemed not to have committed the offence and specifically Lord Irvine commented that the public highway was a public place on which all manner of reasonable activities might take place. Provided those activities were reasonable, they should not constitute a trespass. This judgement is one of a few of the victories which exist for civil liberties and it is interesting to note that the case had to go all the way to the House of Lords before this judgement was given, the lower courts seeming to prefer a more authoritarian interpretation of the legislation.

A question of constitutional balance

This is the backdrop against which we find ourselves and which provides some context for other changes which have taken place over the last 30 or so years, all of which have helped to make it possible for the current government to over legislate to further restrict the liberty and behaviour of individual citizens of the UK. To conclude, and to reiterate what I suggested at the start of this chapter; there appears to be some constitutional factors unique to the United Kingdom – some of which I have highlighted – which have worked to enable successive Governments, but in particular the Government of the last decade, to systematically erode some of the essential civil liberties of its citizens. I have demonstrated that in my opinion these include the nature of the evolved Constitution; its reliance on the inherent flexibility of many of its constitutional procedures; the ability of Government ministers to rely on this flexibility to achieve certain ends – including for example, the prohibition of membership to trade unions. It has also enabled what I consider to be knee jerk legislative responses to perceived social and cultural problems which have not solved those problems but have merely resulted in the proliferation of a much greater degree of social control. Of course, it should be remembered that balancing the need to criminalise certain forms of behaviour for the good of society, against the need to retain essential freedoms and civil liberties is never an easy goal. Indeed the complexities of this issue were wisely summed up by Prins (1996:220) where he wrote:

> There would seem to be some grounds for concluding that we should adopt a very cautious approach to an over-widespread use of the law in matters concerning the management of social and 'personal' ills...Somehow a balance must be achieved between the view of Mr Bumble, who described the law as 'an ass, an idiot' and the jurist Lord Coke, who considered that 'the law is the perfection of reason'.

The question remains however, has the current Government achieved this balance? The following chapter will discuss some of the philosophical and theoretical explanations for the move towards the greater degree of social control which appears to have proliferated during the last ten years.

3

The Culture of Control

Notions of social control

In this chapter I want to explore some of the philosophical and theoretical explanations for the move towards the greater degree of social control which appears to have proliferated during the last few decades, the background to this and to explore the potential problems that this raises. The nature of this book, and in particular the length of this chapter does not allow for the sort of in depth analysis provided, for example in Garland's (2001) book, *The Culture of Control*, but my aim is to highlight some of the salient aspects of what Garland describes as a transformation of both governmental and citizens' attitudes to crime and contemporary crime control both in Britain and the United States of America. I also want to highlight other factors which I perceive as being relevant in explaining theses changes including the demise of policing by consent and the difficulties of reconciling issues of law and morality.

Democracy and crime control

O'Byrne (2002) comments that the concept of an 'open' society of which humanitarianism, equality and political freedoms are the foundations was originally developed by philosopher Henri Bergson. The central tenet is that governments in such societies should be responsible and tolerant with transparent and flexible political mechanisms, in contrast to totalitarian regimes. Writing in the *British Journal of Criminology* in 1996, Garland initially offered some explanations for what he saw as the rise of markedly different strategies of crime control in Britain and the USA, both of which are so-called 'open' societies committed to individual freedoms and civil liberties. Garland asks how are we to explain the excessive concern with penal and social controls that have come to characterise these nations in the past few decades. He has since extended this work (2001) and in so doing accepts that although the work is quite general, that there are benefits to seeing general trends and patterns. He acknowledges that his approach may involve an 'uncomfortable degree of simplification' but stresses its benefits in highlighting 'structural patterns not otherwise available to inspection.' In further self-defence Garland suggests that this is a field which needs more overarching studies. General works may evoke an 'energetic critical response.' Specifically his discussions of the UK and USA are intended to identify the social and cultural changes that may have shaped social relations and to suggest what trans-Atlantic similarities might exist, arising from both political imitation and policy transfer. He argues that the countries have some similarities in their historical development. These, he says, have come about in a manner captured in the concept of 'late modernity' in which shared patterns of 'social, economic and cultural relations' have resulted in an ideology of shared risks and problems regarding crime control. More specifically Garland (2001) argues that current crime control arrangements have been shaped by two underlying social forces which he describes as the 'distinctive social organisation of late modernity' and 'the free market and socially conservative politics' which he suggests began to 'dominate the USA and UK in the 1980s'.

Garland's book cites a series of studies which show how different agencies (the police, prosecution agencies, courts, prisons government and elected officials) were presented with new problems attributable to these social changes. Garland believes these problems mainly stemmed from high crime and disorder rates, and the realisation that the ability of criminal justice to provide security and control crime was limited. His central chapters look at the evidence for governmental understanding of these problems and focuses on how strategies were devised to deal with this (either by adaptation or evasion).

Garland believes his analysis suggests that 'the structures of criminal justice have changed in important ways in recent decades' and the most important changes have been linked with prevailing cultural assumptions in the response to crime. He asserts that a new 'crime control culture' has emerged that involves what he terms new ideas of 'penal-welfarism, a new criminology of control, and an economic style of decision making.' He also indicates how this new 'culture of control' fits in with social and economic policies shared by and heavily influential in both the UK and USA. He does this by illustrating how the historical development of crime control in the UK and USA has been very nearly completely the opposite of what was predicted in the 1970s. Garland suggests that the way we deal with crime is now totally different from the way it was dealt with as recently as 30 years ago, and that nonetheless, the public is accepting of this. His aim is to explain how contemporary responses to crime have come to take their present form, as he believes they have aspects which are both 'novel and contradictory' and his assertion is that the main changes can be categorised as follows:

First, in historical terms, he suggests that recent developments in official policy are actually quite archaic and certainly do not match any predictions that might have been made previously. Many of the elements of the criminal justice system that are around today are at odds with the way things have worked for the majority of the last century. Second within penology, those who work in the business of crime control have seen huge changes in ideology and practice since the 1970s and now there is no official rulebook for this profession. Garland suggests that whilst there used to be a firmer ideology regarding penality, currently there is none because of what he describes as a 'volatile' and prolific government policy. If this field is to improve, he claims that 'textbooks need to be re-written' and basically new, stable ideologies put in place. He aims to identify new rules that are emerging and open these ideas up to informed criticism.

In sociological terms, Garland suggests that crime control has a degree of autonomy but is linked to social institutions and controls. Changing things in the field of crime control is complex and needs to take many issues into account regarding the way society works and reacts to crime. Many different fields link, so in looking at one issue many others must be addressed. Hence, today's field of crime control is the result of political decisions which are administered, but these are related to the new elements of society and culture we see around us. He also suggests that there are a number of indices of change which can be referred to in terms of political policy, the ideologies of crime control organisations, the views of the public and the ideology of criminologists that have occurred in the last 30 years. The most important of these he details as 'the decline of the rehabilitative ideal' meaning that although rehabilitative programs still operate in prisons, they do not profess to be the underpinning ideology of the penal system. Added to this he claims a re-emergence of more punitive sanctions and a return to more overt systems of justice, partly due to a public lack of sympathy towards criminals which in turn have influenced the attitudes of policy makers. In line with what has been seen to be a greater need to protect the public, and flowing from a change of interest away from offenders and towards victims, the safety of the public has been considered more. Risk monitoring has realised a higher profile alongside a perceived need for prisons to incarcerate the dangerous rather than rehabilitating the offender.

Added to these developments, Garland points to the fact that law and order is now a big issue for politicians. Seen as a political vote winner, responsibility for crime reduction is less likely to be devolved to professional experts – although there may be an argument to say that it was never fully enough devolved to experts in the first place. The focus of criminologists has also changed historically, with crime now more often being viewed as a commonplace aspect of modern society and criminals as rational people for whom the solution to increased crime is the reduction of criminal opportunities. A more significant change has been within the academic discipline of criminology itself and what might be called the 'ivory tower syndrome' with the work of many academics becoming less and less applied. Changes in the ideologies and objectives of academics have also occurred alongside changes in the practices of the main crime controlling organisations. In the UK, the police are no longer seen as the sole crime prevention agents but are now much more often viewed as a public service, which is obliged to respond to the constant and unrelenting reform of crime control. The professionalisation of the police has also taken place alongside the development of crime control being seen as an obligation of the state within liberal democracies. Garland believes that indeterminate sentencing and the early release of prisoners from the 1890s to the 1970s achieved a penal system that seemed to respond to public demands for punishment but in reality sentencing and punishments were at the discretion of professionals. This led to tension amongst those who held different ideals. For example, judges and probation officers might not agree as regards different types of sentencing and there might also be tension between the demands of considerations for the offender and demands for protection of the public. Garland believes that these tensions eventually ironed themselves out and have been replaced by a delicate balance of power which is due to practical penal-welfarism rather than any competently thought out ideology. The government is now focused on the sanctioning and rehabilitation of individual offenders rather than the social prevention of crime.

This he compares to the early 1970s in which some American publications of the time presented damaging critiques of penal-welfarism. The most radical of these he describes as the Report for the Working Party of the American Friends Service Committee's *Struggle for Justice* (1971). Its main target was to highlight the discriminatory nature of the power to punish which had been seen as a tool to repress blacks, the young and cultural minorities. He goes on to discuss the report's arguments against compulsory penal treatment and suggests that since this time nearly all US states have repudiated indeterminate sentencing laws with the aim of increasing fairness but without increasing levels of imprisonment.

Garland identifies two sets of transformative forces driving crime control, aside from the purely criminological, social, economic and cultural and political and in an effort to explain this, splits the late 20th century into two sections and describes what occurred in them. First, he suggests that from 1950 to 1973, and in the post war era, both the UK and USA flourished economically as a result of Keynesian economic policies. Production increased and accordingly the affluence of society increased. This economic prosperity in turn provided a driver for civil rights which can be demonstrated in the radicalism of the 1960s, although arguably coincidence does not necessarily equate with causation. From 1970 to 1980 Garland describes a crisis decade in which the Capitalist market undergoes problems, there is high unemployment and large sectors of society fall below the poverty line. He associates changes in the economy and employment with social changes in families. More women began to enter employment; divorce rates increased because women were no longer entirely financially dependent on their husbands and the result was more children living in single parent families. The collapse of the family unit led to more people living alone, younger people moving away earlier, single parents being able to survive on benefits and better healthcare allowing the elderly to live longer and more independently.

Perhaps most interesting is Garland's explanation for how these things have affected crime. He suggests that the move to Capitalism and the emphasis on the greater and more efficient production of goods (especially electronics) has simply meant that there are more things to steal. The mobility of the population has increased due to the expansion in the numbers of cars on the road, resulting in greater mobility for law breakers, a reduction in situational controls and more potential targets for crime. Added to this he feels that young people have grown up in a much less socially regulated, but more materialistic society, with greater expectations and desires for immediate gratification. He highlights two factors in particular that he feels have caused problems in the last third of the 20th century.

First, what he describes as the normality of high crime rates, (which has major implications for government and the agencies responsible for crime control) and second, the acknowledged limitations of the criminal justice state (so much so that when crime rates dropped in the 1990s few experts were willing to attribute this to the effective actions of crime control agencies). Garland believes the state took crime control upon itself, where it once belonged to the institutions of civil society. Now the whole area is too politically potent to be easily dismantled by rational critique and administrative reform. The government needs to withdraw their accountability from the crime control field, but the political costs of this would be disastrous. So, the extent of the problem is either denied, or the sovereignty of the state is reasserted. Here he describes what he means by *acting out* – that the concern is not so much controlling crime, but more with expressing the anger that it provokes. This is stated as the problem which has shaped crime control in the late modern period. *Political actors* have a different agenda from *administrative actors*, they need to consider a wide range of issues in terms of their political appeal on a short term basis, whereas the latter needs to concentrate on the interests of a single organisation over a long term basis. Hence, the political hinders the administrative, and this, he believes, causes problems.

In the 1980s and 1990s crime control began to be more politicised, and the decision making shifted from the administrative more towards the political. He goes on to explain the contradictory ways in which ambivalent state authorities and their various agencies have responded to the predicament over time, sometimes adapting to it in a realistic manner, other times by evading it and *acting out*. This, he suggests, has happened in a number of ways including the professionalisation, rationalisation and commercialisation of justice; a concentration upon consequences (for victims and of the fear of crime); a relocation and redefinition of responsibilities (for example to non-government agencies); and a change in the new criminologies of everyday life (to a set of modern theories stemming from the idea that crime is normal, alongside an aim to embed controls in normal interaction, rather than the higher form of sovereign control and where the criminal is viewed as an opportunistic consumer whose nature cannot be changed but whose access to social goods can be barred). Finally it also occurred as a result of non-adaptive responses such as denial and acting out and the contradictory response – aiming to restore public confidence and be 'tough on crime' which has led to increasing rates of imprisonment in UK and USA.

In essence, Garland suggests that new structures of everyday life have changed people's experiences of crime and insecurity, prompting a build up of a control culture so intense that it undermines the very freedoms it aims to preserve. His claim is that the important similarities between the US and the UK – which he claims do not 'merely stem from political imitation and policy transfer' but from a process of social and cultural change that has recently been altering relations in both societies – mean that crime control in the modern age does more than simply deal with problems of crime and insecurity. It also condones certain responses to these problems that in themselves have an impact. In the US and the UK, 'late modernity' (Garland 1996:194) resides, not just by offenders, but by all of society, in a mode that is more than ever defined by what Mythen (2006:385) calls institutions of 'policing, penality and prevention.' Naturally there is an inherent desire in most cultures, for certain levels of security, for appropriate controls and for the management of risk, but in the US and the UK, the suggestion is that this ideology has taken over and led to an over abundance of regulation, inspection and control. Whilst this might be beneficial for certain sections of society, the question which does not appear to being asked is, how is this negatively affecting others who may be unwittingly caught up in this aspect of a more repressive and intolerant society? Garland's point here is that it is policy which has dictated the balance between individual freedoms and social control over the last 30 years and that:

> Where the liberating dynamic of late modernity emphasised freedom, openness, mobility and tolerance, the reactionary culture of the end of the century stresses control, closure, confinement and condemnation. (1996:195).

Certainly this accords with some of the sentiments expressed in this book and indeed it is possible – as Garland suggests – to demonstrate this in various ways. In 2001 Garland mentioned the use of imprisonment as a form of social control and regulation. In 2008, this example is even more relevant as the figures for the prison population in the United Kingdom stand at over 80,000 compared to 65,298 ten years previously.[1] Arguably the rise in the prison population is not due to an increase in the number of offenders appearing before the courts. Indeed, the government has made it plain that the crime rates have been decreasing during the last ten years. So why has the prison population gone up? Inevitably one of the contributing factors is harsher

---

[1] Figures from The Howard League 2007.

sentencing led by a political climate in which politicians have emphasised that justice must be *seen* to be done, alongside the government's
pledge to be 'tough on crime and tough on the causes of crime' (Blair,
1998:4). In November 2004 the Chief Executive of the National Offender
Management Service (NOMS) told *The Guardian* newspaper that in the
previous year the courts had imprisoned 3,000 people 'for thefts such
as shoplifting or stealing a bicycle, even though they did not have any
previous convictions' (Travis, 2004). Surely this use of indiscriminate
sentencing serves to highlight that the government is using prison as a
quick-fix remedy and not as a last resort.

Arguably – and an issue to which I shall return to later in this book
– the UK is experiencing an increase in State power and influence over
people's daily lives. The Anti-Terrorism Crime and Security Act 2001
has ensured arrested terrorist suspects have their DNA taken and stored
regardless of whether they are charged or not. CCTV surveillance represents what Moran (2005:351) has aptly called 'silent technology.' What
could easily be described as a control or surveillance culture surely means
the potential for abuse is more possible. Arguably this could bring innocent citizens into a situation where state monitoring is the norm.
Certainly the intensification of state power has been more noticeable following the events of 9/11 both in the US and the UK. Does this mean
that we should begin to rethink paradigms of democracy and sovereignty
in the modern world or rather, should we begin to question more directly
the fundamental nature of state power in the modern world? The UK and
US governments certainly appear to have used the events of 9/11 and the
continued threat of terrorism world wide to undermine some fundamental principles underpinning civil liberties.

As Garland (2001) suggests, there does seem to be a perception of high
crime rates as a normal social fact, which in itself emphasises a more
general acceptance of the increased need for law and order and crime control. This can be demonstrated by the findings of the most recent Ipsos
Mori Poll (Duffy *et al.*, 2007) which has shown that most people have a
view about crime and how it is being, or should be, regulated. The problem is that this is not necessarily based on real facts or statistics but is more
to do with 'perceived' knowledge. The poll found for example that people's fear of crime is driven by different factors. The public's political views
often shape their perceptions. For example the research showed that people who voted Conservative in the last election are much more likely to be
dissatisfied with how the government is dealing with crime. In terms of
demographics, older people; the more affluent and those without qualifications tended to have more negative views about crime than younger,

more highly qualified people, or those from minority ethnic groups. The globalisation of information through the media and other mechanisms has also affected perceptions of crime rates. A very pertinent example being that when participants in the Mori poll were asked what they felt were the most important issues facing Britain today, 55 per cent of spontaneous mentions highlighted crime, law and order compared with only 6 per cent, 7 per cent and 8 per cent respectively who said that drug abuse, unemployment and taxation were the most important issues. Interestingly Mori (2007:13) found this figure very large compared to previous years but explained the jump in the percentage of responses about crime to be:

> ...related to the extensive media coverage of the shooting of Rhys Jones, the 11 year old boy from Liverpool.

Over a period of time, the effective control of crime and the routine protection of citizens from crime have come to form a normal regulatory part of the relationship that the state has with its citizens. The development of a professional police force at the beginning of the 19th century and the belief that the police were the sole crime prevention agents added to this. To a certain extent this continues, in spite of legislation which has specifically sought to share the responsibility for crime reduction on a much wider basis through section 17 of the Crime and Disorder Act 1998. Historically, social forces and the mechanical societies that predated the industrial revolution were successful in reducing crime and maintaining social order but these more informal social controls did not last. With the rise of the organic society following the industrial revolution, the professional police force succeeded in regulating crime in society and the state was becoming entrenched as the ultimate law making and governing body, responsible both for creating laws, and punishing those who violated them. Garland (1996) believes that it is precisely this situation which has become unsustainable. Realistically, the state cannot adequately deliver all aspects of control and regulation in a modern society and is therefore doomed to fail.

Perhaps governments have covertly understood this however since a modern attitude to the problem of crime control appears to be to share the responsibility for it more widely across a number of different agencies. The problem here however, is that whilst they may understand that this is necessary, to admit to it would be political suicide. At the same time government policies on crime and disorder appear to have become worryingly knee jerk, reactive and based far too often on the idea of the 'quick fix' rather than being representative of a well considered and designed response to reducing crime and improving public reassurance. Of course, it is politically expedient to be seen to be doing something about crime, disorder, anti social behaviour, football hooliganism and even worse, terrorists, but is the state really doing something worthwhile or are they merely flexing their arm of control and in the process, just restricting citizens unnecessarily?

Public perceptions about crime and the consequent fear of crime have also emphasised the debate about risk. It is not enough that everything we now do is judged against health and safety criteria. This in effect means that some window cleaners do not use ladders because it is thought too dangerous; teachers carry out risk assessments before they take children anywhere and now even academics have to undertake a risk assessment if they want to travel to a conference in certain countries. Seemingly risk is now attached to everything, or so we are to believe. Even certain groups of people appear to have a heightened risk index. For example, ethnic minorities are finding themselves marginalised and incriminated and Morris (2004) reports that in the UK the number of Asian people stopped and searched under anti-terrorism laws, quadrupled in a single year from 744 in 2001/02 to 2,989 in 2002/03. Mythen (2006:381) claims that:

> Through the governmentality lens, the construction of a suspect population is making 'subjects' of certain civilians on the basis of the possession of an ascribed set of ethnic, religious and cultural traits. Unwittingly, innocent people are rendered risk repositories by virtue of sharing some characteristic of a 'typical' terrorist.

Pre-emptive incarceration based on the possibility of future actions has been debated but thankfully left out of the new (UK) Mental Health Act 2007. Preventive detention however is here to stay since the 'terror attacks' of 9/11 and calls for tighter and tighter security are constantly justified on the basis of the need to keep citizens safe. Mythen (2006:390) claims also that:

> ...this is reflected in criminal justice policy which has witnessed a pendulum shift from risk management to risk control...the attack on the World Trade Centre can be viewed as an analogy to a schoolboys' masculinity contest; 'If I don't hit back, he will see that I'm a coward and will do it again.'

As will be discussed in a later chapter, repressive legislation such as the 2000 Terrorism Act has arguably weakened democracy. The so-called 'war on (or against) terror' has justified numerous previously unacceptable measures such as illegal detention and unwarranted forms of surveillance. It could almost be argued that civilisation has wound backwards towards an earlier and more naive era in relation to crime control. Indeed even Durkheim (1973:199) commented that:

> strong political regimes have no need to rely upon intensely punitive sanctions. Punitiveness may pose as a symbol of strength, but it should be interpreted as a symptom of weak authority and inadequate controls.

Similarly Michel Foucault (1977) in his description of the public torture and execution of Robert Damiens the regicide, showed in graphic detail how harsh punishments have been used as public displays of the state's power, designed specifically to reaffirm the force of the law operated through the state. Abu Ghraib is a more recent example of this. Garland (1996:133) comments that:

> Punishment is an act of sovereign valour, a performative action which exemplifies what absolute power is all about. However, although today's democratic regimes do not resemble that of the eighteenth century, whenever state authorities 'wage war on crime', they are deliberately employing the same archaic tactics. The essential attractiveness of the punitive response is that it can be represented as an authoritative intervention to deal with a serious, anxiety-ridden problem. Such action confers the appearance that 'something is being done' here, now, swiftly and decisively.

Governments do have a duty to take steps to protect their citizens. However my argument is that this should never justify the side-stepping of democratic values. Since the Prevention of Terrorism Acts of the 1970s for example, terrorism laws have done little to ensure that society is safe from terrorist attack, but much to infringe the human rights and civil liberties of those living in the United States and United Kingdom. Rather they have satiated a political desire for a 'quick fix' in response to terrorism and arguably have undermined not only civil liberties and human rights but one of the cornerstones of western democracy, namely the presumption of innocence as a core value of once robust democracies.

The concept of human rights was first expressed in the 1948 Universal Declaration of Human Rights, which, according to Davis (2003:94) established:

> the recognition of the inherent dignity and inalienable rights of all members of the human family.

This theory of the fundamental rights which are associated with civil liberties and human rights is often linked to the notion of Locke's ideas on individual liberty. It can also be tied in to Rousseau's notion of the social contract where that contract exists between the state and the individual and each individual agrees to cede some power to the state and to obey its laws in return for the state being the guarantor of the fundamental rights of each of its citizens. Rawls (1999) takes this theory further by arguing that in order to enjoy a society that will provide each of us with the 'good life', it is necessary to live in a society that not only protects fundamental human rights but does so irrespective of a person's standing or class or other individual difference. As Simon Jenkins commented in *The Sunday Times* (5 February 2006):

> Nobody has an absolute right to freedom. Civilisation is the story of humans sacrificing freedom so as to live together in harmony. We do not need Hobbes to tell us that absolute freedom is for newborn savages. All else is compromise.

The demise of policing by consent

Also relevant to the debate about how the regulation of ordinary citizens has changed is the background against which both Conservative and Labour governments have altered the law in relation to police powers and the conduct of investigations. I would suggest that there are a number of reasons for this.

First, from about 1979 there were increases in the numbers of reported criminal offences. As the Conservative Party of the time had campaigned vigorously on the law and order issue, it was perceived as politically vital that the government was seen to be responding to the problem. Second, it was perceived that existing legislation was not working, nor did it have the full confidence of the public at large. Criticisms of police practices were heard in Parliament and in the courts. Third, the image of the police in society had undergone a dramatic transformation. Images of the policeman as the people's friend had long been the type of response many sections of the media had sought to enforce. Perhaps the best example of this was the role model character Dixon of Dock Green. In 1950, BBC television introduced the character of PC George Dixon who quickly came to epitomise the popular image of the friendly, firm and fatherly local policeman. Just ten years later, a survey conducted by the Royal Commission on the Police revealed that nearly 83 per cent of the public had great respect for the police and the Willink Commission (Gilligan & Pratt, 2004) concluded that the findings of the survey constituted an overwhelming vote of confidence in the police, whose relations with the public on the whole were very good.

These findings, made at the beginning of the 1960s appear to reflect the consensus that British policing by consent had reached its zenith in the 1950s and early 1960s due to a number of factors. The police had positive relations with the public from which consequent support flowed. Added to this, wider social factors were also important such as the relative success of the social and economic policies of the time which reduced the amount of conflict in society; the existence of formal channels where political and economic grievances could be articulated, for example elections and trade unions; a relatively homogenous set of values and attitudes within society and also the creation of social agencies which contributed to this vision of peace and tranquillity.

The decline of this golden age of policing came about with changes in police roles. Successful policing had hitherto been based on public consent and explicit cooperation but since the mid-1960s some of the basic principles which underpinned this – such as effectiveness, participation, legitimacy and justice – were gradually eroded, thus undermining the idea of policing by consent. Some interesting explanations have been suggested for this. One is that mass ownership of cars resulted in a distancing of the police and the public. It has been suggested that from around 1954 onwards, the number of vehicles in private ownership doubled and consequently more people began to have contacts with the police in relation to this. It has also been suggested that the Police Act 1964 went a certain way toward centralising the control of police powers, enforcing the role and influence of the Home Secretary and in so doing, curtailing the influence of factors crucial to consensual policing such as local accountability and participation. Finally the conduct of the police themselves came under some scrutiny. Most notably a number of corruption scandals, high profile so-called miscarriages of justice, race issues and what was seen as the increasing politicisation of the police all led to the decline of policing by consent.

Against this backdrop other more recent factors include the relevance of the fact that 'New Labour' was able to form a government in 1997 on the back of what could be described as the 'law and order ticket' and the emergence of what Garland (2001:29) has described as a 'criminal justice state'.

Alongside the demise of policing by consent, certain powers exercised by the police have been augmented. In particular police powers to deal with terrorism have been altered dramatically against the backcloth of the attacks not just on the World Trade Centre, but also in relation to those terrorist attacks which took place in Bali and Madrid in 2002 and in London in 2005. It is inevitable that these events caused a moral panic. All of them were attributed to Al Qaeda and have heightened the sense of fear that many people experience of falling victim to unpredictable attacks which might occur due to suicide bombers. Stone (2006:384) suggests that:

> ...the situation is one in which the rules of the game have changed, and that this justifies increasing the powers of the police and security services.

The British government has in some ways sought to allay such fears within the general population, but at the same time it has also sought to respond by extending police powers. No doubt the argument would be that in order to respond effectively to this type of threat, we must expect a certain reduction in our freedoms because these must be balanced against the need for security. However, it could also be argued that any departure from the essential liberties which are afforded citizens of a democratic society should only take place in the most extreme of circumstances. In such circumstances, perhaps the real question to be asked is, what is the minimum possible departure necessary from essential personal rights and civil liberties in order to assist in the fight against crime or terrorism? Obviously, when governments tell us that we are facing life threatening risks and that some departure from essential freedoms and liberties is necessary to safeguard the security of the majority, we are bound to acquiesce to certain limitations being placed on our civil liberties simply because we are led to believe it is necessary in the interests of national security and the preservation of democracy. However, the question it seems to me that no one is asking is, if civil liberties are to be affected by the push to preserve national security, exactly who is ensuring that our essential and inalienable rights are being compromised in the least possible way? Who for example, was asking these questions when the stop and search powers of the police were extended beyond what are essentially investigative powers and which should be used only for the purposes of crime detection or prevention in relation to a specific individual at a specific time. Under section 43 of the Terrorism Act 2000 for example, the police are able to stop and search a person provided they have 'reasonable suspicion' that s/he is a terrorist. In such a case, the purpose of the search would be to discover whether the person has in his or her possession anything which may constitute evidence. Under sections 44–47 random stop and searching of individuals, their vehicles and any occupants is also allowed for a limited period of time if this is authorised by a senior officer who believes that 'it is expedient to do so' (Elliott & Quinn, 2006:389) in order to prevent acts of terrorism. Any vehicle or person stopped under these powers can be searched, according to McConville (2002:56) for:

> …articles of a kind which could be used for a purpose connected with the commission, preparation or instigation of acts of terrorism.

It could easily be argued that this is a rather vague definition, which merely authorises any sort of search that an officer might wish to carry out. Unlike certain other police powers of stop and search, there is no need to invoke reasonable suspicion in order to carry out of a search and once again we can only deduce from this that the extensive and intrusive nature of these powers is felt to be justified by the threats imposed by terrorist activity. However, one could argue whether the use of these powers involves a potential breach of Article 5 of the European Convention on Human Rights (ECHR).

The Home Office regularly publishes information comparing the number of stop and searches with the ethnic composition of the resident population and these comparisons consistently show that minority ethnic groups are subject to heightened rates of stop and search. According to the latest Home Office research published in March 2006, black people are still six times more likely to be stopped and searched in the street by the police than white people.[2] The figures also showed that whilst Asian people are twice as likely to be stopped by the police, they also appear to face discrimination as victims of crime. Of 59,000 racist incidents recorded by the police, 37,000 were racially aggravated offences, of which one third were cleared up. Bowling and Phillips (2002:138)

---

[2]Travis, A. *The Guardian*, Friday March 31 2006, p. 4.

have previously described this disproportionality as 'the most glaring example of an abuse of police powers.' They argue that the figures show the potential for the misuse of stop and search powers outside of the area of suspected terrorism and comment that explanations for this disproportionality have consistently emphasised the subjectivity of police officers.

In particular the problem of the terrorist suicide bomber has brought to the forefront of discussion the issue of the amount of force which the police may use in arresting a suspected terrorist. The Metropolitan Police has previously been reported as adopting a shoot-to-kill policy (Waddington, 2005) and in relation to this, the killing of Juan Carlos Menenez, on 22nd July 2005 illustrated the problem to tragic effect. He was shot by members of the police as he sat on a tube train. He had apparently been suspected of being a suicide bomber. The legal position as to what the police may or may not do in such a situation is governed by the common law, one provision lying in a British statute, whilst the other exists in Article 2 of the ECHR. The statutory provision to note is section 117 of the Police and Criminal Evidence Act 1984. This empowers a police officer to use reasonable force in the exercise of any of the powers under the Act, including the power of arrest for any offence.

The question that immediately arises is 'what is reasonable?', and more specifically can it ever be reasonable to use *lethal* force? Stone (2006) suggests that the answer to such a question must be no, because if an officer wishes to arrest someone, then the intention is to have a live suspect at the conclusion of this, rather than a dead one. At the same time he cautions that Article 2 of the ECHR must also be considered as well as any domestic provisions which are relevant because this article is specifically concerned with the right to life and is, of course currently emphasised in the UK by the Human Rights Act 1998, which imposes an obligation on public authorities (including the police) to act compatibly with the Convention rights. Article 2 states clearly that the force which can be used in such situations should be 'no more than absolutely necessary', and this is rather different to applying a more objective 'what is reasonable?', test. In October 2006, lawyers acting for the family of Jean Charles de Menezes tried to mount a legal challenge against the decision not to charge individual officers involved in the shooting, concluding that a review of available evidence 'justifies a prosecution for murder'. Lawyers at solicitors Birnberg Pierce sent the Crown Prosecution Service a letter raising serious misgivings over the decision to level health and safety charges at the Metropolitan Police over the shooting. The letter claimed that prosecutors should have considered murder, or at the very least, gross negligence manslaughter. In spite of this however, in October 2007 the case proceeded but on Health and Safety grounds only.

This case can be compared to that of *Edwards v UK* [2002] which established that such a duty *was* violated when a prisoner was killed after being placed in a cell with another known dangerous and unstable prisoner. This had exposed the deceased to 'real and serious risk' of loss of life. So we can deduce from this that if risk is known and quantifiable then Article 2 will be violated. Similarly in *Jordan & Others v UK* [2003] this case stated that failure to properly investigate the lethal shooting of IRA suspects was also a breach of Article 2. Finally in *McCann, Farrell & Savage v UK* [1996] in the attempted arrest and shooting dead of 3 IRA suspects in Gibraltar the court held that it would not be a breach of Article 2 if you shoot dead people you think are about to detonate a bomb. However in this case they said a lack of proper planning meant that the officers had been unable to make a rational decision about when lethal force should be used and that consequently the level of violence used was disproportionate to the circumstances of the case.

The rationale for restriction

Under normal circumstances, if an individual is arrested for a criminal offence, the maximum length of time that this person can be detained without charge is 96 hours. Where that detention is carried out on the basis of terrorism however, the period of detention can be longer. Why should this necessarily be the case? Originally under section 41 of the Terrorism Act 2000 the initial period of time that an individual could be detained was seven days. This was subsequently extended to 14 days by the Criminal Justice Act 2003. Subsequent to the July 2005 London bombings an argument was put forward to raise the length of time to 90 days but after a defeat in the House of Commons a period of 28 days was finally agreed. Fenwick (2002) comments that these moves towards extended detention have not necessarily been as easy as the government might have wished, and specifically in relation to the ATCSA 2001 she comments (2002:729) that:

> If the prospect of smuggling a range of new powers into law under the guise of the urgent need to combat terrorism seemed to leave the Commons relatively unperturbed, the same cannot be said of the Lords.

During the first 48 hours the position of the detainee is comparable to that of a suspected criminal detained under the provisions of the Police and Criminal Evidence Act 1984. The difference comes at the end of the 48 hour period. At that point, the decision about continued detention passes to a Judge. Under the 1984 Act, the power to extend detention rested with the Home Secretary, and appeared to be entirely at his or her discretion. The lack of any judicial review of this extended period brought the British government into conflict with the European Court of Human Rights, in the case of *Brogan v United Kingdom* [1989] there were four applicants who had been detained, on the authorisation of the Home Secretary, for periods of between four days and six hours, to six days and 16.5 hours. The European Court of Human Rights recognised the particular problems presented by terrorist offences. It was also acknowledged that these difficulties might have the effect of prolonging the period during which a person suspected of terrorist offences may, without violating Article 5(3), be kept in custody before being brought before a judge. Stone (2006:396) asks:

> What is the rationale for extended detention in terrorist cases? It cannot be simply that such cases are more complex: serious fraud cases, for example, may be equally involved and contain international elements. Due to the international nature of modern terrorism, there exists the need to employ interpreters, the need to decrypt large numbers of computer hard drives and to analyse the product as well as disclose prior to interview, the need to make safe premises where extremely hazardous material may be found, the need to obtain and analyse communications data from service providers, the need to allow time for religious observance by detainees, and the fact that suspects often use one firm of solicitors which causes delay in the process.

Detention under a law that allows arrest and imprisonment without charge can be equated with a double-edged sword that is just begging to be abused. The fact that one might not be a terrorist will not be the basis for an initial arrest but might be the reason for an eventual release. Arguably the application of this type of process is something which could more easily be equated with the actions of governments that the US and UK say they are at war with. In the volatile aftermath of any terrorist attack, knee jerk responses are, to some extent inevitable. Surely the question that should be posed once the dust has settled is, now that the threat has dimmed somewhat, is it subsequently possible to consider in a measured and balanced way, what changes in the law might be necessary whilst at the same time upholding the principles of the democratic society? A recurring theme in the development of state powers in any democratic society is the tension which arises over the balance to be achieved between the ideals of liberal legalism, with their emphasis on protecting the citizen from the coercive potential of the State, and the need to have a police force with sufficient powers to enforce the law effectively and efficiently. As Stone (2006:397) rightly comments, one of the hallmarks of a strong government ought to be that it should do all it can to protect its citizen's fundamental rights:

> ...even when it is facing new and challenging threats, such as those posed by terrorism in the early 21st century.

Currently it might well be argued that the balance between maintaining adequate public protection, whilst at the same time preserving the rights of the individual, has not been achieved in the most fair way possible and that the numerous justifications which have been made for the manifold increases in restriction have outweighed any of the arguments for the retention of fundamental freedoms and civil liberties. However, as Garland points out, both the political and social climates of the last 30 years in the UK and the USA have facilitated such changes in ways that previously may have been thought impossible.

Law and morality

One further issue is relevant in this context which arises out of the famous Hart-Devlin debate which surrounded the legalisation of homosexuality between consenting male adults. This is the debate about whether there is a role for law at all in matters of morality. Patton (1964:8) suggests that:

> in all communities that reach a certain stage of development there springs up a social machinery which we call law. ... In each society there is an interaction between the abstract rules, the institutional machinery existing for their application, and the life of the people.

McTeer (1995:895) also suggests that:

> Throughout history, law has played an important role in the definition and protection of certain relationships, systems and institutions and in the control of individual and collective human behaviour. Through the use of normative and prescriptive rules, supported by varying

degrees of sanctions, law has been used to create a climate of social order, the usual justification of which has been that it benefits members of society.

It is certainly the case that historically the law was seen as being inextricably linked with issues of morality since medieval law makers – as discussed in the last chapter – were seen to derive their authority directly from God as a 'Divine Right.' In this context laws were respected because they were seen to be connected in a fundamental way, with issues of morality. With the passage of time, the development of science and technology and other such significant changes in society such as a greater degree of secularity, the connection between law, religion and consequently morals has diminished. Today, there appears to be a more general acceptance that whilst there is not necessarily an interdependence between law and morality, it is still most people's perception that the law should work in such a way as to protect society including certain moral aspects, although the morality of society is of course not a static notion. As such, as society's moral outlook changes, so the law must change with it. The problem with this is that how far should the law intervene in matters of morality or personal conscience before it becomes inappropriate? Where should the line be drawn between the legitimate role of the law in such matters – perhaps where it is deemed necessary to protect the public interest – and where issues should be left to an individuals own conscience? This is a particularly difficult question if one accepts that what might have been deemed an acceptable role for the law historically, would not, in the modern world, perhaps be thought of as such. Thus the debate itself is not a static one. In the UK, the Wolfenden Report (1957) was particularly influential in raising the profile of this debate some 50 years ago. The Report suggested that the law which previously made consensual homosexual relations in private an offence should be changed, primarily because the suggestion was that the law had no part to play in decisions about morality. Subsequent to this, both Lord Patrick Devlin (1965) and Professor Herbert Hart (1971) engaged in the debate which has been discussed since by other authors such as George (1990) and Hittinger (1990).

The relevance of this is rooted in the issue of the enforcement of morality and what the basis of decisions should be in circumstances where there is a conflict between individual moral freedom and social control. Specifically within this debate, Lord Devlin addressed himself to two particular issues. First, he asked, has society the right to pass judgement on matters of morals and second, if society has this right, does it also have the right to use the law to enforce it? Devlin's view was that the law *should* be able to intervene in matters of morality, in order to preserve what he called 'society's constitutive morality.' In relation to the Wolfenden Report, Devlin claimed that homosexuality was a threat to society and as such it fell within the domain of public morality, on which the law should pass judgement to preserve social cohesion. Devlin claimed that in order to decide which rules of morality should be enforced, a 'feelings test' should be applied in order to determine the potential for harm to an individual. Whilst Hart agreed with Devlin that if a threat existed, which was sufficient to challenge social cohesion, then the law ought to be able to intervene, he did not agree that homosexuality was an example of this and was clear about his view that in order to prove what constituted true threats to society, then empirical evidence was required. What appears to be the case with these respective positions is that both Devlin and Hart have inherently different values and this then informs each of their arguments in a different way as regards the enforcement of morals. This is precisely why the question of law and morality is so difficult since it must be attached to the current social condition, and the expectations and values of society, but social conditions are not constant. Thus we have a potentially continuous debate about the balance between law, morality, freedom and social control. Whichever position one takes in such matters, there will no doubt be some intellectual philosophy which will support it and in this sense, perhaps this dilemma can never be resolved by reason. For what might be one man's reason may well be another's unreason. Moreover, and in line with the birth of the positivist paradigm within criminology, who should decide what is rational and for whom?

Whilst the debate about homosexuality, the law and morality has seemingly been and gone in liberal Western democracies apart from the USA, today's societies face new dilemmas, resulting particularly from the developments of science and technology in numerous fields which pose new and unaddressed questions. Take for example the case of *Evans v United Kingdom* [2006]. Having lost her ovaries to cancer treatment, previously stored embryos created from Ms Evans' eggs and her ex-partner's sperm represented Ms Evans' last chance to have her own genetic child. With the UK courts having denied her claim to use the embryos against her ex-partner's wishes, Ms Evans went to the European Court of Human Rights where a majority of five to two judges held that UK law did not breach her Convention rights and the fertilised embryos were duly destroyed. In Ireland, in *MR v TR* [2006] another woman was similarly recently refused the right to use stored embryos against the wishes of her estranged husband. These two judgments highlight two important issues. First, the significance that the law has seemingly attached to the role of genetics in parenthood and second, the difficulty of achieving some sort of equality in balancing the competing interests of two potential parents. It also demonstrates clearly that the law appears to be able to make judgements in such matters which arguably are rooted in issues of morality, not just genetics and technology. What was interesting in both of these very difficult cases is that whilst the courts did not appear to have any difficulty with their right to sit in judgement of such matters, at the same time they did not give the fullest consideration to all of the relevant factors. For example, in both cases it seems to have been assumed that genetic links have the same psychological, social and moral significance for men and for women. But in terms of the respective roles of both fathers and mothers and the inherent differences that this has for each, can the courts really be certain that both male and female genetic interests are truly the same and should be treated by the law as such? These challenging cases have required the judiciary to make sense of the inherent meaning of the family, parenthood, gender, and reproduction.

The question remains, how much, if at all, should the law involve itself with matters of morality, particularly if those issues directly affect inherent freedoms of conscience, religion, speech and liberty? The concluding chapter of this book will return to some of these issues, notably the fact that there is currently not a particularly healthy or transparent debate ongoing in relation to these matters currently – possibly with the exception of terrorism. But is this sufficient? As McTeer (1995:903) rightly comments:

> Failure to engage in this kind of debate may lead to a situation where the public discussion of the fundamental issues involved would stagnate at the level of slogans, as in the abortion debate. We must now find new processes and contexts for the resolution of issues which profoundly affect society. Otherwise, we will be faced with *ad hoc* public policy and legislation in an area of extreme importance to the integrity and freedom of both society and the individual...

In summary, during the course of this chapter, I have advanced the argument that there has been a significant move towards a greater degree of social control, particularly during the last decade, which can be explained by reference to a number of factors. First, in spite of an overt commitment to the idea of 'open and democratic societies' attitudes to security and contemporary crime control in both Britain and the United States have undergone something of a transformation towards what Garland (1996) describes as an excessive concern with penality and social control. This can partly be explained by the response of numerous criminal justice agencies to rising crime rates and social changes from which a new 'crime control culture' has emerged. Second, this move has been underpinned by social policy developments which, contrary to what was predicted in the 1970s, have become more oppressive, rather than less so. This development has been encouraged by the intense interest in law and order that politicians in most countries have shown – probably because to pursue these interests is both ideological and pragmatic. Added to this, changes in ideologies about responsibility for crime have not only shaped attitudes, but have also changed the way in which many criminal justice and other agencies now respond to crime and its control. Finally, perceptions about increases in the crime risks to society – both from what we might term 'ordinary' crimes, to the threat posed by terrorism – have increased due both to media and political representations. This chapter therefore provides the theoretical and philosophical backdrop against what I now wish to discuss in the following chapters. Namely a number of very specific examples of what I consider to be excessive restriction of personal liberties through legislation. The following chapter therefore discusses the first of these examples, the notion of detention without trial.

4
Detention Without Trial

In the furtherance of the overall theme of this book, this chapter considers a more specific example of the potential for the restriction of personal liberties which have been facilitated through legislation and highlights my view that current attempts at preventing crime are disproportionate to the risks posed and therefore represent in themselves a different kind of danger. Specifically I want to highlight the undermining of the age old principles of 'innocent until proven guilty' and *habeas corpus* by the move to the detention of terrorist suspects without trial for indefinite periods of time. This practice, which appears to have been justified both in the UK and the USA on the basis of an increased need for security in the wake of terrorist atrocities, has given rise to the previously unacceptable notion of detention without trial. To do this, I want to focus in this chapter on a number of specific matters.

First, I want to focus on the nature of detention without trial, its legalities, the very ancient rule of *habeas corpus* and questions about how the concept has come to exist. I want to highlight what I see as the circumstances surrounding this development by exploring the philosophical and theoretical ideas behind the 'special relationship' between the UK and the US, but more specifically the relationship between Tony Blair and George Bush, and the impact this relationship has had on international policy. I also want to address the issue of human rights and the apparent demise of the presumption of innocence and to focus on how government policies and legislation both in the UK and the US have enabled a distancing from the fundamental principles of human rights. Finally I will highlight the experiences of some of those detained at Guantánamo Bay Prison Camp in Cuba and in Belmarsh Prison in the UK and ask whether their treatment contravenes human rights legislation. Before embarking on the promised examples however, I want to ask a question. Any discussion of civil liberties and restrictions upon people naturally at some point focuses on the fact that arguably certain restrictions upon individual freedom are sometimes necessary and are implemented for the safety and well being of the majority of people. However, the difficulty here of course is that who decides what is reasonable and for whom and in what circumstances? Is there a case to say – for example – that generally you should be allowed to do everything except where explicitly forbidden, or whether there are certain principles which drive the kind of restrictions legitimately imposed?[1] For example, one of these driving forces might be quarantine, where the temporary deprivation of the liberty of an individual could be justified on the grounds of a known and quantifiable health risk. In order to reinforce the point I am trying to make I want to mention two examples which come to mind in relation to the notion of what should and should not be forbidden and under what circumstances.

Researchers at the Centre for Disease Control in Atlanta, USA postulated in the early 1980s that the spread of Aids was most likely to have occurred because of the movements of a single individual around the world which introduced the disease to North America. In order to test this they traced sexual contacts and in 1982 found a man they called patient zero who, through his sexual liaisons could be linked to nine of the first 19 cases in Los Angeles, 22 cases in New York City and nine more in eight other cities – in all, some 40 of the first 248 cases in the US. Shilts (2000) identified this man as Gaetan Dugas, a steward for Air Canada, who travelled extensively and picked up men wherever he went. Dugas developed Kaposi's sarcoma, a form of skin cancer common in AIDS victims, in June 1980, before the epidemic had been perceived by physicians. Told later he was endangering anyone he slept with, Dugas carried on with an estimated 250 partners a year until his death in March 1984. Shilts (2000) argues that the Aids epidemic spread wildly because the federal government put finances ahead of the nation's welfare and

---

[1]For example, prior to the enactment of the Human Rights Act 1998 the legal position in the UK regarding the civil liberties of the individual was premised on the notion of residual rights. That is to say that citizens were made aware of the things they were not allowed to do, as restricted specifically by law, with the assumption that anything which lay outside of these restrictions was allowed. This interpretation seems to have been based on the attitude of British judges that individuals should be free to do whatsoever they wish, without the fear of interference by, or sanction from executive officials or others. Whether this would still be the likely judicial interpretation currently – in the light of more recent legislation – is debatable.

health authorities placed political expediency before the public health. Added to this he claims that some scientists were more concerned with international prestige than saving lives. He suggests that all of these institutions failed the public and from the point of view of this book, it seems strange that in the face of such a health risk, no attempt was made to prevent this man from being at liberty when the risk to the lives of others was known and quantifiable. A somewhat different approach was recently taken in the US in relation to a man who may have exposed passengers on board two trans-Atlantic flights to a dangerous form of tuberculosis. The infected man travelled from Atlanta to Paris and then from Prague to Montreal in May 2007 and was subsequently quarantined by the US Centre for Disease Control. CDC officials said the man was potentially infectious during this period and recommended that crew members and passengers on board the same flights sought medical attention. It is the first such federal quarantine order to be issued in over 44 years. According to the CDC the last such order was issued in 1963, to quarantine a patient with smallpox.

These examples appear to demonstrate that in certain circumstances there may be principles which drive the kind of restrictions that might legitimately be imposed – one of these driving forces being quarantine. However in the former of the two examples the drivers for rational restriction based on a quantifiable risk did not materialise. What does this tell us? Perhaps cynically it could be suggested that where issues of finance, politics or prestige are involved risk factors become subordinate. Could the same be said in relation to issues of national security? More specifically when a threat to the nation is perceived and the organs of government feel the need to be seen to be doing something in the face of a moral panic created by postulations about the war on terror, then arguably this might pave the way for a greater level of restriction based precisely on the importance of political expediency. Perhaps this is also how the idea of detention without trial has become acceptable.

Detention without trial

Detention without trial is sometimes also known as preventive detention and, in the case of Northern Ireland, was also called 'internment'. To be detained without trial essentially means that a people are deprived of their freedom even though they have not been tried or found guilty of any offence in a court of law. This type of detention is normally exercised by the State and according to Jayawickrama (2002) is usually justified on the basis of national security when it is alleged that the person in question poses a threat to the State. Naturally, this is not the only situation in which a person may be detained without trial. For example, in the UK a person may be sectioned under the Mental Health Act 1983 if s/he is deemed (by two independent medical practitioners) to be either a danger to him/herself or to others. Obviously this type of detention is also indefinite and a persons release will be dependent upon the subsequent findings of a Mental Health Review panel. I have also highlighted previously in this chapter, other circumstances where a person may be detained such as quarantine. However, although this concept is not unknown, the purpose of this chapter is to highlight the very particular circumstances where individuals are detained by virtue of the fact that they are thought to be actively involved in terrorist activities and, according to Zinn (2002:453) are known as either 'special interest detainees' or 'illegal combatants.' The right to liberty is of course not absolute and most societies limit this right in certain circumstances where it is deemed, by law to be necessary for the proper functioning of society. Clearly this occurs where imprisonment is the most widely used criminal sanction but this is obviously normally only used where such detention is based on a pre-existing domestic legal norm establishing both the reason and the procedures for that detention, including the transparency of the period of detention and the likely time of release. Under normal circumstances of detention therefore, the law allows individuals to foresee what sort of conduct will lead to detention, that it will not be arbitrary and to have some awareness of the likely period of detention associated with particular criminal sanctions and an expected time for release.

Within most western democracies the assumption is that in a free society citizens are at liberty to go about their business without the need to explain to anyone in authority what they are doing, and without the fear that they may be subject to arbitrary challenge or arrest. The notion of preventive detention undermines this fundamental notion of personal liberty and in so doing is making assumptions about a person's potential risk to society in a subjective way, since any Government which condones this practise has a vested interest in the outcome. Naturally, such decisions are justified on the basis of the need for national security. This has recently been facilitated by the current concern over the so-called 'war on terror' subsequent to the attacks of 9/11 in the USA and the 7/7 bombings in London. In these situations, it is generally claimed that the safety and well being of the majority outweighs an individuals right to personal liberty and the greater the perception of a crisis is, then the easier it is to justify this. However, the problem with this is that how is it possible in such circumstances to determine whether this approach is being abused, or used for the wrong reasons? The cynic might for example argue that it may well be politically expedient for a government to justify this approach by saying that it is protecting the public from terrorism. However, in spite of this the legality of such an approach should be questioned. Whilst the initial power to detain might well be found in a statutory provision of some sort, the problem with this is that the provisions authorising such detention are often framed in broad or vague terms such as 'national security'. Added to this, it is either difficult, or impossible for individuals to determine what circumstances might lead to their release from this type of detention. All of this creates an atmosphere of unacceptable arbitrariness which arguably contravenes some of the basic principles of legality. So what safeguards exist in relation to the abuse of such a power?

The International Covenant on Civil and Political Rights 1966 (ICCPR) currently protects an individual's right to liberty and security of the person, under Article 9. Nowak (1993:160) says that:

> Liberty in this context is interpreted narrowly, basically meaning physical freedom, or freedom from forceful detention...at a certain, narrowly bounded location.

O'Byrne (2002:253) highlights that the Human Rights Committee (HRC) has specified that detention will be deemed to be arbitrary when it is 'unjust', 'inappropriate', 'unpredictable', 'unnecessary', 'unreasonable' or 'unproportional.' Article 9 of the ICCPR also gives several procedural rights of protection from arbitrary detention including the fact that the detainee must be informed of the reasons for his/her arrest and must be given appropriate and relevant legal information in relation to the specifics of any acts or threats that s/he was supposed to be involved in. Consequently it would not be sufficient to justify the detention purely on the basis of a vague or more general accusation about the risk such an individual posed.

Situations of armed conflict give rise to another set of rules for the protection of the individual. These are the rules of international humanitarian law which limit the conduct of states in times of war. The major codified bases of humanitarian law relevant to this are the Geneva Conventions of 1949. Condorelli (2004) suggests that under these Conventions persons are either 'combatants', (meaning that they actively participate in hostilities) or they are 'non-combatants', (meaning those who do not actively participate). These two theoretical groups of individuals have the right to be treated as Prisoners of War (POW) which means they can be detained for as long as active hostilities are taking place but because they have POW status, they are supposed to have special protection. The purpose of their detention therefore is not punishment but simply to prevent them from actively taking part in a war situation. The special status of a POW also means that they are supposed to be released and repatriated as soon as a war situation is at an end because as indicated by De Preux (1960), once active hostilities end there can no longer be any justification for their detention. Whilst the recommendations contained in the Geneva Conventions remain relevant, it should be remembered that they were drafted after the cessation of two conventional world wars. Their relevance to the types of modern warfare and theatres of war which proliferate today might reasonably be questioned. For example, in a conventional war setting the termination of active hostilities could more easily be determined than it is today. In the case of the 'war on terrorism', Mariner (2002) argues that the identification of the cessation of this 'war' becomes virtually impossible, because this phenomenon is both uncertain and ill-defined. Therefore the possibility that identified terrorist 'combatants' may be detained indefinitely becomes highly likely, particularly if there is an assumption that such 'combatants' may at some point take up arms again and re-engage in terrorist action. In such a situation, the so-called 'war on terrorism' has no end and the terrorist detainee has no realistic prospect of release.

Without doubt the assertion would be made that in order to fulfil their function of providing security, law and order, States depend on the power to deprive persons of their individual liberty. Indeed I have already mentioned at the start of this chapter, circumstances such as quarantine, where this might be the case. The problem with this is that this power is likely to be abused particularly when it is used to counter emotive threats like terrorism. Deprivation of liberty is a serious consideration which has been of concern constitutionally for centuries and notably since the time of the Magna Carta 1215 and as subsequently amended and extended. In the present climate, restrictions on the deprivation of essential liberties can be found in both the international law of human rights and in humanitarian laws. Kunschak (2006:29) states that for detention to be considered non-arbitrary and legal under international law a number of conditions have to be satisfied.

Firstly, detention must be objective in each individual case. In human rights law, such grounds must be stated in some prior legal basis and, in addition, comply with standards of basic justice, that is they must be reasonable, appropriate and proportional. Humanitarian law authorises the detention of combatants by reason of their status as POW's as well as the detention of civilians for imperative security reasons of absolute necessity. Secondly, detainees must be told why they have been arrested and detained....... And [any] administrative decision to detain must be reviewed by a neutral third authority, at least at the request of the detainee. This......authority must be impartial and competent and rely on a fair procedure. Additionally, the prohibition of arbitrary detention also involves a temporal element. The basic principle is 'the longer the detention, the higher the probability of arbitrariness'. Although a specific time limit can not be found in human rights law and jurisprudence, the permissible period of administrative detention without trial must be measured in hours or days as opposed to weeks, following which judicial review must commence. Indefinite detention without judicial review is prohibited.

The United States and the 'War on Terror'

The USA has always been rather vocal in support of human rights, but when it comes to combating terrorism it could feasibly be argued that it has rejected certain legal constraints when it comes to the exercise of its foreign policy. In spite of having a constitution that is based on the need to impose checks and balances, the US government could arguably be accused of maintaining an international policy that places no limits on its own actions. Terrorism is of course antithetical to human rights and the indiscriminate targeting of civilians goes against human rights norms. Those who believe in human rights have a direct interest in the success of the anti-terrorism effort, but the tendency of the US government to ignore human rights in fighting terrorism could be seen as dangerously counterproductive. In the latter half of the past century, the United States has enjoyed a position of importance, being seen as a driving force for strengthening the human rights ideal. It took the lead in drafting the Universal Declaration of Human Rights, building the international human rights system and lending its voice and influence on behalf of human rights in many parts of the world (Roth, 2004). However, this support for human rights has been inconsistent and strategic concerns have often taken precedence together with some resistance to applying international law domestically. Despite this, and whatever it actions in reality, the US government has been at the forefront of numerous human rights battles, and has contributed significantly to building a global consensus regarding the importance of human rights as a restraint on legitimate governmental conduct.

〔More recently it could be argued that the US Government's neglect of human rights in the fight against terrorism has been manifested in its treatment of terrorist suspects, notably those detained at Guantánamo Bay〕(I shall return to this particular issue later in this chapter.) Arguably, the US administration has adopted a rather narrow interpretation of aspects of the Geneva Convention, which effectively allows detainees to be kept in long-term arbitrary detention despite international prohibitions. The Third Geneva Convention provides that captured combatants are to be treated as prisoners of war until a "competent tribunal" (Roth, 2004:117) determines otherwise. Under the standards set out in the Convention, detainees such as former Taliban soldiers almost certainly qualify as POWs, whilst many of the detainees who are suspected members of Al Qaeda arguably do not. However, according to Roth (*op cit*) the US administration has refused to bring any of the detainees before a tribunal and continues to claim that none of them qualifies as a POW. It could reasonably be suggested that this represents an abandonment of due process and as such this undermines the basic principles of democracy since the security services cannot be entirely certain in every case that the detained suspects are actually guilty of any terrorist crime unless these cases are individually tried on their own merits. A respect for the law and fundamental rights is what distinguishes democratic systems from the world of dictatorship and tyranny.

〔Detention without trial has most obviously been used as an antiterrorism measure since the terrorist attacks of 9/11. This is relevant, because in countering terrorism, governments frequently choose to ignore existing norms of international law. Interestingly, according to Kunschak (2006:32):

> the use of administrative detention as a means to combat terrorism was hardly considered in the US pre 9/11〕

and he claims that what had been a subject of disinterest latterly came to be one which attracted 'fervent support'. It was only a matter of time before this was placed on a statutory footing and in this case the legislative response to this was the US Patriot Act (2001) which has subsequently allowed the detention of 'unlawful combatants' at Guantánamo Bay – a naval base on Cuban territory occupied by the US on the basis of a lease treaty with Cuba from 1903. The US has jurisdiction and control over the base, but Cuba retains sovereignty. In January 2002, the

US began transferring suspected terrorists to Guantánamo Bay. They were labelled as 'unlawful combatants' and because this is not a label recognised in international law, they have not been afforded the rights that other POW would claim and which were discussed earlier in this chapter. In effect, this has meant that they have been denied their fundamental rights and civil liberties and at the same time have found that they have not been able to legally defend themselves or challenge their detention. So how has this situation been made possible? Any US President has what are known as 'wartime powers'. Part of these powers mean that if Congress gives the President authorisation, in his capacity as Commander in Chief of the US forces, to detain people on the basis of a terrorist threat, then this becomes a lawful exercise of power. Interestingly what also makes all of this possible is US legislation, specifically the US Patriot Act 2001 which, under section 412(a) gives authorisation for the detention of people who are thought to be engaged in terrorist activity.

The United Kingdom and the 'War on Terrorism'

The United Kingdom is no stranger to using indefinite detention as a means of counter-terrorism and did so in Northern Ireland between 1971 and 1975. In line with its ally, the US, the UK has also resorted to indefinite detention without trial as a response to the perceived new threats. The UK, however, did not employ the 'enemy combatant' approach, but has used immigration laws to justify the detention of terrorist suspects. Since 9/11 and following the terrorist bombings of the public transport system in London in July 2005, former Prime Minister Blair stated, according to Elliott & Quinn (2006:265) that; 'the rules of the game had changed' and outlined ideas for amending the law in the UK to tackle this threat to society. Simultaneously, concerns were expressed by civil liberties organisations that the government might respond to these attacks in a way that amounted to a significant attack on individual human rights while at the same time proving to be counter-productive in the fight against terrorism. In March 2005 Parliament adopted a new anti-terrorist law – the Prevention of Terrorism Act. This Act is a modification of Part Four of the Anti-terrorism, Crime and Security Act 2001, the specific provisions of which concern detention of foreigners accused of terrorism expired on March 14, 2005. In so doing, Parliament made it possible for the government to expand the emergency provisions to which foreigners are subjected within the context of war on terrorism to cover the whole population. This change is important because it calls into question the notion of *habeas corpus*, the ancient common law rule which has historically been an important instrument for the safeguarding of individual freedom against arbitrary state action. The newly enacted law arguably attacks the formal notion of the separation of powers (the accepted British principle that the parliament, the supreme law-making body and the judiciary – the supposedly non-political body which interprets the law passed by Parliament, should operate entirely independently). It does this by giving to the Secretary of State for Home Affairs, judicial prerogatives to detain suspects without trial on the basis not of what they have done, but according to what the Home Secretary thinks they could have done or might do in the future. Consequently, this law knowingly turns its back on the rule of law and establishes a new form of political regime. The attacks of September 11, 2001 had allowed the British government to force the urgent adoption of a new anti-terrorist law, the Anti-terrorism, Crime and Security Act, which was enacted on December 14, 2001. In comparison with the Terrorism Act 2000, which is still in force, the 2001 legislation authorised the indefinite detention, without an indictment, of a foreigner suspected of terrorist activities. In particular Article 21 allows for indefinite incarceration based on a certificate issued by the Secretary of State for Home Affairs:

> The Secretary of State may issue a certificate under this section in respect of a person if the Secretary of State believes that (a) the person present in the United Kingdom is a risk to national security, and (b) suspects that the person is a terrorist.

No objective fact is necessary to justify the decision, and the time limit for 'conviction' is entirely subjective. The certificate issued by the Home Secretary permits the detention of the accused person within the terms of the Immigration Act of 1971, i.e. for the purposes of either expulsion or return to the country of origin. The possibility of detention for an indefinite period is necessary when expulsion is prevented by an international agreement. The person has a choice between remaining in indefinite detention in the UK or returning to his/her country of origin and being subjected there to a whole set of proceedings that are exceptional under the terms of international law. Most often, the countries of origin of the incarcerated persons are infamous for their systematic violations of human rights. By permitting potentially unlimited detention, this Act effectively suspends the law for all persons not having either British citizenship or legal residence and those who do not have the right of protection as refugees. Therefore, the suspension of *habeas corpus* is less extensive than in the United States, where all foreigners are affected. In order to pass this law, the British government instituted an exception to the European Convention on Human Rights. This exception is based on the notion of a state of emergency and is thus an exception to Article 5, paragraph 1 of this convention, which guarantees the liberty of persons. According to Article 15 of the convention, exceptional measures must be limited strictly to the minimum necessary as required by the situation. As judged by the Special Immigration Appeals Commission (SIAC), this is not true of unlimited detention. Elliott & Quinn (2006) suggests that the SIAC was created in order to assume some control over detentions. Interestingly, this Act does not allow for appeals to be made before this Commission.

(Under the ATCSA 2001, nine foreign nationals were certified as suspected terrorists and detained without trial. The legality of this detention has been challenged through the courts in the case of A and Z and others v Secretary of State for the Home Department (2005) UKHL 71. Some of the applicants had been detained in a high security prison for three years, with no prospect of release or trial. Due to the importance of the case, nine judges in the House of Lords heard the case instead of the usual five and the House held that the detentions were unlawful. By late 2004, the British Law Lords ruled that, because only foreigners suspected of being capable of, or implicated with, terrorist acts, could be detained without trial, that such anti-terrorist law was discriminatory, disproportionate and unlawful under Article 14 of the European Convention on Human Rights.) It was subsequently proposed that rather than abolishing this measure, the power of detention without trial should be extended to all British citizens as well as foreign nationals. This caused an outcry on behalf of human rights and the principle of the burden of proof (an accused person is innocent until proven guilty), central to English constitutional tradition since the Magna Carta in 1215. On December 22, 2004, the Secretary-General of the Council of Europe demanded the immediate abrogation of the 2001 Terrorism Act stating that:

(Anti-terrorist legislation in the United Kingdom must be changed immediately. We will not win the war on terrorism if we undermine the foundation of our democratic societies.[2])

Subsequently, this legislation was repealed and replaced by the Prevention of Terrorism Act which was passed on March 11, 2005. This

---

[2]Statewatch News Online, December 22, 2004.

authorises the Home Secretary to initiate control orders over a person, potentially leading to house arrest, in cases where he has reason to suspect that an individual is or was implicated in an action linked with terrorism. The implementation of house arrest is the first time that this measure has been used in the UK. Up to 16 different restrictions can be placed on an individual who is subjected to a control order, examples being the use of electronic tagging, surveillance, permission to search their premises and a curfew order. Such orders are made by the High Court following an application by the Home Secretary and imposed where an individual is suspected of having been involved in terrorist-related activity. Breach of a control order, without reasonable excuse, is a criminal offence punishable by up to five years imprisonment (Elliott & Quinn, 2006).

Interestingly, justification for the decision to place a person under supervision is not founded upon objective facts, but in the suspicion that falls on that person or in the intention that is attributed to that person. Terrorist activity is defined in the PoTA 2005 (Art 1(9)) as:

The commission, preparation or instigation of acts of terrorism;
Conduct which facilitates the commission, preparation or instigation of such acts, or which is intended to do so;
Conduct which gives encouragement to the commission, preparation or instigation of such acts, or which is intended to do so;
Conduct which gives support or assistance to individuals who are known or believed to be involved in terrorism-related activity.

Therefore the law does not appear to concern itself with definite acts, but punishes assistance to persons who are simply suspected of activities or intentions linked to terrorism. Arguably this notion is indeterminate and subjective. Its area of application is vast, nearly unlimited and wholly unverifiable. What is an activity linked to terrorism? Is it, for example, to have engaged in accommodating persons who later were suspected of participating or of having had the intention of participating in actions designated as terrorist? Does it include belonging to a support group for political prisoners?

The relevance of *habeas corpus*

According to Paye (2005) the writ of *habeas corpus* has historically been an important instrument for the safeguarding of individual freedom against arbitrary state action. Considered the hallmark of western liberty, *habeas corpus* has its origins in the Magna Carta dating back to 1215 and as previously indicated in chapter 2, there is however, nothing whatever to commemorate anything British about Magna Carta. It is not surprising that the Americans have sought to commemorate what in effect gave them the basis of the American Bill of Rights and what was the original document for their principle that: 'No person shall...be deprived of life, liberty or property without due process of law.' But considering that this place also gave the British what could be described as the most potent symbol of freedom under law in western civilisation, one might have thought we would want to celebrate that in some way – perhaps with our own monument or even a plaque?

As highlighted by both Elliott & Quinn (2006) and Paye (2005), the writ of *habeas corpus* is a judicial mandate to a prison official ordering that an inmate be brought to the court so it can be determined whether or not that person is imprisoned lawfully and whether or not should be released from custody. The right of *habeas corpus*, or rather, the right to petition for the writ, has long been celebrated as the most efficient safeguard of the liberty of subjects. The 'Great Writ' ended the king's power to kidnap people, lock them in dungeons and never bring them to court. The habeas story began in an English meadow at Runnymede on June 15, 1215, when dissident English nobles forced King John to sign the Magna Carta, a contract limiting the power of the king in exchange for his right to rule. John was an autocrat and an ineffectual war king. He had alienated the papacy, the aristocracy, the French and imposed ruinous taxes, all of which prompted a war. As a result, England's barons forced John at sword-point to sign the Magna Carta, which began the transformation of *habeas* from a tool to bring people to trial to a legal action allowing detainees to challenge the lawfulness of their detention. Today, *habeas* is arguably the single most important legal lever to prevent unjust and indefinite imprisonment. *habeas corpus* identifies what distinguishes authority under the law from authority that merely purports to be, but is not the law. It is a core democratic principle. If one is to view the United States and United Kingdom as free and democratic societies, it is of cardinal importance that these principles are upheld. To threaten *habeas corpus* tears at the very fabric of the rights of the nation because when a person is arrested under false charges or without charge, that person has a right to petition a court to ask that this is justified under law. Accordingly the state must justify its right to detain a person under law or that person must be set free.

Over the past 200 years, political systems in the Western world have increasingly experienced significant developments with regard to the institutions on which they are built, the values that societies uphold and the preferences and attitudes that their citizens and leaders express. Political stability has been attained through the introduction of constitutional orders, a settled framework of government, and reliable procedures to ensure leadership succession. The terrorist attacks on the World Trade Centre on the 11th September 2001 had unprecedented ramifications for international politics. One could argue that the events of 9/11 have reconfigured the meaning of terrorism in the West and rendered it more powerful. The type of terrorism which emerged that day has not only altered the way liberal democracies define and execute their foreign and defence policies, but it has also affected their ability to attend to policy objectives domestically. Wilkinson suggests (2006:79) that by definition terrorist groups are making a war on legality and that their claim is that the 'ends justify their means' and they are for 'true justice' in order to avenge the injustices and judicial procedures they view with such hatred and contempt. The notion of a 'New terrorism' has seeped into political language and public discourse intensifying the feeling that we are living in risky times. It has been suggested by Mythen (2006:379) that new forms of terrorism have become a 'leitmotif' of the age. But what exactly is 'new' about new terrorism? It is easy to see why terrorism has become a fundamental political concern in western capitalist cultures. Terrorist acts have disrobed the liberal myth that the state is capable of providing order and control over its territory (Garland, 1996).

Since 9/11 the public have become accustomed to reminders that a new type of risk has emerged. The unpredictability of terrorism has arguably forced governments to admit that they cannot guarantee public safety and the threat of crime, or more specifically the threat of terror, has become a routine part of modern consciousness. Both politicians and the media are in part responsible for perpetuating the notion that crime is now an everyday risk to be routinely assessed and managed. Added to this, what is also dangerous about the present climate of fear is that it has no apparent time limit and unlike historic wars, no foreseeable end. Although President Bush chose to define the struggle against terrorism after September 11 as a war, it might have been more appropriately described as a worldwide law enforcement effort against a criminal gang. However, the idea of a war against terror remains, and that makes the need for vigilance against abuse of power the more acute. Post 9/11, the State has clearly extended its power on the basis of the need to address the new risk to society. This has been achieved in many different ways including through new legislation, by bureaucratic expansion, increased surveillance capacity and greater data collection. Surveillance, however, is not constant, nor can anyone currently claim that it is uniformly efficient or fool proof.

The Terrorism Act 2000, The Anti-Terrorism Crime and Security Act 2001 and the Prevention of Terrorism Act 2005 in the UK and the US Patriot Act 2001 all represent important extensions of state power which have been passed by Parliament in the usual way. Much of this legislation has provided the police with greater powers specifically in the areas of stop and search, detention and it has also introduced new offences such as 'supporting terrorism'. In addition, the Government campaign to extend pre-charge detention for those suspected of terrorist offences to 28 days limit was secured in the Terrorism Act 2006 (Moran, 2005). The debate to extend this further to 42 days trundles inexorably on. Added to this, Control Orders can now be applied to individuals on the basis of intelligence presented to special tribunals as opposed to the standard judicial process. Subsequently, if a person is identified as being involved in terrorist related activity s/he may become the subject of a control order which has the potential to impose a wide range of restrictions such as wearing an electronic tag, refraining from contact with specified individuals or movement outside a demarcated area, being subjected to curfews, and house arrest, to name but a few.

Whilst these restrictions are applicable to the UK domestically, terrorism is inherently international and the Al Qaeda movement is now perceived as being the most serious threat now faced by the international community. Although it has global networks, it is widely believed that local and regional groups plan and carry out attacks and also recruit new militants and suicide bombers by providing ideological leadership and inspirations to potential followers. Wilkinson (2006:193) describes them as an 'incorrigible group' and warns that there is no feasible political or diplomatic route to resolving this sort of conflict within the civilised world, not least because the debate on the morality of terrorism will always be doomed to failure. The cliché that 'one man's terrorist is another man's freedom fighter' (Wilkinson, 2006:207) simply reflects the paradox that many groups use terror in pursuit of a cause that most liberal people would also consider just. It is simply that their methods involve fundamental attacks on the human rights of fellow citizens. Democracies are clearly vulnerable to terrorist attacks because the openness of such societies makes it easy for extremists to exploit democratic freedoms with the aim of destroying them. If prolonged, terrorism can be very damaging to the democratic governments and societies that experience it. However, just as damaging could be contraventions of the human rights of citizens by Government campaigns against terrorism.

Guantánamo Bay and the campaign against terror

⌈The treatment of detainees at Guantánamo Bay remains the subject of much debate and contention.⌉This detainment camp, which serves as a joint military prison and interrogation centre, has occupied part of the United States Navy base at Guantánamo Bay Cuba, since 2002. The detention area has three camps: Camp Delta, Camp Iguana, and Camp X-Ray.[3] Subsequent to the September 11 attacks on the World Trade Centre there appears to have been a reflex reaction demonstrated in part by the Bush administration that the newly named 'war on terror' should be fought according to new rules, since – as the White House chief Counsel, Alberto Gonzales, put it in a memo to President Bush on 25 January 2002, 'the war against terrorism is a new kind of war' (Von Ness, 2003:7) in which there would be no place for old-fashioned structures such as the Geneva Convention on the treatment of prisoners of war. Von Ness (2003:8) thus demonstrates that this war on terror had rendered the convention virtually 'obsolete' whilst Rose (2004:2) has described Guantánamo Bay as a 'legal black hole' effectively beyond the reach of any jurisdiction. Arguably, perhaps this was the intention. Certainly one of its most salient features is that Guantánamo and its prisoners are effectively beyond both American and international law. ⌈Rose (*op cit*) cites a French detainee as saying;

> If you want a definition of this place, you don't have the right to have rights.⌉

Amnesty International released their 'Memorandum to the U.S. Government on the Rights of People in U.S. Custody in Afghanistan and Guantánamo Bay' in 2002 which criticised the failure of the US Government to comply with standards of international law in the detention and treatment of detainees both in Afghanistan and Guantánamo

---

[3]Now closed.

Bay. It summarised the specific concerns of both the humanitarian and legal communities and stated that the US Government had:

Transferred and held people in conditions that may amount to cruel, inhuman, or degrading treatment, and that violate other minimum standards relating to detention;

Refused to inform people in its custody of all their rights;

Refused to grant people in its custody to legal counsel, including during questioning by US and other authorities;

Refused to grant people in its custody access to the courts to challenge the lawfulness of their detention;

Undermined the presumption of innocence through a pattern of public commentary on the presumed guilt of the people in its custody in Guantánamo Bay;

Failed to facilitate prompt communications with or grant access to family members;

Undermined due process and extradition protections in cases of people taken into custody outside of Afghanistan and transferred to Guantánamo;

Threatened to select foreign nationals for trial before military commissions;

Raised the prospect of indefinite detention without charge or trial, or continued detention after acquittal, or repatriation that may threaten the principle of non-refoulement ('non-return' – laws which protect refugees from being returned to places where their lives or freedoms could be threatened.)

Wilkinson (2006:560) describes Guantánamo Bay as an 'anomaly' where human rights and legal protection do not exist and where torture is rife and doctors have abandoned their ethical responsibilities. The first detainees arrived in January 2002 but in spite of the fact that they had been captured in Afghanistan – with whom the US had said it was at war – they were not detained as prisoners of war, but as 'unlawful combatants.' The effect of this labelling has effectively been to deny them any rights under the Geneva Conventions. Lewis (2004) suggests that few of the individuals who have passed through Guantánamo or are still imprisoned there were actually involved in any active capacity in killing Americans and that the individuals who really fit this description – and are now in US custody – have never actually been detained in Cuba. Most of the Guantánamo prisoners – who come from over forty different countries worldwide – are probably innocent of involvement in anything that could be described as terrorist activity. Added to this, they have never been charged with terrorist crimes, will most probably never be charged and have merited no right to a fair trial – being effectively deemed guilty until proven innocent. The isolation of this site at the south eastern tip of Cuba only serves to reinforce the cliché, 'out of sight out of mind' and as a result, those detained there have been denied access to due process. Many prisoners past and present have given consistent and repeated testimony of serious abuse and ill-treatment. There is also significant evidence both from United States officials and in government documents, of widespread abuse at the camp. The British detainees known as the Tipton Three (Lewis, 2004) alleged they were repeatedly beaten, shackled in painful positions for long periods and subjected to strobe lighting, loud music and extremes of hot and cold – all intended to have a profound psychological impact. Other detainees have suffered beatings, sexual assaults and death threats. At least one man was 'water boarded'.[4]

The United States administration and the United States military have sought to justify this detention by saying that it is a special programme of measures and does not amount to torture. Whilst it is true that based on European decisions about what amounts to torture, there is a very stringent test, the Red Cross have already reported that detention at Guantánamo has caused psychological suffering that has driven inmates mad, with scores of suicide attempts and three inmates killing themselves in 2006 (Dodd, 2004). One official investigation found an inmate had been sexually humiliated and forced to perform dog tricks on a leash. It said the conduct was 'abusive and degrading but not torture'. In a UK court hearing over Guantánamo, a senior British Judge Mr Justice Collins declared 'America's idea of what is torture is not the same as ours'. Wilkinson (2006) reports that the United Nations has confirmed evidence of torture, and that Amnesty International has declared Guantánamo 'the gulag of our time.' One of the United States founding fathers, Thomas Jefferson, stated: 'He who trades liberty for security deserves neither and will lose both'. Adorned on the walls of the Guantánamo camp is its mission statement: 'Honour-bound to defend freedom'. After five years of Guantánamo, one could ask, does society feel safer?

It is interesting at this point to draw a parallel here with the story of the Soledad brothers, their treatment and what this ultimately led to in the US in terms of indeterminate sentencing. George Jackson, one of

---

[4]This is the process of being tied to a board and placed under water so that the prisoner has the sensation of drowning.

those subsequently known as the Soledad brothers was accused at the age of 16 of stealing $71 from a gas station. He refused to show remorse for this crime and received an indeterminate sentence of one year to life in which his case was reviewed annually. Jackson was never granted parole and spent the rest of his life in prison. Whilst incarcerated at Soledad Prison in Salinas, California, he became politicised and began studying the theories of Mao Zedong, Frantz Fanon, and Fidel Castro. He developed strong ideas viewing capitalism as the source of the oppression of people of colour, and became the leader in the politicisation of Black and Chicano prisoners in Soledad. On January 16, 1970 in response to the death of three Black Muslims, a white guard (John Mills) was killed; Jackson, Fleeta Drumgo, and John Clutchette were accused of the murder. The three became known as the 'Soledad Brothers'. The fate of the Soledad Brothers became an international cause célèbre which focused on the treatment of blacks in prison. The publication of Jackson's book Soledad Brother that same year added to his visibility. For many supporters the issue was the belief that the Soledad Brothers were victims of a prison conspiracy. In August 1970, Jackson's teenage brother Jonathan was killed in the Marin County Courthouse in an attempt to rescue his brother. After being transferred to San Quentin Prison, three days before he was to go to trial, George Jackson was killed by prison guards. The official report said that he was armed and had participated in a prison revolt earlier in the day, which had left five men (two guards and three prisoners) dead. Accounts of this incident however remain conflicting. Many in the Black Power Movement and the New Left eulogised Jackson as a martyr and a hero. The importance in this story is that the US moved to determinate and guideline sentences on the basis that you should be punished for what you did not who you are. Arguably society should have come a long way post-Soledad in respect of the rights of prisoners but this does not appear to be the case with regard to the unintended effects of what is now referred as Homeland Security legislation.

Running through this record of the war on terror is a single theme: the unlimited power of the United States administration to override treaties, conventions and laws in times of war. If Guantánamo has provided but a few meagre scraps of information, it has also become an icon of oppression throughout the developing – and especially the Muslim – world. Guantánamo is cited time and again as a rallying point for Jihad, as a justification for creating more suicide 'martyrs', the London bombings in 2005 are a poignant example. Terrorism has discovered a new vogue: the decapitation of western hostages in Iraq and Saudi Arabia videotaped before and during their executions in orange costumes, in deliberate imitation of the detainee uniform in Guantánamo.

⌈The victim-as-warrior mentality which swept the United States after 9/11 appears to be giving way to a climate in which it is becoming possible to address the morality of an institution such as Guantánamo; to ask whether holding such numbers in such conditions outside the scope of the rule of law truly serves the values which the United States nation and its constitution seek to represent. Guantánamo is having a radicalising effect in the Islamic world today. The case that Guantánamo is legally and morally questionable is overwhelming. But according to the terms of its own stated mission – to stop further terrorist attacks – it has proved ineffective. ⟩

Is detention without trial a credible approach to dealing with suspected terrorists?

In its response to 9/11 the United States administration and British government not only adopted the language of a 'war on terror' deploying troops in Afghanistan to topple the Taliban and moving on to attack Iraq, but it also decided to circumvent, if not entirely abandon the criminal justice system as a means of dealing with suspected terrorists. Suspected terrorists captured in Afghanistan were labelled 'enemy/unlawful combatants' and detained without trial in Guantánamo Bay Prison Camp in Cuba. Instead of indicting prisoners suspected of terrorism for trial in federal courts, the United States administration devised a system conducted by the military. Suspects were denied access to legal representation and the standards of proof were much less rigorous than those used in the federal criminal courts. What possible justifications can there be for the abandonment of due process? Proponents who see themselves as fighting what could be described as the 'Third World War' argue that the only way to deal with terrorists is to suppress them with crushing military force on the assumption that 'the only good terrorist is a dead terrorist' (Wilkinson, 2006:61). The belief is that crushing the Al Qaeda network justifies any means and that terrorists have forfeited any human rights. It is also argued that criminal courts are cumbersome, too slow and unpredictable in their results, and because detained suspects are already deemed guilty, trials before a court of law would be an expensive waste of time. Those in favour of this position may also take the view that in some circumstances inhumane and degrading treatment of suspects and even torture may be justified in the name of the 'war on terror'. However, by abandoning due process under the rule of law and by violations of the human rights of suspects, are the United States administration and British governments not betraying the values and principles of the foundation of democracies they seek to defend? Is it justice to deny captives who may have to suffer decades of imprisonment any opportunity to prove their innocence before a court of law?

Even when a person's safety is threatened by terrorist activities, it remains of critical importance that these safeguards are able to protect the individual from unlawful actions by the government. This position is a fundamental part of the rule of law. How can governments defend the individual while also tackling the terrorist threat? At present, detainees have a right to appeal to a special tribunal, presided over by judges of the High Court. The Special Immigration Appeals Commission (SIAC) deals with appeals from people the Home Secretary wants to deport on grounds of national security (Crahan *et al.*, 2004). Under the auspices of the 2001 Anti-Terrorism, Crime and Security Act, a detained suspect can request a hearing, which takes place behind closed doors. The detainees are not told the charges against them. Questionably, unless there are circumstances in which privacy is essential for justice to be done, court hearings held behind closed doors are undesirable. As former Lord Chief Justice Woolf asserts, 'secret courts are an affront to our liberty' (*The Mail on Sunday*, 2006). Alternatively, using ordinary courts would ensure judges wider discretion to go behind closed doors when this were deemed necessary to protect the confidentiality of covert security activities. However, two principles would have to be observed by the courts. First, proceedings must be held in public whenever possible and when there is no threat to national security. Secondly, the person detained should be charged and tried whenever this is a realistic possibility. If this is not possible, detention should be limited to the period absolutely necessary; and in any event should be subject to a limit laid down by Parliament. Such an example is provided by Northern Ireland. The 'Diplock courts' (Wilkinson, 2006:246) were established in 1972 in order to address the problem of paramilitary violence through means other than detention. These courts attempted to overcome the widespread jury intimidation associated with the Troubles by trying suspects in front of a judge alone. The Diplock Courts contributed to the provision of justice in the most difficult of times. Unlike the secret tribunals, they are 'open' to public scrutiny. Thus, an 'open' society is open to accountability. Additionally, courts should be allowed to rule on the lawfulness of any new government proposal that might seriously infringe the rights of the individual. Crucially this ruling would be made before any such procedure is introduced. Thus, the courts would be able to provide an advisory declaration on the lawfulness of what is proposed. The government would then know beforehand whether what it proposed did indeed comply with the law. The detainee would avoid illegal detention. Even if the suggestion was turned down, a crisis would be avoided in which a decision is 'taken in haste but repented at leisure' (*The Mail on Sunday*, 2006).

⌐ The security threat posed by terrorism should not obscure the importance of human rights. How can the security authorities be sure that detained suspects are in fact guilty of any terrorist crime? Are we to believe that intelligence agencies are always correct in their information? Military or police action can be seductive. It leaves the impression that the problem is being addressed head-on. Concern with human rights, by contrast, may seem peripheral, of long term utility, undoubtedly, but not an immediate priority. This view is profoundly mistaken. An anti-terrorism policy that ignores human rights is a gift to terrorism. It reaffirms the violent instrumentalism that breeds terrorism and undermines the public support needed to defeat it. A strong human rights policy cannot replace the actions of security forces, but it is an essential complement. A successful anti-terrorism policy must endeavour to build strong international norms and institutions on human rights, not provide a new rationale for avoiding and undermining them.⌐

How does a society assess how much of its values should be surrendered in order to increase protection from terrorist attacks? The inner strength of a liberal democracy against terrorism lies in its citizens' determination not to allow terrorists to 'impose by bomb and gun what they cannot achieve by ballot box' (Wilkinson, 2006:181). Democratic governments must in all circumstances, try to avoid, on the one hand, appeasement or weakness in response to terrorism, and suspending democracy in the name of defending it. There is no universally applicable counter-terrorism policy for democracies. Every conflict involving terrorism has its own unique characteristics. The tightrope between under-reaction, or toleration of terrorism, on the one hand, and draconian overreaction, leading to serious infringement of civil liberties, on the other, is pitched at a different height and angle in each case. In devising effective countermeasures against terrorism one must not lose sight of what terrorism is all about. It is indiscriminate on a major scale intended above all to provoke panic and other reactions that can be harnessed to serve the purposes of the perpetrators. Whether it is panic or other forms of reaction, it is but a means to an end. In the case of Al Qaeda its objectives include starting and sustaining a "jihad" (Tsang, 2007:93) against the West led by the United States, for which inflaming public opinions in the Islamic world against the West is essential. Consequently, a western democracy that overreacts to the threats of the global terrorism to the extent of breaching the rights of the individuals, wilfully or unwittingly, furthers the cause of Al Qaeda. In discussing the key elements of a successful strategy to counter Al Qaeda it remains of cardinal importance to ensure that basic civil liberties and the rule of law are upheld even in a severe terrorist emergency. There is no alternative to upholding human rights when confronting the threats from modern global terrorists. For new democracies there is a 'modelling effect' through the behaviour of so-called mature democracies. If an established democratic power utilises military tribunals in non-war settings, claims 'exception' from the Geneva Conventions or international law, or advocates the use of torture, this sets a precedent and an example for others. Indeed, the suspension of *habeas corpus* and the detention of individuals without trial at Guantánamo Bay are indicative of this point.

It is also worrying that the United States administration and British government have used the attacks of September 11th as an excuse to push through legislation which erodes civil liberties. It is not moral to try to pretend that the risk of terrorism has increased. It has not. It is the perception of risk which has increased. Both governments would do well to learn from history and realise that the first step is the most profound. Once the first step towards the erosion of civil liberties has been taken it is relatively easy to gradually erode as much as possible. When detention without trial was introduced in Northern Ireland in response to terrorism, the Catholic community was alienated, there was an increase of membership to the terrorist groups and the level of violence increased. Did the British government, in this instance, expect this legislation to be any more successful? Arguably, the legislation has given Al Qaeda the best propaganda necessary and has aided its terrorist recruitment campaign.

Detention without trial is an anathema in any country which observes the rule of law and arguably is another example of the current government's capacity to increasingly legislate to criminalise more and more behaviour. Surely laws are designed to prevent or reduce crime, not to increase the capacity for more crimes? In short, the question one should ask is does the introduction of more and more legislation reduce more crime or does it actually increase the potential for crime, and if this is the case should we not be decrying this and asking the government to account for it? Why do governments continue to legislate if this is the case? The possible explanations for this are twofold. Many of these statutes have been ill-thought through, are over-complicated and highly unlikely to achieve the aims expected of them. The anti-terrorist legislation is knee jerk and is an ill thought through response to the terrible atrocities to which society is frequently vulnerable. Do political leaders believe that all social problems can be resolved through the statute book? Whilst no-one would diminish 9/11 or any other terrorist act, a badly conceived of and executed response does not help solve the problem. Arguably, such responses are a simplistic way of demonstrating that governments are 'being seen to be doing something'. Again, that does not make for either good law or provide a solution to the problem.

Detention without trial is certainly an infringement – and a dangerous one – of civil liberties. However, terrorism is equally a dangerous abuse of civil liberties. It appears to be a case of trading off one hazard against the other. Concern arises when detention under a law that allows arrest and imprisonment without charge is a double-edged sword just begging to be abused. Theoretically, any individual could be taken off the street and locked up at the whim of the local police force. In short, the fact that a person might not be a terrorist will be the reason for their eventual release, rather than their initial arrest. This genre of jurisdiction has hitherto been a hallmark of the draconian governments that the United States and United Kingdom have encountered regarding the 'war on terror'.

5

Football Banning Orders

In this chapter I want to focus on a rather different type of restriction, namely the Football Banning Order which was enacted under the Football (Disorder) Act 2000. I wish to highlight not only the nature of this type of restriction, but also importantly, the way in which it has been implemented and question whether it is another example of imposing what might be called 'quasi-criminal sanctions' on people in much the same way as the Anti Social Behaviour Order. Whilst there was a burst of interest regarding the legality of football banning orders around the time of a famous Court of Appeal decision in the case of Gough – which I will consider specifically later in this chapter – this issue has mostly been ignored. However, there is more scope for debate regarding the legality of these types of sanctions and perhaps even to put forward an argument that if any one of these quasi-criminal sanctions are questioned, then all of them would collapse. Whilst currently football banning orders and the way they have been implemented are assumed to be acceptable because of the judgement in Gough I want to highlight the fact that, with the exception of the work of James & Pearson (2006) there has simply not been a full intellectual engagement of the issue.

Football hooliganism

One of the interesting things about the concept of 'football hooliganism' is that it has never been defined nor is there agreement between writers, football experts or academics about what it constitutes, what causes it and its true extent. One of the major writers in this area – Dunning (2000:142) – suggests that the label football hooliganism:

> Lacks precision and is used to cover a variety of forms of behaviour which take place in more or less football-related contexts.

It is not clear whether 'football hooliganism' only refers to crimes committed specifically in relation to football or the arena of football itself, or whether it refers to more specific football-related offences such as throwing missiles onto the pitch or fighting with rival fans in the vicinity of the stadium. Many of the types of behaviour routinely associated with the 'football hooligan' are non-violent and can include verbally abusing or threatening the opposition, drinking heavily, congregating in large crowds or general match day high spirited behaviour. Other forms of less acceptable behaviour have also come to be associated with the sport such as racist hate speech – both in relation to fellow spectators and players on the pitch. The interesting dichotomy here is whether these more undesirable behaviours are labelled under the umbrella of general anti social behaviours or whether in fact they should be seen as 'football-related' behaviours and what the implications in either case might be.

Frosdick & Marsh (2005) state that there are differences between organised violence between two hooligan 'firms' and a spontaneous pitch invasion. Both behaviours involve different individuals with differing motivations but they still both come under the current definition of what constitutes 'football hooliganism'. Currently both the media and politicians use the term 'football hooliganism' as an umbrella for a number of forms of deviant behaviour. The term appears to include many forms of threatening, verbal and physical violence which occur in football-related contexts. It is interesting to note however that all of these types of behaviours can also be manifested in numerous other contexts such as in a pub or club on a Saturday night. Frosdick & Marsh (2005) also indicate that incidents like these, although removed from the football stadium, can still carry the label 'football hooliganism' and as a result, the term football hooliganism appears to cover a wide spectrum of different behaviours. Recent legislation aimed at football supporters has been interpreted by critics such as Williams (2001) as increasingly criminalising the 'normal' activities of football spectators. The Football (Offences) Act (1991) created three new football-related offences; pitch invasion, missile throwing, and indecent/racist chanting (Brick, 2000) and it could be argued that an increasing number of previous 'non-hooligan' fans are being labelled as 'hooligan' due to the ever increasing number of behaviours and activities constituting football hooliganism. As a result, Frosdick & Marsh (*op cit*) suggest that the type of behaviour considered as constituting football hooliganism is changing as a result of this legislation and ideas about what is deviant inside the football stadium have led to traditional fan behaviour, involving the frequent use of hate speech becoming criminalised. This suggests an ever increasing trend towards the legislative regulation of behaviour within society in general, with football supporters being continually and perhaps incorrectly demonised as a result. In addition, Brick (2000) claims that such legislative interventions are occurring at a time when issues of social regulation have taken an increasingly moralistic stance, with less tolerance for violent and threatening behaviour. Current police statistics on football related arrests suggest that the hooligan label is somewhat unhelpfully all-inclusive, allowing the 'normal' football spectator to quite justifiably ask; are we not all football hooligans?

Football hooliganism is not a recent phenomenon. Violence has always been associated with football, whether in the form of two opposing players making a physical challenge for the ball during a match or with two rival fans fighting. Spectator violence at football matches dates back to the earliest forms of the game and as a result there have been calls to control the game, with legislation being implemented to prevent spectator violence since the 14th century. During these times, football was a game for entire villages with loose rules, often descending into full-scale rioting and violence. It has been suggested by Pratt & Slater (1984) that when such violence occurred, it was an expression of local community and a form of solidarity rather than the sole actions of a 'lunatic' minority as is often the case today.

Holt (1989) tracks the emergence of the 'modern game' as occurring in 1863 with the formation of the Football Association. Subsequently, the structure of domestic football was significantly altered with clubs, players and supporters being regulated more stringently. Despite such regulation, football-related disorder still continued into the 20th century, although as Dunning *et al.* (1988:74) state:

> A number of indications combine to suggest that incidents of crowd disorderliness declined in England between the wars.

Such a decline occurred as football became more 'respectable' in this era with regards to paying spectators and the players themselves. If any incidents of disorder did take place, they took the form of verbal protests rather than organised or spontaneous acts of violence. As a result this era has since been labelled the 'golden era' of the domestic game and one free from football hooliganism as we know it. It is widely suggested that the present day understanding of football hooliganism started in the 1960s. Prior to this, the phenomenon of football hooliganism was paid little attention by both the popular press and society in general. However, during the 1960s media coverage of football matches began to increase, with incidents of disorder being reported just as often as the match itself. As a result of the press reporting more regularly on acts of football-related violence, the term 'football hooliganism' was born. Furthermore, this increase in the frequency of such reports contributed to the impression that football hooliganism was rapidly increasing within the domestic game in Britain. According to Dunning (1999:132):

> From the late 1960s until around the middle of 1990, soccer hooliganism was routinely regarded as one of England's major social problems.

In addition, the 1960s and 1970s were also a period of rising juvenile crime rates and significant media concern regarding the deviant behaviour of young people in general, sparking a 'moral panic'. This moral panic focused on the emergence of a variety of 'threatening' youth subcultures such as the 'skinhead' and the 'teddy boy', who it is claimed became increasingly attracted to football in order to act out their violent and deviant actions (SNCCFR, 2002). For such sub-cultures, the football grounds were seen as being arenas which accepted and tolerated individuals indulging in violent behaviour with little or no chance of being caught and punished. During this time, acts of hooliganism often focused on defending your supporters' territory in the stadium from invasion by rival fans, with violence being seen as a legitimate means of achieving this aim and thus became the prominent way for members of such sub-cultures to resolve their problems. However Frosdick & Marsh (2005) note that although such practices seemed to be menacingly aggressive, in reality, serious injuries were quite rare. The link between youth sub-cultures and football hooliganism at this time fashioned the idea that football hooliganism was a manifestation of wider social problems rather than solely the result of violently predisposed males. A report by the Home Office (2001) into football-related disorder claimed that the phenomenon should be seen as groups of alienated young males demonstrating their many frustrations in both an anti-social and violent way. If this is true, then one could argue that football hooliganism would be a thing of the past if other social problems were successfully dealt with – but would continue to grow if such social problems remain unchecked.

A great deal of research[1] into the phenomenon of football hooliganism tends to suggest that football hooligans are generally young males who have low-level jobs and come from predominantly working-class backgrounds. However, following extensive research into the phenomenon, sociologists have come to believe that there is no simple explanation behind football hooliganism. Manser (2000) even goes as far as saying that 'to define a football hooligan is just as difficult as defining a murderer'. This emphasises the fact that each individual is motivated in unique ways. In addition, research suggests that modern day football hooligans come from all walks of life and are no longer solely young males from working-class backgrounds. An article by Mary Riddell,[2] referring to hooliganism in Albufeira during the Euro 2004 championship in Portugal claimed that:

> Those accused of involvement in drunken violence included a grandson of a chief of police and a child of an Oxford don.

This highlights the problems of identifying exactly who the football hooligans are. Williams (2001) suggests that it is not the activity engaged in which leads to the successful application of the 'hooligan' label, but the type of person involved. Therefore, disorder involving a businessman would be more likely to be viewed as boisterous high-jinks rather than hooliganism. If this is the case then perhaps it would be better to label such individuals who engage in violence while intoxicated as being 'aggressive drunks' and a product of societies drinking culture rather than 'football hooligans'? The inability to determine the nature of hooliganism is partly due to this lack of definition around the phenomenon. Although stereotypes remain, the majority are now outdated, with research indicating that hooligans can be anyone. Or perhaps there is another explanation – the fact that an increasing amount of 'normal' football-related behaviours are being criminalised by an ever increasing amount of legislation?

---

[1]Including that carried out by the Sir Norman Chester Centre for Football Research (SNCCFR), University of Leicester, whose work can be accessed at; www.le.ac.uk/resources/factsheets/fs1.html
[2]*The Guardian*, 20th June, 2004.

The current nature of the problem

Pratt & Slater (1984) have suggested that since the late 1960s, violence and the expectation of violence at football matches appears to have become a permanent characteristic of the sport. The emergence of hooligan minority groups attaching themselves to all domestic clubs in Britain as well as the national teams of England, Scotland and Wales has provoked a wide range of official responses. Wide-spread concern with football-related disorder commonly arose in conjunction with specific football-related disasters. One of the most famous in Britain is the Hillsborough stadium disaster of 1989 when 96 Liverpool fans were crushed to death against a perimeter fence. Although football hooliganism was not the sole causal factor, the subsequent report into the disaster by Lord Justice Taylor (1990) highlighted bad planning and 'drunken yobs' as being to blame.

Following the Taylor report, Brick (2000) suggests that football in Britain has become increasingly connected with a culture of regulation. Standing terraces were replaced by 'all-seater' stadia for the majority of league clubs and increased stewarding at matches was introduced to make football a safer spectator venue. The 'gentrification' of the game at domestic level has also arguably taken place, which has culminated in the inception of the F.A. Premier League. New marketing of the game has been aimed at attracting a 'new' and more family-based, audience to football games. However, it is argued that such measures have only succeeded in displacing the problem of football hooliganism from the stadium to the community. It has been suggested by Pratt & Slater (1984) that the various measures suggested by the Taylor report have improved the safety of football spectators' attending matches, but has not been particularly effective in curbing football hooliganism. This is largely because incidents of hooliganism still occur today, but *outside* the stadium environment. Therefore, such measures have merely displaced the problem of football hooliganism from the football stadium to the community, making it increasingly difficult to confine and control. In addition, one could also argue that this displacement, coupled with technological advances such as mobile phones, have made hooliganism a more accessible form of behaviour for like-minded individuals. Organised forms of football hooliganism involving two sets of willing participants now tend to take place away from the stadium. In a study by Armstrong (1998) concerning the Sheffield United hooligan firm known as 'The Blades', it emerged that the vast majority of hooliganism took place between consenting adults and away from the public eye.

This suggests that the average spectator will not encounter many incidents of hooliganism on match days. It also suggests that the displacement of hooliganism will make it increasingly difficult to detect, catch and arrest perpetrators. This has in part led to an increasing intelligence led policing approach to football hooliganism with its reliance of surveillance and police 'spotters'. Some criminologists might describe this change in location of football-related disorder as 'positive displacement'. This is because the relocation of football hooliganism away from the grounds has led to violence being confined to places away from both police and public view. Thus the overall effects of football-related disorder are likely to be less damaging because large numbers of innocent people are far less likely to witness football hooliganism. However, critics could also claim that incidents of football hooliganism have not decreased but have merely taken on a different mantle. It has been claimed by Frosdick & Marsh (2005:38) that:

> between 50 per cent and 60 per cent of reported incidents of football hooliganism take place away from the ground.

This supports the notion that intensive social controls during the match period and in the stadium have displaced the phenomenon to town centres, licensed premises and public transport systems. In addition, Garland & Rowe (2000) suggest that together with the advent of organised football violence, the experience of watching football matches has also been displaced from the stadium as a result of rising ticket prices. Many people now tend to watch live matches on big screens in public houses and incidents of spontaneous disorder could arguably be just as likely to break out there. Today, it is very unlikely for members of the general public and football crowd to witness incidents of football hooliganism, as it occurs out of sight. This gives the general perception that levels have decreased, but in fact sceptics have argued that they have just stayed the same.

This makes it difficult to ascertain the true extent and nature of the problem today. In addition, the continued media amplification of football hooliganism makes the public remain fearful of its occurrence, even though the vast majority of hooligan incidents occur 'out of sight'. It could be argued that keeping the public fearful allows the government to gain support for unnecessary and draconian legislation to tackle the problem. One such recent attempt to combat football hooliganism has been the introduction of the international Football Banning Order.

Legislative aims

Football hooliganism has been prominent on the political agenda in Britain since the mid 1960s. It could be argued that recent concerns about football hooliganism are the result of the amplification process from media reports of disorder involving England fans. However, this concern may have also manifested itself as a result of the embarrassing scenes of rioting involving England fans at recent international matches and tournaments. State responses to football disorder, or as stated above 'football hooliganism' have typically resulted in numerous pieces of football specific legislation coupled with innovations in public order policing tactics (McArdle, 2000). A number of football-specific statutes have been introduced since 1985, with the sole aim of reducing the occurrence and re-occurrence of English football hooliganism both at home and abroad (James & Pearson, 2006). These statutes highlight the desire of the New Labour government to be seen as being responsive to popular concerns and 'moral panics'. As a result, football-related statutes have created a number of new 'football-related offences', and have also promoted continued attempts to regulate and control the 'normal' match-day behaviour of football fans. An analysis of some of the key pieces of football-related legislation is important in order to highlight how current measures, such as the Football Banning Order, have materialised.

It could be argued that previous attempts to legislate against football hooligans have achieved mixed success. Initial attempts to control and prevent football hooliganism tended to focus on the common-sense assumption that football disorder and alcohol are strongly related. It was widely assumed that excessive alcohol consumption made a number of football fans more aggressive and less inhibited by the presence of existing organs of social controls such as the police. In 1985, the Sporting Events (Control of Alcohol) Act was introduced to reduce levels of crowd disorder by restricting the sale of alcohol before, during and after a football match (Pearson, 2000). If the causal link between alcohol and hooliganism were sufficiently established then the regulation of alcohol in the context of football matches would be a necessary form of social control. Initial attempts to control the movements and freedom of supporters emerged with the creation of the Football Spectators Act 1989. This piece of legislation saw the introduction of 'restriction orders', intended to prevent supporters convicted of football-related offences from leaving the country when England teams played abroad (Pearson, 2000). Yet at this time 'football-related offences' were narrowly defined and as a result, only a small minority of individuals could be prevented from travelling abroad. This severely limited the effectiveness of the Act. This stumbling block was addressed by the inception of the Football (Offences) Act 1991 which widened the definition of football-related offences by creating new offences covering incidents such as pitch invasion, missile throwing and racist or indecent chanting. However, as the nature of football hooliganism has changed over the years, with incidents of disorder moving away from the stadium, such pieces of legislation have had limited effect. Football fans are constantly subjected to all manners of highly restrictive social-control measures today, even though the vast majority of football matches pass without any incidents of football hooliganism. As a result of technological advances such as increases in the use of CCTV on match days and the creation of the Football Intelligence Unit (FIU), football spectators are now placed under a much higher level of surveillance. In addition to this, numerous restrictions on movement have continued to be placed upon 'away' supporters at matches in attempts to limit the likelihood of trouble. Such restrictions may take the form of banning away supporters from certain pubs in the area on match days or keeping them confined in the stadium after the final whistle. However, Murphy and his colleagues (1990) argue that although controls imposed by central government have become more all-embracing and sophisticated, so to have football hooligans become more organised, using more sophisticated strategies to evade detection by the police. Despite a dramatic fall in football-related arrests over the past decade, it has been claimed that football hooliganism remains a pressing social problem today, which continues to tarnish Britain's reputation overseas. Such arguments largely surfaced following the behaviour of England fans in Marseilles during the 1998 World Cup and in Charleroi (Belgium) during the Euro 2000 tournament. As a result, the government deemed it necessary to draft the Football (Disorder) Bill which contains the controversial football banning order powers.

Football banning order legislation

For the last decade, New Labour has pursued populist policies aimed at dealing with both criminal and quasi-criminal behaviour deemed to be a social problem. Pearson (2006) claims that the media construction of 'football hooliganism' has influenced the response of the government to football-related disorder both domestically and when the national team play abroad. Media reports about incidents of football hooliganism tend to exaggerate its occurrence and severity with most articles condemning English fans. As a result, football hooliganism becomes defined as a pressing social problem, which largely results in the implementation of reactionary statutes, often within months of widely reported 'disorder' which have been deemed to shame the reputation of the nation.

Football banning orders are not a new idea, and date back to the restriction orders found in the 1986 Public Order Act. This piece of legislation contained 'exclusion orders' which could be served upon those convicted of football-related offences (Stott & Pearson, 2006) and it has been claimed that these powers led to the break up of a number of domestic hooligan firms during the 1980s (Frosdick & Marsh, 2005). In addition, the Football Spectators Act 1989 was implemented following incidents of football hooliganism during the 1988 European championships held in Germany (Stott & Pearson, 2006). This statute gave Magistrates the power to impose banning orders that prevented those convicted of football-related offences from leaving the UK when English club sides or national team was playing abroad (James & Pearson, 2006). Prior to the creation of these powers, hooligans could only be prevented from attending football matches if the club in question banned that person from entering their ground under the clubs own rules. The Football Spectators Act 1989 was therefore deemed necessary, as the existing measures had limited scope, only banning fans from the stadium where they had committed an offence. This meant that they remained free to watch other domestic and international matches at other stadia. As a result, fans could not be prevented from travelling abroad, and during this period, numerous disturbances and riots involving England fans occurred abroad. It was therefore believed that implementing Banning Orders upon conviction of a football-related offence would prevent convicted individuals from travelling, thus reducing disorder abroad.

Following disorder at the England v Ireland match in Dublin (1995) it was deemed that existing legislation remained ineffectual at preventing English football disorder abroad. This is because it emerged that although Banning Order powers were in place, the UK police authorities were aware of the attendance of many 'known hooligans' at the match (Stott & Pearson, 2006). However, the police could not stop their attendance as very few were subject to international banning orders. In addition, conviction of a football-related offence remained difficult due to the narrow definition of such offences, resulting in defendants being tried under public order legislation instead. Incidents of football crowd disorder continued to occur at major international tournaments throughout the 1990s. During the 1998 World Cup the media extensively highlighted major incidents of disorder involving England fans in Marseilles. As a result, the definition of 'football-related' was further extended to encourage the imposition of more Banning Orders. In addition, Magistrates were given the power to order that individuals convicted of football-related offences surrender their passports when the England and Welsh national teams played abroad. The introduction of this measure signalled the first significant attempt to restrict the movements of known hooligans in order to prevent disorder from occurring at international matches. However, even the introduction of these new measures failed to prevent football crowd disorder during the European Championships held in Holland and Belgium in 2000.

Large-scale disorder in Charleroi, Belgium resulted in 965 English citizens being arrested (Gough & Smith, 2002), demonstrating that current provisions remained insufficient to prevent English fans from becoming involved in football disorder overseas. Therefore the UK government decided to strengthen the existing powers further by introducing the Football (Disorder) Act 2000. This need for additional powers was further emphasised by the reluctance of host countries to prosecute offenders of football hooliganism. Instead, individuals were merely deported, which only encouraged a repeat pattern of misbehaviour which existing legislation could not prevent (Home Office, 2005).

Pearson (2002) claims that the Football (Disorder) Act has been the most dramatic legal attempt to deal with football hooliganism and is one of the most significant pieces of legislation affecting civil liberties in the UK today. The Act was passed in late July 2000 as a response to numerous reports of football crowd disorder involving England fans during Euro 2000 and introduced highly restrictive Banning Orders. According to the Home Office (2005) the Act demonstrated to governments and police forces across Europe that the UK was taking effective steps to prevent English troublemakers from travelling to matches overseas. Reducing the number of known hooligans from travelling abroad should both reduce the occurrence of disorder and put host nations at ease. Moreover, it was hoped that by doing this, host police forces would begin to treat the large number of visiting English fans on the basis of their behaviour rather than their reputation. This is important, as the nature of police and crowd relations are an important factor in the escalation of crowd disorder.

It has been claimed by Pearson (2005) that the purpose of the Act is to protect the public, both here and abroad, from the 'evil' of football hooliganism. In order to achieve this aim and reduce hooliganism by English fans abroad, the Act contains powers to impose football banning orders, which aim to prevent future disorder in relation to football matches by significantly restricting the civil liberties of football fans. Football Banning Orders originally prevented those convicted of football-related offences from attending future football matches, in the hope that the removal of trouble makers would lead to a reduction in disorder (James & Pearson, 2006). Today, football banning orders are viewed as being the cornerstone of the Home Office's strategy to prevent football disorder abroad by English football fans (Pearson, 2005). The underlying rationale of football banning orders is that major incidents of football crowd disorder during international tournaments are caused by the convergence of individuals and hooligan groups, who are predisposed towards violence (Stott & Pearson, 2006). Therefore, if these individuals and organised groups are prevented from attending, then large-scale incidents of disorder can be avoided or at least minimised.

The Football (Disorder) Act 2000 amalgamated domestic and international banning orders, which was necessary as only a minority of individuals subject to domestic banning orders could be prevented from travelling overseas under previous legislation (Home Office, 2005). Under the 2000 Act, once a Football Banning Order is imposed, its domestic application remains automatic, but its international application is activated by the Football Banning Order Authority (FBOA), who analyse the risk associated with each match taking place outside the UK which involves English or Welsh teams (James & Pearson, 2006). All Banning Orders are activated for every England match and also when the team the banned person supports plays in Europe. As a result of this amalgamation, it is hoped that a far larger number of known hooligans can be prevented from organising and taking part in football hooliganism both domestically and abroad.

Furthermore, the Act widened the scope of Banning Orders made upon a criminal conviction. The Act made an allowance for Football Banning Orders to be imposed even where the conviction was not 'football related' (James & Pearson, 2006). This essentially widened the scope of offences which could lead to the imposition of banning orders, thus allowing Orders to be more widely imposed. Secondly, section 14B of the Football (Disorder) Act 2000 introduced a new and highly controversial form of football banning order, known as a Banning Order 'on complaint'. Essentially this allowed a football banning order to be imposed upon an individual who had *not been convicted* of any offence, but who had been identified by the police as having 'caused or contributed' to violence or disorder in relation to football matches. Prior to this development, Football Banning Orders could only be imposed following conviction of a football-related offence (Home Office, 2005).

It is important to distinguish between these two different forms of Banning Orders as they have differing impacts on the individual. Following the conviction of a football-related offence, a Football Banning Order 'on conviction' can be imposed. Under section 14A of the Football (Disorder) Act a Banning Order can be imposed if the court is satisfied that there are 'reasonable grounds to believe that imposing a Banning Order would help to prevent violence or disorder in connection with any regulated football match' (Gough & Smith, 2002). A Banning Order made following a conviction may last for a minimum period of three years and a maximum of five years (Frosdick & Marsh, 2005). However, under the Act, Football Banning Orders can also be imposed 'on complaint' if two conditions are satisfied, namely:

1. Whether the suspect has at any time caused or contributed to any violence or disorder in the UK or elsewhere.
2. That the court is satisfied that there are reasonable grounds to believe that imposing a Banning Order would help to prevent violence or disorder at or in connection with any regulated football match.

(James & Pearson, 2006)

There are two important differences between Banning Orders made 'on conviction' and those made 'on complaint' under the Football (Disorder) Act 2000. Firstly, Banning Orders made 'on conviction' do not require the prosecution to prove the defendant's previous involvement in violence or disorder as this has already been proven by the preceding trial. However, where no conviction is secured, the chief police officer for the area where the suspected hooligan resides can apply for a Football Banning Order 'on complaint' to the Magistrate's Court. Such orders can be imposed on the basis of police suspicion that the suspect *may* in the future become involved in a football-related offence. If this suspicion is based upon past misdemeanours, then one potential problem here could be the nature and extent of the suspect's past involvement in disorder. Is a drunken scuffle after a night out sufficient? If this is the case, then the new powers contained in the Football (Disorder) Act 2000 make it possible to impose a Football Banning Order made 'on complaint' on an individual with no previous history of 'football-related violence'. This has fuelled the argument that Football Banning Orders are not just targeting football hooligans, but can be used against any individual. According to Robb (2000), merely being captured on CCTV close to an incident of disorder could be enough for a Banning Order to be placed on someone. Furthermore, Williams (2001) has claimed that Football Banning Orders 'on complaint' operate in a similar way to Anti Social Behaviour Order's in that they allow bans/constraints on individuals on the basis of criminal law, but crucially do not require subjects to be found guilty of a criminal offence. Therefore, it is important to critically evaluate this piece of legislation due to the seriousness of the human rights concerns surrounding the imposition of Football Banning Orders, particularly when they are made 'on complaint'.

Following the introduction of the Football (Disorder) Act 2000, the number of football banning orders imposed has risen dramatically. It has been noted by Pearson (2005) that there were 106 Football Banning Orders prior to its inception. Since then this number rose to 2,188 in 2004 and it has been estimated that there were 3,286 Banning Orders in force by the beginning of the 2006 World Cup in Germany (James & Pearson, 2006). This increase is likely to have occurred due to the general assumption that the 2006 World Cup in Germany would be 'high risk' due to its proximity to England, encouraging a larger number of spectators to travel. In addition, Pearson (2005) has suggested that this increase is also partly due to the introduction of Banning Orders 'on complaint', which have been imposed upon an increasing number of individuals 'suspected' of future involvement in football hooliganism. However, as these powers do not require a conviction, one must question whether they are being used proportionately. If a large number of Banning Orders made 'on complaint' are being imposed when football hooliganism is in decline, then this would suggest that they are being used in an arbitrary and disproportionate fashion. What remains difficult to ascertain however is whether this rise has resulted from an increase in football hooliganism, or whether it represents a government which wants to be seen as being responsive to media-constructed 'problems'. Certainly, research by Frosdick & Marsh (2005) amongst others seems to suggest the latter.

Within two years of the introduction of the Football (Disorder) Act, the 2002 World Cup staged in Japan and South Korea passed off peacefully with no reported incidents of crowd disorder involving England fans. However, one must be careful when suggesting that this 'success' was the result of this new piece of legislation. Although the new powers may have prevented some known troublemakers from making the journey, it is widely agreed that the absence of disorder is more attributable to the distance and expense involved for those intending to attend the tournament. As a result, the number of Banning Orders continued to rise, with their effectiveness soon to be tested during the 2004 European Championships held in Portugal. Despite this tournament being deemed 'high risk' with regard to disorder, the tournament passed off without major incidents of disorder, despite the large number of England fans attending.

However, the British media were quick to report incidents of disorder involving England fans on two separate occasions in the resort of Albufeira. These incidents led to the arrest of 52 UK citizens and three Football Banning Orders being issued (Home Office, 2005). However, the incidents did little to damage the perceived effectiveness of Banning Orders as the disorder occurred in a resort occupied by a large percentage of British holiday makers, and mainly involved groups of drunken English 'yobs' rather than England football fans. Furthermore, it could be argued that the behaviour witnessed in Albufeira is more symbolic of an alcohol-related social problem evident in all UK cities every Friday and Saturday evening rather than the manifestation of football hooliganism. Home Office statistics from the 2005–06 season highlighted a 7 per cent decrease in the number of arrests for football-related offences, which signified a 22 per cent reduction since 2003–04 despite rising attendances at matches in England (Home Office, 2006). Furthermore, the statistics also showed a 17 per cent reduction in arrests made when English club teams play in European competitions at home and abroad. In keeping with the majority of academic research on domestic hooliganism, statistics from 2004–05 provide evidence that small-scale incidents of largely orchestrated violence continue to occur domestically, though often at locations away from the football ground and public eye, with 59 per cent of total football arrests occurring away from football grounds (Home Office, 2005). These statistics highlight the decline in domestic football disorder, despite the number of Football Banning Orders issued since the Football (Disorder) Act 2000 constantly rising. Therefore, one must begin to question whether such a response is actually necessary to control and reduce football hooliganism. This is important due to the severe implications which Football Banning Orders have on individual civil liberties.

A new form of legislation?

It has been claimed by Pearson (2006) that the desire of New Labour to be seen as being responsive to popular concerns and moral panics such as football hooliganism has led to a plethora of legislation which bridges both criminal and civil law. In essence, Football Banning Orders target anti-social and yobbish conduct, which is on the very limits of criminal law, even though it may cause distress to members of the public. Furthermore, as the majority of anti-social misdemeanours are minor, it has become difficult to prevent their occurrence using the normal criminal law process. This is primarily due to the high standard of proof needed when action is taken under criminal law proceedings. The Football (Disorder) Act 2000 has been labelled as being a 'hybrid law' due to the fact that the legislation was imposed in response to criminal conduct, is supported by criminal law sanctions but operates under civil proceedings (Pearson, 2006). It has been claimed that although Football Banning Orders are civil in character, the measures contained in section 14B of the Football (Disorder) Act, notably Banning Orders made 'on complaint' are both radical and tough (Home Office, 2005). However, if one were to believe the moral panics surrounding football hooliganism, then one would be led to believe that such measures provide a proportionate response to the phenomenon of English football-crowd disorder. In response to the Football (Disorder) Act 2000, civil libertarians have claimed that imposing quasi-criminal sanctions on the basis of civil proceedings leads to an infringement of a citizen's human rights (Pearson, 2006). This is especially in relation to Articles, 5, 6 and 8 of the Human Rights Act 1998.

James & Pearson (2006) feel that the hybrid character of the Football Banning Order is what makes it such an effective tool in preventing banned individuals from attending domestic matches or travelling abroad to international matches. This is due to the fact that any breach of a Football Banning Order constitutes a criminal offence, which could lead to the imposition of a fine or even imprisonment. Furthermore, breaching a Banning Order also constitutes being a football-related offence, which could lead to the imposition of a Football Banning Order 'on conviction'. This becomes problematic when one considers that some individuals subject to Banning Orders 'on complaint' have never been convicted of an offence of violence or disorder in connection with a regulated football match. If they breach their order they commit a criminal offence, which could lead to a Banning Order 'on conviction' being imposed on them (James & Pearson, 2006). As a result, the individual is further punished as they are subject to a Banning Order for a much longer period of time, and have a criminal conviction on their record. This 'hybrid law' is not solely used against football hooligans, but can also be seen in response to anti-social behaviour in the form of Anti-Social Behaviour Orders (ASBOs). However, such 'hybrid' legislation has led to concerns regarding the numerous powers which severely restrict the freedom of individuals, who may not have been found guilty of any criminal offence and the fact that such civil proceedings provide fewer protections for defendants. As a result of its hybrid nature, James & Pearson (2006) have claimed that Football Banning Orders present a number of legal conundrums in determining what evidence should be accepted and what standard of proof should be applied. These issues have been the main focus of numerous attempts to challenge the imposition of Football Banning Orders made 'on complaint'. The first and perhaps most notorious challenge was the case of *Gough and Smith v Chief Constable of Derbyshire (2002) EWCA Civ 351, CA.*

In October 2000, Gough and Smith were made the subject of football banning orders which prevented them from attending certain matches In England and Wales and also from travelling abroad to attend fixtures. Gough and Smith's argument was that the restrictions imposed on them were not lawful. Specifically that the banning orders violated EC law in a way which ought to render them void and further that they violated certain articles of the European Convention on Human Rights. There does not appear to have been any argument about the fact that both Gough and Smith had previously been involved in hooligan related incidents since information had been gathered by Derbyshire police through the football intelligence system co-ordinated by the National Criminal Intelligence Service (NCIS) about their behaviour. In all, 15 profiles for Gough and 21 for Smith had been put before the court to evidence the occasions when they had both been involved in disturbances involving opposing football fans. However, there are a number of problems with this case with regard to the rule of law, the presumption of innocence, EU rights and the ECHR. The ban on foreign travel and the confiscation of passports of individuals issued with banning orders raises problems regarding the right of UK citizens to leave their territory as granted by the EC Treaty (Council Directive 73/148/EEC, Articles 1–2). Gough and Smith argued that member states could only deny citizens their fundamental rights under this Treaty on the grounds of public policy if this denial could be justified under the principle of proportionality. It is accepted that member states have the right to limit cross-border movement for legitimate public policy aims (e.g. on the grounds of national security or public health), but it was argued that this could only be legitimate if it was a propor-tionate response to the problem in question. Gough and Smith also claimed that the restrictions placed on them amounted to a criminal penalty that was being imposed in relation to a civil law procedure and that as such this limited their protection in terms of the standard of proof utilised and the admissibility of evidence.

Further they challenged the procedure used to impose the FBO's on Complaint under Article 6 of the ECHR, which provides for the right to a fair trial and grants additional protections to those under a 'criminal charge'. In particular, Article 6(2) states that, 'Everyone charged with a criminal offence shall be presumed innocent until proved guilty according to law,' and Article 6(3)(d) grants the right, 'to examine or have examined witnesses against him and to obtain the attendance and examination of witnesses on his behalf under the same conditions as witnesses against him' to anyone in a criminal trial.

In spite of these weighty arguments the Court of Appeal in Gough only briefly considered the effect of the banning orders upon the defendants. Although the court accepted that there might be an argument to suggest that in the case of Gough the effects of the banning orders were not sufficiently severe to warrant classification as a criminal penalty, the Court instead focused primarily on the intention behind the imposition of the Football (Disorder) Act (that was preventative and not punitive), and the stated (civil) court procedure, before ruling that Article 6 had not been infringed. The judgment was therefore highly contentious on the grounds that it did not pay sufficient attention to the nature of the offences or the penalty and instead relied in a circular way upon the domestic classification of the proceedings by the legislature.

James & Pearson (2006:529) state that:

> The apparent concessions of the Court of Appeal in *Gough* towards civil libertarian concerns over proportionality in particular have taken much of the sting out of criticisms from fans groups about the risk of innocent supporters being given unnecessary bans. However, our own research has suggested that there are fundamental problems with Football Banning Orders imposed under both sections 14A and 14B and that this will have a serious negative impact upon both their ability to prevent football-related disorder and to have their draconian conditions justified under the principle of proportionality.

By way of explanation, the doctrine of proportionality is a method of testing whether member states actions are compatible with convention standards. If a member state says that they acted in a legitimate way regarding the public interest the EC asks whether the action taken was proportionate to the aims pursued and whether the reasons given are relevant and sufficient. In the case of Bowman v UK [1998] the applicant distributed literature in the 1997 elections about the views of the main candidates on abortion. She was taken to court under section 75 of the Representation of the People Act 1983 because she spent more than the £5 allowed on this by the Act. Bowman took her case to the European Court under Article 10 saying it was her right to freedom of expression. In upholding her claim, the court held (1) some legitimate limit on expenditure was right to ensure fairness between candidates but (2) that section 75 imposed an unnecessarily severe restriction on the dissemination of opinions and that (3) it was a bit odd when national political publicity campaigns in England have no such financial restrictions on them.

In conclusion I feel that the evidence presented in this chapter demonstrates a number of important things. Recent legislation aimed substantially at football supporters has been interpreted by critics such as Williams (2001) as increasingly criminalising the 'normal' activities of football spectators. Further, that following the introduction of the Football (Disorder) Act 2000, the number of football banning orders imposed has risen dramatically. It has been noted by Pearson (2005) that there were 106 Football Banning Orders prior to its inception. Since then this number rose to 2,188 in 2004 and it has been estimated that there were 3,286 Banning Orders in force by the beginning of the 2006 World Cup in Germany (James & Pearson, 2006). It also demonstrates that court orders that seriously infringe the rights of fans who have been convicted of no offence cannot be considered proportionate under EU and ECHR law in spite of the judgement in the case of Gough and that this in turn raises important questions about the efficacy and justifiability of football banning orders as a long-term strategy for the management of football 'hooliganism'.

Perhaps one of the key questions which should be asked is, why has a link specifically been made between football and disorder whilst it has not been made between either other sports or professions? In a personal conversation with my long time friend and colleague Professor Ken Pease, he aptly commented that if cooks were occasionally violent (I'm talking about you, Ramsey) you wouldn't have a Cuisine Banning Order. He said that for him the strangeness is choosing a *specific* context within which behaviour which is *generally* objectionable is dealt with.

Finally I could not complete this chapter without mentioning some of the questions which also remain over the way in which cases of violence between footballers are dealt with by normal criminal law (while the managers and others say that the criminal law ought to keep its nose out.) For example, the tackle by Dean Saunders on Paul Elliott which ended his career whilst at Chelsea FC. In this particular case, Dean Saunders, (who at that time was playing for Liverpool FC) was acquitted of recklessness and negligence because the Judge was of the view that he had merely been attempting to make a legitimate challenge. Roderick (1999) suggests that these cases, and other less high-profile ones, expose some interesting discrepancies and injustices in terms of the intersections between violence, law and professional football. In this sense, this case can usefully be compared to that of Gordon Watson who was seriously injured during a first division match in 1997 and which left him with a double fracture of the leg requiring five operations and the insertion of a metal plate. Watson sued Kevin Gray, who made the tackle, for negligence at the High Court in Leeds and was eventually awarded £900,000. Roderick (1999) highlights that soccer pundit Jimmy Hill said the tackle was the worst he had seen in 50 years of football.

So how are such matters dealt with and by whom, and does this explain how such discrepancies can occur? Most incidents are dealt with by the FA who have an internal disciplinary mechanism within which players who break the rules can be punished. Generally speaking, although it is possible that the FA's decision could be made the subject of judicial review, they tend not to be because the law has always treated on the pitch incidents as private incidents and probably also because the perception is that those who play, do so at their own risk. Thus, this has become one of the legal 'grey' areas with certain types of injury seemingly acceptable or expected and therefore legitimised. Cases which appear to fall outside this category are those in which players – due to the seriousness of the injury – have to seek compensation for a ruined career. In legal terms this throws up all sorts of questions about the dividing line between those on the pitch injuries deemed to be acceptable and those not and how the court distinguishes between the two. It may be that the decision in the Gray case sets a precedent which may make football safer and footballers more cautious about reckless tackling but this remains to be seen. Whatever the case, it remains true for the supporters of this game – and according to Pearson (2006:125) that:

> The desire of the New Labour Government to be seen as responsive to popular concerns and moral panics over hooliganism and anti-social behaviour is resulting in the increased use of legislative responses that bridge criminal and civil law. Anti-Social Behaviour Orders and Football Banning Orders are two key examples of this 'Hybrid Law', imposed as a response to criminal conduct, supported

by criminal law sanctions, but operating under a civil law procedure providing fewer protections for defendants. These hybrid orders have the power to severely restrict the freedom of individuals who have not been found guilty of any criminal offence...

The next chapter will deal with the last of my specific examples of legislative restriction.

6
Secure Borders

In this chapter, which is the penultimate chapter and the last one in which I discuss specific examples of legislation which I believe demonstrate a propensity for the over restriction of the public and the move towards the covert diminution of civil liberties, I want to consider a number of issues. First I wish to highlight the primary legislation with which British Customs and Excise personnel work. This is the Customs and Excise Management Act 1979 and specifically sections 35, 64, 78 and 163A under which persons can be detained indefinitely without being told why even though they are not classed as being under arrest. I will also consider United States customs administration and laws which have recently been strengthened in relation to ports and borders under the Secure Borders Initiative in the attempt to prevent terrorism and illegal migration as a result of the events of 9/11.Third, I will focus on recent changes in the mobility of population between countries within the European Union, specifically those which have emanated from the Schengen Agreement 1985 and the Prüm Convention 2005. Finally I will highlight recent extradition legislation applying between the UK and the US and ask how it works in practice in relation to both security ands the rights of individuals.

Border security in the UK

Within the UK, all ports have a policing strategy which involves screening passengers and freight for signs of human trafficking or for illegal goods or equipment that could be used for terrorist activity. In relation to this, the government's Counter-Terrorism and Intelligence Directorate works closely with the Immigration and Nationality Directorate within which the Border and Immigration Agency is a new executive agency of the Home Office. This Agency has responsibility for managing immigration control in the UK and considers applications for permission to stay, citizenship and asylum. HM Revenue and Customs has responsibility for border controls. The primary legislation with which customs and excise personnel in the UK work is the Customs and Excise Management Act 1979. In most cases, when customs and excise personnel challenge people whom they do not intend to arrest, or who are unlikely to be arrested, there is a duty to inform the detained person why they are being stopped and challenged, and a duty to tell them that they are free to leave. In these circumstances, there are no reasons on the face of it for concern. More problematic are the cases where these criteria do not apply and where, throughout the challenge and detention by customs and excise, a person will not actually be under arrest, but according to the primary legislation with which customs and excise work, that person *will* be under an obligation to remain where they are irrespective of the fact that they are not being arrested. This raises interesting questions concerning both the nature of this legislation, the powers that it confers on individuals in the employment of the customs and excise service, the way in which it may be applied in practice and what the intention of Parliament was in passing this legislation, which arguably severely restricts the personal freedom and civil liberties of those who find themselves detained under one of the sections for which the duty to inform does not apply. It is these specific parts of the Customs and Excise Management Act 1979 with which I particularly wish to deal.

Under section 78, customs and excise have the power to control persons either entering or leaving the United Kingdom. This power relates specifically to the issue of what is known as 'chargeable duty' and the requirement to declare goods subject to it. Section 78 is applied in Customs controlled areas at both ports and airports and the parts of section 78 which are particularly pertinent are subsections (2) and (3). Taking section 78(2) first, this states that:

> Any person entering or leaving the United Kingdom shall answer such questions as the proper officer may put to him with respect to his baggage and anything contained therein or carried with him and shall, if required by the proper officer produce the baggage and any such thing for examination at such a place as the Commissioners may direct.

The interesting thing about this particular subsection of the Act is that it means that either inbound or outbound, an officer can lawfully intercept a traveller and ask that person whatever questions the officer considers necessary to satisfy the officer that the traveller is not doing anything which may contravene the regulations in force at the time. This can potentially relate to any matter including drugs, pornography, weapons, cash, cigarettes, intellectual property rights and foodstuffs. In fact the possibilities appear almost limitless. Added to this, in principle, once a person has been stopped (inbound), s/he can be kept at the customs and excise 'bench' for as long as the detaining officer wishes. It is the case that under the Human Rights Act, whatever decisions the officer makes in relation to this sort of detention must be both proportional and fair but it is unclear what sort of test would be applied to ensure that the basis on which any decision made, was both proportional and fair in the circumstances. The fact remains that because of this, a detainee cannot be kept indefinitely. However, if the enquiries are felt to be meaningful, there is realistically no limit to the detention until the officer reaches the point where the detainee must either be released or arrested.

What is not generally known is that this power also allows an officer to stop a traveller outbound, the main focus of this being, at present, cash. Since the introduction of the Proceeds of Crime Act 2002, customs and excise officials have been able to seize cash which they believe to be from the proceeds of crime. Currently, any amount in excess of £5,000 is seizable, if discovered. Customs and Excise frequently target outbound and in bound passengers to and from what they call 'high risk' countries such as the so-called 'Golden Triangle' countries of South East Asia, Burma, Laos and Thailand and also the 'Golden Crescent'[1] countries of Pakistan, Afghanistan, Iran and South America, because they believe that significant quantities of both cash and drugs are moved in and out of theses countries. Should a passenger be stopped, an officer is entitled to ask that passenger anything s/he wishes in order to establish whether the passenger is carrying cash, either on their person or in any 'checked in' luggage. In these circumstances a passenger is obliged to answer any questions put to him/her and if the officer suspects that s/he may have cash in 'checked in' luggage, then they can have it removed from the aircraft for examination. If cash is found, the officer then

---

[1]The Golden Triangle is one of Asia's two main illicit opium-producing areas. It is an area of around 350,000 square kilometres that overlaps the four countries of South-East Asia, Myanmar (previously Burma), Laos, Vietnam and Thailand. Along with Afghanistan in the Golden Crescent (together with Iraan and Pakistan), it has been one of the most extensive opium-producing areas of Asia and of the world since the 1950s.

requires an explanation as to why and for what purpose the passenger has that cash in their possession. Following detection of the cash, it can be either 'detained' or 'seized' by customs officials and either way further questions will be asked.

All of this of course takes time and one of the considerations for the passenger is whether or not they are going to make the flight that they intended to. This involves an interesting choice for the passenger who must ask him or herself 'do I stop and continue to answer questions and therefore miss my flight, or do I leave the cash in detention with Customs and deal with it on my return?' Anecdotally, customs and excise officers have informed the author that they have experienced frequent instances of passengers missing their flight *and* having their cash seized; the inference drawn by them from this being that the movement of cash was the sole purpose of travel.

It is unlikely that an arrest would take place in the circumstances described, unless money laundering was *known* to be taking place, therefore throughout these whole proceedings the passenger is, in effect, not arrested but merely detained.

Moving on to section 78 subsection (3), this part of the Act states that:

> Any person failing to declare anything or to produce any baggage or thing as required by this section shall be liable on summary conviction to a penalty of three times the value of the thing not declared or the baggage or the thing not produced as the case may be or [level 3 on the standard scale], whichever is the greater.

In a nutshell, section 78(3) gives customs the power to levy a penalty if a passenger does not stop and answer questions as required under section 78(2). Further, and notwithstanding the effect of section 78(3), there is still also the possibility of an arrest for obstruction under the Commissioners for Revenue and Customs Act 2005, (CRCA) sections 30–33. This Act of Parliament combined the Inland Revenue and HM Customs and Excise into a single government department, HM Revenue and Customs. The Act also established the Revenue and Customs Prosecutions Office, and provided for inspections of HMRC by HM Inspectors of Constabulary to ensure that it complies with the law. In combining the two revenue departments into one, the Act implemented the recommendation of the O'Donnell Review. The Act provides for the new department to inherit the powers of the old departments, pending a comprehensive review of revenue powers. Following some controversy in the Parliamentary debates, the Act expressly provides for a duty to keep information confidential, with criminal penalties for wrongful disclosure.

The specific offences which are contained in the CRCA 2005 are as follows. First, the offences of impersonation under section 30, where a person will be guilty of an offence should they pretend to be a commissioner or an officer of revenue and customs in order to obtain:

(a) admission to premises,
(b) information, or
(c) any other benefit.

Second the offence of obstruction, under section 31 if a person without reasonable excuse obstructs:

(a) an officer of Revenue and Customs,
(b) a person acting on behalf of the Commissioners or an officer of Revenue and Customs, or
(c) a person assisting an officer of Revenue and Customs.

Third, under section 32 the offence of assault of an officer of Revenue and Customs and finally, section 33 gives an authorised officer of Revenue and Customs the power to arrest a person without warrant if the officer reasonably suspects that the person:

(a) has committed an offence under section 30, 31 or 32,
(b) is committing an offence under any of those sections, or
(c) is about to commit an offence under any of those sections.

In all cases if found guilty, the penalties are a fine, possible imprisonment for a period of up to 51 weeks or both and interestingly, where the line is drawn between levying a civil penalty under section 78(3) and arresting a person under the CRCA 2005 would depend on the nature of the failure to comply.

The next power of interest is that contained in section 163A which gives officers the power to search articles. This power was designed to assist officers when dealing with suspects who have actually already passed the duty point and may indeed be in the community at large and who might be under the surveillance of customs and revenue officers. Specifically, section 163(A) states that:

(1) 'Without prejudice to any other power conferred by the Customs and Excise Act 1979, where there are reasonable grounds to suspect

that a person in the United Kingdom (referred to in this section as 'the suspect') has with him or at the place where he is, any goods to which this sections applies, an officer may;
  (a) require the suspect to permit a search of any article that he has with him at that place, and
  (b) if the suspect is not under arrest, detain him (and any such article) for as long as is necessary to carry out the search.
(2) The good to which this section applies are dutiable alcohol liquor, or tobacco products, which are;
  (a) chargeable with any duty of excise and
  (b) liable to forfeiture under the Customs and Excise Acts
(3) Notwithstanding anything in subsection (4) of section 24 of the Criminal Law (Consolidation) (Scotland) Act 1995 (detention and questioning by customs officers) detention of the suspect under subsection (1) above shall not prevent his subsequent detention under subsection (1) of that section.

The introduction of section 163A is relatively recent and was intended to target the growing trend in the bootlegging of cigarettes, tobacco and alcohol. Prior to its introduction, customs officials had no power outside of customs controlled areas, to challenge an individual they thought might be carrying bootlegged goods, unless they decided to exercise a power of arrest. So interestingly, section 163(A) significantly extended their powers to target travellers outside of the normal customs controlled areas. To illustrate this, one example might be where observations are being conducted on some premises and for example, an individual left those premises carrying a bag that may or may not contain cigarettes. It may be inappropriate to arrest for two reasons; first, the bag may not contain cigarettes at all or second it may not contain the quantity of cigarettes that might justify an arrest. What section 163A does however, is enable customs and excise officials to challenge an individual and detain that person for as long as it takes to search the bag. In such a case, the issue of proportionality would have to be considered and therefore under normal circumstances this type of detention could not be for too long since it would only take a limited amount of time to search a bag or bags. Once a search is complete however, officers can effect an arrest if they wish, or simply seize the goods and let the suspect go.

Under section 35, every ship arriving at a port, and every aircraft arriving at any place within the United Kingdom from anywhere at all outside of the United Kingdom, is required to produce an section 35 report. This report is supposed to contain 'such particulars as the Commissioners may direct'. This section has direct relevance both to shipping and to aircraft but the author was unable to locate anyone at a UK port who was able to give advice as to how this would apply specifically to shipping of various kinds. In relation to aircraft, the main thrust of this section appears to be that an airline must provide customs officers with a section 35 report (called a manifest) of the passengers in transit. Customs and excise officers known to the author have reported that most airlines comply readily, but some are less keen. This apparently sometimes results in a situation where the manifest does not arrive with customs until five minutes before the plane is due to land. Officers find this unsatisfactory because they feel that it gives them little time to properly examine the manifest and to deal with any information that it may provide. In situations like this, section 35 actually gives customs officers the power to refuse to allow the aircraft to land, however, in reality this is unlikely to happen because of the health and safety implications that it might have. I have been made aware by customs employees however, that airlines which are reluctant to provide the manifest, or which do so, but not in sufficient time to allow officers to examine it have been told that unless the manifest is produced at a reasonable time, customs would refuse to allow the passengers to disembark from the aircraft. In situations where airtime journeys are considerable, passengers obviously wish to disembark as soon as possible after landing and therefore any delay could obviously cause a great deal of tension for the airline and particularly its crew, and its schedule. Customs officers therefore find that this sort of warning usually encourages airlines to produce manifests in good time.

Also of relevance is the role of Immigration. Under the Immigration Act 1971 section 4, immigrations officers have the power to refuse entry to any non-UK citizen until satisfied that they are suitable within the confines of the Act. This detention might be for a short time, whilst enquiries are made or for a longer period until either a return flight is available or the person in question is sent to a detention centre. This provision refers to non-UK citizens only and under these circumstances, they are never actually deemed to be in the country.

Border security in the US

It is clear that subsequent to the events of September 11, 2001 there was a sea change in the climate of fear which existed in relation to what the US government describes as their 'Homeland' (meaning domestic) security.

In this changed social environment many Americans became susceptible to influences which may have persuaded them that the preservation of their safety was of more value than their privacy or civil liberties. Within this political and social climate also, President George W. Bush described what he called the *War on (or against) Terrorism*. Whether this is an accurate description of events is a matter of some debate, but without question what it undoubtedly did lead to in the US was increased military operations, economic measures and political pressure on groups it accused of being terrorists, as well as on governments and countries accused of sheltering them. The attacks on the United States were also judged to be within the parameters of the North Atlantic Treaty Organisation, with NATO declaring that section 5 of the military alliance had been met, making the US 'war on terror' the first time since its inception that NATO would actually participate in a war.

Clearly the attacks on the World Trade Centre focused the government upon issues of domestic security and legislators were quick to create new laws and a new cabinet-level federal agency – the Department of Homeland Security. In particular the newly enacted USA Patriot Act 2001 gave law enforcement agencies sweeping search and surveillance powers over US citizens. The following year, the Information Awareness Office (IAO) was created as a means of initiating what has been called a programme of Total Information Awareness (TIA). The aim of this was to develop the technology to facilitate the collection and processing of huge amounts of information about every person in the United States. The types of information that the IAO gathers includes internet activity, credit card and airline ticket purchase histories, information on car rentals, medical records, drivers' licenses, utility bills, tax returns, and other similar information.

A major part of this push for greater security within the US has been the Secure Borders Initiative (SBI). This plan for greater security and the reduction of illegal migration includes:

- More agents patrolling borders and ports of entry to enforce immigration laws
- Expanded detention and removal capabilities
- Upgrading of the technology used in controlling borders
- Increased investment in infrastructure improvements at borders including additional physical security in order to reduce illegal border crossings
- Increased interior enforcement of immigration laws

Added to this, the Homeland Security Appropriations Act was subsequently passed. This included an increase in funds enabling an additional 1,000 Border Patrol agents to be appointed, increases in criminal investigators, detention beds, fugitive operations teams, and Immigration Enforcement agents to be made and approximately 250 new criminal investigators to be appointed with the intention of better targeting the human smuggling organisations and other criminal groups that the US felt were exploiting their borders. The Department of Homeland Security (DHS) have also suggested changes to their technology and infrastructure which have included what they term as a mix of current and next generation technology with appropriately trained personnel with the goal of ultimately having the capacity to integrate multiple state of the art systems and sensor arrays into a single comprehensive detection suite. The move to better technology will include improved security in the areas between ports of entry by integrating and coordinating the use of technology including more Unmanned Aerial Vehicles (UAVs), aerial assets, remote video surveillance camera systems, and sensors.

In terms of what they call 'interior enforcement' the DHS stated their aim to strengthen efforts to target those who enter the US illegally by enforcing laws and making sure that the removal (of people) could be achieved. The measures suggested included the implementation of an employer self-compliance programme that linked government and business in an effort to reduce the employment of unauthorised aliens in specified industries. This partnership would assemble a 'best practice' methodology that employers would use to minimise known vulnerabilities in the legally required employment eligibility verification process. Added to this, they instigated the Criminal Alien Program (CAP) which seeks to identify and remove all incarcerated criminal aliens from the United States. Key to this effort is identifying and screening foreign born aliens incarcerated in federal, state and major metropolitan jails and putting them through deportation proceedings prior to their release. Their goal for CAP is to screen 90 per cent of all foreign born aliens in state and federal jails by 2009 and by 2010, a large percentage of aliens in major metropolitan jails.

At an international level, the US government has long maintained that border-related crime affects communities on both sides of land boundaries, and that therefore a shared approach should be paramount in disrupting criminal groups. The SBI was designed to be implemented in a way that draws in the Governments of both Mexico and Canada. At the same time the DHS has also signaled its commitment to working with other governments to ensure the timely provision of travel documents in order to remove the backlog of nationals in US detention facilities and to safely and quickly repatriate migrants back to their own countries.

As if all of this were not enough, the Unites States felt that the events of September 11, 2001 highlighted the need to enhance the overall security of the US food supply. As a result of this, Congress passed and the President signed into law the Public Health Security and Bioterrorism Preparedness and Response Act of 2002. This Act included a number of provisions designed to improve the food safety efforts of the Food and Drug Administration (FDA) in cooperation with US Customs and Border Protection (CBP), including new authority to protect the food supply against terrorist acts and other threats. Most recently, in August 2007, the US announced further steps that they intend to implement by the end of 2008. These include the recruitment of an extra 18,000 border patrol agents, 300 miles of vehicle barriers, 105 extra border cameras and an extra 370 miles of fencing. The US has also reiterated its commitment to the policy of the 'catch and return' of all illegal aliens found crossing the border and their intention to strengthen this policy by providing over 30,000 more detention beds to hold immigrants until they can be returned to their place of origin. The US has also said that it will continue to push for the establishment of biometric identification requirements at all borders as well as promises to strengthen worksite and domestic enforcement of security measures.

As if to add insult to injury and in the post-9/11 landscape, where various high-tech security systems are vying for supremacy and a lasting relationship with the government, Applied Digital Solutions (ADS) of Palm Beach, Florida wants its piece of the pie. The move to high-tech security systems has sparked a renewed debate over how best to profit from emergent identification technologies whilst maintaining a fair balance between civil liberties and the increased need for homeland security. ADS took the opportunity to announce the existence of something they call the 'verichip' – an identification chip which can be injected under the skin. Critics of the chip express concerns over the spectre of persons being injected with the chips against their will, perhaps surreptitiously in conjunction with a routine vaccination. In addition, they are concerned about the possibility of such chips eventually being mandated by the government as a form of ID. Lest we should imagine that only the Americans have determined to secure their borders in this way, we need look no further than the plans which have recently made in relation to Europe and the UK.

European security

Writing in 2004, Apap and Carrera state that (2004:1):

> Contemporary challenges to traditional concepts of security, and especially to the distinction between internal and external security, has stimulated justifications across Europe for a significant increase in state practices involving intrusive surveillance, policing, and restrictive measures toward people in general.

They go further in suggesting that in some instances, this change may have resulted in the erosion of civil liberties, human rights, and the rule of law. Therefore, the practices implementing the Schengen borders regime merit special attention. The Schengen Agreement of 1985 and the Schengen Convention of 1990 that implemented it were intended to establish, through an intergovernmental approach, the application of 'the principle of the free movement of persons' within the European borders. The Single European Act, which came into effect on July 1, 1987, by introducing Article 14 into the EC Treaties (formerly, Article 8a), stipulated that the European Community should adopt measures aimed at achieving 'a market without frontiers'. So what is the current position in Europe as regards borders and security?

In 1985 the Schengen Agreement was reached amongst some European countries which allows for the abolition of systematic border controls and some common policy on the temporary entry of persons (including the Schengen Visa), the harmonisation of external border controls, and cross-border police co-operation. Before Schengen, Belgium the Netherlands and Luxembourg had already given up the borders controls which had previously existed between them but in spite of this it took until 1995 for the first member states to agree to sign up to it. These included Belgium, France, the Netherlands, Germany, Sweden, Portugal and Spain. Currently, the UK and Ireland have not yet signed, although they share what is known as a common travel area with no border controls and hypothetically Ireland could join the Schengen Agreement without affecting its common travel area with the UK which remains reluctant to agree to shared border controls and work permit systems. This means that an unusual situation exists whereby the UK and Ireland are both signatories in terms of police cooperation but not in terms of factors relating to border control, asylum and visas. This situation has even been criticised by the House of Lords who have said that it restricts the possibilities for fighting cross-border crime since as a result the UK does not share access to common data bases on suspects. The effect of Schengen, for those participating countries, is that most border posts have been closed and travellers no longer have their identities checked when they are crossing EU borders. There is no necessity to get visas to travel within any of the Schengen countries and all participating countries check the identity of incoming and out going travellers. Under Article 2.2 of the Schengen Agreement, it is possible for a country to reinstate its border controls temporarily. This is most likely to happen for reasons of national security and has occurred a few times, for example in France after the 2005 London Bombings and in 2004 in Portugal during the European Football Championships. It is also possible for the police to travel between countries and to share information about people through the Schengen Information system.

In 2005, France, Spain, Germany, Austria, Belgium the Netherlands and Luxembourg signed up to a new visa information sharing system known as the Prüm Convention. The origin of this idea came on the back of the Madrid bombings in 2004 and subsequently allows the signatory countries to this agreement to exchange any DNA or fingerprint data they have on the basis of preventing terrorist activity. This system is set, in the future to become the largest biometric database in the world and is scheduled to be rolled out in 2009. This in itself is of significance since the European security agenda and the associated use of biometric techniques appear to signal a significant increase in the securitisation of Europe. Arguably this directly challenges Europe's commitment to the principles of freedom, democracy and justice. The implementation of such techniques to service immigration and internal security priorities (such as combating terrorism) may even compromise EU legitimacy and more worryingly still it implies that in the future, ordinary citizens could, in certain circumstances, be conceived of as suspects.

The future for UK border security

It has been estimated that around 200 million passengers passed through UK airports in 2003 and that if growth continues as predicted, by 2030 this will increase to as many as 600 million passengers. The government has made no secret of the fact that these increases in travel, together with the fear of international terrorism, has resulted in their proposals to tighten and automate security at borders under a £400m e-Borders project, which will use biometrics and databases to check the identity of passengers even before they travel to the UK. As a result of this, any airline that fails to submit passenger lists, or carries passengers that have been refused by the UK, will face a penalty. The system will also record details of who has left the country, making it easier to spot visitors that overstay. The Home Office has said that e-Borders will be fully operational by March 2014 but that the programme will continue to roll out incrementally to major air, sea and rail ports to ensure complete coverage of international services in and out of the UK by 2010 with the remaining small air and sea ports covered in the last stage of the programme from 2010–14. Many UK passports now include a biometric identifier which has been the result of the push for increased security. However, under the proposed e-Borders programme, airlines will have to provide advance passenger information (API) and passenger name records (PNR) electronically. Passenger details – including names, dates of birth, nationality and passport details – will be checked against government databases before passengers board a flight and essentially means that UK authorities will be able to stop undesirable passengers from even travelling to the UK. Any airline that fails to submit passenger lists, or carries passengers that have been refused by the UK, will face a penalty. The Home Office has said that the passenger data provided by the airlines will allow the border agencies to identify what they describe as 'persons of interest' in order to target them for 'further action' but do not say what this might be. In essence it might range from getting immigration officers from the intelligence unit to operate surveillance on a particular flight, or calling in the police to arrest a passenger wanted for questioning. The Home Office claims that this database of information and the increased collection of biometric data will make it harder for people to conceal their identity and will make it easier to remove those who have no right to be in the country. Several projects that will feed into the bigger programme are already in operation, including Project Semaphore – a prototype system – and Project Iris, which uses biometrics to identify frequent travellers.

In March 2007 a new Home Office Document 'Securing the UK Border: Our Vision and Strategy for the Future' was produced in which the government and the foreign and commonwealth office set out their aims for the future security of the UK's borders. This document sets out what the government sees as 'the exponential growth in global movement' which creates new challenges which demand a new doctrine for the national border. Within the foreword to this document it is claimed that (2007:2):

> Border control can no longer just be a fixed line on a map. Using new technology, particularly biometrics, and new approaches to

managing risk and intelligence, we must create a new offshore line of defence, checking individuals as far from the UK as possible and through each stage of their journey. Our aim is to make legitimate travel easier, yet prevent those who might cause us harm from travelling here. We want the UK to be attractive and welcoming to business, tourist, student and family visitors, skilled migrants and returning nationals and residents, but halt those with no right to come to this country well away from our shores. This approach cannot be taken forward by a single government department acting alone. It requires coordinated support of government, international partners and industry to succeed. We will consult those who can assist in the initiatives outlined in this paper as we proceed and develop new mechanisms for co-operation. This strategy is a part of the radical reform of the UK immigration system begun last July. It provides a vision for the future for our border and visa operations and sets out practical steps as to how we will get there. It is part of our wider migration message, whether in-country or abroad, of supporting those with entitlements and penalising those without. A strong border is good for travellers, good for industry, national security and the economy. A strong border is what the public demand and is what we will deliver.

The timetable set out for change in the UK within this document is as follows:

2006–2007

- Pre-arrival data covering 20 million passenger movements on 55 routes
- Roll-out of first phase of biometric visas
- Intelligence-led exit controls in place at selected ports, supported by mobile
- teams and pre-arrival data
- Roll-out of e-passport readers at UK and juxtaposed control ports
- Specific arrangements for short-term students coming here for six months or less
- Legislation on new powers introduced
- Pilot of uniforms at borders

2007–2008

- Pre-arrival data covering 30 million passenger movements over 90 routes

- Global roll-out of biometric visas complete
- Further development of intelligence-led exit controls, supported by pre-arrival outbound data
- Visa Waiver Test run against all non-EEA countries
- Review of Direct Airside Transit Visa (DATV) regime and Transit without
- Visa (TWOV) concession
- Commercial partnership arrangements in place to deliver more efficient and customer-orientated visa service
- Risk Assessment Units rolled out to cover 75 per cent of all visa applications
- Consultation on changes to rules for visitors
- Roll-out of Tier 1 of Points Based System
- Consultation on introduction of English language testing for those seeking to settle in the UK through marriage
- Clarifying processes – introduce new application forms and guidance for entry clearance staff, applicants and sponsors
- Inter-agency border co-operation framework agreed
- 4CG data-sharing framework agreed
- Visible, uniformed border service in place at major ports, including Heathrow Terminal 5

2008–2009

- Pre-arrival data covering 100 million passenger movements over 90 routes
- Biometric immigration documents introduced for people here for work or study
- Changes to visa regimes
- Roll-out of remainder of Points Based System
- Changes to rules for visitors (following consultation)
- Inter-agency border co-operation framework implemented
- Uniform standards in place for all frontline border control staff

2009–2010

- Biometric-enabled automated clearance points implemented at selected ports
- Fingerprint biometric included in UK passport
- Majority of passenger traffic covered by e-Borders
- 4CG data-sharing framework in place
- Introduce an Authority to carry scheme

2010–2011

- Unique, secure identity required for all non-EEA nationals travelling to the UK
- 95 per cent of passenger traffic covered by e-Borders
- Biometric-enabled automated gates at all major ports

Reproduced from Home Office (2007:25) Securing UK Borders. London: Home Office

If this document is anything to go by, we are set then to experience even greater restriction and control over our movements world wide within the next five years. So what of the ideology of freedom of movement, particularly as suggested within the European Union? Arguably the right to freedom of movement is a fundamental one, inherently linked to the status of individuals as citizens of the European Union in which it is not only assumed, but highlighted within a recently adopted Directive on the rights of citizens of the Union and their family members, that people should be able to reside or move freely within Member States. Indeed were we not to understand that this was one of the actual benefits of membership of the EU? How then can this be possible in the current climate? In the light of the sorts of pro-security policies which currently proliferate both within Europe and in relation to the Unites States of America, it will surely become increasingly difficult to uphold the principles of free movement and to make residence rights more inclusive, even in an enlarged Europe. We can only begin to guess at what the impact of this might be on the ideology of freedom of movement. Added to this concern is surely that whilst many people might argue that stronger border controls are necessary in the light of an increased fear of terrorism – and persist in emphasising the old chestnut that 'if you have nothing to hide, why worry about greater intelligence?' – this conveniently side steps the debate about whether technology is always fool proof. Arguably not, since how many of us have experienced mistakes with the low level technology that we currently utilise such as the internet, our banks and ID fraud? How likely is it that cases of mistaken identity will occur and if they do, who will question this new technology? Greater restrictions on civil liberties and on people's movements mean that this issue must not be side stepped, but where is this debate occurring? There have already been numerous examples of so-called reasonable restrictions which have subsequently been used for less than reasonable reasons.

Civil liberties and extradition

One such example is the recent use of the Extradition Act 2003. The new act has been attracting attention from civil liberties groups, because of the way in which it changes extradition procedures from the previous legislation. Specifically, Part 1, which applies to seven EU countries, removes the need, in cases of extradition, for an evidential burden. Part 2 (which relates to non-EU countries) keeps the burden, but 42 countries, including the US, have been granted a fast track process by the UK, which allows them to provide 'information' rather than 'prima facie evidence' that a crime has been committed. The new legislation has been severely criticised for being one sided and yet another example of the UK allowing itself to be treated like the US's poodle which will inevitably lead to injustice. There have been calls for extraditions to the US to be suspended because it effectively allows British citizens to be sent to the US without proof of the case against them – but there is no reciprocal arrangement. The crux of the argument is that Britain should not enforce a treaty which the Americans have failed to ratify. The British government has since argued that the arrangement means both countries have to produce an equivalent level of legal evidence when seeking extradition from the other nation but is this strictly the case?

Take for example the case of Alex Stone, a blind 34 year old man who in 2003 travelled to America to meet a woman he had met over the internet. All was well until Stone was accused by the woman's family and the police, of causing harm to her child (by another relationship) in the form of broken bones. Advised by an American lawyer to return to the UK, since he had neither been arrested nor charged, he returned home only to find that the British police were looking for him and that he was to be extradited back to the US under new laws contained in the Extradition Act 2003. This Act had already been the subject of debate amongst some M.P.'s who had been campaigning to have it overturned. The Act replaced the need for American Prosecutors to show a prima facie case when asking British courts to extradite. This basically means that the American authorities did not need to provide evidence for the extradition to take place although ironically it remains the case that British courts do not have the same power to extradite American suspects because this would break the terms of the American constitution which demands that a requesting country demonstrates 'probable cause' that the person to be extradicted is actually guilty of the crime in question. In 2005, Stone was taken to Gatwick by the extradition squad and under guard by American marshalls, was removed to a jail in Missouri where he spent 23 hours a day locked in a cell. His blindness obviously made this a more isolating experience that it would for people without this disability. After six months his parents were able to secure bail for him and he lived in a motel until evidence emerged that he could not have injured his girl friend's child because the injuries predated his arrival in America and it was subsequently found that another child in the family – with whom Stone had had no contact – had suffered similar injuries. In spite of this, Stone was asked to take a polygraph test – which he passed – and was then given the choice of pleading guilty to the minor offence of leaving the country during a police investigation instead of the original charge of assault, which would have carried with it a penalty of 10–30 years imprisonment.

It is interesting to compare this case with that of the Muslim cleric Abu Hamza al-Masri who is currently serving a seven year sentence in Belmarsh prison for inciting murder and race hate. Although the City of Westminster Magistrates court have already approved the extradition, this has yet to be ratified by the Home Secretary. The American authorities want to put Abu Hamza on trial in America for eleven charges including funding terrorism, organising a terrorist training camp in Oregon between 1998 and 2000, and conspiring to take 12 Westerners hostage in Yemen in 1998. An earlier extradition hearing was told the hostages, which included two Americans, were abducted partly to gain the release of Abu Hamza's stepson, Mohsen Ghailan, and five others.

It is alleged Abu Hamza gave advice to the hostage-takers and provided them with a satellite phone. Four of the captives – Britons Margaret Whitehouse, a teacher from Hampshire; Ruth Williamson, an NHS employee from Edinburgh; university lecturer Peter Rowe, from Durham and an Australian, Andrew Thirsk – were killed after Yemeni authorities tried to rescue them. The American charges carry a potential jail sentence of 100 years and Abu Hamza was arrested on an extradition warrant issued by the US government in May 2004 but the process was put on hold while he stood trial in Britain and attempted to appeal against his UK convictions. A decision by the House of Lords in January 2007 to refuse him leave to make a further appeal against his convictions left the path clear for the present proceedings and once tried in the US, Abu Hamza would have to return to the UK to complete his jail term before being extradited if any sentence was handed down to him by an American court. However, unlike that of Alex Stone, this situation has yet to be resolved since there has still been no word from the Home Secretary Jacqui Smith about the British Government's intentions in respect of this matter. In the face of Abu

Hamza already having being convicted of crimes in this country, the seeming reticence of the government to resolve this situation seems slightly odd when compared with their lack of interest in the less high profile case of Alex Stone.

Whilst Abu Hamza currently avoids extradition, Alex Stone is not alone in his less than fortunate case. Three British bankers lost their High Court battle against being extradited to America to face charges relating to the collapse of the energy trading company Enron in 2001 due to inflated profits and hidden debts. The case against the three men, David Bermingham, Gary Mulgrew and Giles Darby, has been heavily criticised because current extradition laws mean that the US is not required to provide "prima facie" or solid evidence of wrongdoing in order to facilitate the extradition of a UK citizen. On the other hand Britain still has to provide evidence of probable cause in the same circumstances. The three men have been accused of seven counts of 'wire fraud' in the US as well as conspiring with former Enron executives over the sale of part of the company in the year 2000, which apparently made them over £4 million. Although previously Lord Justice Laws ruled that the case was 'perfectly properly triable' as well as being 'unduly simplistic to treat the case as a domestic English affair' in the US, their lawyer, Mark Spragg has been reported as warning that the judgement in respect of the three men could have far-reaching consequences.

It is interesting to compare these three cases, all of which could be viewed as test cases of the British Government's Extradition Act 2003, which was, of course developed in the wake of the 9/11 attack in 2001. It is probably not unfair to suggest that the US justice system has a long and aggressive extra-territorial reach, and the concern here is that the potential to apply for the extradition of UK citizens for allegedly criminal conduct committed against UK institutions might increase in the future far beyond those cases which have been highlighted here. Added to this it could surely be argued that forcing them to stand trial in the US may be a breach of European Human Rights law. Comparing these three cases it is interesting to note both the differences but also the similarities between them and to ask on what basis different decisions appear to have been made. Would it be fair for example to suggest that the British government was using its citizens as a form of 'political currency'? Even if this is not the case, the facts appear to suggest some serious inconsistencies with the application of this legislation are evident, which have the potential to create an unequal political balance between the UK and the US and which ultimately the government may come to regret on the basis that they have arguably entered into an agreement with the United States, the end result of which gives British citizens much less rights than American citizens.

Other examples of the power of the customs and excise agency in the UK have been reported in the media. For example it was reported by the BBC on 20th Oct 2004[2] that the European Commission was to take legal action against Britain over cross-Channel shoppers, by confiscating goods such as cheap alcohol and cigarettes if they believe they have not been brought into the country for personal use. Under EU rules, people can buy alcohol and cigarettes abroad (where taxes are lower) and bring them into Britain without paying British excise duties. However, Customs officers have seized goods and impounded cars when shoppers come back with large amounts of goods which they intend to sell to friends and family. The Treasury has claimed that this causes a revenue loss to them every year of approximately £3 billion but the European Commission felt that this kind of treatment was actually disproportionate for these types of minor offence. As a result the [then] Chancellor Gordon Brown had to agree that Customs should let first-time offenders keep their cars and goods but that they should pay any duty that was evaded plus a fine. The fact that they were able to do this in the first place might appear strange to anyone with some vague knowledge of the law since this practice amounted to a reversal of the burden of proof, and was therefore always likely to be out of kilter with Article 9 of the Council Directive 92/12/EEC, as incorporated into English law by the Excise Duty (Personal Reliefs) Order 1992.

Perhaps the most relevant case which articulates this situation is that of *R (on the application of Hoverspeed Ltd) v HM Customs and Excise* [2002] EWHC 1630 reported on by Joshua Rosenberg in the Telegraph on 1st August 2002. The case established that customs officers had no right to stop and search returning cross-channel travellers for alcohol and tobacco unless they had 'reasonable grounds' for suspicion. Rosenberg (2002)[3] reported that the High Court commented that customs had:

> Not embraced the world of an internal market where excise goods can move freely across internal frontiers, subject only to checks

---

[2]http://news.bbc.co.uk/1/hi/uk/3758476.stm
[3]http://www.telegraph.co.uk/news/main.jhtml?xml=/news/2002/08/01/ncust01.xml

made where there are reasonable grounds for suspecting that an individual traveller holds alcohol or tobacco for a commercial purpose and not for his own use. Customs officers said in this particular case that they did not believe that one of people involved – a Mr Wilkinson – had bought 10,000 cigarettes for his personal use and seized all the goods and the car. The Court commented that Customs and Excise had not explained the reasons why they stopped Mr and Mrs Andrews and Mr Wilkinson, and because they suggested in their evidence that they might stop passengers for legally inadmissible reasons, they did not prove to the court that there were reasonable grounds for stopping the car and questioning the occupants. They therefore held that the car and the goods should not have been confiscated because it was a disproportionate response to the situation.

The ruling is important because it was made under European Community law which provides for free movement of both people and goods within the internal market. Added to this, the Human Rights Convention does not permit a public authority to act in a disproportionate way when forfeiting a person's property, however keen it is on a harsh deterrent policy for the greater public good.

In a recent edition of Consilio, Couser (2007)[4] commented on this situation in the following way:

If Parliament passes a law tomorrow that legalises the possession of cannabis, it is not for enforcement agencies such as the police or Customs & Excise to second-guess the wisdom of that move. The same ought to be true in this situation, where a defective statutory instrument has failed to give effect properly to a European Regulation. At the root of this matter is the thorny question of how the government is to raise sufficient revenue to give effect to its fiscal promises, but that is a political issue upon which civil servants should hold their peace. There can be little doubt that those who flout the law should be punished, but granting virtually limitless powers to enable Customs to harass individuals when they have no reasonable grounds for suspecting guilt of anything other than a desire to emulate Sir Winston Churchill's drinking habits is simply going too far... Whatever HM Customs & Excise might happen to think on the matter, there can be no possible

---

[4] www.spr-consilio.com/couser3.html

justification for reversing the burden of proof in order to turn day trip-
pers into criminals.

And so to the future and the continued debate about balancing security
and liberty. In the UK, from August 2007 immigration officers began
patrolling Gatwick Airport for the first time as part of a move by the
Home Office to make borders more secure The BBC reported (24th August
2007) on the plans to make – as stated by government – borders more
secure starting with new look passport control workers in uniform
which create a more visible and intimidating presence to deter oppor-
tunists and fraudsters. A Panorama programme in 2006 did not help
matters by showing an undercover reporter getting into the UK using a
fake Latvian passport. Plans to merge immigration and customs and
plans for the single border force have however been criticised for not
specifically bringing the police into the equation.

In the US, President Bush continues to push for greater shake ups of the
immigration system to secure the nation's borders. In April 2007, he
inspected a new device, the unmanned spy plane which now patrols the
border with Mexico. President Bush has praised this development but said
that more needs to be done to stop people entering – or as President Bush
recently termed it, 'sneaking into' – the US. If this sounds bad enough,
right wing republicans have dismissed the beefing up of the borders that
he has already initiated and have said that his measures are too liberal in
the light of the fact that 10,000 illegal immigrants try to gain access to
the US each week. What they did not mention however was that of these,
1 in every 1000 dies of heat exhaustion and 1 in 3 are caught by authorities. President Bush has not yet managed to secure laws to grant visas for
the unallocated workers currently living in the US. These examples illustrate that undoubtedly the threat of terrorism both in the UK, Europe and
further abroad, have exacerbated the range of measures that have recently
been implemented to counter this threat. One of the justifications for
this has been that the particular threats of terrorism which we now face
in the aftermath of 9/11 and 7/7, to name just two examples, are new,
and that co-operation between countries – particularly the US and UK
– are required in order to bring perpetrators to justice and keep citizens
safe. However, is terrorism really new and therefore are these wide ranging
measures really justified? Terrorism is not new, but then we must consider whether there is anything inherently different about the current terrorist threat particularly from international terrorists either linked to or
associated with al-Qaeda in comparison with that which has faced before.
The international nature of such terrorism and the methods by which it

is organised and perpetrated within a diffuse and global world structure does indeed present new challenges for governments and enforcement agencies. Added to this globalisation of terrorism are new methods and unusual weapons facilitated by the modern technological world. The increased use of mobile phones, the internet and satellite technology have all contributed to the challenge to preserve security, but at what price is this carried out? Governments need to remain aware that there is a balance to be struck here and that whilst one of any governments responsibilities is to protect its citizens from such threats, in assessing what appropriate steps should be taken, it is also their responsibility to protect civil liberties with no less vigour.

7
Implications for Crime Reduction and Criminology

In this book I have sought to give some specific examples of what I consider to be unjustified and unnecessary legal restrictions upon individuals and to detail some of the motives behind this. I began by asking a number of questions which in the course of the last six chapters, I hope I have at least answered in some way. In Chapter 1, I asked whether the present government really does have a mania for legislation, concluded that it seems to, and discuss what the explanation for such a mania could be. I sought then to produce some topical evidence for the glut of legislation which has reached the statute books over the last ten years and the background to this. More laws, I argue, do not necessarily make for less crime but sometimes serve only to criminalise more and more behaviour. In Chapters 2 and 3 I focused on some of the possible reasons for the proliferation of restrictive legislation over the last decade and which could be considered to have impacted upon our essential rights and liberties as citizens. Moreover, I mused about whether this represents a new form of social or even moral control. In Chapters 4 to 6 my aim was to highlight some particularly interesting areas in which to concentrate this argument and to present to the reader some detailed examples which demonstrate the point. In this final chapter my aim is to ask, why might it be wrong to over-legislate and what implications are arising from this, first in terms of the success of balancing individual rights and liberties against the need for security and second, for the academic discipline of criminology?

I am keenly aware that the examples given here represent only a fraction of those that could have been discussed. In fact, writing this book has simply heightened my awareness that I have merely scratched the surface of this important area and that more attention should be drawn to these and other related issues by academics, and the general public, many citizens being only too well aware from personal experience, how ill thought through and knee-jerk legal measures can indict the innocent. It is also pertinent to point out that the role the government has played in all of this should not be underestimated. Arguably one of the factors on which an effective government ought to be judged is its commitment to civil liberties. The Blair-Brown administration has recently become the longest serving Labour Government in history. During its tenure in office, more legislation has reached the statute books than was the case for any other government – and more is to follow. Aside from examples already detailed in this book, it is enlightening to mention briefly some of the other suggestions that have been, or are being made as this book goes to press.

Within the criminal justice sphere we have seen greater limitations suggested on the right to a trial by jury, the argument here being that some cases are considered by the government to be too complex for juries to understand. The double jeopardy rule has been under discussion again after it was severely circumscribed under the Criminal Justice Act 2003. In November 2007, the government was again considering the penalties for speeding with suggestions being made for tougher penalties and the possibility of banning drivers after they incur only six points rather than 12, as well as the potential for speed cameras to identify motorists who then may be awarded 12 points in one 'go' rather than three, depending on how fast they are going. It has also been interesting to see the debate on National identity Cards come and go. Labour has had an on off love affair with this idea for some time, predictably sparking a vigorous debate. On the one hand proponents have argued that if individuals have nothing to fear or to hide, then identity cards should not be a problem. Civil libertarians however have made strenuous representations against these cards which they have said will be extremely technical, possibly containing biometric information which would be linked to a central database. Once this is achieved, it is argued that it would pave the way for further developments such as a national DNA database. It is probably a rational thing to be a little sceptical about such developments, if only on the basis that common sense tells us that technology is not yet developed to the point where by the government could assure us categorically that mistakes with such technology would never be made. Certainly on the back of the loss of Child Benefit Information which included the personal details and bank accounts of some 25 million people, it is surely not surprising that many people would see identity cards as being no safer and as having the potential to turn innocent people into possible suspects. More recent examples will be mentioned later in this chapter. After scathing reports in *The Times* (Gibb & Ford, 2007) perhaps the government ought not to be surprised that a return to the ID card debate would be currently inadvisable. The loss of 25 million child benefit records (including mine) in November 2007 has merely served to demonstrate that mistakes affecting the security of people's lives can now be made as a result of both human and technical error. The same *Times* report indicated that one man had resigned as a result of the loss of two Compact Discs which contained not only child benefit information, but also other sensitive information (such as names, dates of birth, National Insurance numbers and bank details) which it was reported had not been removed from the CDs because the process for doing so was too complex and would cost too much. Although the Prime Minister, Gordon Brown was reported as saying at the time that he acknowledged the government's duty to protect the public, the loss of this information represents a palpable failure to do so.

2012 has been earmarked (if years have ears) as the year that the full national identity register is supposed to be instituted. Anyone applying for a passport will have their fingerprints and eye scans placed on the register. Although there is an opt out clause to begin with, the government has said that after this date anyone renewing or getting a passport will automatically be included. The government has successfully jumped through all the legal hoops necessary and big contracts have probably been signed with Capita or EDS, but in reality what will this mean? Commenting in the *Guardian* (2008) Jackie Ashley recently said:

> We know that millions of sensitive details will be lost. We know that material of huge use to criminals will be sent in the post, stolen, mislaid, dropped in car parks, will fall off the back of lorries and will be sent by accident to radio talk show hosts. We know this because whatever the system, whatever the rules, from Tyne and Wear to Iowa City, they are operated by humans. And people get bored, tired, drunk, have bad days, think they're about to be fired, are greedy and, in general, make mistakes. The government is going to introduce a single system for all our identities. And I promise, you can't trust it. First, it will leak like a battered old bucket. Oh yes, there will be ministerial statements. Apologies. Inquiries. Expensive new IT consultants will be brought in. Tough and unbreakable procedures will arrive. And still it will leak like a battered old bucket – except that it will be the most expensive battered old bucket in the history of the world, and we will keep pouring in money to the IT industry in the years to come. Second, it will be riddled with errors. Great-grannies will be jumped on by armed police at Newcastle airport because of an administrative or human error.

Identities will be confused. And third, whatever promises there are about keeping some things, health things, or criminal record things, off one database, these walls will be breached. There is always an emergency, a special case, on the way.

Mistakes like this can also give rise to other, unforseen problems such as the scam US web site Fullreleases.com, which, shortly after the loss of the data, was encouraging people to view their website for a payment of $29.95. They publicised several files called 'child benefit' – thereby implying that they contained the missing data – but if any payment was made to the site, the files highlighted as 'child benefit' files, could not be accessed. This development merely goes to show that the law must continually play 'catch up' with ingenious criminals and therefore further demonstrates that mistakes, ill thought through or knee-jerk responses to situations will probably not be successful. In January 2008 (BBC 18/01/08) it was also reported that hundreds of documents which contained personal data such as benefit claims, mortgage payments and copies of passports were found by a member of the public dumped on a roundabout near Exeter. The same person reported that he had found similar documents in November 2007. Is there something special about roundabouts in Exeter, or is it a general pattern to be discerned? This new batch of missing sensitive data merely compounds problems already known to exist after it came to light also in January 2008 that details of hospital patients were lost by the NHS and a Ministry of Defence laptop stolen in Birmingham contained personal information relating to the Royal Navy, Royal Marines and the Royal Air Force.

Perhaps inevitably the debate about anti terrorism measures and specifically the further extension of the current 28 day pre-charge detention time limit has still not been resolved. In 2005, Prime Minister Tony Blair was initially defeated when he tried to raise the limit to 90 days, and was thus forced to settle on 28 days for holding suspects without charge. The police currently claim that the growing complexity of terror plots that rely on hi-tech secure computer networks means they may need more time to investigate before they have enough evidence to bring charges. But opponents say none of the terror cases brought so far required suspects to be held for the full 28 days. Home Secretary Jacqui Smith has said that a range of judicial safeguards will be put in place to prevent abuse of this extension which would include requiring the approval of a High Court judge, the Director of Public Prosecutions and the Home Secretary before a suspect could be held for more than 28 days. Such promises have done nothing however to allay the fears of those who claim that not only is the extended detention proposal an affront to civil liberties, but that it will merely provide yet another opportunity for anti terror legislation to be used in an indiscriminate way, probably against those citizens who least deserve it. One example of this is the protests which took place at RAF Fairford where anti-terrorism laws were used to try to prevent citizens making these lawful protests and arguably also to deny people their basic rights of association, movement and freedom to protest. It was also here, for example that an anti-terrorist order was served on an 11 year old girl.

And so the debate about the detention of terror suspects trundles on inexorably. In November 2007 (Brogan, *The Times*, 2007) it was again reported that the government wished to extend the 28 day limit on detaining suspected terrorists but that it would come under fierce opposition not just from Conservatives but also from their own back-benches which could mean an embarrassing defeat for Gordon Brown whose Home Secretary, Jacqui Smith has proposed a maximum period of up to 56 days. It appears however, that there is little support for the variation from the current 28 days, which can also be extended to 30 days if a state of emergency is declared under the Civil Contingencies Act 2004. This however, would only be declared in the most grave situations – for example if a number of airports were attacked simultaneously – and therefore it is clear that the Government wishes to extend the period of detention without having to resort to emergency measures.

Aside from the restrictions that could be imposed upon us in the name of national security, other forms of moral control continue to proliferate. In January 2008 (BBC 01/02/08) it was reported that patients with unhealthy lifestyles may be penalised under a proposed NHS constitution being considered as part of Lord Darzi's review of the NHS, ahead of the National Health Service's 60th anniversary. Newspaper reports had indicated smokers and obese people could be refused treatment whilst Prime Minister Gordon Brown claimed that a constitution would only set out patients' rights and responsibilities. Dr Peter Carter, general secretary of the Royal College of Nursing, was reported as saying that his members would debate the contents of any constitution in the coming months and that should such a constitution reduce the day-to-day influence of politicians in the NHS, that would be a positive step, but ultimately taxpayers would still need to be able to hold politicians to account. The problem with this proposition is that in essence what the government could be suggesting is a form of conditional delivery of NHS services, which given the reasons for its initial inception as universal care, free at the point of use appears wholly unsatisfactory.

Also recently reported (January 2008) is the suggested installation of border-style security arch metal detectors in hundreds of schools in England, in an effort to reduce knife crime and deal with violent behaviour. Although the most recent plan – announced by Home Secretary Jacqui Smith on BBC's Andrew Marr programme – is said to have the backing of both senior teachers and the police, this announcement again seems to disregard the fact that there might be a balance to be achieved between promoting security and the preservation of privacy. Apparently the details of this plan are to be unveiled in a new Home Office Report; the 'Tackling Violence Action Plan' which the government has promised will be available within the next few weeks.

In the same month it appears that private companies are also imposing new restrictions on the public in an apparent effort to dictate how parents should spend their leisure time with their children. It came to light in the media on 4th January 2008 that the JD Wetherspoons pub chain has decided that adults with children will only be allowed two alcoholic drinks whilst on their premises. Although the chain has no official signage alerting customers to this development, the company has said[1] that it felt uncomfortable with children being on the premises for long periods, supposedly because of lack of play facilities, and that it has told its managers that it will be left to their discretion whether or not to offer parents soft drinks. This restriction extends beyond the parents of children to those who may simply be with them and their parents. However, in spite of saying that their concern was over lack of play facilities, the chain has already contradicted itself by saying that refusal will be at the discretion of pub managers, who could even deny parents soft drinks. Wetherspoons has claimed that the reason for these restrictions is its keenness to comply with child cruelty laws under UK Licensing legislation. This appears an overly narrow interpretation of an Act which has previously been interpreted as applying to the environmental conditions and the segregated areas available for children.

Whilst it must be true that companies should be able to impose conditions on those using their premises, both for their own safety and the safety of others, this move to dictating how many drinks, either soft or alcoholic a parent should consume, does appear to be rather over-controlling Indeed are we to understand from this that the only people who become the worse for wear for drink are parents, and that the majority of them do this whilst their children are with them? Surely this cannot be the case and even if it were, is it really up to breweries and pub chains to impose sanctions on those people? It is true that the British have not had a distinguished tradition of taking their children out with them for

---

[1]http://news.bbc.co.uk/go/pr/fr/-/1/hi/uk/7170939.stm 2008/01/04

meals and other occasions when compared with some of our European friends such as the French and the Greeks. However, when they do take them out, is it really rational to suggest that this sort of measure is justified. If so, this surely implies that most parents are irresponsible and incapable of making their own decisions about their children. Arguably if this type of action is widely condoned it demonstrates just how far we are down the slippery slope of widespread personal restriction and just how much our civil liberties and our power to decide for ourselves is being undermined. It also raises the question of intent versus capability. If this kind of measure is indeed possible because of legislation previously enacted by the Government it merely demonstrates that almost every type of legislation can be abused and that sooner or later it probably will be.

In order to understand some of the implications for crime reduction of what has been discussed in the previous chapters, we should perhaps remind ourselves of it's (albeit recent) historical context. Of particular importance is the emergence of crime prevention as a separate policy issue in the 1970s due, according to Tilley (2005:267):

> ...to rising crime rates, disillusionment with traditional crime control methods and evidence that situational methods could be effective.

Tilley suggests that certain alterations have taken place within the types of formal or policy approaches taken to crime reduction which in turn have led both to innovative ways of rethinking crime reduction, as demonstrated by aspects of the Crime and Disorder Act 1998 (for example spreading more widely the responsibility for crime reduction as laid out in section 17), but arguably also to the approach which this book has highlighted. That is, a criminal justice approach to reducing crime, not solely based on reducing opportunities and widening responsibility but based also quite firmly in the notion of legislating to further criminalise activities and modes of behaviour previously not thought to be criminal. The background against which this policy trend has been facilitated in Britain can be detailed as being due to two particular factors.

First, Tilley (2005) suggests that subsequent to the Second World War and with the rise of the welfare state and the general upward trend in social circumstances, the Government and the public did not anticipate that crime would be a big problem. He points out however (2005:267) that:

> ...improved social conditions were not, it appeared, being matched by falling crime rates.......[and] these circumstances created an appe-

tite for alternative ways of thinking about crime and ways to control it.

So it was that crime reduction or – as it was more popularly referred to until recently – crime prevention, took on a more specific importance for policy makers and in particular of course, the Home Office which still has the main responsibility for crime reduction in England and Wales.

At the same time, Tilley (2005) points out that the development of the new discipline of criminology truly began to take off and crime reduction as a specific focus of interest for certain academics, also began to see a growth. Arguably this was facilitated by two further factors. First, the advent of what is now known as 'situational crime prevention' and second, the fact that some of those academics who were particularly interested in this method of crime prevention, were also at the time to be found working within the Home Office itself and therefore in a position to influence policy making within this area. I have mentioned in another publication[2] that perhaps the best examples of this are Ken Pease and Ron Clarke whose publications – including those they undertook for the Home Office at this time – changed the face of crime reduction entirely.[3]

---

[2]Moss, K. (2008) (ed.) *Crime Reduction: Critical Concepts in Criminology Series*. London: Routledge.

[3]Dr. Ronald Clarke is currently University Professor at the School of Criminal Justice, Rutgers University. Ron Clarke is internationally renowned as a leader in innovative crime prevention. He is one of the pioneers of situational approaches to crime and has worked extensively on the development and synthesis of situational approaches to preventing crime. He was employed for 15 years in the British government's criminological research department, where he had a significant role in the development of situational crime prevention and the British Crime Survey. Clarke has written on numerous crime related topics including *Designing Out Crime* (HMSO 1980, with Pat Mayhew), *The Reasoning Criminal* (Springer-Verlag 1986, with Derek Cornish), *Situational Crime Prevention: Successful Case Studies* (Criminal Justice Press, 1997), *Superhighway Robbery* (Willan Publishing, 2003, with Graeme Newman) and Crime Analysis for Problem Solvers (US Dept of Justice, 2005, with John Eck).

Professor Ken Pease (OBE) is currently Visiting Professor of Crime Science at the Jill Dando Institute of Crime Science, University College London and at the University of Loughborough. He has held chairs at the Universities of Manchester and Saskatchewan. A psychologist by training, he has been responsible for some of the most innovative, rigorous yet practical work in crime reduction in the last 20 years. His work on the prevention of repeat burglary in Kirkholt led to a 70 per cent reduction in crime and spawned replications all over the UK, the US, Australia and many other countries. Alongside Nick Ross he conceived and coined the term 'crime science' and has done more than any other scholar to integrate serious scientific methods into crime reduction. Testament to the far reaching effect of Ken's work is the recently published book, 'Imagination for Crime Prevention: Essays in Honour of Ken Pease'. Monsey: Criminal Justice Press.

I have also mentioned previously (Moss & Stephens, 2006) that one of the main problems which has beset criminological thinking until very recently is that it hinged on the offender and what to do about him (or her). Conventional criminology had focused in the main on the motivation and disposition of offenders and how to deal with them to alter this. Thus criminology had traditionally sought to understand criminals, but had not necessarily used this knowledge to prevent crime. In contrast to this, the focus of crime reduction – given that crime is harmful to social structures and individuals – is to reduce crime, or the seriousness of crime by analysing it and formulating crime reductive approaches to diminish it. In order to achieve this, three approaches to crime reduction have been distinguished. First, what might be termed the structural approach, which concentrates on the 'root causes' of crime including social deprivation and unemployment. Second, the inherent approach where crime is thought to be a product of personal or genetic factors and finally the situational approach. Here crime is thought to be the result of circumstances or the right opportunities being present to facilitate it.

Crime reduction should really take into consideration all the relevant factors, but realistically most do not, preferring to specialise in one of them. As a result there are both historical and current classifications and theories of crime prevention as well as debates about what should be prevented and what is preventable. The most recent of these paradigms suggests that changes in the social and physical settings in which crime occur can reduce its frequency and/or impact. This is sometimes referred to as Primary Prevention and usually means reducing the opportunities for crime without making reference to characteristics of the criminals themselves. All of these developments have contributed to the debate about where the future of crime reduction lies but this is not as simple as it might sound. The problem remains the issue of balance between crime reduction and any negative or restrictive impact or influences this might have on people generally. The focus of this book has really hinged on the difficulty of balancing civil liberties against crime prevention and how this is achieved, and whether or not successfully. Whilst being mindful of the ways in which crime can better be prevented, citizens also need to retain an element of choice in the decisions that they make. As so succinctly put by Pease (1998:963):

> A society in which more crime is prevented is not necessarily a more pleasant society. The burdens and restrictions imposed on people to

prevent crime must be balanced against the harm caused by the crime prevented.

Of course it is true that crime is an ever changing phenomenon. Things that used to be crimes are no longer – such as adult male consenting homosexuality: things that used not to be crimes now are, such as the rape of a wife. According to Pease (2002:967):

> The constant factor necessary for sustainable crime reduction is the motive to 'go with the flow'; to understand changing opportunities for crime and to head them off or minimize their impact.

So is it possible to work to reduce crime but at the same time protect civil liberties given the huge changes that have taken place world wide in terms of the potential to commit crime and can criminology – or any other discipline for that matter – work to protect civil liberties whilst at the same time working to reduce crime?

Dershowitz, A. (2006:1)[4] comments that:

> It is five years since the attacks on the World Trade Center and the Pentagon, but Western democracies have not even begun to address seriously, and in a nuanced way, the moral and intellectual challenges posed by the relatively new phenomenon of mass-casualty suicide terrorism. The traditional paradigm by which we have long confronted harmful conduct – waiting until the harm occurs and then punishing the harm-doer to deter others – cannot work with the suicide terrorist who welcomes the ultimate punishment. A new paradigm, relying more on anticipatory and preventive measures, must be considered. But such measures carry with them considerable dangers to civil liberties. The debate thus far has been largely an unilluminating clash of ideological extremes with one side arguing against any compromise with the old deterrent-civil liberties model, and the other side insisting that the need to prevent mass-casualty terrorism trumps traditional concerns over civil liberties. What has been missing from the debate thus far is a willingness to adapt old approaches to new realities.

What does Dershowitz mean by these new realities? It is simply that at both ends of the spectrum, whether planning or trying to thwart terrorist plots or other mass-casualty scenarios, the requirement is one

---

[4]http://findarticles.com/p/articles/mi_qa3724/is_200609/ai_n1670520

of strategic planning, innovative thinking and exploitation. Perhaps the only difference that Dershowitz refers to is the element of luck in these matters and how that yields success or failure. For the terrorist, one success and many failures still has a huge effect on society, but for those whose role is in preventing or reducing crime, one failure is still one too many. Added to this, the age old notion that the ultimate penalty – death – is the ultimate deterrent matters not in such scenarios. For the suicide bomber, death is the ultimate reward in a culture where the moral and legal constraints of democracy matter not. Democracies are fettered – we hope – by an inability to use the tyrannical methods employed by people such as Hitler and Stalin, whom Dershowitz (2006:1)[5] also explains:

> ...surveilled everyone, using family members and friends as spies (imagine what they would have done with modern technology). They deterred terrorists who were themselves prepared to die by punishing their kith and kin (as when Reinhard Heydrich was killed by a Czech terrorist and Hitler ordered the mass murder of the entire village of Lidice). They criminalised all advocacy of terrorism (and even peaceful advocacy of change). They restricted movement in and out of the country and required everyone to carry identification cards ('your papers, please!'). Perhaps most important, they exercised total control over the media and forbade reporting of terrorist acts (thereby denying terrorists the ability to communicate widely their 'propaganda by deed').

It is inconceivable that any democracy should now suggest that such methods should be used in the so-called 'war on terrorism' but in reality, how far are we from a situation where crime prevention begins to violate both legal and moral norms? The manifold increases in the restriction of people generally in terms of both international and domestic security have been identified in this book. I have attempted to highlight a few of these in relation to a few areas – detention without trial, border security measures and closer to home, the implementation of football banning orders – but the problem remains that most people do not see themselves in any of these categories and as such do not feel threatened by any of these restrictive measures. It may the case that most people are not putting two and two together and cannot see the whole picture with regard to the slow but certain diminution of our civil liberties and freedoms. This is not to suggest that we should succumb to some paradigm of maximalist civil liberties, but rather that instead of accepting without question extreme ways

---

[5]http://findarticles.com/p/articles/mi_qa3724/is_200609/ai_n16705207

of confronting the current problems of 21st century crime – including terrorism – that we should begin an informed debate about how to combat these problems without succumbing to the same immorality as those we seek to castigate. We know all too well that governments of the past have used immoral means of discovery and scrutiny. Dershowitz (2006) aptly reminds us that the US, bugging was evident in relation to both the Watergate affair and in relation to Martin Luther King prior to his assassination. In the UK, powers to detain prisoners of war during the Second World War were abused by the Churchill government. We know all of this with hindsight, and what more will we ultimately find out about our present governments and the tactics they have used in the fight against crime? In the UK, the Crime and Disorder Act 1998 stated that we could share data if it was with the sole purpose of preventing crime (section 115) but more seems to have been made of the Data Protection Act 1998 which states when we can't share information. This sort of confusion and the lack of clarity which emanates from ill thought through and knee jerk legislation predictably results in a lack of trust. A degree of cynicism and a measure of scepticism are an essential part of a healthy democracy, and indeed may be what has perhaps been lacking of late. The price of liberty is indeed eternal vigilance. This does not, however, mean that imaginative thinking about crime reduction should be hindered. It is surely possible to strike a balance between reducing crime and preserving civil liberties and privacy.

On example of this is given by the present writer (Moss, 2006) in which the devising and implementation of the Nottingham Burglary Risk Index (Brix) is discussed. A particular interest in how information sharing between agencies could reduce crime within the East Midlands was highlighted by the [then] Crime Reduction Director for the Government Office who provided analytical capability to all Crime and Disorder Reduction Partnerships in the region in an effort to move to evidence-led crime reduction. Two years into the project it became clear that there was a need to determine the focus of data required to make specific reductions of particular crimes. For this reason, the Nottingham Brix was developed which suggested that two residential areas should be chosen in order to develop a risk index for domestic burglary. As Moss states (2006:191):

> The intention of the project was to draw up a risk assessment instrument based upon accepted and proven risks rather than those that could best be described as anecdotal or experiential.

And further, the beauty of this research project was; Moss (2006: 192)

> ...that all information at the point of use had the personal elements deleted and was therefore entirely anonymous.

It is not clear whether any lessons have been learnt from the Nottingham Brix, but at the very least, it certainly demonstrates that it is possible to gain relevant and useful crime reductive information without compromising people's privacy. It is also possible to suggest therefore that structures could be implemented which – as in the Nottingham Brix – could assure confidentiality.

The famous quotation by Benjamin Franklin – those who would give up essential liberty, to purchase a little temporary safety, deserve neither liberty nor safety' – is relevant. Perhaps the most important words here are 'liberty' and 'safety' for it is us who should decide what these terms mean and which are of the greatest importance to us in a democratic society. The freedom to speak, to express, to protest, and to dissent are the forms of liberties which are essential to any democracy and must never be compromised, even if it means giving those with radical and unpalatable views the right to be heard. As long as that debate continues, we can be sure democracy survives. So is there room for hope? Two recent examples perhaps demonstrate that free speech is not entirely stifled in the UK. Writing in the *Guardian* (2006) George Monbiot discussed the case of Stephen Green, head of the organisation called Christian Voice. Green had been arrested under the Public Order Act 1986 for handing out leaflets at the gay and lesbian festival in Cardiff stating that homosexuality could be compared to incest and that the continuation of such a lifestyle would lead to hell. He was arrested and charged under the Act for using 'threatening, abusive or insulting words or behaviour within the hearing or sight of a person likely to be caused harassment, alarm or distress thereby'. Subsequently however, the Crown Prosecution Service decided to drop the case. Green is a well known figure, some of whose exploits include trying to have the Jerry Springer Opera banned on the grounds of blasphemy, and infamous for saying that Hurricane Katrina was a judgement from God due to the indecency of the lives of people in New Orleans. Although by most people's standards, Stephen Green might well be described as intolerant and offensive, Monbiot is quick to remind us that be this as it may, the law under which Green was arrested was just as illiberal.

Although his leaflets were, by all accounts offensive to homosexuals, the Crown Prosecution Service probably realised that his actions did not suffice for this. However, Monbiot also comments that had the police used different legislation, they would doubtless have been successful. The legislation to which he refers is the Protection from Harassment Act 1997 and the Serious Organised Crime and Police Act 2005. In the former, only 'speech' is required to cause alarm or distress and this does not need to be threatening abusive or insulting but does need to occur to the same person more than once. At the time of drafting the government claimed that the Protection from Harassment Act would protect people from stalkers and assured us that there were a number of defences, but having the right to exercise free speech or to protest is of course, not one of these. The Protection from Harassment Act has since been used to prosecute those guilty of dissent such as peaceful animal rights protestors. Aside from this possibility, the police could also have arrested Stephen Green under the Serious Organised Crime and Police Act 2005 for 'harassment intended to deter lawful activities'. Under this Act, alarm or distress needs only be caused to 'two or more persons'. So Green would only have had to hand his leaflets out to two people to be in breach of the Act, which does not include a defence for peaceful protest. Monbiot (2006)[6] comments that:

> Luckily, the police – fuddled like everyone else by the size and complexity of the Act – have not yet grasped its full implications, though they have used another of its sections, which bans us from demonstrating near parliament without their permission. But it can't be long before they realise how powerful they have become. When they do, they will abandon the acts passed under Conservative governments by bleeding-heart liberals such as Leon Brittan and Michael Howard, in favour of the much more draconian laws propelled through a dozy parliament by Tony Blair.

We may not like what Green has to say, nor the way in which he says it, but nevertheless he should be allowed to say it, and public

---

[6]http://www.guardian.co.uk/commentisfree/story/0,,1886186,00.html

opinion, not the law, should decide whether he has gone too far. More succinctly put by Voltaire:

I disapprove of what you say, but I will defend to the death your right to say it.

Arguably in the UK – and depressingly – it appears that recent legislation has negated this. These Acts allow the police to decide who may speak, what they may say and even where they can say it. The case against Green may have been dropped, but not for the right reasons and only because they used the wrong Act.

More recently (McSmith & Taylor, 2007)[7] it was reported that protestors had stormed the Oxford Union in protest against a debate which included the controversial historian David Irving (jailed for three years in Austria for denying the Holocaust) and the BNP leader Nick Griffin. After some delay because of the sit down protest, the debates went ahead. The President of the Oxford Union claimed to be disappointed that the police had given the protestors a chance to storm the building; however, once again we have a classic example of the right to speak freely and the right to protest coming head to head. In this case we could say that both the protestors and the debaters got a fair chance to air their respective views and in this sense we are undoubtedly better off than jurisdictions such as the Sudan, where, in the same month that the Oxford Union debacle was taking place, a British teacher was arrested after being accused of insulting the Islamic Prophet by allowing her pupils to name a toy bear Mohammed. Whether this could indeed be construed as an insult to Islam is one which has not yet been resolved by the Muslim community – some believing that only boys may bear the name and that to give it to toys and pets amounts to idolatry, whilst others argue that it should not be a problem as long as the naming was not intended to cause offence. In fact the Islamic Society sold a soft toy made for British Muslim children named Adam the Prayer Bear – Adam also being the name of a Prophet. The British teacher may have had to face a public flogging, jail or both but was allowed to return to the UK after intercession by two British Muslim peers.

Striking a balance between protecting fundamental rights and freedoms and preserving security, law and order is difficult but the debate itself sensitises one to the issues. Obviously all states should have dual responsibilities to preserve both in the most consistent and lawful way

---

[7]http://www.independent.co.uk/news/uk/politics/the-uprising-against-facism-students-storm-oxford-union-debate-760584.html

possible. Not all ills can be cured by way of legislation. If Bentham, the great founding father of criminology were around today might he have argued that in these troubled times, his utilitarian view would be that the security of the many outweighs the rights of the few? I do not think so since true democracies must have a commitment to the funda- mental notion of the rule of law alongside the liberty of the individual. It is this commitment which ought to prevent democratic governments from responding to criminal or security threats in an arbitrary way, which compromises the liberty and privacy of ordinary individuals. Certain rights should be non negotiable, for example, the right to life, the pro- hibition of torture, the right to a fair trial and the presumption of innocence – some of which I have highlighted previously. But the reality of our situation is that we know these rights have already been violated by countries that pride themselves on their commitment to democracy. This is in spite of the fact that both the European Con- vention on Human Rights as well as the Human Rights Act 1998 has expressly recognised such rights. Perhaps one of the problems is that whilst the tenor of these aspirational documents is to recognise the protection of everyone in society, it is still possible for states who have signed up to them, to derogate from them if they can justify this on the basis of an emergency. A good example of this is provided by the cases of *A and others v Secretary of State for the Home Department*; and *X and another v Secretary of State for the Home Department [2004] UKHL 56*. The background to these two cases are the 11 September 2001 attacks in the United States. The UK government's reaction to these attacks was to introduce Part 4 of the Anti-terrorism, Crime and Security Act 2001 which extended powers to detain foreign nationals against whom no action was being taken with a view to deportation. It was clear from the outset that this would be inconsistent with Article 5(1) of the Convention for the Protection of Human Rights and Fundamental Freedoms 1950, which guarantees a person's right to liberty. In order to get around this problem the government then made the Human Rights Act 1998 (Designated Derogation) Order 2001, in the form of a Statutory Instrument (SI 2001/3644) by which it sought to derogate from its obligations under Art 5(1) on the basis that a public emergency threatening the life of the nation, within the meaning of Art 15(1) existed in the United Kingdom. The appellants were non-UK nationals and were suspected international terrorists who had been detained under part 4 of the Act. None had been the subject of any criminal charge and in none of their cases was a criminal trial in prospect. They all challenged the lawfulness of their detention contending that it was inconsistent with obligations binding on the United Kingdom under the convention which had subsequently also been given domestic effect by the Human Rights Act 1998 and that as such the United Kingdom was not legally entitled to derogate from those obligations. They also claimed on appeal that there had not been a 'public emergency threatening the life of the nation' within the meaning or Art 15(1), and therefore that the steps taken by the government in derogation of its obligations under Article 5 were disproportionate and discriminatory under the terms of the Convention. Interestingly however, the House of Lords held that they had not shown a strong enough argument to warrant the displacement of UK government's decision that there was a 'public emergency threatening the life of the nation' within the meaning of Art 15(1). This only confirms that conventions or legislation which have been designed specifically to safeguard against these sorts of abuses of civil liberties are powerless in the face of an argument concerning national security and the inherently flexible approach which we are told needs to be taken and which in some cases, can amount to restrictions on fundamental rights. If we are to be magnanimous about this issue, we might well countenance some limitation of fundamental rights if properly justified and proportionate, but the fact remains that there are surely certain principles on which there can be no compromise and arguably the right to a fair trial is one of these. This is precisely the reason why the UK (in spite of its own track record at Belmarsh) has been unable to accept that the US military tribunals of those detained at Guantánamo Bay represent a sufficient guarantee of a fair trial in accordance with international standards.

However, what Britain does stand accused of along side the US are cases of extraordinary rendition. What exactly does this mean? Extraordinary or what is occasionally known as irregular rendition is the process whereby a person is transferred from one jurisdiction to another, outside of the normal legal channels or processes. An allegation which has been made in conjunction with this is that such people have either been tortured whilst in transit or have been taken to areas where it is known that they will be tortured. According to a Report of the European Parliament in February 2007 it is alleged that the CIA has sanctioned over 1000 such flights and as such has been in contravention of Article 3 of the UN Convention against Torture (UNCAT) which states that:

1. No State Party shall expel, return ('refouler') or extradite a person to another State where there are substantial grounds for believing that he would be in danger of being subjected to torture.

2. For the purpose of determining whether there are such grounds, the competent authorities shall take into account all relevant considerations including, where applicable, the existence in the State concerned of a consistent pattern of gross, flagrant or mass violations of human rights.

In spite of the fact that no jurisdiction has admitted to this wholly extra-legal conduct it has been suggested that this practice has increased since the terror attacks of 9/11. There have been a number of well known cases of rendition, some of which precede the attack on the twin towers in the US. One such is the case of the Achille Lauro[8] hijackers who were forced by the US fighter planes to land at a NATO airbase which effectively put them within the judicial reach of the US Government. It has also apparently been used in the mid-1990s by the CIA in their attempts to track down Islamic militant organisations such as Al Qaeda. Since 9/11 further allegations have been made, mainly in the media, that the US had subjected hundreds of people who have been suspected of being terrorists, to extraordinary rendition. In 2005 it was reported in the Washington Post (Priest 2005) that:

> Members of the Rendition Group follow a simple but standard procedure: Dressed head to toe in black, including masks, they blindfold and cut the clothes off their new captives, then administer an enema and sleeping drugs. They outfit detainees in a diaper and jumpsuit for what can be a day-long trip. Their destinations: either a detention facility operated by cooperative countries in the Middle East and Central Asia, including Afghanistan, or one of the CIA's own covert prisons – referred to in classified documents as 'black sites,' which at various times have been operated in eight countries, including several in Eastern Europe.

Perhaps the most well known case where an allegation of extraordinary rendition has been made is the case of Khalid El-Masri. El-Masri was a German national, although he had been born in Kuwait. He alleged that in 2003, whilst on holiday in Macedonia, he was kidnapped by local police who held him for three weeks before turning him over to

---

[8]The Achille Lauro first made headlines in 1985 when it was hijacked by Palestinian guerrillas off the Somali coast. In 1994 a fire started in one of the cabins and the ship finally sank two days after as a salvage vessel towed it to Kenya.

CIA agents. He claimed that he was drugged and transferred to an American run prison in Afghanistan where he was held for five months, was beaten, kept in solitary confinement and was interrogated before suddenly being released by being dumped on a road in Albania. In an effort to substantiate his story, El-Masri has had strands of his hair analysed in order to prove his whereabouts and since this time American agents have admitted kidnapping him but said it was a case of mistaken identity. In this instance, it could be called a case of 'erroneous' or mistaken rendition, where an entirely innocent person is subject to rendition. Such claims have not been restricted to foreign countries. A number of allegations that British airports have been used by the CIA for extraordinary rendition flights have also been made and in July 2007, the government's Intelligence and Security Committee released their Rendition Report, detailing US and UK activities and policies (Grey, 2006 and Thompson & Paglen, 2006). Whilst it is the case that any state that is a signatory of the UNCAT which passes an individual to another state "where there are substantial grounds for believing that he would be in danger of being subjected to torture" would be in breach of their treaty obligations, the US only ratified the treaty with certain reservations, declarations, and understandings, which may alter the nature of their treaty obligation with regard to UNCAT Article 3. Congressional Record S17486-01 II.3 reads 'the United States understands the phrase, "where there are substantial grounds for believing that he would be in danger of being subjected to torture," as used in Article 3 of the Convention, to mean "if it is more likely than not that he would be tortured."' This 'understanding' with regard to US ratification perhaps increases the difficulty of proving a treaty violation (USS Treaty No.100–20). Since this time, the UN Committee against Torture (Fisher 2006) has said that the US should stop holding detainees in alleged secret detention facilities, and should publicly condemn any such policy.

Realism dictates that in the globalised world countries cannot, and perhaps should not tackle these problems alone. The sharing of data, information, experience and resources is important in successfully tackling and dealing with threats. However, we should not forget that we have many hard-fought rights such as the right to privacy, the right to property, the right to free speech and the right to life. If those rights are actively threatened by criminals, terrorists and even governments there must be a duty and responsibility to help protect them through practical measures. The problem in achieving this is in achieving the right balance and a proportionate and effective result.

The implications for criminology or whose war is it anyway?

Since the events of September 2001 it seems that we are now living in a world that is characterised by fear and subsequently obsessed with security. In this sense perhaps those attacks were unfortunately successful. A decade ago it might have been unthinkable for criminologists or indeed anyone involved in crime reduction within the democratic world to imagine that we could see the demise of some of our basic democratic principles. Who would have thought that the notion of *habeas corpus* – traceable to the 13th century – and the concept of 'innocent until proven guilty' would be so easily dismissed and that people would be held without trial, sometimes for years both here in the UK and in the US – a country which openly claims to be a champion of human rights and personal freedoms. More surprising perhaps is the fact that relatively few people appear to be speaking out about these developments, including academics that arguably ought to be interested in them. It is somewhat ironic that similar developments in other countries such as Iraq, Libya and Saudi Arabia have received huge comment, but arguably, when Britain and the US perpetrate similar behaviour in respect of innocent people, many seem to turn a blind eye or accept the justification which is often given for it, that it is part of the 'war against terror.'

It seems to me somewhat dangerous for any of us to turn a blind eye to these developments, particularly those of us who ought to be speaking out against them. The systematic disintegration of various human rights and personal freedoms has happened before. We have only to remind ourselves of some of the genocides of the 20th century in Germany and Rwanda, and currently that in Darfur – to name but a few. Let's not forget also the segregation of blacks and whites in America and the McCarthy communist witch hunts. In all of these cases, certain groups of people were persistently attacked purely on the basis of their religious, ethnic or political beliefs. It is not as if we do not have experience of this historically, but to my thinking, it seems that the state's potential to repress is now on a much wider scale.

In this book I have written in general terms about some of the recent ways in which we continue to be restricted, including the move to greater surveillance, and the proliferation of legislation outlawing hundreds of types of behaviour. I have also given the reader a flavour of these moves by providing, in a small number of cases, some specific evidence for this in relation to three particular issues, namely detention without trial, the implementation of football banning orders and the moves towards greater border security and restriction on travel both in Europe and the US. Many more examples could have been given but the length of this publication does not allow for this. Hopefully I and others will write much more about these issues in the future. What troubles me the most about the issues I have raised is that I consider there is not enough open debate about them. For sure, there is some, but it is not a wide debate and certainly I do not see 'criminologists' – whatever that title means – speaking out about them. I feel they should perhaps take more responsibility for furthering this debate and that to date there has been a strange silence in this quarter about the current repressive attitudes of the state. After all, it was, amongst others, the 'new' criminologists like Taylor, Walton and Young (1973) who challenged orthodox positivist thinking about crime and called for the abolition of the power to criminalise what they saw as human diversity. Their concern with the enlarged power of the state is no less relevant today than it was in the 70s but criminology as a discipline does not appear to be commenting on it in the same way. Is this due to complacency, are academics just not interested in this area of research or does something else drive it? I have written before (Moss, 2006:184) that one of the problems with criminology is that most of its research interests are money and outcome driven. The discipline preaches flexibility in dealing strategically with crime but this approach means that what drives the research is what the policy makers wish to fund. Thinking imaginatively about crime, and of course criticising the state's approach to crime, human rights and personal freedoms, is not therefore something which is likely to attract large amounts of funding. Added to this, given that future research assessment exercises are likely to take a metric form, then the push to undertake greater amounts of funded research may well obscure other types of research which are arguably no less worthwhile, but which are not likely to attract funding. Certainly, researching the restrictive legislative practices of the government is not something I imagine will be government funded. This poses a problem because it potentially stifles the most innovative or ground breaking research.

To be fair, criminologists are not the only people who have such problems, and indeed neither are they the only people who have spoken out in defence of such matters, but my point is that *someone* (aside from charities like Amnesty International and others) needs to take responsibility for raising new awareness about the diminution of our human rights and freedoms and the growing repressiveness of the state, be it lawyers, criminologists or whoever might be interested in taking up the cudgels in defence of the helpless, the expendable, the dissenters, the protestors and others deemed undesirable by a society driven by law making and surveillance on a grand scale. The history behind the growth of criminology as a scholarly discipline lends weight to my argument because it is the social science which has always been most closely associated with the criminal law, and as my argument is that the law is once again becoming the primary instrument of oppression, perhaps that is why criminologists should take up this cause. If we look for one moment at the work, for example of Cesare Beccaria, John Stuart Mill and Jeremy Bentham it is plain to see that the birth of criminology was assisted by the types of challenges that these writers made, on the barbaric and inconsistent operation of the criminal justice systems of the 18th century. These ground-breaking writings did much to highlight the inadequacies of a criminal justice system whose operation might only be fair to those who were moneyed, in power or with some authority. They also highlighted the plight of those not so fortunate who found themselves at the mercy of this system. Later on this type of work was developed by writers such as Michel Foucault who focused on his own ideas of the repression of a bourgeois state. There are those who agree with such sentiments and those who do not. The important thing however, is that the debate was kept alive. There is a history therefore of criminology being associated with the prevention of abuses by the state and perhaps that is why I look to criminology to take up this role once more. They are not, of course, the only possible contenders but are certainly a good place to start. If modern criminologists were to follow some of the footsteps of their predecessors, they would not simply sit back and allow the sorts of injustices I have referred to in this book. They would speak out, as did Beccaria and Bentham before them, in defence of society's underdogs, and would not become the silent participants of increasingly authoritarian states. The evidence for this however is not encouraging.

Criminologists around the world seem to me to be strangely silent in relation to many of the issues I have raised here and many others besides. Perhaps they no longer see these issues as being part of their domain, and would rather leave it to other organisations such as Liberty and Amnesty International. But although the work of these agencies is a valuable contribution, this surely does not negate the need for academics to involve themselves in an informed debate about such matters and once more to be in a position to raise awareness at all levels about the importance of other aspects of society besides security – namely human rights, privacy, freedom of expression and other essential liberties about which we appear to be increasingly complacent. Is it possible that the discipline of criminology has been castrated by successive governments whose narrow policies about crime have been the only drivers of the issues that have more recently been studied by criminologists the world over? Academics have increasingly been caught between 'a rock and a hard place' with the pressure to secure research funds. Initially this could be secured from governments as long as the findings were supportive of political policies – something which in itself flew in the face of the objectivity those academics prided themselves in bringing to the research table. Over a period of time, research by academics appears to have been neglected in favour of the move to the research consultant, who, with the money in his pocket rather than in the University coffers probably felt more compelled to have the 'right findings' for the funders. The result for criminology has been that its focus has narrowed and become more circumscribed with the ultimate danger of criminology becoming totally irrelevant.

It appears that fears about levels of crime and security both at national and international levels have also eclipsed the work that 'old' criminology used to do. This was waging its own war against social ills such as poverty, unemployment, drugs and crime. All that seems to have been forgotten since much of the emphasis of time, resources, policies and manpower now seems to be directed against a more international and global threat whilst the well being of societies is largely forgotten. Criminology now seems to be driven by politicians who set their own agendas. Even getting money from charities to carry out research is difficult – unless of course your idea fits in with one of their 'current strands of interest.' Writing this reminds me of the many times I, like thousands of academics, have applied for research funding unsuccessfully. In academe, a long standing joke is that if you are lucky your success rate might be that one out of every six applications is successful. My research has revolved around a number of aspects relating to crime reduction and in one notable example I twice applied to the Economic and Physical Research Council (EPSRC) for funding to develop a virtual reality 'walk through' of planned housing estates in order that police and planners could assess the security features of the new housing developments prior to them being built. Maybe it wasn't the best idea in the world, (but pretty practical – and maybe this was the problem) but when I found out later that one of the researchers who *had* been funded was an Oxbridge Don who wanted to research the tapestries of Northern France, I inevitably became a little cynical of the process.

In my opinion, if criminology as a discipline is to survive and continue to have something useful to say, both to students and to the world in general, then it needs to transform itself; to reinvent itself in a meaningful way. This will be difficult particularly for those of us for whom the next Research Assessment Exercise (RAE) is already being discussed, although we are told it will now be called the Research Excellence Framework (REF). What is also certain is that it will be driven by metrics, one of which will be the success of funding applications and the amounts of money brought into each institution – but where will this money come from and what sort of hoops will we have to jump through to get it? Is this really the way to drive the most imaginative and best quality research? Added to this it will also apparently include a process called 'bibliometrics' whereby we will also all be judged based on how many times we have been cited by others in (certain) academic journals. Whilst one person may well be very successful at securing large amounts of funding to pursue government approved research on the hot topic of the moment, another may be singularly unsuccessful in securing any funding at all because that person's research interest is simply not 'fundable.' This does not necessarily mean not worthwhile though – does it? As I said previously, in my own case, I don't think there will be much funding to assess the restrictive legislative practices of the UK government and its impact upon civil liberties. This may be something I have to pursue in my own time, whilst grappling with other projects which tick the REF boxes.

So what can criminology do about this before it folds completely or before it ceases to be empirical and scientific and instead becomes merely philosophical or normative? The first thing it needs to do is acknowledge that a change needs to take place. At this moment, and as someone who has had the great fortune to work, and be associated with, some of the best criminologists involved in this discipline, I envy terribly the fact that they are all now either retired or at the point of retirement. What a blessing it would be not to have to think about the future, but for those of us left it is absolutely necessary and something which 'some' criminologists such as Fattah, have already predicted (2003:26) when he commented that:

> Criminology's fate would be sealed were criminologists to maintain their present silence, were they to become the tools of oppressive regimes and governments, were they to refrain from criticising those in power and denouncing their abuses and excesses, were they to abstain from expressing critical, unconventional, controversial views, or were they to lack the courage to loudly and publicly defend their views and their convictions.

References

Adam, B. & van Loon, J. (2000) 'Repositioning Risk: The Challenge for Social Theory', in Adam, B., Beck, U. & van Loon, J. (eds) *The Risk Society and Beyond.* London: Sage.

Allen, J. (2004) 'Power in its institutional guises', in Hughes, G. & Ferguson, R. (eds) *Orderly Lives, Family, Work and Welfare.* London: Routledge.

American Friends Service Committee (1971) *Struggle for Justice.* Report for the Working Party of the American Friends Service Committee.

Apap, J. & Carrera, S. (2004) Maintaining Security within Borders: Toward a Permanent State of Emergency in the EU? *Alternatives: Global, Local, Political,* Vol. 29.

Arendt, H. (1963) *On Revolution.* New York: Viking Press.

Armstrong, G. (1998) *Football Hooligans: Knowing the Score.* Oxford: Berg.

Ashby, D.I. (2005) Policing Neighbourhoods: Exploring the Geographies of Crime, Policing and Performance Assessment. *Policing and Society,* 15: 413–447.

Ashley, J. (2008) 'The National ID Register will Leak Like a Battered Bucket'. *The Guardian,* 21 January www.guardian.co.uk/commentisfree/story/0,,2244088,00. html accessed 21 January 2008.

Ashworth, A. (2004) Social Control and Anti Social Behaviour: The Subversion of Human Rights? 120 *Law Quarterly Review.*

Back, L., Crabbe, T. & Solomos, J. (2001) *The Changing Face of Football: Racism, Identity and Multiculture in the English Game.* Oxford: Berg.

Bacon, F. (1605) *The Advancement of Learning.* Book 1, Ch 5, Sect 8.

Bagehot, W. (1928) *The English Constitution.* Oxford: Oxford University Press.

Bale, J. (1993) 'Sport, Space and the City', cited in Frosdick, S. & Marsh, P. (2005) *Football Hooliganism.* Cullompton: Willan Publishing.

Barnaby, F. (2003) *How to Build a Nuclear Bomb and Other Weapons of Mass Destruction.* London: Granta.

Berry, J. (2006) *The Guardian* UK News Section, May 6th, p. 7.

BBC (2007) 'Police reject UK rendition claims'. *BBC News Online,* June 9, 2007 http://news.bbc.co.uk/1/hi/uk/6736227.stm accessed July 15 2007.

Bichard, Michael Sir (2004) The Bichard Inquiry Report. London: Stationery Office.

Blackstone, W. (1979) *Commentaries on the Laws of England: A Facsimile of the First Edition of 1765–1769.* University of Chicago Press.

Blair, T. (1998) *The Third Way.* London: Fabian Society.

Bovard, J. (2004) *The Bush Betrayal.* Basingstoke: Palgrave Macmillan.

Bowling, B. & Phillips, C. (2002) 'Race and Crime', in Maguire, M. *et al.* (eds) *Oxford Handbook of Criminology* OUP.

Brick, C. (2000) 'Taking Offence: Modern Moralities and the Perception of the Football Fan', *Soccer and Society,* 1 (1): 158–172. London: Routledge.

Bright, M. (2006) 'The rhetoric of reform has made legislation appear necessary when most of what is contained in this bill could be done without passing new laws'. *New Statesman,* March 20th 2006 http://www.newstatesman.com/200603200004 accessed June 15, 2006.

Brogan, B. (2007) *The Times,* 16 November.

Brookes, S., Moss, K. & Pease, K. (2003) Data Sharing and Crime Reduction: The Long and Winding Road. *Crime Prevention and Community Safety: An International Journal,* 5 (4): 7–14.

Brown, A. (2004) Anti-Social Behaviour, Crime Control and Social Control. *The Howard Journal of Criminal Justice,* 43 (2): 203–211.

Brownlie, I. (2003) *Principles of Public International Law.* New York: Oxford University Press.

Bullock, K., Moss, K. & Smith, J. (2000) Anticipating the Impact of Section 17 Crime and Disorder Act 1998. *Home Office Briefing Note 11/00.* London: HMSO.

Burbach, R. & Clarke, B. (2002) *September 11 and the U.S. War: Beyond the Curtain of Smoke.* San Francisco: City Lights Books and Freedom Voices Press.

Burns, V. (2005) *Terrorism: A Documentary and Reference Guide.* Oxford: Harcourt Education.

Campbell, B. & Dawson, A. (2001) 'Indecent Exposures: Men, Masculinity and Violence', in Perryman, M. (2001) *Hooligan Wars.* London: Mainstream Sport.

Chakrabarti, S. (2005) Presumption of Guilt, *The Guardian,* Saturday April 16, http://www.politics.guardian.co.uk/attacks/comment/0,,1461277,00.html accessed 6 May 2007.

Chang, N. (2002) *Silencing Political Dissent: How post-September 11 Anti terrorism Measures threaten our Civil Liberties.* New York: Seven Stories Press.

Chief Constable of Greater Manchester v Clarke, cited in James, M. & Pearson, G. (2006) 'Football Banning Orders: Analysing Their Use in Court', *Journal of Criminal Law ,* 70 (6): 509–530.

Chomsky, N. (1989) *The Culture of Terrorism.* London: Pluto Press.

Chomsky, N. (2001) *9-11.* New York: Seven Stories.

Claude, J. (1998) 'Policing and Security: Terrorists and Hooligans', *Sport and Society,* 1 (2) 145–160. London: Routledge.

Cockfield, C. & Moss, K. (2002) Sex, Drugs and Broken Bowls: Problems of Crime Reduction in Public Conveniences. *Community Safety Journal.*

Cohen, S. (1985) *Visions of Social Control: Crime, Punishment and Classification.* Cambridge: Polity Press.

Cohen, S. (1972) *Folk Devils and Moral Panics,* 1st Edition. London: Routledge.

Cohen, S. (2002) *Folk Devils and Moral Panics,* 3rd Edition. London: Routledge.

Cohen, S. (1985) *Visions of Social Control: Crime, Punishment and Classification.* Cambridge: Polity Press.

Cole, D. & Dempsey, J. (2002) *Terrorism and the Constitution: Sacrificing Civil Liberties in the Name of National Security.* New York: The New Press.

Condorelli, L. & Naqvi, Y. (2004) 'The war against terrorism and jus in bello: Are the Geneva Conventions out of date?', in Bianchi, A. (ed.) *Enforcing International Law against Terrorism,* p. 25. Portland: Hart Publishing.

Cook, H. (1992) 'Preventive detention-international standards and the prevention of the individual', in Frankowski, Stanislaw & Shelton, D. (eds) *Preventive Detention: A Comparative and International Law Perspective.* Norwell, MA: U.S.A.

Coughlin, C. (2005) *American Ally: Tony Blair and the War on Terror.* New York: Ecco.

Couser, J. (2007) 'James Couser considers the use of imprisonment in recent land law dispute cases and the use of power by H M Customs', *Consilio*. www.spr-consilio.com/couser3.html accessed 5/12/07.

Crahan, M., Goering, J. & Weiss, T.G. (2004) *The Wars on Terrorism and Iraq: Human Rights, Unilateralism, and U.S. Foreign Policy*. London: Routledge.

Danchev, A. (2007) Human Rights and Human Intelligence, in Tsang, S. *Intelligence and Human Rights in the Era of Global Terrorism*. London: Praeger Security International.

Davis, H. (2003) *Human Rights and Civil Liberties*. Cullompton: Willan Publishing.

De Preux, J. (1960) *Commentary: III Geneva Convention Relative to the Treatment of Prisoners of War*. Geneva: International Committee of the Red Cross.

Dean, M. (1999) 'Risk, Calculable and Incalculable', in Lupton, D. (ed.) *Risk and Socio-cultural Theory: New Directions and Perspectives*. Cambridge: Cambridge University Press.

Dershowitz, A. (2006) Five Years On. What if it happens again: The greatest threat to civil liberties would be another atrocity like 9/11. *The Spectator*, 2 Sept 2006.

DeSmith, S.A. (1998) *Constitutional and Administrative Law*. Harmondsworth: Penguin.

Devlin, Lord Patrick (1965) *The Enforcement of Morals*. London: Oxford University Press.

Dicey, A.V. (1915) *Introduction to the Study of the Law of the Constitution*. History of Economic Thought Books. McMaster University Archive for the History of Economic Thought, edition 8.

Dinstein, Y. (1981) 'The right to life, physical integrity, and liberty', in Henkin, L. (ed.) *The International Bill of Rights: the Covenant on Civil and Political Rights*, pp. 128–129. New York: Columbia University Press.

Dodd, V. (2004) 'Guantánamo Britons sue Rumsfeld', *The Guardian*, 28 October.

Dorfman, G. (2005) *Trouble at Number Ten*, Readers Digest, No.1 accessed 06/02/07. www.hoover.org/publications/digest/3001151.html

Downes, D. (1997) What the Next Government Should Do About Crime, *The Howard Journal of Criminal Justice*, 36 (1): 1–13.

Duffy, B., Wake, R., Burrows, T. & Bremner, P. (2007) *Closing the Gaps: Crime and Public Perceptions*. London: Ipsos Mori Social Research Institute.

Dunning, E., Murphy, P. & Williams, J. (1988) *The Roots of Football Hooliganism: An Historical and Sociological Study*. London: Routledge.

Dunning, E. (1999) *Sport Matters: Sociological Studies of Sport Violence and Civilisation*. London: Routledge.

Dunning, E. (2000) 'Towards a Sociological understanding of Football Hooliganism as a World Phenomenon', *European Journal on Criminal Policy and Research*, Vol 8, 141–162.

Dupont, D. & Pearce, F. (2001) 'Foucault contra Foucault: Rereading the "Governmentality" Papers', *Theoretical Criminology*, 5: 123–158.

Durkheim, E. (1973) *On Morality and Society*. London: University of Chicago Press.

Elliott, C. & Quinn, F. (2006) *English Legal System*. London: Pearson.

European Parliament Report (2007) 'EU endorses damning report on CIA', *BBC News Online*, February 14, 2007. Accessed 14 Feb 2007.

Ewald, F. (1991) 'Insurance and Risk', in Burchell, G., Gordon, C. & Miller, P. (eds) *The Foucault Effect: Studies in Governmentality*. London: Harvester Wheatsheaf.

Evans, R. & Rowe, M. (2002) 'For Club and Country: Taking Football Disorder Abroad'. *Soccer and Society*, 3 (1): 37–53. London: Routledge.

Fattah, E. (1997) *Criminology at a Crossroads: The Future of Criminology in a Rapidly Changing World*. Criminology Graduate Alumni Meeting, Vancouver, December 2, 2003.

Feldman, D. (2002) *Civil Liberties and Human Rights in England and Wales*, 3rd edition. Oxford University Press.

Felson, M. & Clarke, R.V. (1998) *Opportunity Makes the Thief: Practical Theory for Crime Prevention*. Police Research Series Paper 98. London: Home Office, RDSD.

Felson, M. (1994) *Crime and Everyday Life: Insights and Implications for Society*. London: Pine Forge Press.

Fenwick, H. (2002) The ATCSA 2001: A proportionate response to 11 September? *Modern Law Review*, 65 (5): 724–762.

Finn, G. (1994) 'Football Violence: A Social Psychological Perspective', in Giulianotti, R. *et al.* (1994) *Football, Violence and Social Identity*. London: Routledge.

Fisher, W. (2006) US Groups Hail Censure of Washington's 'Terror War', *Inter Press Service*, May 20, 2006, accessed 10 Feb 2008.
http://www.mwglobal.org/ipsnorthamerica.net/_authors/wfisher.php

Fiske, R. (2003) 'Double Standards, Dubious Morality and Duplicity of this Fight Against Terror', *The Independent*, 4 January 2003.

Flynn, E. 'Counter-terrorism and Human Rights: The View from the United Nations', *European Human Rights Law Review, 29*.

Foster, S. (2003) *Human Rights and Civil Liberties*. Harlow: Longman.

Foucault, M. (1977) *Discipline and Punish: The Birth of the Prison*. London: Allen Lane.

Foucault, M. (1991) 'Governmentality', in Burchell, G., Gordon, C. & Miller, P. (eds) *The Foucault Effect: Studies in Governmentality*. London: Harvester Wheatsheaf.

Franck, T. (2004) 'Criminals, Combatants, or What? An Examination of the Role of Law in Responding to the Threat of Terror', *American Journal of International Law*, 98: 686.

Fraser, D. (2006) *A Land Fit For Criminals: An Insider's View of Crime, Punishment and Justice in the UK*. East Sussex: The Book Guild Ltd.

Frey, B.S. (2004) *Dealing with Terrorism: Stick or Carrot?* Cheltenham: Edward Elgar.

Frosdick, S. & Marsh, P. (2005) *Football Hooliganism*. Cullompton: Willan Publishing.

Furedi, F. (2002) *Culture of Fear: Risk Taking and the Morality of Law Expectation*. London: Continuum.

Furedi, F. (2005) 'Terrorism and the Politics of Fear', in Hale, C., Hayward, K., Wahidin, A. & Wincup, E. (eds) *Criminology*. Oxford University Press.

Garland, D. (1996) 'The Limits of the Sovereign State: Strategies of Crime Control in Contemporary Society', *British Journal of Criminology*, 36: 445–471.

Garland, D. (2001) *The Culture of Control: Crime and Social Order in Contemporary Society*. Oxford University Press.

Garland, J. & Rowe, M. (2000) 'The Hooligan's fear of the Penalty', *Soccer and Society*, 1: 144–157.

Gearty, C. (2005) 11 September 2001, Counter-terrorism, and the Human Rights Act, *Journal of Law and Society*, 32 (1): 18–33.

George, R.P. (1990) 'Social Cohesion and the Legal Enforcement of Morals: A Reconsideration of the Hart-Devlin Debate', *American Journal of Jurisprudence*, 35 (15): 8.

Gibb, F. & Ford, R. (2007) Law chiefs see no case for longer detention of terrorist suspects. *The Times*, November 22, 2007, accessed Feb 10 2008. http://www.timesonline.co.uk/tol/news/politics/article2917711.ece

Giddens, A. (1998) 'Risk Society: The Context of British Politics', in Franklin, J. (ed.) *The Politics of Risk Society*. Cambridge: Polity Press.

Gill, M, Bryan, L., Allan, J. (2007) Public Perceptions of CCTV in Residential Areas: 'It is not as good as we thought it would be', *International Criminal Justice Review*, Volume 17, Number 4, pp. 304–324.

Gill, M. Little, R. Spriggs, A. and Collins, K. (2006/7) What Do Murderers Think About the Effectiveness of CCTV? *International Journal of Security Education*, Volume 2, Number 1, pp. 11–17.

Gill, M. and Loveday, K. (2003) What offenders Think About CCTV?, in Gill, M. (ed.) *CCTV*. Leicester: Perpetuity Press.

Gill, M. & Spriggs, A. (2005) *Assessing the Impact of CCTV, Research, Development and Statistics Directorate*. London: Home Office.

Gilligan, G.P. & Pratt, J. (2004) *Crime, Truth and Justice: Official Inquiry, Discourse, Knowledge*. Cullompton: Willan Publishing.

Giulianotti, R., Bonney, N. & Hepworth, M. (1994) *Football, Violence and Social Identity*. London: Routledge.

Gough & Smith v Chief Constable of Derbyshire (2001) Royal Courts of Justice, EWHC Admin 554 cited in James, M. & Pearson, G. (2006) 'Football Banning Orders: Analysing Their Use in Court', *Journal of Criminal Law*, 70 (6): 509–530.

Gough & Smith v Chief Constable of Derbyshire (2002) Judgement as approved by the Royal Courts of Justice, EWCA Civ 351, Smith Bernal Reporting: London.

Grey, S. (2006). *Ghost Plane: The True Story of the CIA Torture Program*. New York: St. Martin's Press.

Gross, E. (2001) Human Rights, Terrorism and the Problem of Administrative Detention in Israel: Does a Democracy have the Right to Hold Terrorists as Bargaining Chips? *Arizona Journal of International and Comparative Law*.

Hart, H.L.A. (1971) *Law, Liberty and Morality*. NY: Stanford University Press.

Haubrich, D. (2003) September 11, Anti-Terror Laws and Civil Liberties: Britain, France and Germany Compared. *Government and Opposition Ltd.* Oxford: Blackwell.

Haubrich, D. (2006) Modern Politics in an Age of Global Terrorism: New Challenges for Domestic Public Policy, *Political Studies*, 54: 399–423.

Heymann, P. (2003) *Terrorism, Freedom and Security*. Cambridge: The MIT Press.

Hitchens, P. (2003) *A Brief History of Crime*. Atlantic Books.

Hittinger, R. (1990) 'The Hart-Devlin Debate Revisited', *American Journal of Jurisprudence*, 35 (47): 49.

Hoffman, B. (1999) 'Introduction', in Lesser, I., Hoffman, B., Arquilla, J., Ronfeldt, D., Zanini, M. & Jenkins, B. (eds) *Countering the New Terrorism*. Santa Monica: Rand.

Hoffman, D. (2003) *Human Rights in the UK: A General Introduction to the Human Rights Act 1998*. Harlow: Longman.

Holt, R. (1989) *Sport and the British*. Oxford University Press.

Home Office (1960) *Royal Commission on the Police Interim Report* London: HMSO.

Home Office (2007) *Securing the UK Border: Our Vision and Strategy for the Future*. London: HMSO.

Home Office (2001) *Working Group on Football Disorder Chaired by Lord Bassam: Report and Recommendations*. London: Home Office.

Home Office (2004) *Home Office Statistics on Football-related Arrests and Banning Orders*: Season 2003/2004, www.homeoffice.gov.uk/docs3/football_stats2004pdf accessed 15/08/07.

Home Office (2005) *Football (Disorder) Act 2000: Report to Parliament*. London: HMSO.

Home Office (2006) 'Statistics on Football-Related Arrests and Banning Orders Season 2005/06.' www.homeoffice.gov.uk/documents/football-arrests-0506 accessed 15/08/07.

Hor, M. (2005) 'Law and Terror: Singapore Stories and Malaysian Dilemmas', in Ramraj, V., Hor, M. & Roach, K. (eds) *Global Anti-terrorism Law and Policy*. Cambridge: Cambridge University Press, pp. 273–300.

Howard League (2007) Prison Statistics at http://www.howardleague.org.uk/ accessed 24 August 2007.

Hudson, B. (2003) *Justice in the Risk Society*. London: Sage.

Human Rights Watch (2002) *Presumption of Guilt: Human Rights Abuses Post-September 11 Detainees*, HRW Report, 14 (4). http://hrw.org/reports/2002/us911/USA0802.pdf accessed 08/05/07.

Human Rights Watch (2003) *In the Name of Counter-Terrorism: Human Rights Abuses Worldwide*. A Human Rights Watch Briefing Paper for the 59th Session of the United Nations Commission on Human Rights, March 25 (2003). http://hrw.org./un/chr59/counter-terrorism-bck.pdf accessed 08/05/07.

Ishay, M. (2005) Human Rights in the Age of Empire, in Bronner, S.E. (ed.) *Planetary Politics: Human Rights, Terror and Global Society*, pp. 204–217. Oxford: Rowman and Littlefield.

James, M. & Pearson, G. (2006) 'Football Banning Orders: Analysing Their Use in Court', *Journal of Criminal Law*, 70 (6): 509–530.

Jayawickrama, N. (2002) *The Judicial Application of Human Rights Law: National, Regional and International Jurisprudence*. Cambridge University Press.

Jenkins, S. (2006) 'These cartoons don't defend free speech, they threaten it'. *The Sunday Times*, 5 February, 2006. http://www.timesonline.co.uk/tol/comment/columnists/simon_jenkins/article727080.ece accessed 8 Feb 2008.

Jenkins, P. (2003) *Images of Terror: Fanaticism and the Arms of Mass Destruction*. New York: Oxford University Press.

Jennings, I. (1940) The Law and the Constitution. *Modern Law Review*, 3 (4) (April 1940): 321–322.

Jennings, I. (1959) *Cabinet Government*. Cambridge: Cambridge University Press.

Kellner, D. (2002) 'September 11 and Terror War: The Bush Legacy and the Risks of Unilateralism', *Logos*, 1: 19–41.

King, M. & Knight, M. (1999) *Hooligan: 30 Years of Hurt* . London: Mainstream Sport.

Kunschak, M. (2006) Creating Legal Black Holes? Terrorism and Detention without Trial: Towards a Changing Rule in International Law. Unpublished M.Phil Dissertation, University of Cape Town, School of Advanced Legal Studies.

Larch-Grove, R. (1999) 'Masculinity, Violence and Football Hooliganism'. www.footballhooligans.org.uk.

Laquer, W. (2003) *No End to War: Terrorism in the 21st Century*, London: Continuum.

Lesser, I., Hoffman, B., Arquilla, J., Ronfeldt, D., Zanini, M. & Jenkins, B.M. (1999) *Countering the New Terrorism*. California: RAND.

Lewis, A. (2004) *Are We Better Off? One Liberty at a Time*. http://www.motherjones.com/news/feature/2004/05/04_403.html

Lodge, J. (1988) *The Threat of Terrorism*. London: Harvester Wheatsheaf.

Lord Justice Taylor (1990) Final Report into the Hillsborough Stadium Disaster, London: HMSO.

Lupton, D. (1999) *Risk*. London: Routledge.

Lustgarten, L. (2002) The Parable of the Terrorist. *The Times Literary Supplement* (5195): 15–15.

Lyon, D. (2003) Technology vs 'Terrorism': Circuits of City Surveillance since September 11th, *International Journal of Urban and Regional Research*, 27 (3): 666–678.

Lord Hailsham of Marylebone (1985) The British Legal System Today. *Modern Law Review*, 48 (1) (Jan 1985): 114–116.

Maghan, J. (1998) Terrorist Mentality, in *Psychology and Criminal Justice: International Review of Theory and Practice*, pp. 335–345. New York: Walter de Gruyter.

Maguire, M., Morgan, R. & Reiner, R. (2002) *The Oxford Handbook of Criminology*, Third Edition. Oxford University Press.

Manser, R. (2000) *Old Image: New Imagination. A Focus on Football Hooligan Stereotyping*. Unpublished MSc Social Research and Evaluation Dissertation, University of Huddersfield.

Mariner, J. (2002) 'Indefinite Detention on Guantánamo', *Find Law's Writ*, 28 May 2002. http://writ.findlaw.com/mariner/20020528.html (accessed January 2007).

Marsh, P., Carnibella, G., Fox, A., Fos, K., Marsh, J. & McCann, J. (1996) *Football violence in Europe: A Report to the Amsterdam Group*. The Social Issues Research Centre: Oxford Press.

Mayhew, C. & Clarke, R. (1989) Crime as Opportunity: A Note on Domestic Gas Suicide in Britain and the Netherlands. *British Journal of Criminology* 29: 35–46.

McArdle, D. (2000) 'Missing the Target: Legal Responses to Football Hooliganism', in McArdle, D. *From Boot Money to Bosman: Football, Society and the Law*. UK: Cavendish Publishing.

McConville, M. (2002) *The Handbook of the Criminal Justice Process*. Oxford University Press.

McDonald, N. & Sullivan, S. (2003) 'Rational Interpretation in irrational times: the third Geneva Convention and the "War on Terror"', *Harvard International Law Journal*, 44: 301.

McSmith, A. & Taylor, J. (2007) The Uprising against Fascism: Students Storm Oxford Debate. *The Independent*, 27 November, 2007. http://www.independent.co.uk/news/uk/politics/the-uprising-against-fascism-students-storm-oxford-union-debate-760584.html accessed 12 May 2008.

McTeer, M.A. (1995) A Role for Law in Matters of Morality. *McGill Law Journal*, 40: 890–903.

Meek, J. (2005) 'They Beat me from all Sides', *The Guardian*, January 14, 2005 http://www.guardian.co.uk/germany/article/0,2763,1390258,00.html accessed 06/02/08.

Monbiot, G. (2006) 'I'm Glad the Case Against this Ranting Homophobe was Dropped.' *The Guardian*, 3 October, 2006. http://www.guardian.co.uk/commentisfree/story/0,,1886186,00.html accessed 12 May 2008.

Moran, J. (2005) State Power in the War on Terror: A Comparative Analysis of the UK and USA. *Crime, Law and Social Change*, 44: 335–359.

Morgan, C. (2007) *The Times*, 24 September 2007.

Morgan, M. (2004) 'The Origins of New Terrorism', *Parameters*, Spring Edition: 29–43.

Morgan Report (1991) *Safer Communities: The Local Delivery of Crime Prevention through the Partnership Approach*. London: HMSO.

Morris, N. (2004) 'Muslim Anger at Stop and Search Statistics', *The Independent*, 3 July 2004.

Moss, K. (2003) The Good, the Bad or the Ugly? What will the New Planning out Crime Guidance Look Like and What Should it Look Like? *Community Safety Journal*, 2 (1) June 2003.

Moss, K. (2006) The Future of Criminology in Moss, K. & Stephens (eds) (2006) *Crime Reduction and the Law*. London: Routledge.

Moss, K. (2008) (ed.) *Crime Reduction: Critical Concepts in Criminology*. London: Routledge.

Moss, K. & Ardley, J. (2007) The Nottingham Burglary Risk Index in Farrell, G. *et al.* (eds) *Imagination for Crime Prevention: Essays in Honour of Ken Pease*. Monsey: Criminal Justice Press.

Moss, K. & Stephens (eds) (2006) *Crime Reduction and the Law*. London: Routledge.

Moss, K. & Pease, K. (2004) Data Sharing in Crime Prevention: Why and How? *Crime Prevention and Community Safety: An International Journal*, 6 (1): 7–12.

Moss, K. & Seddon, M. (2001) Crime Prevention and Planning: Searching for Common Sense in Disorder Legislation. *Crime Prevention and Community Safety: An International Journal*, 3 (4): 25–31.

Moss, K. & Pease, K. (1999) Crime and Disorder Act 1999: Section 17. A Wolf in Sheep's Clothing? *Crime Prevention and Community Safety: An International Journal*, 1 (4): 15–19.

Munro, C. (1999) *Studies in Constitutional Law*. 2nd edition. London: Butterworths.

Munro, C. (1987) *Studies in Constitutional Law* .1st edition. London: Butterworths.

Murphy, P., Williams, J. & Dunning, E. (1990) *Football on Trial: Spectator Violence and Development in the Football World*. London: Routledge.

Mythen, G. (2004) *Ulrich Beck: A Critical Introduction to the Risk Society*. London: Polity Press.

Mythen, G. and Walklate, S. (2006) Criminology and Terrorism, Which Thesis? Risk Society or Governmentality? *British Journal of Criminology*, 46: 379–398.

Newton, R. (2004) 'Fight, Fight Wherever you May Be: A Critical Analysis of the Nature and Extent of Football Hooliganism', in Frosdick, S. & Marsh, P. (2005) *Football Hooliganism*. Cullompton: Willan Publishing.

Neuman, G. (2004) 'Comment, Counter-terrorist Operations and the Rule of Law', *European Journal of International Law*, 15: 1019.

Norris, C. & Armstrong, G. (1999) *The Maximum Surveillance Society: The Rise of Closed Circuit Television*. Oxford: Berg.

Nowak, M. (1993) *UN Covenant on Civil and Political Rights: CCPR Comm*entary, Kehl: NP Engel.

Nyerere, J.K. (1967) *Freedom and Unity: Uhuru na umoja: A Selection of Writings and Speeches, 1952–65*. London: Oxford University Press.

O'Byrne, D.J. (2002) *Human Rights: An Introduction*. Harlow: Longman.

O'Day, A. (2004) *Dimensions of Terrorism*. Aldershot: Ashgate.

O'Donnell, G. (2004) Financing Britain's Future CM 6163 London: Home Office. www.hm-treasury.gov.uk/media/3/2/odonnell fore_ch1_245[1] accessed 24/01/08.

Parmar, I. (2005) 'I'm proud of the British Empire': Why Tony Blair backs George W. Bush', *The Political Quarterly*, 76 (2): 218–231.

Patton, G. W. (1964) *A Textbook of Jurisprudence*. Oxford: Clarendon Press.

Paye, J. C. (2005) The End of Habeas Corpus in Great Britain, *Monthly Review*, 57(6): 1–9.

Pearson, G. (2000) 'Legislating for the Football Hooligan: A Case for Reform', in Greenfield, S. & Osborn, G. (eds) *Law and Sport in Contemporary Society*. Frank Cass Publishers.

Pearson, G. (2002) 'A Cure Worse than the Disease? Reflections on Gough and Smith v Chief Constable of Derbyshire', *Entertainment and Sports Law Journal*, Sept 2002.

Pearson, G. (2005) 'Qualifying for Europe? The Legitimacy of Football Banning Orders on Complaint Under the Principle of Proportionality', *Entertainment and Sports Law Journal* Sept 2005.

Pearson, G. (2006) 'Hybrid Law and Human Rights – Banning and Behaviour Orders in the Appeal Courts', *Liverpool Law Review*, 27 (2): 125–145. New York: Springer.

Pease, K. (1998) *Repeat Victimisation: Taking Stock* (1998) Home Office Research and Planning Unit Paper 90. London: Home Office.

Pease, K. (2002) Crime Reduction. In Maguire M. *et al.* (eds) *Oxford Handbook of Criminology*, 3rd ed., pp. 947–979. Oxford: Clarendon.

Pennant, C. & Nicholls, A. (2006) *Thirty Years of Hurt. The History of England's Hooligan Army*. UK: Pennant Publishing.

Pratt, J. & Slater, M. (1984) 'A Fresh look at Football Hooliganism', in *Leisure Studies*, 3 (2): 201–230.

President Bush 'Statement by the President in His Address to the Nation', 11 September 2001 www.whitehouse.gov/news/releases/2001/09/20010911-16.html Accessed 24 January 2007

Preist, D. (2005) The *Washington Post*, December 4, 2005.

Prins, H. (2007) Fifty Years 'Hard Labour' (A Personal Odyssey). *The Howard Journal of Criminal Justice*, 46 (2): 176–193.

Prins, H. (1996) *Offenders, Deviants* or Patients? 3rd edition. London: Routledge.

Reiner, R. (2002) 'Media Made Criminality', in Maguire, M. *et al.* (eds*) Oxford Handbook of Criminology*. Oxford: OUP.

Riddell, M. (2004) *The Guardian*. 20 June 2004.

Robb, M. (2000) *Football (Disorder) Act 2000*. http://www.magnacartaplus.org/bills/football/index.htm accessed 16/08/06.

Rawls, J. (1999) *A Theory of Justice*. London: Oxford University Press.

Rehman, J. (2003) *International Human Rights Law: A Practical Approach*. New York: Longman.

Rehn, E. (2003) 'Excessive Reliance on the Use of Force Does Not Stop Terrorism', in Hoeksema, T. & ter Laak, J. (eds) *Human Rights and Terrorism*. Holland: NHC/OSCE.

Riddell, P. (2003) *Hug them Close: Blair, Clinton, Bush and the 'Special Relationship'*. London: Politico's.

Roderick, M. (1999) *'Hard Cases in Court'*. Singer and Friedlander Football Review 1998–1999 Season. Produced in association with and hosted by The Centre for Research into Sport and Society at theUniversity of Leicester www.le.ac.uk/sp/sf-review/98-99/98article5.html accessed 9 Nov 2007.

Rose, D. (2004) *Guantánamo: America's War on Human Rights*. Open Democracy Ltd.

Rosenberg, J. (2002) The Telegraph accessed 5 December 2007. www.telegraph.co.uk/news/main.jhtml?xml=/news/2002/08/01/ncust01.xml

Roth, K. (2004) 'War in Iraq: Not a Humanitarian Intervention', in *Human Rights Watch World Report*, January 2004, at http:www.hrw.org/wr2k4/3.htm accessed 06/08/08.

Sassoli, M. (2004) 'The status of persons held in Guantánamo under international humanitarian law. *Journal of International Criminal Justice*, 2: 96.

Sontag, S. (2004) 'What Have We Done?' *The Guardian*, 24 May 2004.

Sparks, R. (2001) 'Degrees of Estrangement: The Cultural Theory of Risk and Comparative Penology', *Theoretical Criminology*, 5: 159–176.

Statewatch News Online, December 22, 2004, www.statewatch.org/news/archive2004.htm

Stenson, K. (2003) 'The New Politics of Crime Control', in Stenson, K. and Sullivan, R. (eds) *Crime, Risk and Justice*. Cullompton: Willan Publishing.

Steyn, Lord Johan (2003) Lecture to the British Institute of International and Comparative Law, November 2003. Cited in Lewis, A. (2004) *Are We Better Off? One Liberty at a Time*. www.motherjones.com/news/feature/2004/05/04_403.html

Stone, J. (2006) Police Powers and Human Rights in the Context of Terrorism, *Managerial Law*, 48 (4): 384–399

Sugiyama, C. (1996) *Lauderdale's notes on Adam Smith's Wealth of Nations*. London: Routledge.

Shilts, R. (2000) *And the Band Played on: Politics, People and the Aids Epidemic*. USA: St Martins Press.

Scarman, L. (1975) English Law: The New Dimension, *Modern Law Review*, 38 (5) 589–590.

Scottish Education Department (1977) 'Report of the Working Group on Football Crowd Behaviour' (The McElhone Report) cited in Frosdick, S. & Marsh, P. (2005) *Football Hooliganism*. Cullompton: Willan Publishing.

Sir Norman Chester Centre for Football Research (SNCCFR) (2002) 'Football and Football Hooliganism' , University of Leicester. www.le.ac.uk/resources/factsheets/fs1.html.

Stephens, M. (2000) *Crime and Social Policy*. London: Gildredge Press.

Stott, C., Hutchinson, P. & Drury, J. (2001) 'Hooligans abroad? Inter-group Dynamics, Social identity and Participation in Collective 'Disorder' at the 1998 World Cup Finals', *British Journal of Social Psychology*, 40: 359–384.

Stott, C. & Pearson, G. (2006) 'Football Banning Orders, Proportionality and Public Order Policing', *Howard Journal of Criminal Justice*. 45 (3): 241–254.

Tadros, V. & Tierney, S. (2004) The Presumption of Innocence and the Human Rights Act, *The Modern Law Review Limited*, 6, 7(3): 402–434.

Taft, W.H. (2003) The Law of Armed Conflict after 9/11: Some Salient Features, *Yale Journal of International Law*, 28: 319.

Taylor, Walton & Young (1973) *The New Criminology: For a Social Theory of Deviance*. London: Routledge and Kegan Paul.

Thompson, A.C. & Paglen, T. (2006). *Torture Taxi: On the Trail of the CIA's Rendition Flights*. Hoboken, New Jersey: Melville House.

Toynbee, P. (2006) *The Guardian*, 31 January 2006.

Travis, A. (2004) Blunkett on Film Sways Judges, *The Guardian*, 17 November 2004.

Travis, A. (2006) 'Unequal use of stop and search against ethnic minorities', *The Guardian*, Friday March 31 2006, p. 4.

Tilley, N. (2005) Crime Reduction: A Quarter Century Review, *Public Money and Management*, October 2005: 267–274.

Trivizas, E. (1981) 'Sentencing the Football Hooligan', *British Journal of Criminology*, Vol. 21, No. 4.

Tsang, S. (2007) *Intelligence and Human Rights in the Era of Global Terrorism*. Westport, Connecticut: Praeger Security International.

USS Senate (1988) Convention Against Torture and Other Cruel, Inhuman Or Degrading Treatment Or Punishment. United States Senate, Resolution ratifying Treaty Number 100-20. The Library of Congress May 20 1988 http://thomas.loc.gov/cgi-bin/ntquery/z?trtys:100TD00020: accessed 09/02/08.

US Department of Defence (2002) 'News Briefing, Secretary Rumsfeld and General Myers', 11 January 2002. www.defenselink.mil/transcipts/2002/t01112002_t0111sd.html accessed 30 January 2007.

Vierucci, L. (2003) 'Prisoners of War or Protected Persons qua Unlawful Combatants? The Judicial safeguards to which Guantánamo Bay Detainees are Entitled', *Journal of International Criminal Justice*, 1: 284–301.

Von Ness, P.M. (2003) *Guantánamo Bay Detainees: National Security or Civil Liberty?* Pennsylvania: U.S. Army War College.

Waddington, P.A.J. (2005) 'Slippery Slopes and Civil Libertarian Pessimism', *Policing and Society*, Volume 15, Issue 3,September 2005, 353–375.

Waddington, P.A.J. (2007) Someone's got their eye on you. *Jane's Police Review*, March 23 2007.

Wakefield, A. (2003). *Selling Security: The Private Policing of Public Space*. Cullompton: Willan Publishing.

Walker, C. (2005) Intelligence and anti-terrorism legislation in the United Kingdom, *Crime, Law and Social Change*, 44 (4-5): 387–422.

Wheare, K.C. (1951) *Modern Constitutions*. Oxford University Press.

Wade, J. H. (1972) *Morals and the Enforcement of Values: An Analysis of the Hart-Devlin Debate*. Unpublished LLM.

Wade, H.W.R. (1980) *Constitutional Fundamentals*. The Hamlyn Lectures, 32nd series.

Welch, M. (2003) 'Trampling Human Rights in the War on Terror: Implications to the Sociology of Denial', *Critical Criminology*, 12: 1–20.

Wilkinson, P. (2006) *Terrorism versus Democracy: The Liberal State Response*. London: Frank Cass.

Williams, J. (unknown) 'Hooliganism, "New" Football and Social Policy in England', Sir Norman Chester Centre for Football Research, University of Leicester.

Williams, J., Murphy, P. & Dunning, E. (1989) *Hooligans Abroad*. London: Routledge.
Williams, J. (2001) 'The Costs of Safety in Risk Societies', *Journal of Forensic Psychiatry*, 12 (1) April 2001. London: Routledge.
Wolf, D. (2006) Censorship wasn't all bad. *The Spectator*, 4 February, 2006.
Wolfenden, Sir John (1957) *Report of the Committee on Homosexual Offences and Prostitution*. Cmnd 247, London: HMSO.
Wood, D. M., Ball, K., Lyon, D., Norris, C. & Raab, C. (2006) *A Report on the Surveillance Society: for the Information Commissioner*. Surveillance Studies Network. London: Information Commissioner's Office.
Woolf, Lord. Former Lord Chief Justice (2006) 'Secret courts are an affront to our Liberty', *The Mail on Sunday*, 15th October 2006.
Zinn, H. (2002) *Terrorism and War*. London: Seven Stories.

Legislation, Treaties and Agreements

Anti-Terrorism, Crime and Security Act 2001
Bermuda Agreement 1946
Case of Proclamations 1611
Chequers Estates Act 1917
Civil Aviation Act 1982
Civil Contingencies Act 2004
Commissioners for Revenue and Customs Act 2005
Crime and Disorder Act 1998
Criminal Justice Act 2003
Criminal Justice and Public Order Act 1994
Crime and Security Act 2001
Criminal Law (Consolidation)(Scotland) Act 1995
Customs and Excise Management Act 1979
Dangerous Dogs Act 1991
Extradition Act 2003
European Convention on Human Rights 1953
Elections and Referendums Act 2000
Football (Disorder) Act 2000
Football (Offences) Act 1991
Football Spectators Act 1989
Freedom of Information Act 2000
Highways Act 1980
Homeland Security Appropriations Act 2007
Human Rights Act 1998
Human Rights Act 1998 (Designated Derogation) Order 2001
Immigration Act 1971
International Covenant on Civil and Political Rights 1966
Mental Health Act 1983
Military Commissions Act 2006
Official Secrets Act 1911
Police and Criminal Evidence Act 1984
Police Act 1996

Protection from Harassment Act 1997
Public Health Security and Bioterrorism Preparedness and Response Act of 2002
Public Order Act 1986
Prevention of Terrorism Act 2005
Proceeds of Crime Act 2002
Prum Convention 2005
Representation of the People Act 1983
Racial and Religious Hatred Act 2005
Secure Borders Initiative
Serious Organised Crime and Police Act 2005
Sexual Offences Act 2003
Single European Act 1987
Schengen Agreement 1985
Scotland Act 1998
Sporting Events (Control of Alcohol) Act 1985
Statute of Westminster 1931
Terrorism Act 2006
Terrorism Act 2000
USA Patriot Act 2001

Cases

A and Others v Secretary of State for the Home Department and H and Another v Secretary of State for the Home Department [2004] UKHL 56
A and Z and others v Secretary of State for the Home Department [2005] 2 AC 68 (HL)
Attorney General v De Keysers Royal Hotel [1920] AC 208
Attorney General v Jonathan Cape Ltd [1976] QB 752
Beatty v Gilbanks [1882] 9 QBD 308
BBC v Johns [1965] 1 All ER 923
Bowman v UK [1998] 26 EHRR 1
Brogan v UK [1989] 11 EHRR 117
Burmah Oil v Lord Advocate [1965] AC 75
CCSU v Minister for the Civil Service 3 All ER 935
Chandler v DPP [1964] 3 All ER 142 HL
DPP v Jones [1999] 2 AC 240 HL
Edwards v UK [2002] 35 EHRR 19
Ellen Street Estates v Minister of Health [1934] 1 KB 590
Evans v United Kingdom (2006) Application No. 6339/05 Strasbourg, 7 March at http://news.bbc.co.uk/1/shared/bsp/hi/pdfs/07_03_06_echr.pdf accessed 14 February 2008
Gough and Smith v Chief Constable of Derbyshire [2001] EWHC 554
Handyside v UK [1979–80] 1 EHRR 737
Ireland v UK [1979–80] 2 EHRR 25
Jordan & Others v UK [2003] 37 EHRR 2
Kent v Metropolitan Police Commissioner [1981] The Times, 15 May
Laker Airways v Department of Trade [1977] QB 643
McCann, Farrell and Savage v UK [1996] 21 EHRR 97

MR v TR, Dr. A Walsh, Dr. D Walsh, Sims Clinic Ltd and the Attorney General, unreported, Irish HC (McGovern J.), 15 November 2006.
Plattform 'Artze fur das Leben' v Austria [1991] 13 EHRR 204
R (on the Application of Hoverspeed Limited) v HM Customs and Excise [2002] EWH 1630
Redmond v Bate [1999] All ER 864
R v CICB ex parte Lain [1967] 2 All ER 770
R v Hampden [1637] 3 St Tr 825

Index